THE UNITED KINGDOM'S STATUTORY BILL OF RIGHTS
Constitutional and Comparative Perspectives

PROCEEDINGS OF THE BRITISH ACADEMY · 183

THE UNITED KINGDOM'S STATUTORY BILL OF RIGHTS
Constitutional and Comparative Perspectives

Edited by
ROGER MASTERMAN
& IAN LEIGH

Published for THE BRITISH ACADEMY
by OXFORD UNIVERSITY PRESS

Oxford University Press, Great Clarendon Street, Oxford OX2 6DP

First edition published in 2013

British Library Cataloguing in Publication Data
Data available

Library of Congress Cataloging in Publication Data
Data available

Typeset by
New Leaf Design, Scarborough, North Yorkshire
Printed in Great Britain by
TJ International Ltd, Padstow, Cornwall

ISBN 978–0–19–726537–6
ISSN 0068–1202

MIX
Paper from responsible sources
FSC www.fsc.org FSC® C013056

Contents

Notes on Contributors

Merris Amos is a member of the Department of Law, Queen Mary, University of London. Her teaching and research primarily concerns the Human Rights Act 1998 and she is the author of a number of publications in this field. At present she is completing the second edition of *Human Rights Law* (2006).

Sir Jack Beatson is a Justice of the High Court of England and Wales (Queen's Bench Division), Queen's Bench Liaison Judge (Administrative Court) for the Midlands and Wales, a Fellow of the British Academy for the Humanities and Social Sciences, and an Honorary Fellow of Brasenose and Merton Colleges, Oxford, and St John's College, Cambridge. He was formerly Rouse Ball Professor of English Law at the University of Cambridge, Founder Director of the Cambridge Centre for Public Law, a Law Commissioner for England and Wales, and a member of the Competition Commission. His most recent book on a public law topic (with S. Grosz, T. Hickman and R. Singh) is *Human Rights: Judicial Protection in the UK* (2008).

Petra Butler is an Associate Professor at Victoria University of Wellington and an Associate Director of the New Zealand Centre for Public Law. Her experience encompasses common law, as well as mixed and civil law jurisdictions having studied in Germany, clerked at the South African Constitutional Court and worked in New Zealand for the last 14 years. She is a fully qualified German lawyer and admitted as barrister and solicitor of the High Court of New Zealand. Her main interests include domestic, comparative and international human rights law. She has published widely in these areas, including (together with Andrew Butler) a major text book on the New Zealand Bill of Rights Act 1990. She has also consulted with government on human rights issues, most recently on the implementation of the Convention on the Rights of Persons with Disabilities and on major Bill of Rights cases.

Alice Donald is Senior Research Fellow in the Human Rights and Social Justice Research Institute at London Metropolitan University. Her recent research reports include *Developing a Bill of Rights for the UK*, commissioned by the Equality and Human Rights Commission. Alice was formerly a journalist and editor at the BBC World Service.

Simon Evans is Professor of Law at the Centre for Comparative Constitutional Studies, Melbourne Law School, University of Melbourne. He has broad interests in constitutional and administrative law, particularly in common law and Commonwealth countries. His current project analyses the powers and accountabilities of the executive branch of government in comparative context; he recently completed a project investigating the capacity of parliaments to protect human rights and the effectiveness of the Commonwealth model of human rights protection.

Helen Fenwick is Professor of Law at Durham Law School and a Human Rights Consultant to Doughty Street Chambers in London, one of a group of Chambers specialising in human rights litigation. She specialises in human rights, counter-terrorist law and policy, public protest, media law and the Human Rights Act. She is the author of *Civil Rights: New Labour, Freedom and the Human Rights Act* (2000), *Media Freedom under the Human Rights Act* (2006, with G. Phillipson), *Text, Cases and Materials on Public Law and Human Rights*, 3rd edn (2010, with G. Phillipson) and *Civil Liberties and Human Rights*, 4th edn (2007).

Ian Leigh is Professor of Law at Durham Law School. He is a member of the Durham University Human Rights Centre and the Durham Global Security Institute. He has taught at several UK universities and held visiting appointments at the universities of Otago, Florida, Virginia, Melbourne and at Osgoode Hall Law School. His major publications include (with Roger Masterman) *Making Rights Real: The Human Rights Act in Its First Decade* (2008) and (with Rex Ahdar) *Religious Freedom in the Liberal State*, 2nd edn (2013).

Sir Anthony Mason AC KBE was a Justice of the High Court of Australia from 1972 to 1987 and Chief Justice from 1987 to 1995. He was Commonwealth Solicitor-General from 1964 to 1969 and a Judge of the NSW Court of Appeal from 1969 to 1972. Until recently, he was Chancellor of UNSW, National Fellow at the Research School of Social Sciences at the ANU, a Judge of the Supreme Court of Fiji and President of the Solomon Islands Court of Appeal. In 1996–97 he was Arthur Goodhart Professor in Legal Science at Cambridge University. Since 2001 he has been Distinguished Visiting Fellow at the ANU College of Law. Sir Anthony has been a non-permanent Judge of the Hong Kong Court of Final Appeal since 1997. He holds honorary doctorates from the Australian National University and Sydney, Melbourne, Monash, Griffith and Deakin universities, UNSW and the universities of Oxford and Hong Kong.

Roger Masterman is Reader in Law at Durham Law School. His research interests lie in constitutional law and reform, and he is the author of a number of pieces on the Human Rights Act 1998, including (with Ian Leigh) *Making Rights Real: The Human Rights Act in Its First Decade* (2008). His most recent book is *The Separation of Powers in the Contemporary Constitution: Judicial Competence and Independence in the United Kingdom* (2011).

C. R. G. Murray was appointed to a lectureship in law at Newcastle University in 2007, having completed his undergraduate and postgraduate degrees at Durham University. His current research ties together the fields of national security law, legal history and public law. His prominent articles include "In the Shadow of Lord Haw Haw: Guantánamo Bay, Diplomatic Protection and Allegiance" [2011] *Public Law* 115 and "We Need to Talk: 'Democratic Dialogue' and the Ongoing Saga of Prisoner Disenfranchisement" (2011) 62 *Northern Ireland Legal Quarterly* 57.

Aidan O'Neill QC is a barrister at Matrix Chambers. He is qualified to appear as counsel in England and Wales and in Scotland and has appeared as senior counsel before, among other tribunals, the UK Supreme Court, the Judicial Committee of the Privy Council, the House of Lords, Court of Justice of the European Union and the European Court of Human Rights. He has published extensively, particularly in the fields of human rights, constitutional law and EU law. His most recent book is *EU Law for UK Lawyers*, 2nd edn (2011).

Gavin Phillipson is Professor of Law at Durham Law School and has published extensively in the fields of human rights and constitutional law.

Sir Rabinder Singh is a Justice of the High Court of England and Wales (Queen's Bench Division). At the time of writing he was a barrister at Matrix Chambers, London. He is an Honorary Professor of Law at the University of Nottingham. His publications include (with J. Beatson, S. Grosz and T. Hickman) *Human Rights: Judicial Protection in the UK* (2008).

Julia Watson is an associate to the Honourable Chief Justice French at the High Court of Australia, and was previously an associate to the Honourable Justice Kenny at the Federal Court of Australia. Julia Watson holds a masters degree in Public Policy from the University of California, Berkeley, and is currently completing a masters degree of Laws at the University of Melbourne. She is particularly interested in public law and human rights, and was closely involved in the drafting of the Charter of Human Rights and Responsibilities Act 2006 (Vic) in her capacity as Researcher to the Solicitor-General for Victoria, Ms Pamela Tate SC.

Acknowledgments

This collection arose out of a British Academy-funded conference, held at St John's College, Durham University, over the 24th and 25th September 2010, to mark the tenth anniversary of the full implementation of the Human Rights Act 1998. We are grateful to all those who attended and contributed to the discussions, and to Francesca Klug, Tom Poole, Roger Smith and John Wadham for agreeing—in at least one instance at very short notice—to deliver papers. The majority of the essays in this volume were first presented at this event, and have been revised and amended in the light of the discussions and subsequent developments. Petra Butler and Gavin Phillipson both kindly allowed themselves to be commissioned to produce their respective essays following the conference. Our gratitude is owed to all of our contributors, a number of whom have showed remarkable forbearance and tolerance in the face of repeated, and increasingly desperate, correspondence regarding deadlines. Finally, our thanks are also due to James Rivington and Brigid Hamilton-Jones at the British Academy for efficiently encouraging us towards submission.

RMWM and IDL
May 2012

Synopsis

By providing enforceable remedies for breaches of Convention Rights in domestic courts, and in allowing judges to scrutinise parliamentary legislation on human rights grounds, the United Kingdom's Human Rights Act 1998 marked a sea-change in the relationships between the individual and the state, and between the courts and the political branches of government, as they had been traditionally understood.

Despite the undeniable practical importance of the Human Rights Act, widespread political and popular scepticism over the nature of rights adjudication and the relationship between human rights laws and—for instance—measures designed to combat terrorism and crime has prevented the Human Rights Act from being seen as an established and essential part of our constitutional structures. This uncertainty has not, however, prevented the Human Rights Act from exerting significant constitutional influence within the United Kingdom, within the framework provided by the European Convention and European Court of Human Rights, and beyond.

This edited collection of essays therefore seeks to chart the lasting constitutional impact of the Human Rights Act at a point when its political future is far from assured. To that end, the essays examine the relationships between the Human Rights Act and domestic constitutional doctrine, with the Convention's enforcement bodies at Strasbourg and with statutory Bills of Rights in other common law jurisdictions. Further, the collection goes on to examine the permanence of changes initiated in domestic legal reasoning and process—including to judicial technique and in advocacy—before finally turning to examine how the experience of the Human Rights Act might influence the future development of a Bill of Rights for the United Kingdom.

1

The United Kingdom's Human Rights Project in Constitutional and Comparative Perspective

ROGER MASTERMAN AND IAN LEIGH

Introduction

NARRATIVES ON THE UNITED KINGDOM'S HUMAN RIGHTS ACT (HRA)—passed in 1998 and coming into effect, for the most part, in October 2000[1]—are typically characterised by their paradoxical nature. During its short existence the Act has been variously portrayed as both democratic and counter-majoritarian,[2] as an effective remedial instrument and as a 'futile' gesture,[3] as a virtually entrenched cornerstone of our constitution and as an ordinary statute susceptible to the ebb and flow of contemporary political opinion.[4]

In the legal realm, far-reaching statements of the Act's significance are not hard to find. The Act is hailed as a 'constitutional statute' which enjoys the limited protection from implied repeal that that status conveys.[5] It has been termed a 'higher-order' provision,[6] and has been referred to as one of the foundations of a new constitutional order, under which the established doctrine of parliamentary sovereignty—and therefore the primacy of political

[1] The protections afforded by the Human Rights Act 1998 had been operational in respect of the activities of the devolved administrations since their establishment in 1999 (see Scotland Act 1998, Northern Ireland Act 1998 and Government of Wales Act 1998).
[2] Cf. *A and others v Secretary of State for the Home Department* [2004] UKHL 56; [2005] 2 A.C. 68, at [42] (Lord Bingham) with J. Allan, "Portia, Bassanio or Dick the Butcher? Constraining Judges in the Twenty-first Century" (2006) 17 K.C.L.J. 1.
[3] Cf. K. D. Ewing, "The Futility of the Human Rights Act" [2004] P.L. 829 with A. Lester, "The Utility of the Human Rights Act: A Reply to Professor Ewing" [2005] P.L. 249.
[4] Cf. *Jackson and others v Her Majesty's Attorney-General* [2005] UKHL 56; [2006] 1 A.C. 262, at [102] (Lord Steyn) and The Conservative Party, *Invitation to Join the Government of Britain* (2010), p.79.
[5] *Thoburn v Sunderland City Council* [2002] EWHC 195 (Admin); [2003] Q.B. 151.
[6] F. Klug, "A Bill of Rights: Do We Need One or Do We Already Have One?" [2007] P.L. 701, at 708.

Proceedings of the British Academy, **183**, 1–22. © The British Academy 2013.

actors within the constitutional sphere—has irreversibly conceded ground to the substantive constitutional morality of the rule of law.[7] From this perspective, the Act is marked out as having tempered the absolutism of Dicey's conception of the legal powers of Parliament,[8] and has been argued to have helped to cement the United Kingdom's transition from parliamentary to constitutional democracy.[9]

Yet at the 2010 general election, the future of the HRA provided the backdrop to one of the many inter-party skirmishes of the election campaign, with the Conservative Party committed to its repeal and replacement with a British Bill of Rights.[10] In this sphere, the 'higher order' and 'constitutional' epithets count for little. The responses of the law and of politics could hardly be more starkly opposed.

Responses to the Act, and the protections it provides, have been—and continue to be—polarised. As a result, the broad-based 'culture of rights'[11] that the first Blair administration promised would be generated by its human rights project has failed to materialise. In the context of this continued popular and political uncertainty, this book seeks to examine the undoubted influence of the HRA across the three constitutional spheres within which it can be seen to operate: within the un-codified constitution of the United Kingdom, within the context of the supervisory jurisdiction of the European Court of Human Rights (ECtHR), and, finally, on the international plane as the subject of ongoing transnational 'conversations' on rights and the instruments that protect them.[12] In order to assess the potential legacy of the HRA—and to provide a counterpoint to the Act's continued political fragility—the authors seek to identify trends and developments that hold the potential to outlast the Act that gave rise to them.

This volume brings together a collection of internationally-renowned scholars and lawyers in order to examine the lasting constitutional legacy of the HRA at a time when its political future is yet to be secured. In the context of debates over the introduction of a Bill of Rights for the United Kingdom, this set of essays examines the clear effects of the Act on constitutional doctrine, on the formal (and informal) interactions between the branches of

[7] See, for instance, V. Bogdanor, *The New British Constitution* (Oxford: Hart Publishing, 2009) and *Jackson v Attorney-General* [2005] UKHL 56, paras [104]–[107] (Lord Hope).

[8] A. V. Dicey, *An Introduction to the Study of the Law of the Constitution*, 3rd edn (London: Macmillan, 1889).

[9] J. Jowell, "Beyond the Rule of Law: Towards Constitutional Judicial Review" [2000] P.L. 671.

[10] The Conservative Party, *Invitation to Join the Government of Britain* (2010), p.79. The Labour Party and Liberal Democrats campaigned for the retention of the Act: Labour Party, *A Future Fair for All* (2010), p.93; Liberal Democrats, *Manifesto 2010* (2010), p.94.

[11] HL Debs, vol.582, col.1228, 3 November 1997 (Lord Irvine of Lairg QC).

[12] C. McCrudden, "A Common Law of Human Rights?: Transnational Judicial Conversations on Constitutional Rights" (2000) 20 O.J.L.S. 499.

government (at central and devolved levels), and on legal reasoning within, and before, the courts. It examines the nature of the relationships between national bodies and the enforcement structures of the European Court of Human Rights, examining the capacity of decision-making under the HRA to generate an extra-jurisdictional influence on decisions taken by the Convention on European Human Rights (ECHR). The migration of constitutional ideas and of jurisprudential trends of reasoning is also examined beyond the Convention system; with the interplay between the Human Rights Act, the New Zealand Bill of Rights Act, the Victorian Charter of Rights and the Australian Capital Territory (ACT) Human Rights Act demonstrating the spread of the statutory Bill of Rights model within systems of parliamentary sovereignty and the continued exchange of ideas across the common law world. Finally, the book turns to the United Kingdom's own Bill of Rights debate, asking what lessons from the HRA experiment—and from other jurisdictions' experiences of Bill of Rights design—can be carried forward to the debates over the future course of rights protection in the United Kingdom and what shape a future Bill of Rights for the United Kingdom might take.

The Human Rights Act 1998: A Short History

May 1997 saw the election of the first Blair administration with manifesto commitments to implement an unprecedented array of constitutional reforms: the abolition of the hereditary principle as a criterion governing membership of the House of Lords, the enactment of Freedom of Information legislation, devolution to Scotland, Wales and Northern Ireland, reform of the party funding mechanisms and reform of the House of Commons were all a part of the new government's ambitious scheme.[13] The introduction of a statute designed to incorporate the European Convention on Human Rights into domestic law was one of the key elements of this new constitutional landscape. The enactment of the HRA in 1998 marked the culmination of a 30-year campaign for access to the Convention rights in domestic courts[14] and, for many, provided a tonic for the steady erosion of civil liberties that had taken place during the preceding years of Conservative rule.[15]

The structure of the HRA differed from that associated with *constitutional* Bills of Rights elsewhere. The Labour government was careful in its

[13] *New Labour: Because Britain Deserves Better* (London: Labour Party, 1997).
[14] See, for example, A. Lester, *Democracy and Individual Rights* (London: Fabian Society, 1969); Lord Scarman, *English Law: The New Dimension* (London: Stevens & Sons, 1974).
[15] R. Dworkin, *A Bill of Rights for Britain* (London: Chatto & Windus, 1990); K. D. Ewing and C. A. Gearty, *Freedom under Thatcher* (Oxford: Oxford University Press, 1990).

attempts to provide a *statutory* protection for rights, while ultimately preserving the primacy of Parliament. As a result, the judges would not find themselves empowered to strike down legislation which contravened the requirements of the Convention, but would instead be permitted to interpret statutory language—so far as that was possible—in order to achieve compatibility.[16] If such an interpretation was not possible, then the Act provided courts with a novel, non-coercive, remedial order—the declaration of incompatibility[17]—which would serve to highlight to the government and Parliament the specific inconsistency between domestic statute and the Convention rights.[18] Hence, parliamentary sovereignty was preserved through denying the courts the power to invalidate legislation,[19] and by leaving the elected branches of government with the choice of whether or not to remedy legislation that the courts had identified as contravening the standards required by the Convention. While the protections to be afforded by the Act extended to *all* public bodies—making it unlawful for them to act in a way which was incompatible with one or more of the Convention rights[20]—and to private persons exercising public functions,[21] Parliament was explicitly excluded from potential liability.[22] Under the provisions of the Act, legal scrutiny was designed to run in train with 'political rights review'.[23] Upon introducing draft legislation into Parliament, the responsible minister would be required to make a statement as to the compatibility of the proposed measure in order to provoke rights-focused scrutiny.[24] Ultimately, however, Parliament's legislative power would not be subject to substantive restrictions; the autonomy of the legislature was, in form at least, preserved. In setting up this division of power, the HRA attempted to reconcile an expanded role for the judges in rights protection, with traditional constitutional doctrine and the scrutiny mechanisms of the political constitution.

Yet, in other respects, the HRA was a marked departure. While sovereignty was essentially preserved, the separation of powers—the constitutional division of labour between courts, executive and Parliament—was in practice quite radically altered. The HRA provided the courts with the tools to hold the executive to account for breaches of fundamental rights, and to scrutinise

[16] HRA 1998, s.3(1).
[17] HRA 1998, s.4.
[18] HRA 1998, s.1(1).
[19] See, for example, HC Debs, vol.306, col.722, 16 February 1998 (Jack Straw).
[20] HRA 1998, s.6(1).
[21] HRA 1998, s.6(3)(b).
[22] HRA 1998, s.6(6).
[23] The phrase is Janet Hiebert's. See J. L. Hiebert, "New Constitutional Ideas: Can New Parliamentary Models Resist Judicial Dominance When Interpreting Rights" (2003–04) 82 *Texas Law Review* 163.
[24] HRA 1998, s.19.

parliamentary legislation—traditionally substantially immune from such scrutiny[25]—for compatibility with the protections afforded by the Convention rights. These new powers of review were, prior to the implantation of the HRA, thought of as being beyond the constitutional Rubicon.[26] As a result, the classic account of sovereignty, under which Parliament legislated subject to no constitutional reservations,[27] had—though ceding to the courts these powers of proto-constitutional review—arguably given way to a more cohesive system of checks and balances.

The design of the HRA therefore attempted to blend the radical with the orthodox; rights would be judicially protected, but not at the (explicit at least) expense of Parliament's sovereignty. It is perhaps no surprise then that, as a result, much of the substantive debate over the correct application of the HRA is to be found in the reconciliation of this expanded judicial role with the ideal of democratic governance.[28] In spite of its novel structure, the HRA has not been allowed to escape the anti-democratic accusations that dog constitutional Bills of Rights.[29] And for all its successes in making available remedies for the infringement of individual rights,[30] nor has it been able to escape the suggestion—levelled by Lord McCluskey on its introduction—that the Act would provide 'a field day for crackpots, a pain in the neck for … legislators and a goldmine for lawyers'.[31] Throughout its short life the Act has provoked opposition from the popular press and (on occasion) from across the political sphere. It has become commonplace to read that the HRA provides convicted criminals with a 'right' to pornography,[32] that a culture of compensation—fuelled by the HRA—is 'running riot' in the United

[25] Cf. the limited exceptions to this rule in *R. v Secretary of State for Transport Ex p. Factortame (No.2)* [1991] 1 A.C. 603 and *Jackson v Attorney-General* [2006] 1 A.C. 262.

[26] F. Klug, "The Human Rights Act—A 'Third Way' or 'Third Wave' Bill of Rights" [2001] E.H.R.L.R. 361, at 370. Ewing has described the change brought about by the HRA as 'unquestionably the most significant formal redistribution of political power in this country since [the Parliament Act] 1911, and perhaps since [the Bill of Rights] 1688' ("The Human Rights Act and Parliamentary Democracy" (1999) 62 M.L.R. 79, at 79).

[27] G. Marshall, *Constitutional Theory* (Oxford: Clarendon, 1971), p.74.

[28] For one of the most compelling attempts to address this particular issue, see C. A. Gearty, *Principles of Human Rights Adjudication* (Oxford: Oxford University Press, 2004).

[29] A. M. Bickel, *The Least Dangerous Branch: The Supreme Court at the Bar of Politics* (Indianapolis, IN: Bobbs-Merrill, 1962); J. Waldron, "The Core of the Case against Judicial Review" (2006) 115 *Yale Law Journal* 1346.

[30] L. Matthews, S. Sceats, S. Hosali and J. Candler, *The Human Rights Act: Changing Lives* (London: British Institute of Human Rights, 2008).

[31] *Scotland on Sunday*, 6 February 2000.

[32] See "Tories Target Human Rights", *Daily Telegraph*, 17 August 2004. Far from being successful, the applicant—the convicted serial killer Dennis Nilsen—was in fact denied leave to appeal at permission stage.

Kingdom,[33] that the Act allows judges to wantonly interfere with executive decisions in defiance of 'common sense',[34] provides an invitation to the unelected judges to illegitimately engineer a legal right to privacy,[35] and so on. A Department of Constitutional Affairs Review of the Act, published in 2006,[36] did little to correct the series of damaging myths and half-truths that had by that point virtually drowned out discussions of the Act's merits. By 2012, little had changed—the Equality and Human Rights Commission concluded in a far-reaching review that the Convention and HRA were a firm foundation but that, nevertheless, the government had some way to go (not least in its policies and legislation) in ensuring that the Convention rights were enjoyed by everyone living in Britain.[37] To say that the Act has 'failed to attract sufficient symbolic significance to become embedded in the national consciousness' is something of an understatement.[38]

Yet, at the same time, the Act *has* brought discussions of rights to the fore in both legal and political contexts. The protections afforded by the Act have formed the hub of discussions over the necessity and proportionality of anti-terrorism legislation,[39] have informed debates over, inter alia, the legal status of same-sex partnerships,[40] acquired gender recognition,[41] the availability of enforceable privacy rights against the press,[42] and have served to underpin

[33] Michael Howard MP, "Time to Liberate the Country from Human Rights Laws", 18 March 2005. At the time of Howard's speech, damages had actually been awarded in a mere three cases under the HRA. See I. Leigh and R. Masterman, *Making Rights Real: The Human Rights Act in Its First Decade* (Oxford: Hart, 2008), pp.273–82.

[34] Comments attributed to Tony Blair in the aftermath of the 'Afghan Hijackers' decision—*R. (on the application of S) v Secretary of State for the Home Department* [2006] EWHC 1111 (Admin)—("Afghans Who Fled Taliban by Hijacking Airliner Given Permission to Remain in Britain", *Guardian*, 11 May 2006). On appeal, the Court of Appeal found the criticised decision to have been 'impeccable' (*R. (on the application of S) v Secretary of State for the Home Department* [2006] EWCA Civ 1157).

[35] See the widely publicised comments of Paul Dacre (editor of the *Daily Mail*) in response to a series of decisions taken in the High Court by Mr Justice Eady; "The Threat to Our Press", *Guardian*, 10 November 2008; "Judge Has Created Privacy Law by Back Door, Says *Mail* Editor Paul Dacre", *The Times*, 10 November 2008.

[36] Department for Constitutional Affairs, *Review of the Implementation of the Human Rights Act* (July 2006), on which see Joint Committee on Human Rights, *The Human Rights Act: The DCA and Home Office Reviews* (2005–06), HL278/HC1716.

[37] Equality and Human Rights Commission, *Human Rights Review 2012* (Manchester: Equality and Human Rights Commission, 2012).

[38] Francesca Klug, "Enshrine These Rights", *Guardian*, 27 June 2006, and letter to *Observer*, "Parliament—A Danger to Freedom", 9 April 2006.

[39] See, for example, *A and others v Secretary of State for the Home Department* [2004] UKHL 56; [2005] 2 A.C. 68; Joint Committee on Human Rights, *Counter-terrorism and Human Rights: Bringing Human Rights Back In*, HL86/HC111 (March 2010).

[40] Civil Partnerships Act 2004.

[41] Gender Recognition Act 2004.

[42] *Campbell v Mirror Group Newspapers* [2004] UKHL 22; [2004] 2 A.C. 457.

reform of the structure of government itself.[43] Giving effect to the HRA has prompted changes to the cultures and processes of political and legal decision-making which might be seen to have lasting impact, within the constitution, on the United Kingdom's relationships with Strasbourg, and in the international context in which the credence of legally enforceable human rights continues to gain currency.

Part I—The Human Rights Act in Constitutional Perspective

The relationship between political and judicial power is a vexed one, especially controversial in a state—such as the United Kingdom—that lacks a foundational constitutional document from which the elected branches and judiciary draw their powers. The absence of a written constitution has necessarily shaped the particular form that controversy over judicial supremacism has taken in the United Kingdom. Commentators on all sides appeal to the twin doctrines of the rule of the law and parliamentary sovereignty, but ambiguity about these key concepts and their specific application gives considerable scope for disagreement and misunderstanding.

The most generous version argues that there is no conflict of values over the Human Rights Act 1998, that the scheme itself has created an entirely new constitutional model within which parliamentary sovereignty and judicial supremacism have been reconciled. This scheme of rights protection has been variously labelled the British,[44] Westminster[45] or new Commonwealth model.[46] Supporters of this view emphasise that the interpretive power in s.3(1) is the Act's main remedial tool, stress the primacy of the political inherent in the declaration of incompatibility under s.4 and remind us that the courts have no power to strike down primary legislation for incompatibility with the Convention. The role of legislatures in rights scrutiny and protection under the new Commonwealth model provides a foil to, and is designed to avoid, excessively robust judicial enforcement.[47] As a result, it is argued that the

[43] Constitutional Reform Act 2005.

[44] By the Home Secretary responsible for its introduction, Jack Straw.

[45] D. Erdos, *Delegating Rights Protection: The Rise of Bills of Rights in the Westminster World* (Oxford: Oxford University Press, 2010).

[46] S. Gardbaum, "The New Commonwealth Model of Constitutionalism" (2001) 49 *American Journal of Comparative Law* 707; S. Gardbaum, "Reassessing the New Commonwealth Model of Constitutionalism" (2010) 8 *International Journal of Constitutional Law* 167.

[47] For example, D. Nicol, "Law and Politics after the Human Rights Act" [2006] P.L. 722; D. Feldman, "The Impact of Human Rights on the UK Legislative Process" (2004) 25 *Statute Law Review* 91; J. Hiebert, "Parliament and the Human Rights Act: Can the JCHR Help Facilitate a Culture of Rights?" (2006) 4 *International Journal of Constitutional Law* 1; J. Hiebert, "Parliamentary Bills of Rights: An Alternative Model?" (2006) 69 M.L.R. 7; J. Hiebert, "Interpreting a Bill of Rights: The Importance of Legislative Rights Review" (2005) 35 *British*

new Commonwealth model holds the potential to avoid the charges of judicio-centricity that have been levelled at other, constitutional, rights instruments.

Academic sceptics meanwhile decry the inability of judicially policed rights instruments to effectively manage the competing imperatives of individual liberty and democratic governance. As such, many commentators have added the HRA to the canon of legislative and other developments that have in recent years precipitated the steady decline of representative, and participatory, democracy and cemented the 'juridification' of the constitution.[48] Continued debate over the seemingly irreconcilable paradigms of representative governance and the judicial protection of human rights—and the successes or otherwise of the HRA's pragmatic middle ground between challenges of remedial inadequacy and judicial overkill[49]—is unsurprising and an inevitable consequence of the counter-majoritarian tendencies of legal rights instruments.[50]

However, whether there is a real difference between the Westminster model and conventional 'strong form'[51] review depends crucially on institutional behaviour—both of the courts and of politicians.[52] On the one hand, much has been written of judicial self-restraint within this model which, now that earlier terminological confusion has been settled,[53] is invariably referred to as 'deference'.[54] This suggests that institutional conflict can be avoided by judges

Journal of Political Studies 235; J. Hiebert, "A Hybrid Approach to Protect Rights? An Argument in Favour of Supplementing Canadian Judicial Review with Australia's Model of Parliamentary Scrutiny" (1998) 26 *Federal Law Review* 115; C. Evans and S. Evans, "Legislative Scrutiny Committees and Parliamentary Conceptions of Human Rights" [2006] P.L. 785.

48 For example, M. Bevir, "The Westminster Model, Governance and Judicial Reform" (2008) 61 *Parliamentary Affairs* 559.

49 See, for example, C. A. Gearty, "Reconciling Parliamentary Democracy and Human Rights" (2002) 118 L.Q.R. 248; A. Kavanagh, *Constitutional Review under the UK Human Rights Act* (Cambridge: Cambridge University Press, 2009).

50 J. Allan, "Bills of Rights and Judicial Power: A Liberal's Quandary" (1996) 16 O.J.L.S. 337.

51 The terms 'strong' and 'weak' review were coined by the US scholar Mark Tushnet and have been widely adopted. See, for instance: M. Tushnet, "New Forms of Judicial Review and the Persistence of Rights- and Democracy-based Worries" (2003) 38 *Wake Forest Law Review* 813.

52 See also W. Sadurski, "Judicial Review and the Protection of Constitutional Rights" (2002) 22 O.J.L.S. 275.

53 Early case law referred to a 'discretionary area of judgment' especially in relation to the restriction of qualified rights: *R. v DPP Ex p. Kebilene* [2002] A.C. 326, at 381 (Lord Hope).

54 J. Jowell, "Deference, Servility, Civility or Institutional Capacity" [2003] P.L. 592; M. Hunt, "Sovereignty's Blight: Why Contemporary Public Law Needs the Concept of 'Due Deference'", in N. Bamforth and P. Leyland (eds), *Public Law in a Multi-layered Constitution* (Oxford: Hart Publishing, 2003); Lord Steyn, "Deference: A Tangled Story" [2005] P.L. 346; A. Kavanagh, "Deference or Defiance? The Limits of the Judicial Role in Constitutional Adjudication", in G. Huscroft (ed.), *Expounding the Constitution: Essays in Constitutional Theory* (Cambridge: Cambridge University Press, 2008), p.184; A. Young, "In Defence of Due Deference" (2009) 73 M.L.R. 554.

recognising the limitations of their role and the greater legitimacy of political actors, at least in relation to certain types of question that may arise for interpretation under the HRA.

On the other hand, are those who argue that the differences between strong- and weak-form review are cosmetic or minimal because of the constraints within which the executive and Parliament operate, both politically and legally. Commentators such as Keith Ewing argue that once the courts have declared legislation incompatible the ability of Parliament to disregard this judgment is theoretical only.[55] In practice nearly all declarations of incompatibility have been 'followed', giving rise to the suggestion that the elected branches do so as a matter of routine.[56] But what does this show precisely? The same comment could be made of adverse judgments from the European Court of Human Rights against the United Kingdom. In both cases one could conclude that the United Kingdom is a state governed by the rule of law in which judgments from independent courts are highly respected. To suggest that this somehow demonstrates that parliamentary sovereignty is a dead letter is to ignore two important points. First, there is the possibility that an exceptional case may arise. The very fact that questions about whether certain counter-terrorist powers or prisoners' voting rights judgments should be implemented arise affirms that all involved believe in the existence of the exception.[57] Secondly, we can refer to what Ronald Dworkin calls, in another context, the distinction between 'strong' and 'weak' discretion.[58] Even if, after a period of suitable observation, we were to conclude that the practical effect of a declaration of incompatibility is in end result tantamount to a strike down of legislation, political actors nevertheless retain decisive influence over the timing, the form and the extent of legislative change by way of response. The inability of the courts to legislate in a judgment that is fact- and context-specific (often referred to as a constraint on the interpretative power under s.3) is a real practical constraint.

In "The Human Rights Act, Dialogue and Constitutional Principles", Gavin Phillipson considers different perspectives on the relationship between the HRA and existing constitutional principles. Identifying two contrasting views on the matter, corresponding broadly to the political–liberal constitutionalist divide, he argues that each contains something of a paradox. Phillipson then goes on to consider two more specific views of the HRA which impliedly or explicitly seek to 'read down' the powers it grants the judges: one accuses the judges of having over-used their powers under the HRA, reducing

[55] K. D. Ewing, "The Futility of the Human Rights Act" [2004] P.L. 829.

[56] Kavanagh, "Deference or Defiance?, p.214.

[57] See Chapter 3, this volume.

[58] R. Dworkin, "The Model of Rules I", in *Taking Rights Seriously* (Cambridge, MA: Harvard University Press, 1978), p.33ff.

its distinctiveness as a 'third wave' or 'dialogic' Bill of Rights; the other suggests that the judicial role in such dialogue should be regarded as merely 'proposing principles' to the other branches. Neither view can be squared, Phillipson suggests, with the political and legal realities; considering the recent governmental reaction to the Sex Offender Register judgment, he contends that it is not the judges but the democratic branches that currently pose the biggest obstacle to genuinely principled dialogue on rights controversies.

However, the democratically appealing claim that Parliament has a role to play in the protection of human rights itself conceals a number of difficulties. First, the arrangements of the Coalition formed in 2010 force a sober reassessment of exactly why supporters of the political constitution[59] can claim moral superiority for Westminster over the 'colonels in horsehair'. Even in those narrow areas where controversial human rights questions are in issue, the Coalition partners have found the need to compromise on manifesto commitments endorsed by the electorate. Both parties have had to revise their human rights policies in order to form a working partnership: for the Conservatives this has meant postponing their ambitions to replace the HRA, for the Liberal Democrats it has meant, inter alia, watering down their plans to scrap Control Orders. At the time of writing some of these disagreements remain unresolved, notably the future of the HRA itself.[60] Accountability for these decisions is at best the nebulous one of accountability to the electorate at the next election. Then there is the question of whether the effectiveness of Parliament's role in rights scrutiny lives up to the democratic ideal.

Central to this calculation is the place of the Joint Committee on Human Rights (JCHR) within the scheme for human rights protection. Commentators have argued that the shift in the JCHR's work from its early emphasis on Bill scrutiny for Convention compatibility towards thematic reporting and monitoring of compliance with incompatibility judgments has been beneficial. The JCHR is much admired overseas as a model for parliamentary scrutiny of human rights.[61] Nevertheless, measuring the true impact of the Committee's

[59] A body of 'rights sceptical' scholarship in this vein builds on the seminal work of the late John Griffith, "The Political Constitution" (1979) M.L.R. 1. Thomas Poole summarises Griffith's position as a belief that rights discourse corrupts law and politics: T. Poole, "Tilting at Windmills? Truth and Illusion in 'The Political Constitution'" (2007) 70 M.L.R. 250. For examples of more recent rights-sceptical scholarship, see T. Campbell, K. D. Ewing and A. Tomkins (eds), *Sceptical Essays on Human Rights* (Oxford: Oxford University Press, 2001); K. D. Ewing, *The Bonfire of the Liberties: New Labour, Human Rights and the Rule of Law* (Oxford: Oxford University Press, 2010).

[60] On which see Chapters 12 and 13, this volume, and The Commission on a Bill of Rights, "A UK Bill of Rights? The Choice Before Us" (December 2012).

[61] The Council of Europe has called on national parliaments to strengthen their protection of human rights: Committee on Legal Affairs and Human Rights, *National Parliaments: Guarantors of Human Rights in Europe* (Rapporteur: Mr Christos Pourgourides), Parliamentary Assembly Doc.12636 (6 June 2011), http://assembly.coe.int/ASP/Doc/XrefViewPDF.asp?FileID=12866&Language=EN.

work is far from simple. Recently published quantitative research confirms that the JCHR's reports have been referred to with greater frequency in parliamentary debates since 2005–06.[62] This, however, masks repeated citation by a small number of MPs and peers and a high proportion of self-citation by some JCHR members.[63] The same study could point to only a small number of instances (16 over 5 years) where amendments to Bills before Parliament could be clearly attributed to JCHR reports, although the 'educative' effect in raising awareness of human rights among parliamentarians is almost certainly broader. After more than a decade of the JCHR's operation it would appear that the creation of a rights culture is not yet secure where parliamentary debate is concerned.

Parliamentarians were naturally keen to safeguard under the Act their own freedom of action as legislators. While the HRA provides that decisions of public bodies[64]—or private bodies exercising public functions[65]—are unlawful insofar as they contravene the requirements of one or more of the Convention rights, legislative decisions taken by Parliament which are similarly incompatible with the Convention rights remain of full legal effect.[66] In order to preserve the ability of Parliament to legislate subject to no legal constraints, domestic courts may not strike down or otherwise invalidate primary legislation which contravenes the requirements of the Convention. Instead, the HRA—under s.4—provides that courts might issue a declaration of primary legislation's incompatibility with the Convention. Such a declaration is of no legal effect on the parties to the case, on government or on Parliament. The coercive force of a declaration of incompatibility instead can be found in the political pressure that will result from the finding of a superior court that domestic legislation does not meet the standards which the United Kingdom can be expected to adhere as a party to the European Convention on Human Rights.[67] While in practice, the issue of a declaration of incompatibility has resulted in legislative change—or of the initiation of a process designed to assess the legislative incompatibility—such change has not necessarily been a timely or direct response to the declaration issued.

The novelty of this process has given rise to much discussion about its place within 'dialogue' between the courts and the political branches of the

[62] M. Hunt, H. Hooper and P. Yowell, *Parliaments and Human Rights: Redressing the Democratic Deficit* (AHRC, 2012).

[63] Hunt, Hooper and Yowell, *Parliaments and Human Rights*, p.24.

[64] HRA 1998, s.6(1).

[65] HRA 1998, s.6(3)(b).

[66] HRA 1998, ss.3(2) and 4(6).

[67] Though, as we have seen, the difference between the declaration of incompatibility and a clear power of 'strike down' has been argued by some to be of form alone. See, for example, T. Campbell, "Incorporation through Interpretation", in T. Campbell, K. D. Ewing and A.Tomkins, *Sceptical Essays on Human Rights* (Oxford: Oxford University Press, 2001).

state. One judge has gone so far as to remark that declarations of incompatibility are 'essentially political in character rather than legal'.[68] Indeed there is some debate over whether it can be seen as a remedy at all because of the lack of tangible individualised benefits to the litigant to whom a declaration is awarded, both in domestic law and from the perspective of effectiveness under Article 13 of the Convention system as a whole.[69] In "The Continuation of Politics, by Other Means: Judicial Dialogue under the Human Rights Act 1998", Colin Murray examines the declaration of incompatibility within the broader context of interaction between the judiciary and the other branches. Murray's analysis suggests that post-HRA 'dialogue' should be understood against a wider time-frame and in the context of more informal modes of interaction. Seen in this way the volume and intensity of judicial attempts to promote law reform have grown since 2000 but this process is by no means such a constitutional novelty as some have suggested. Nevertheless at times there has been a lack of parliamentary engagement, so much so that the judges have frequently been 'dancing without a partner' or with one that shows at best only token interest.

In one part of the United Kingdom—Scotland—the effect of incorporation of Convention rights has produced dramatic constitutional change since the powers of the Scottish Parliament and Scottish ministers are limited by the HRA, in contrast to Westminster. In a historical survey, "Back to the Future? Judges, Politicians and the Constitution in the New Scotland", Aidan O'Neill QC shows how the UK Supreme Court's handling of Scottish criminal appeals is, on the one hand, providing an injection of external influence to a criminal justice system that remained distinct and to some extent isolated since the Act of Union. On the other hand, as O'Neill demonstrates, this development is proving immensely controversial with Scottish politicians and judges, so much so that it has become a prominent issue in debates about Scotland's future.

Part II—Domestic Protections within a European Framework

Consideration of the effectiveness of domestic human rights protection cannot take place without placing the HRA in the context of the Convention system as a whole. More than 50 years after hearing its first case the European

[68] *A v Secretary of State for the Home Department* [2004] UKHL 56; [2005] 2 A.C. 68, at [145] (Lord Scott).

[69] See, for example, *R (on the application of Chester) v Secretary of State for Justice* [2009] EWHC 2923 (Admin); [2010] H.R.L.R. 6; *Burden v United Kingdom* (2008) 47 E.H.R.R. 38. For commentary, see Leigh and Masterman, *Making Rights Real*, ch.5.

Court of Human Rights is a victim of its own success. The growth in the Court's workload and the expansion of the Council of Europe after 1989 produced a backlog of more than 120,000 petitions, although this is beginning to reduce as a result of implementing procedural reforms under Protocol 14 to the Convention. The growing reach of the Convention jurisprudence under the 'living tree' doctrine intermittently causes an acute political reaction from some governments. In the United Kingdom's case, the Court's decisions concerning prisoners' voting and deportation of terrorist suspects are instances in point. One possible solution to workload and controversial decisions would appear to be to give greater prominence to national protection of human rights and to restrict the role of the European Court of Human Rights.[70] It is no surprise then that the UK government used its chairmanship of the Council of Europe in 2011–12 to promote an intergovernmental declaration (the Brighton Declaration) that stressed the principle of subsidiarity in reform of the Court.[71] Apart from exhortations that the Court should give greater prominence to the margin of appreciation, in practical terms this translated into a proposal that cases be inadmissible as manifestly ill-founded if they have been properly considered by a domestic court according to well-established Convention jurisprudence unless the European Court of Human Rights considers that a serious question of interpretation is raised.[72] If this proposal becomes a treaty amendment the treatment of Strasbourg jurisprudence by domestic courts will be increasingly important in future.

The Convention rights as given effect by s.1(1) of the HRA enjoy a symbiotic relationship with the Convention rights as enforced by the European Court of Human Rights. Though the HRA is an instrument passed by the Parliament of the United Kingdom, its effects and implications cannot be fully assessed without reference to the provisions of the treaty to which it gives further effect, or to the decisions of the Strasbourg-based enforcement bodies that police member states' obligations under the Convention. The domesticated Convention rights cannot therefore be completely divorced from their Strasbourg cousins, for it is in the European Convention and its attendant jurisprudence that authority as to their meaning and scope of application can be found.[73] The relationship between the Convention organs and national authorities is not—contrary to the frequent claims of politicians—however, one directional. The 'living' jurisprudence of the European

[70] See Chapter 13.

[71] High Level Conference on the Future of the European Court of Human Rights, Brighton Declaration, 19 April 2012, http://www.coe.int/en/20120419-brighton-declaration/.

[72] Brighton Declaration, at [15.d].

[73] A. Kavanagh, *Constitutional Adjudication under the UK Human Rights Act* (Cambridge: Cambridge University Press, 2009), p.156.

Court of Human Rights on the meaning and interpretation of the Convention feeds on decisions taken by the national authorities of member states. The interpretations of the rights enforced at the national level under the HRA are therefore linked to those enforced by the European Court of Human Rights, and vice versa. The primary contributors to this particular 'dialogue' on the content of the protections afforded by the Convention prior to the implementation of the HRA were the Strasbourg enforcement bodies and the UK Parliament, with the unincorporated Convention being—for the most part—of limited utility in the hands of domestic courts.[74] In permitting Convention questions to be posed in domestic courts, the HRA enabled, for the first time, UK courts to be regarded as being legitimate contributors to this inter-institutional debate.

The very fact of an existing substantial body of jurisprudence from the European Court of Human Rights interpreting the meaning of Convention rights (and binding the United Kingdom) necessarily means that so-called 'dialogue' models of rights have only a limited sphere in which to operate. But setting the structural constraints imposed by the Convention itself to one side, the HRA has seen the development of a home-grown limitation on the powers of courts to effectively contribute to this wider discussion on the meaning of the Convention. Roger Masterman's essay, "Deconstructing the Mirror Principle", examines the idea that domestic courts should, in giving effect to the Convention rights at the domestic level, do 'no more, but certainly no less'[75] than the European Court of Human Rights. This so-called 'mirror principle'[76] has become something of a mantra for the higher courts in giving effect to the HRA, but—as Masterman argues—provides an inaccurate and inadequate account of the processes of reconciling Strasbourg authority with domestic common law and statute. On this analysis, the notable decision of the UK Supreme Court in *R. v Horncastle*[77] forms a part of a much broader trend away from unquestioning or slavish implementation of the Strasbourg jurisprudence at the domestic level.

In "From Monologue to Dialogue: The Relationship between UK Courts and the European Court of Human Rights", Merris Amos considers the interplay between courts at the national and Strasbourg levels from a different angle, demonstrating—and providing a further argument on which to reject

[74] *R. v Secretary of State for the Home Department Ex p. Brind* [1991] 1 A.C. 696.

[75] *R. (on the application of Ullah) v Special Adjudicator* [2004] UKHL 26; [2004] 2 A.C. 323, at 20 (Lord Bingham).

[76] On which see J. Lewis, "The European Ceiling on Rights" [2007] P.L. 720; R. Masterman, "Aspiration or Foundation? The Status of the Strasbourg Jurisprudence and 'the Convention Rights' in Domestic Law", in H. Fenwick, G. Phillipson and R. Masterman, *Judicial Reasoning under the UK Human Rights Act* (Cambridge: Cambridge University Press, 2007).

[77] [2009] UKSC 14; 2 A.C. 373.

the 'mirror principle' in so doing—that decisions of the UK courts are closely scrutinised (and responded to) by the European Court of Human Rights. In assessing the state of this emergent dialogue, Amos examines how it impacts on the relationships between the UK authorities and the Convention organs, and its consequences for effective rights protection at the national level.

Part III—A Permanent Revolution in Legal Reasoning?

In Part III the focus of the discussion turns to the emerging record of responses to rights-based argument among members of the United Kingdom's highest courts, the ability of judges to produce reasoning that is persuasive to international judges, the continuing utility of the common law in protecting human rights, and the differing techniques of legal argument required of advocates advancing human rights claims.

The ways in which legal argument and reasoning have adapted to the incorporation into UK law of a substantial body of extrinsic law are topics worthy of specific investigation in considering the long-term impact of the HRA.[78] It can be argued that, since, unlike many European legal systems, the common law underwent no historical process of 'reception' of Roman Law, the infusion of Convention jurisprudence represents the greatest injection of external juristic material since its formative medieval period.[79] This development raises a number of pertinent questions: the tensions and differences if any between indigenous methods of rights protection and the Convention approach; the effect on procedural aspects of 'lawyering', namely litigation strategy, advocacy and proof; the impact on the means by which judicial decisions are reached and justified or presented.

Sir Jack Beatson, in "Human Rights and Judicial Technique", provides a judicial perspective on the impact of the Act on public law litigation and statutory interpretation. He argues that the impact of the HRA should be assessed in the context of a broader revolution in public law since the 1960s. On this measure the Act has led to changes of a different order to the developments in the period between 1963 and 1984,[80] when modern public law was formed in the United Kingdom but, he suggests, these changes are not irreversible. The tension between the competing interpretations of the HRA itself

[78] For a study of the impact on the Appellate Committee of the House of Lords, see T. Poole and S. Shah, "The Law Lords and Human Rights" (2011) 74 M.L.R. 79.

[79] Although Lord Denning famously described European Community law as 'an incoming tide' (see *Bulmer (HP) Ltd v J Bollinger SA* [1974] Ch. 401, at 418–19) the pervasiveness and reach of the Convention rights are significantly greater by virtue of the general application of the HRA.

[80] The dates respectively of the seminal decisions in *Ridge v Baldwin* [1964] A.C. 40 and *Council of Civil Service Unions v Minister for the Civil Service* [1985] A.C. 374.

(highlighted above by Gavin Phillipson) plays out ultimately at this level of judicial technique. While the dominant view is that the HRA simply provides a domestic remedy for breach of the United Kingdom's international obligations[81] there are nevertheless continuing indications of an alternative view that it is a constitutionally significant measure creating a new domestic law of human rights.[82]

Human rights adjudication has introduced new terminology, especially proportionality[83] and the related question of the 'necessity' of restrictions on qualified rights.[84] The questions raised are whether, or to what extent, this modifies the conventional view that a court should not substitute its judgment for that of the official or public body under review and the differences between these new concepts and those under common law public law. Beatson considers here the implications of the use of 'deference', 'respect', 'margin of discretion', 'institutional capacity or competence' or 'weight' used to describe what used to be called 'justiciability'. Moreover there are constraints which result from the adversarial nature of adjudication and ways of dealing with them: the judges are not dealing with constitutional questions in abstract.

Specific consideration is given to the idea of common law fundamental rights.[85] While there is some debate about the origins of these rights[86] their potential significance is clear. In the short term, reliance on established common law doctrine is one means by which hostility to the HRA and European Convention can be deflected by pointing to the *Britishness* of at least some human rights standards. In the longer run, fundamental common law rights are a resource available to rights-conscious judges if a future government were to repeal or substantially amend the Act, without allowing domestic law to return (as Sir Jack Beatson puts it) to the 'wilderness years'.[87] Nevertheless, the status of the common law rights jurisdiction leaves some unresolved questions. Some have clear parallels with the operation of the HRA itself, such as the at times unclear relationship between the twin-track approaches taken by

[81] See, for example, Lord Bingham's speech in *R. (on the application of SB) v Denbigh High School Governors* [2006] UKHL 15, at [29].

[82] For example, Lord Scott in *R. (on the application of Animal Defenders International) v Secretary of State for Culture, Media and Sport* [2008] UKHL 15, at [44]–[46].

[83] *R. (Daly) v Secretary of State for the Home Department* [2001] 2 A.C. 532, at [26]–[27]. See generally J. Beatson, S. Grosz, T. Hickman, R. Singh with S. Palmer, *Human Rights: Judicial Protection in the United Kingdom* (Sweet & Maxwell: London, 2008), pp.195–254.

[84] Especially ECHR, arts 8–11.

[85] *R. v Lord Chancellor Ex p. Witham* [1998] Q.B. 575; *R. v Secretary of State for the Home Department Ex p. Simms* [2000] 2 A.C. 115.

[86] Leigh and Masterman, *Making Rights Real*, pp.10–12.

[87] Beatson, Grosz, Hickman, Singh with Palmer, *Human Rights: Judicial Protection in the United Kingdom*, pp. 82 and 378.

the Convention and domestic law. Others arise independently; for instance, how the judiciary should approach the restriction of common law fundamental rights without the benefit of a text like the Convention which sets out the grounds for limitation. Yet more are common to rights discussions across the globe, where seeking to legitimise the increased susceptibility of policy decisions to judicial rights-based scrutiny is a perennial concern. But for those seeking to reform the bases on which human rights are protected in the United Kingdom, addressing all of these questions will be an essential precursor to the introduction of any successor instrument to the HRA which is designed to be consistent with our constitutional heritage.

The changing judicial role under the HRA is accompanied by implications for legal procedure. Sir Rabinder Singh explores a number of these in his essay, "The Impact of the Human Rights Act on Advocacy". The implementation of the Act has affected the kind of evidence which it is necessary and appropriate to deploy in litigation, whether the advocate is acting for the claimant or for the defendant. Where the court is required to adjudicate on the compatibility of primary legislation with the Convention rights,[88] questions may arise as to the extent to which it is permissible to refer to statements made in Parliament in order to support or challenge the compatibility of primary legislation. The traditional rule that disclosure is not automatic in public law proceedings, in contrast to ordinary civil litigation, has been modified in order to allow the court to perform its role under the HRA to decide questions of proportionality.[89] Litigation under the HRA is more likely than traditional judicial review to require live evidence and cross-examination when it is necessary to decide disputed facts where previously there would have been written evidence only.[90] Moreover the expanded canvas of human rights litigation has made the courts more receptive to third-party interveners, especially statutory bodies (for instance the Equality and Human Rights Commission) and NGOs, in proceedings under the HRA, placing special responsibilities upon advocates.[91]

[88] A contrast can be seen between what is permissible within the constitutional principles of the United Kingdom (e.g. *Wilson v First County Trust (No.2)* [2004] 1 A.C. 816) and what may be done by the European Court of Human Rights (e.g. *Hirst v United Kingdom (No.2)* (2006) 42 E.H.R.R. 849).

[89] *Tweed v Parades Commission for Northern Ireland* [2007] 1 A.C. 650.

[90] For example, *R (Wilkinson) v Broadmoor Special Authority* [2002] 1 W.L.R. 419; cf. *R (N) v M* [2003] 1 W.L.R. 562.

[91] Interveners often add value to a case but care needs to be taken that the intervener does not become 'an additional counsel for one of the parties': *E v Chief Constable of the RUC* [2009] 1 A.C. 536, at [2]–[3] (Lord Hoffmann).

Part IV—The Human Rights Act on the International Plane

The HRA is arguably as notable for those comparable instruments from which it took inspiration as those constitutional templates which were rejected by its framers. In fact, as Conor Gearty has argued, it is in the rejection of the 'orthodox precedents' of constitutional Bills of Rights—specifically, those that enable the courts to invalidate primary legislation—that the 'genius' of the HRA can be found.[92] Questions of constitutional design and of the migration of institutional and jurisprudential models[93] form the subject of Part IV, which examines the impact of the HRA, and judicial approaches to its interpretation, in Australia, New Zealand and Hong Kong. In the context of recently-enacted Bills of Rights Acts in Victoria and the Australian Capital Territory, and the Australian government's consultation on a national Bill of Rights for Australia,[94] the influence of the HRA model has been apparent in the design of, and proposals for, Australian Bills of Rights.[95] The New Zealand Bill of Rights Act (BORA) has served as inspiration for the HRA, and in turn has seen jurisprudential developments in the United Kingdom considered in the decisions of the New Zealand Supreme Court.

The potential for statutory Bills of Rights to reconcile the imperatives of individual rights with those of democratic governance is the core feature which distinguishes them from more obviously constitutional instruments. The relative force of the sovereignty doctrine, and its ability to condition the nature of judicial interpretative techniques under their respective rights instruments, is considered by Sir Anthony Mason in the context of developments in Australia, New Zealand and Hong Kong. Comparing those jurisdictions with the experience under the HRA, Sir Anthony argues in "Human Rights and Legislative Supremacy" that constitutional and political cultures are as relevant to the operation of a constitutional or statutory rights instrument as the provisions of the instrument itself. In "Australian Bills of Rights and the 'New Commonwealth Model of Constitutionalism'", Simon Evans and Julia Watson address the influence of the HRA on the design and implementation of the ACT HRA and, in particular, the Victorian Charter of Rights and Freedoms. While the Victorian Charter shares structural similarities with the HRA, a number of subtle linguistic and substantive differences give that

[92] C. Gearty, *Can Human Rights Survive?* (Cambridge: Cambridge University Press, 2006), pp.94–98.

[93] On which, see generally S. Choudhry (ed.), *The Migration of Constitutional Ideas* (Cambridge: Cambridge University Press, 2007).

[94] http://www.humanrightsconsultation.gov.au/.

[95] C. Evans and S. Evans, *Australian Bills of Rights: The Law of the Victorian Charter and the ACT Human Rights Act* (Chatswood, NSW: LexisNexis Butterworths, 2008).

instrument a different character to its United Kingdom counterpart.[96] Evans and Watson address issues of convergence and divergence between the United Kingdom's HRA and the Australian experience of statutory rights protection.

Given that the HRA itself is the product of constitutional borrowing—taking much of its inspiration from the earlier New Zealand Bill of Rights Act—Petra Butler's essay on the relationship between the HRA and the BORA, "Cross-fertilisation of Constitutional Ideas", is of a slightly different order, charting the symbiotic relationship between the two rights instruments. While the HRA was closely modelled on the BORA, it differs in a number of notable respects. First, the HRA's interpretative clause is linguistically stronger than its New Zealand counterpart.[97] Secondly, the HRA provides for judicially enforceable remedies, and for the novel declaration of incompatibility. While the BORA contains no express remedies clause, implied remedies have been read into its provisions through judicial interpretation. The implication of a general remedies provision into the BORA pre-dated the implementation of the HRA,[98] but the subsequent development of an implied declaration of inconsistent interpretation has a clear heritage in the HRA's own declaration of incompatibility. Further to this, the New Zealand Supreme Court has relied heavily on UK case law—particularly in resolving issues concerning the available interpretative latitude under s.6 of the BORA and the degree of deference to be afforded to the elected branches of the state. As Butler's essay demonstrates, the exchange of constitutional ideas between common law courts is a vibrant, two-way, process.

Part V—Amendment, Repeal or a Bill of Rights for the United Kingdom?

Following the establishment of the Conservative–Liberal Democrat Coalition government in May 2010, the Conservative policy to repeal the HRA was replaced by an apparently watered-down commitment to establish a Commission to:

[96] On which, see R. Masterman, "Interpretations, Declarations and Dialogue: Rights Protection under the Human Rights Act and Victorian Charter of Rights and Responsibilities" [2009] P.L. 112.

[97] Section 6 of the New Zealand Bill of Rights Act 1990 provides: 'Whenever an enactment can be given a meaning that is consistent with the rights and freedoms contained in this Bill of Rights, that meaning shall be preferred to any other meaning.'

[98] *Simpson v Attorney-General (Baigent's Case)* [1994] 3 N.Z.L.R. 66.

> … investigate the creation of a British Bill of Rights that incorporates and builds on all our obligations under the European Convention on Human Rights, ensures that these rights continue to be enshrined in British law, and protects and extends British liberties.[99]

This signalled something of a reprieve for the HRA, certainly in comparison with earlier Conservative statements indicating that it would be repealed and replaced with a British Bill of Rights (without the promises to continue to enshrine Convention obligations in British law and build upon them).[100] Advocates of the HRA had expected a period of frantic debate and defence after the election. Instead, at least in the short term, potential reform of the Act was effectively kicked into the long grass. The Bill of Rights Commission was appointed in March 2011 and reported in December 2012. Initial speculation suggested that the Commissioners were unlikely to be able to agree a firm template for either change or stasis. Those predictions have proven accurate; though a majority of the Commission agreed that there are weighty arguments in favour of establishing a UK Bill of Rights the Coalition looks likely to give the HRA further time to establish itself within judicial and legal culture.[101]

The effect of financial cuts cannot be ignored. The Commission for Equality and Human Rights may have been spared from sudden quangocide (after appearing on an initial leaked list of public bodies under consideration for culling)[102] but it is nevertheless listed as a public body over which ministers have obtained powers in the Public Bodies Act 2012[103] to modify constitutional arrangements, funding arrangements and to amend or transfer functions. Even following the survival of the Equality and Human Rights Commission, the scale of the economies announced by the Ministry of Justice has serious implications.[104] The practical impact of the HRA will be muted by cuts to legal aid which may severely curtail its deployment in increasing the accountability of public power. The search for economies in the health field may likewise have broad implications for disabled groups.[105]

In the longer term more fundamental debate about repeal of the HRA will surely re-emerge, particularly as a by-product of the Coalition partners wishing to reassert clearer identities as the next election approaches. Whereas the Conservative Party manifesto for the 2010 general election pledged to

[99] *The Coalition: Our Programme for Government* (2010), p.11.

[100] For instance, D. Cameron, "Balancing Freedom and Security—A Modern British Bill of Rights", speech to the Centre for Policy Studies, London, 26 June 2006.

[101] The Commission on a Bill of Rights, "A UK Bill of Rights? The Choice Before Us" (December 2012).

[102] *Daily Telegraph*, 23 September 2010.

[103] Schs 3–5.

[104] Ministry of Justice, *Proposals for Reform of Legal Aid in England and Wales*, November 2010.

[105] Equality and Human Rights Commission, Parliamentary Briefing on Health and Social Care Bill, January 2011.

repeal the HRA and replace it with a 'modern, British Bill of Rights', the Liberal Democrats advocated a written constitution as, among other purposes, the vehicle for consulting upon additional rights to the HRA and the mechanism for enforcing them, and committed to a citizens' convention to determine its contents, subject to a national referendum. The process of reform is still highly pertinent, especially in the light of the majority findings of the Bill of Rights Commission. The United Kingdom could benefit in this regard from studying overseas experiences, as Alice Donald argues in her essay, "A Bill of Rights for the United Kingdom? Lessons from Overseas". From an examination of processes for developing Bills of Rights in several Commonwealth jurisdictions she distinguishes between elite-led (Canada and New Zealand) and more participatory processes (Australia and Northern Ireland). Meanwhile some, over time, became a hybrid of the two (South Africa). Donald identifies the methods and approaches that might be used to create a 'UK' or 'British' Bill of Rights, and places these in the context of the emergent idea of participation as both a right and a precondition to democratic legitimacy and popular ownership of the resulting constitutional document. As she acknowledges there are obstacles to the creation of consensus in favour of a new Bill of Rights, including low levels of public understanding and enthusiasm for the project, and the legal, constitutional and political implications of devolution. Nevertheless, based upon the evidence from comparable jurisdictions, Donald proposes principles which might underpin the conduct of any future process in the United Kingdom and against which it might be held up to scrutiny.

Moreover, the Coalition is proceeding to repeal statutory initiatives taken by preceding Labour governments—notably in the field of counter-terrorism—which, in practice, challenged its commitment to its own creation, the HRA. Several landmark changes have been announced: repeal of the Identity Cards Act 2006 and the destruction of information recorded in the National Identity Register, the proposed reduction of the power to detain suspected terrorists without charge to 14 days, narrowing the use of stop-and-search powers and the replacement of Control Orders with Terrorism Prevention and Investigation Measures. In "Conservative Anti-HRA Rhetoric, the Bill of Rights 'Solution' and the Role of the Bill of Rights Commission", Helen Fenwick argues that these initiatives should not be mistaken for a pro-rights stance within government, arguing that the Conservative agenda clearly appears to be to enhance the autonomy of the Westminster Parliament at the expense of both Strasbourg's influence and the maintenance of ECHR standards. Against this backdrop, Fenwick examines the role of the Bill of Rights Commission, considering the potential for any future Bill of Rights to rebalance the relationships between Parliament and courts (both domestic and European) through diluting the influence of Strasbourg jurisprudence (via a revision of the duty under s.2(1) HRA) or inserting a 're-balancing' provision in a new Bill of Rights going beyond the exceptions and derogation system of the ECHR.

At a time when the future of the HRA is yet to be determined, our hope is that this collection of essays will make a significant contribution to assessing the lasting impact of the United Kingdom's human rights project, and towards shaping the nature of the debates yet to come.

Part I

The Human Rights Act in Constitutional Perspective

2

The Human Rights Act, Dialogue and Constitutional Principles

GAVIN PHILLIPSON

Introduction

THIS ESSAY IS CONCERNED WITH THE EVOLVING RELATIONSHIP between the existing, but fluid UK constitution and the Human Rights Act (HRA) at a general and two more specific levels. The general question is simply posed. What is the relationship between the HRA and the existing principles of the UK constitution—themselves often notoriously hard not to pin down or agree upon? One basic response to this question—one that some of my previous writings have been premised upon—is that this relationship operates as a kind of one-way street: it is about, and only about, how far the HRA is transforming the existing constitution. Those of us who have been enthusiastic supporters of the HRA have often been eager, perhaps over-eager, to argue for that transformative effect to be of maximum possible extent.[1] Even those, such as Aileen Kavanagh, who have eschewed such 'maximalist' readings of judicial power under the HRA, have nonetheless energetically defended the radical reinterpretation exercises carried out in cases such as *R. v A*[2] and *Ghaidan Mendoza*,[3] while arguing also that the effect of s.4 declarations of incompatibility may realistically be regarded as approaching the constitutional potency of the strike-down powers of the US courts.[4] The opposite viewpoint is concerned with how far the HRA must itself be read in the light of pre-existing constitutional principles. It is immediately apparent that those who believe that the

[1] See, for example, G. Phillipson, "(Mis)Reading Section 3 of the Human Rights Act" (2003) 119 L.Q.R. 183; "Deference, Discretion and Democracy in the Human Rights Act Era" (2007) 60 C.L.P. 40.
[2] *R. v A (Complainant's Sexual History) (No.2)* [2002] 1 A.C. 45 (HL).
[3] *Ghaidan v Godin-Mendoza* [2004] 2 A.C. 557. See, for example, Kavanagh's response to critics such as Danny Nicol in articles such as "Unlocking the Human Rights Act: The 'Radical Approach' to Section 3(1) Revisited" [2005] 3 E.H.R.L.R. 259; for her fullest analysis and defence of the s.3 case law, see A. Kavanagh, *Constitutional Review under the Human Rights Act* (Cambridge: Cambridge University Press, 2009), pp.19–90.
[4] Kavanagh, *Constitutional Review*, pp.416–21, esp. 418.

Proceedings of the British Academy, **183**, 25–49. © The British Academy 2013.

powers the HRA gives to the judges are or should be 'read down', or conditioned by existing constitutional principles—particularly the democratic positivism represented by the orthodox view of parliamentary sovereignty—tend to be sympathetic to what can broadly be termed 'political constitutionalism'.[5] This question therefore not only tends to open up what we might crudely call a 'legal *versus* political constitutionalism' divide in scholarship; I shall argue that it poses something of a paradox for scholars on both sides of that divide too.

Proceeding on from the general question, I will then come to two more particular issues, which arise from the tendency of those in the political constitutionalist school to (in my view) 'read down' judicial powers under the HRA. These relate to the two key powers that the Act gives to courts in relation to legislation: s.3, the obligation to interpret legislation compatibly with Convention rights 'so far as is possible' to do so, and s.4, the power to make a (non-binding) declaration of incompatibility, where a statute is found, inescapably, to violate a Convention right.[6] A common narrative about s.3 is that, as the comparative scholar Stephen Gardbaum has recently suggested, the courts have used this novel power in a more far-reaching way than many expected[7]; the second part of this essay explores whether this is actually the case, given governmental and parliamentary expectations at the time the HRA was passed. The second specific point, which relates to s.4, explores how realistic in practice is a popular way of accounting for, or accommodating, the courts' s.4 declaratory powers within a political constitutionalist reading of the UK polity: namely 'democratic dialogue', and in particular the weak form of dialogue argued for by Danny Nicol and Tom Campbell, which Tom Hickman has critically dubbed 'principle-proposing dialogue'.[8] This approach will be considered in the light of two recent episodes: the protracted saga sur-

[5] Scholars in this school tend to have serious reservations about Bills of Rights, in essence because they see such instruments as taking decisions that should properly be reached by the people through their elected politicians out of Parliament and into the courtroom; as such they amount to 'a denial of participatory citizenship' (J. Waldron, "A Right-based Critique of Constitutional Rights" (1993) 13 O.J.L.S. 18). For this reason they are either hostile to the HRA or argue that it should be given effect in a restrained manner by judges, as discussed below. For a recent collection of essays evincing these broad tendencies, see T. Campbell, K. D. Ewing and Adam Tomkins (eds), *Sceptical Essays on Human Rights* (Oxford: Oxford University Press, 2001) and *The Legal Protection of Human Rights: Sceptical Essays* (Oxford: Oxford University Press, 2010). See also the works cited in note 32 below.

[6] Such a declaration, according to s.4(2)(b), 'does not affect the validity, continuing operation or enforcement of any incompatible primary legislation …'.

[7] S. Gardbaum, "How Successful and Distinctive is the Human Rights Act? An Expatriate Comparativist's Assessment" (2011) 74 M.L.R. 195, at 201.

[8] T. Hickman, "Constitutional Dialogue, Constitutional Theories and the HRA 1998" [2005] P.L. 306.

rounding Control Orders between 2005 and 2010 and the recent, remarkable government response to the 2010 Sex Offender Register judgment[9] of the Supreme Court. It will be argued that these episodes reveal a governmental and parliamentary attitude that is simultaneously more constitutionally 'respectful' of the courts' role in declaring the law than 'weak form' dialogists would like, while also showing rank contempt for the notion of honest dialogue about human rights controversies that their theories hope to advance. The conclusion will be that it is, ironically, the democratic branches, rather than liberal judges, who turn out to be the contemporary enemies of 'weak form' dialogue.

The Human Rights Act and the Constitution: Two Broad Views

Under the traditional UK constitution, the key principles were the political accountability of the executive branch to Parliament, and the sovereignty of Parliament, itself of course accountable to the people once the United Kingdom became a democracy; the judges were confined to a modest role in policing a narrow, formal conception of the rule of law, very much in the shadow of parliamentary supremacy. How far has the HRA changed this? A very large question of course, not to be tackled in a single essay, but what I want to highlight is how approaches to this question—including how it is posed—cannot help but fall into—or open up—the division between legal and political constitutionalism that I posed above. We can sketch two basic, contrasting views, which bear directly upon not only a range of specific interpretive issues raised by the HRA, but also the assessment of the overall significance of the Act. These interpretive issues, all of which are keenly contested, include in particular: (a) the role of judicial deference in reviewing decisions of the elected branches[10]; (b) the extent to which the courts can redefine the

[9] *R. (on the application of F) v Secretary of State for the Home Department* [2010] UKSC 17; [2011] 1 A.C. 331.

[10] See, for example, P. Craig, "The Courts, the Human Rights Act and Judicial Review" (2001) 117 L.Q.R. 589; R. Edwards, "Judicial Review under the Human Rights Act" (2002) 65 C.L.J.; F. Klug, "Judicial Deference under the Human Rights Act" (2003) 2 E.H.R.L.R. 125; J. Jowell, "Judicial Deference: Servility, Civility or Institutional Capacity?" [2004] P.L. 592; Lord Steyn, "Deference: A Tangled Story" [2005] P.L. 346; M. Hunt, "Sovereignty's Blight: Why Contemporary Public Law Needs the Concept of 'Due Deference'", in N. Bamforth and P. Leyland (eds), *Public Law in a Multi-layered Constitution* (Oxford: Oxford University Press, 2003), p.340; T. R. S. Allan, "Human Rights and Judicial Review: A Critique of 'Due Deference'" (2006) 65(3) C.L.J. 670; A. Kavanagh, *Constitutional Review*, chs 7 and 8; A. Kavanagh, "Defending Deference in Public Law and Constitutional Theory" (2010) 126 L.Q.R. 222; T. R. S. Allan, "Judicial Deference and Judicial Review: Legal Doctrine and Legal Theory" (2011) 127 L.Q.R. 96; A. Young, "In Defence of Due Deference" (2009) 72 M.L.R. 554.

meaning of legislation to conform with the Convention rights[11]; and (c) how declarations of incompatibility under s.4 HRA should be constitutionally conceptualised.[12] But the difference between the two views is not simply the different answers they give to these specific questions, although they do tend to give different ones[13]; from it also follows two sharply opposing analytical perspectives through which the interface between the HRA and traditional constitutional principles is itself approached.[14]

Under the first view, broadly associated with the school referred to variously as 'liberal normativists' or 'legal constitutionalists', the HRA amounts to a hugely significant re-orientation of the UK constitution away from its traditional majoritarian basis. The HRA, despite its relative weakness as a merely statutory 'Bill of Rights', formally subject by its provision to parliamentary supremacy, is seen as marking a signal change in the judges' formerly narrow procedural role, and a major rebalancing of the three arms of government in favour of the judiciary. In turn, under this view, the interpretation of the HRA itself should be driven by the overriding objectives of ensuring maximal protection for, and further development of, the Convention rights[15] and be strongly informed by the Convention's implicit requirement that questions concerning rights are primarily for *judicial* determination, as they are at Strasbourg. As Nicol puts it, under this view, 'The homespun idiosyncrasies of the HRA's structure should be played down in favour of the overriding aim of ensuring real and effective protection of human rights.'[16]

It is well known that, particularly in relation to the three interpretive issues mentioned above, the HRA allows for a degree of judicial choice between the use of what may be crudely termed its 'pro-rights' provisions (most importantly, ss. 6(1)[17] and 3(1)), and its 'pro-sovereignty' aspects (ss. 6(2),[18] 3(2)[19] and 4)—and thus gives rise to what may be seen as a 'sliding scale' of judicial power.[20] Under the rights-driven interpretative approach, the dial of judicial power is generally turned up quite high (although scholars within this school

[11] Considered below, at pp.32–38.
[12] Considered below, at pp.38–49.
[13] C.f., for example, the sharp disagreement between Nicol and Kavanagh over the constitutional propriety of a series of decisions under s.3 HRA, considered below.
[14] These two contrasting approaches are sketched here in only the most general terms; there are of course important nuances within them not considered here.
[15] See, for example, Masterman's essay in this volume, Chapter 5.
[16] D. Nicol, "Are Convention Rights a No-go Zone for Parliament?" [2002] P.L. 438.
[17] Providing that public authorities act unlawfully if they act in a way that is incompatible with a Convention right.
[18] Allowing for executive violations of Convention rights in reliance on incompatible statutes.
[19] 'This section … (b) does not affect the validity, continuing operation or enforcement of any incompatible primary legislation …'.
[20] Phillipson, "Deference, Discretion and Democracy in the Human Rights Act Era", at p.76.

differ of course about just how high it may permissibly go).[21] The result is that the judicial role, at least under some readings, may become elevated to such an extent as to give rise to 'bi-polar sovereignty', with the rule of law and protection of fundamental rights given equal or near-equal status with the supremacy of Parliament to which they were previously so firmly subordinated. Under this view, then, the HRA plays a major road in reconceptualising—even transforming—the UK constitution, alongside other developments such as the EU law and devolution; it becomes 'the nexus to a new legal order of European human rights law'.[22]

In sharp contrast, under the second view, associated with the 'political constitutionalist' school, the HRA has a narrower role. There are many different aspects to this perspective but two are perhaps of central importance. First, rather than being seen as a transformative turning point, the HRA is regarded as a practical tool for enabling easier access to British citizens, in domestic courts, to the same limited set of rights that Strasbourg enforces.[23] Second, the s.4 declaratory power is seen not as giving domestic courts the right authoritatively to declare what the Convention rights require, but merely to make helpful suggestions as to what (in their contestable view) they *may* mean—an issue discussed further below.

In turn this means that, when assessing and interpreting the HRA, instead of asking how far the Act should change our view of the constitution, such a view focuses instead upon the way in which traditional constitutional principles must shape our view of the HRA.[24] Such views tend to stress the continuing operation of what can be termed the 'constitutional constraint' on judges, represented by the separation of powers and the primacy of Parliament's democratic role as law-maker.[25] Under this view, the courts must grant considerable deference to the elected branches of government, continue to develop the common law only incrementally, and take particular care to ensure that 'interpretation' of legislation never tips over into effectively rewriting it and thus usurping the democratically mandated role of the legislature.

[21] See, for example, p.25 above, contrasting Kavanagh's views to the 'maximalist' readings; and Hickman's criticism of 'Incorporationists' for over-playing the judicial role in protecting rights in "Constitutional Dialogue, Constitutional Theories and the HRA 1998".

[22] Nicol, "Are Convention Rights a No-go Zone for Parliament", at p.438.

[23] See, generally, C. Gearty, *Principles of Human Rights Adjudication* (Oxford: Oxford University Press, 2004), pp.9–13, 25.

[24] Thus Gearty's main work on the interpretation of the HRA and ECHR promises to place it in its 'constitutional, institutional and political context': *Principles of Human Rights Adjudication*, at pp.3–4. He does acknowledge, however, that the HRA is shaped by, but also will reshape, the existing constitution: see, for example, p.208.

[25] See, for example, Gearty, *Principles of Human Rights Adjudication*, at pp.117–22, 142–45.

It seems evident that over-concentration on one viewpoint will tend to limit one's ability to appreciate the complex interplay between the HRA and the existing constitution and I believe that some of my own writings have been limited in this way. I have therefore started to perceive a greater need to consider the 'fit' of the HRA within the existing constitution; in this respect it seems sensible to suggest that the relative influence each has on the other will vary depending upon, amongst other things, the particular provision under consideration. Thus it seems to follow that, where the effect of the Act's provisions are ambiguous, as they are, notoriously, in relation to its impact in the private sphere on common law,[26] existing constitutional principles must exert a greater gravitational pull on the interpretation of the Act than where provisions are clear and explicit. Hence I have recently set out an argument with my colleague Alex Williams[27] that the 'horizontal effect' puzzle posed by the HRA cannot ultimately be solved simply by consideration of the provisions of the Act itself or even of the Convention rights. These provisions indeed set up something of a contradiction: the inclusion through subss. 6(1) and 6(3) of judges within those public authorities bound to act compatibly with the Convention rights has led many to argue that judges must act compatibly even when dealing with a common law dispute between private parties, going so far as to create brand new causes of action in doing so[28]; but such a suggestion is in strong tension with the Act's presumably deliberate silence on private law and common law and its clear suggestion[29] that private bodies are *not* bound to respect the Convention right (and therefore should not be rendered indirectly bound via the judges' obligations in this respect). Hence, to solve the horizontal effect puzzle, we must turn to existing constitutional principles governing the role of the judiciary. These we argue provide the 'constitutional constraint' of incrementalism, supplying the necessary definition of, and

[26] See the sharp differences of view expressed in J. Morgan, "Questioning the 'True Effect' of the Human Rights Act" (2002) 22 L.S. 259, at 260–61; D. Beyleveld and S. Pattinson, "Horizontal Applicability and Horizontal Effect" (2002) 118 L.Q.R. 623, at 664; M. Hunt, "The 'Horizontal Effect' of the Human Rights Act" [1998] P.L. 423; W. Wade, "Horizons of Horizontality" (2000) 116 L.Q.R. 217; R. Buxton, "The Human Rights Act and Private Law" (2000) 116 L.Q.R. 48; G. Phillipson and A. Williams, "Horizontal Effect and 'the Constitutional Constraint'" (2011) 74(6) M.L.R 878. It is now also well known that the courts appear to have taken different views on this issue in different cases and refused thus far to provide a general resolution of it: for recent discussion, see G. Phillipson, "Privacy and Breach of Confidence: A Clear Case of Horizontal Effect?", in David Hoffman (ed.), *The Impact of the UK Human Rights Act on Private Law* (Cambridge: Cambridge University Press, 2011).

[27] "Horizontal Effect and 'the Constitutional Constraint'"

[28] See, for example, Morgan, "Questioning the 'True Effect' of the Human Rights Act"; Beyleveld and Pattinson, "Horizontal Applicability and Horizontal Effect"; Wade, "Horizons of Horizontality".

[29] In s.6(5), as well as s.6(1).

limitation upon, the judicial role in developing common law compatibly with the Convention rights.

Thus both of the basic views above are incomplete on their own. To focus only on how the HRA changes the constitution misses the inevitable question of how far the constitution governs how we approach the HRA in the first place—as in the horizontal effect example. But, equally, the argument that the interpretation of the HRA's provisions must be governed by traditional principles is also a very partial one: first it can lead to the kind of doctrinal messes we have seen when judges have tried to water down the s.6(1) head of judicial review down into a muddled kind of heightened *Wednesbury*.[30] But second, going too far in 'reading down' the plain terms of the HRA—itself after all an Act of Parliament—risks disrespect to Parliament's sovereignty, itself the paramount principle of the traditional constitution. And this leads us to the possible paradox mentioned at the beginning of this essay. On the one hand, enthusiasts for the HRA essentially rely on parliamentary sovereignty in order to assert that Parliament can, and has, transformed the traditional constitution through enacting the HRA; and yet they are often the very people who are opposed to the Diceyan doctrine of sovereignty that gives Parliament this very transformative power. On the other hand, those political constitutionalists, who seek through interpretation of the HRA to turn *down* its dial of judicial power, are in the end appealing to principles of the UK constitution—the separation of powers and a particular view of parliamentary democracy—and asserting (in effect) that Parliament cannot change these things, or at least should be presumed not to have done so. Under this view, legislation like the HRA, which seemingly seeks to transform such principles, instead finds itself reinterpreted by them.[31] At its highest, those who resist expansive readings of the Act's constitutional significance—particularly the interpretive power given to judges in s.3 HRA—seem to rely in doing so on Parliament's *in*ability to change certain constitutional fundamentals. And yet it is these political constitutionalists who are generally most supportive of a traditional view of parliamentary sovereignty, which entails that any and every principle other than the basic sovereignty of Parliament itself is open to change by Parliament. These arguments are explored further in what follows in the context of the arguments around s.3 HRA.

[30] For a trenchant critique of this tendency, see I. Leigh, "Judicial Review after the Human Rights Act", in H. Fenwick, G. Phillipson and R. Masterman, *Judicial Reasoning under the UK Human Rights Act* (Cambridge: Cambridge University Press, 2007).

[31] I discuss below an arguable example of such an instance in relation to s.3 and *Bellinger v Bellinger* [2003] 2 A.C. 467: see pp.35–36.

The Exercise of Interpretive Power under s.3 HRA: Exceeding Legitimate Expectations?

A fashionable narrative about the HRA emanating from the political constitutionalist school argues that what was at best a doubtful enterprise has been made worse by the courts' over-use of their powers under that Act: to be more precise, their over-use of some powers and under-use of others. Under this view, a 'major gap' between 'theory and practice' has opened up, with the result that, in the view of many, 'the HRA has proven to be less distinctive from US-style constitutionalism than initially claimed or hoped'.[32] This is because, as Gardbaum puts it:

> [T]he courts have treated the section 3 interpretive duty as a very strong one and as the primary remedy for rights violations under HRA. As a result, courts have ... not relied on section 4 declarations as the main structural vehicle for the legislative final word as much as some expected or hoped.[33]

Gardbaum expresses broad support for the HRA, but even his overall conclusion is that, because of the above tendency, 'the balance of power has ... gone a little too far in the judicial direction'.[34] Others have been far less temperate: the most vituperative criticism has come from James Allan, who has recently announced that 'the Human Rights Act makes me angry' and furiously attacked the courts' use of section 3 in cases like *Ghaidan Mendoza*[35] as an illegitimate and dishonest 'Sankey Hanky Panky tree-shaping job'.[36] Others, though seemingly more able to control their emotions, have nevertheless strongly criticised certain uses by the House of Lords of s.3 as excessive

[32] Gardbaum, "Successful and Distinctive", at p.196. It should be noted that Gardbaum is *identifying*, not endorsing this view. He states that 'it is a composite rather than a specifically attributable one, putting together and perhaps pushing to an extreme position, the reactions of several commentators, including J. Hiebert "New Constitutional Ideas: Can New Parliamentary Models Resist Judicial Dominance When Interpreting Rights?" (2004) *Texas Law Review* 1963; D. Nicol, "The Human Rights Act and the Politicians"(2004) L.S. 451; and, in the New Zealand Bill of Rights Act context, G. Huscroft, "Civil Remedies for Breach of the Bill of Rights", in P. Rishworth, G. Huscroft, S. Optician, R. Mahoney (eds), *The New Zealand Bill of Rights* (Melbourne: Oxford University Press, 2003) 837'. He might have added to this list James Allan (below) and Mark Tushnet, for example, "New Forms of Judicial Review and the Persistence of Rights—And Democracy-based Worries" (2003) 38 *Wake Forest Law Review* 813.

[33] Gardbaum, "Successful and Distinctive", at p.201.

[34] Gardbaum, "Successful and Distinctive", at p.205.

[35] *Ghaidan v Godin-Mendoza* [2004] 2 A.C. 557.

[36] J. Allan, "Statutory Bills of Rights: You Read Words In, You Read Words Out, You Take Parliament's Clear Intention and You Shake it All About", in Campbell, Ewing and Tomkins (eds), *The Legal Protection of Human Rights: Sceptical Essays*, p.115.

and illegitimate.[37] The substantive merits of this argument as it concerns particular judgments have now been debated many times, and I do not seek to go over this well-trodden ground again. Instead, I propose a simpler argument: that the judges, in using s.3 in far-reaching ways, are simply doing Parliament's bidding, and (with reference to the paradox suggested above) that it seems strange for those who cavil against any judicially imposed limits on what Parliament may instruct thus to be so critical of mere judicial obedience to Parliament's will.

The obvious and common response to this point is to argue that the courts' actual uses of s.3 have gone well *beyond* Parliament's intention. Thus, to make out my argument, I will first have to refute this commonly-held view. To do so, I will contend, is in fact surprisingly easy: we simply need compare a few statistics with some very well known *Pepper v Hart* statements made at the time of the passage of the HRA through Parliament. The declared expectations of government and Parliament, when the HRA was passed, are well known. It was said repeatedly by the government, when the Human Rights Bill was before Parliament, that '*in almost all* cases, the courts will be able to interpret ... legislation compatibly with the Convention'; s.4 would therefore be needed only for the 'rare cases where that cannot be done'.[38] The Lord Chancellor indeed went so far as to declare during the Third Reading in the Lords that the effect of s.3 would be such that, 'in 99 per cent of the cases that will arise, there will be no need for judicial declarations of incompatibility',[39] and in the first major s.3 case, *R. v A (No.2)*,[40] these statements were duly cited by Lord Steyn as evincing parliamentary approval for very strong uses of s.3. And reasonably so: after all, if s.3 was to take care of the vast majority of legislative Convention incompatibility then it would clearly have to be used in a very far-reaching manner indeed.

Thus, even assuming that the Lord Chancellor was employing some poetic licence in his '99 per cent' claim, or that the government underestimed the amount of incompatible provisions on the statute book, *Parliament's* expectations, in the light of such statements, must have been that s.3 would be the default remedy, the one used in the overwhelming majority of cases, while s.4 would be used, as the Home Secretary put it, only 'rarely'. What then has been the balance between the use of these two sections in practice? Half the

[37] See, for example, D. Nicol, "Gender Re-assignment and the Transformation of the Human Rights Act" (2004) 120 L.Q.R. 194. Elsewhere he has written of the House of Lords decision in *R. v A* as 'an all-male Appellate Committee ... blinded by its zeal for the rights of male defendants, falling into line with base prejudice': "Law and Politics after the Human Rights Act" [2006] P.L. 722, at 739.

[38] Jack Straw, HC Debs, col.778, 16 February 1998 (emphasis added).

[39] HL Debs, col.840, 5 February 1998.

[40] [2002] 1 A.C. 45, 67.

answer is well known: according to a recent report by the Ministry of Justice, there have been 27 declarations of incompatibility, of which 8 were overturned on appeal.[41] It is much more difficult to ascertain the total number of uses of s.3, since no central record is kept[42]; it would be an interesting, though painstaking, research project to establish a definitive figure. As a rough guide, though, Clayton and Tomlinson found 24 uses of s.3 by the end of 2008[43]; there has presumably been a handful of other cases since then,[44] but even so, the total number seems likely to be only around 30 or so at most. As Clayton and Tomlinson comment, this is 'a relatively small number'[45]: it is not even twice the total number of declarations sustained on appeal. Hence a rather striking fact emerges: the government told Parliament that it expected the ratio of s.3 to s.4 uses to be something like 99:1. Instead, it has been around 60:40. That looks like a far more *restrained* use of s.3 than the democratic branches expected or intended and far *more* uses of s.4 than they envisaged. Thus my first point is a simple one: it is hard to argue that the courts have used their s.3 powers far more than Parliament intended given that their actual use has been much *less* than Parliament was told to expect when it passed the HRA. Moreover, the reason for this seems fairly clear: recent analysis of declarations of incompatibility by Alison Young has found that 14 resulted from cases in which courts concluded that it would be incompatible with a fundamental feature of the legislation in question to reinterpret it in the way required to achieve compatibly.[46] In other words, the declarations have happened because courts have taken seriously the limits on their powers represented by s.3.

However, another reason why the balance between the two sections has been much more even than anticipated has been judicial application of the

[41] Ministry of Justice, *Responding to Human Rights Judgments: Report to the Joint Committee on Human Rights on the Government's Response to Human Rights Judgments 2010–11* (September 2011).

[42] The major cases, besides *R. v A* and *Ghaidan*, include: *R. v Offen* [2001] 2 All E.R.154; *R. v Lambert* [2002] 2 A.C. 545; *R. (Hammond) v Secretary of State for the Home Department* [2005] UKHL 69; *Secretary of State for the Home Department v MB* [2007] UKHL 46; *Secretary of State for the Home Department v AF (No.3)* [2009] 3 W.L.R. 74; *R. v Holding (Terence Anthony)* [2005] EWCA Crim 3185; *Sheldrake v DPP* [2004] UKHL 43; *R. (MB) v Secretary of State for the Home Department* [2006] EWCA 1000; *Financial Times v Interbrew* [2002] E.M.L.R. 24; *R. (Middleton) v West Somerset Coroner* [2004] 2 A.C. 182; *R. (O) v Harrow Crown Court* [2007] 1 A.C. 249; *R. (Wright) v Secretary of State for Health* [2008] Q.B. 422.

[43] R. Clayton and H. Tomlinson, *The Law of Human Rights*, 2nd edn (Oxford: Oxford University Press, 2009), p.191.

[44] Of which the most notable is *AF (No.3)*, discussed below at pp.41–44.

[45] Clayton and Tomlinson *The Law of Human Rights*, at p.191.

[46] A. Young, "Is Dialogue Working under the Human Rights Act?" (2011) P.L. 773, at 780–81 and appendix 2. In some of these instances there were further reasons for refraining from using s.3, discussed below.

tendency, identified in the general discussion above, to read the HRA in the light of, rather than as transforming, existing constitutional principles. My argument, then, is that, while courts have been notoriously bold in their use of s.3 in a handful of cases,[47] they have also read some restrictions into the terms of s.3 itself, albeit that these are context specific and do not always apply. It is worth emphasising this point, because the contrary has been so energetically maintained. James Allan, for example, has argued that the judges have *reinterpreted* s.3 'as granting [them] a licence to rewrite (short of some indeterminate point called "vandalism") all other legislation'[48]; in other words, that they have 'read up' s.3 to give themselves more power than Parliament ever envisaged. To examine this point it is first necessary to consider the legislative choice Parliament made, in adopting the particular language used in s.3(1) HRA. As Lord Steyn remarked in *R. v A (No.2)*[49]:

> The draftsman of the Act had before him the slightly weaker model in section 6 of the New Zealand Bill of Rights Act 1990 but preferred stronger language. Parliament specifically rejected the legislative model of requiring a reasonable interpretation.

When Parliament deliberately rejects an amendment limiting the courts to only reasonable reinterpretations, as it did,[50] it must be taken to have intended some pretty strong rereadings of other legislative provisions. Note that we can here refer quite safely to Parliament's intention: while this is normally a doubtful notion, rejection of an amendment gives rise to an objectively ascertainable intention on Parliament's part, arising from the undisputed legislative history.

The second point, then, is that given the particularly strong wording chosen by Parliament it was not necessary for courts to 'read up' their powers under s.3—since they were very strong as granted. Rather, what has happened is that courts have read their interpretive powers under s.3(1) in the light of background constitutional principles governing the judicial role. They have, in other words, read some limits into the use of s.3 that are not plainly necessitated from the wording of the provision itself. The result has been that courts in practice operate as if s.3(1) provided: 'as far as possible—*and if constitutionally appropriate*—primary and secondary legislation shall be read and given effect in a way that is compatible with the Convention rights'.[51] Thus, even in cases in which it would have been linguistically possible—even easy—

[47] Most notably, *R. v A*; *Lambert*; *Offen*; *Ghaidan*; *Hammond*; *MB*; *AF (No.3)*.

[48] Allan, "Statutory Bills of Rights", at p.115.

[49] [2002] 1 A.C. 45, at 67.

[50] HC Debs, vol.313, cols 421–22, 3 June 1998.

[51] This is the basic conclusion arising from what I believe to be the best analytical account of the exercise of the courts' powers under s.3—that provided by Kavanagh in chs 1–5 of *Constitutional Review*.

to change the meaning of the statutory words, courts have held back because they have considered that the change that would be made—even though only one of interpretation—would have such far-reaching implications that the matter should be considered by Parliament after a s.4 declaration. This point arose particularly clearly in the now well-known decision of *Bellinger v Bellinger*.[52] In that case, the House of Lords was manifestly able to remedy the incompatibility in the relevant statute as a matter of linguistic 'possibility': only a single word—'female'—required reinterpretation so as to include post-operative male–female transsexuals and thus satisfy the requirements of Article 8 of the European Convention on Human Rights (ECHR).[53] But, as Kavanagh has noted, their Lordships thought it 'preferable to leave the issue to be reformed by Parliament, so that it [could] be done in a comprehensive fashion, rather than by means of piecemeal, incremental steps'.[54] As Masterman has put it, 'addressing the wider ramifications of such [a change] was felt to be beyond the constitutional competence of the court'.[55] In other words, their Lordships, not uncontroversially, read the limits of the interpretative obligation imposed by s.3(1) in the light of the limits to the judicial role they saw as prescribed by the constitutional background. Nor was this an isolated expression of such principles: in *Ghaidan v Mendoza* the House of Lords reaffirmed that courts should not use s.3 to take decisions inappropriate to their role and capacities because of their 'exceedingly wide ramifications'[56] or where they raised 'issues of social policy which ought to be left to Parliament and not decided by judges".[57] This then is an example of the HRA taking colour and meaning from the constitutional soil in which it has been planted.

Furthermore, Young's analysis of declarations of incompatibility to date finds that nine of them were made in part because the courts found that there was a choice of ways of rendering the legislative scheme compatible with the Convention, and considered that the choice to be adopted ought to be left to Parliament.[58] Since the HRA does not contain any explicit or implicit provision

[52] [2003] 2 A.C. 467. Another instance cited by Young of a case in which courts felt that Parliament was better able to provide the large-scale reform required was *R. (on the application of M) v Secretary of State for Health* [2003] EWHC 1094 (Admin): see Young, "Is Dialogue Working under the Human Rights Act?", appendix 2.

[53] As argued by T. Hickman, "Constitutional Dialogue, Constitutional Theories and the HRA 1998" [2005] P.L. 306, at 330; G. Phillipson, "Deference, Discretion and Democracy in the Human Rights Act Era" (2007) 60 C.L.P. 40, at 65.

[54] A. Kavanagh, "The Elusive Divide between Interpretation and Legislation under the Human Rights Act 1998" (2004) O.J.L.S. 259, at 272.

[55] R. Masterman, *The Separation of Powers in the Contemporary Constitution* (Cambridge: Cambridge University Press, 2011), p.165.

[56] *Ghaidan*, p.124, per Lord Nicholls.

[57] *Ghaidan*, p.137, per Lord Millett.

[58] Young, "Is Dialogue Working under the Human Rights Act?", at 780–81 and appendix 2.

to this effect, this may be seen as a further limitation upon s.3(1) that has been read into it by courts.

Overall, then, the result has been that the courts have used their s.3 power somewhat *less* than Parliament would have expected.[59] In turn, therefore, the charge that courts have somehow exceeded their powers under the Act turns out to be hard to sustain: critics of the courts appear to be reduced to a position that amounts to little more than complaining about judicial obedience to a statute—this despite the fact that such critics are generally rather keen on such obedience. Of course such critics might reply simply that the HRA is a bad statute—so that their target is not judicial *interpretation* of the HRA, but the Act itself, so that the UK experience simply shows why even statutory Bills of Rights are a thoroughly bad idea. This no doubt is what James Allan, for example, would say. Others, such as Gearty and Nicol, are on the record as not opposing the HRA per se but as simply arguing for a particular approach to it. But here the lurking paradox rears its head again. To argue that the courts are, or should be, bound by principles constraining their use of the HRA is to depend, at least in part, on those principles being binding on an Act of Parliament. But this is at least somewhat in tension with the democratic positivist view, under which the law is simply what Parliament says it is, and the role of the courts is to give effect to Parliament's clear intent. To critique what the judges have done, and argue for more restraint, involves commentators in implicitly suggesting that, when Parliament uses formulations like 'so far as is possible to do so' in s. 3 HRA, the courts should read them down. But this would allow judges to tell us what Parliament 'really' meant.[60] It would come close to requiring the judges to read the HRA as if Parliament had decided instead to use the weaker formulation of the New Zealand Bill of Rights Act, which depends upon legislation being open to more than one interpretation and merely instructs courts to 'prefer' the interpretation that is consistent with the relevant rights and freedoms.[61] It may be doubted whether

[59] It might also be noted that in *R. v A* itself, as in a number of other cases, the Secretary of State intervened on behalf of the government, inviting the court to read down the legislative provision in question. Of course the executive cannot determine what parliamentary language means, but the fact that one of the two democratic branches, which drafted and introduced the legislation in question, itself invited the court to undertake the radical rereading it did rather undercuts the argument that the courts are running amok, vandalising legislation and frustrating democracy.

[60] Gearty has also advanced the narrower textual argument that s.3(2) HRA provides grounds for reading restrictions into s.3(1) HRA, in "Reconciling Parliamentary Democracy and Human Rights" (2002) 118 L.Q.R. 248, an argument, however, that I believe remains unconvincing as a matter of pure statutory interpretation: see G. Phillipson, "(Mis)Reading Section 3(1) of the Human Rights Act" (2003) L.Q.R. 183 and Gearty's reply, "Revisiting Section 3(1) of the Human Rights Act" (2003) 119 L.Q.R. 551.

[61] New Zealand Bill of Rights Act, s.6.

such suggestions are consistent with allegiance to parliamentary sovereignty and loyalty to Parliament's intention.

'Tell Us Your Truth about Rights, but Please Not Too Loud'[62]

We may now turn to the second key power the HRA gives courts in relation to legislation, the more obviously 'dialogic' power to make declarations of incompatibility under s.4. The basic concept of 'democratic' or 'constitutional dialogue' is considered at length in Colin Murray's essay in this volume,[63] and it is unnecessary to go over that ground here. My concern in this essay is with the particular *variant* of 'dialogue' advanced by Danny Nicol and Tom Campbell and critiqued by Tom Hickman[64] as 'principle proposing' dialogue. This position is one of three that Hickman sketches. The first, following Danny Nicol,[65] he dubs 'incorporationist': a view held by those who he thinks would have preferred a full blown Bill of Rights and who try, in his view, to 'read up' the HRA so that it can give the judges something close to the powers possessed by Supreme Courts in Germany and the United States.[66] While critical of this tendency, his real target is the other extreme, proponents of 'weak form' dialogue.[67] Scholars in this school view a s.4 declaration not as the determination of the law, but the proffering of a view to Parliament—which Parliament is properly entitled to disregard if it takes a different view of the rights' controversy in question.[68] A declaration of incompatibility may properly be disregarded, because, as Campbell puts it, the 'interpretation of the ECHR is a matter of moral reasoning in which courts have no special expertise and in connection with which their decisions have no special legitimacy'.[69] Hence any determinations the courts make of what the Convention requires are only 'provisional'.[70] Thus, under this viewpoint, 'The function of

[62] Adapted from Nicol, "Law and Politics", at p.745.

[63] See Chapter 4, this volume.

[64] Hickman, "Constitutional Dialogue, Constitutional Theories and the HRA 1998".

[65] See Nicol, "Are Convention Rights a No-go Zone for Parliament?", at p.438.

[66] His chief target in this respect being the author of this essay.

[67] His own preferred view, a middle ground that he calls 'strong form dialogue', arguably remains a little enigmatic but is not our concern here.

[68] See, for example, F. Klug, "Judicial Deference under the Human Rights Act" (2003) 2 E.H.R.L.R 125, at 132.

[69] T. Campbell, "Incorporation through Interpretation", in Campbell, Ewing and Tomkins (eds), *Sceptical Essays on Human Rights*, p.99.

[70] Campbell, "Incorporation through Interpretation", p.99.

the courts is to propose principled arguments for resolution by the political branches ... .'[71]. As Hickman sees it:

> [T]he courts are transformed from arbiters of rights, albeit subject to legislative overrule, to a form of privileged pressure group whose function it is to raise good reasons why a litigant's interests should be respected. It abandons the idea that the courts should hold government to fundamental principle and the law and repositions the courts within the forum of ordinary politics, providing not a check or balance, but counsel.[72]

Thus, courts, in Hickman's memorable phrase, 'provid[e] minorities with little more than judicial signatures on their petitions to Parliament'.[73] A more nuanced account is provided by Young, who has argued that courts should use s.4 declarations where the rights issue is 'contestable', thus recognising the need for parliamentary input on a difficult rights question.[74]

The purpose of this section is to examine recent episodes of 'dialogue' in order to test the reality against these accounts, particularly those under which s.4 declarations are a way of courts telling Parliament (in Nicol's words), '[T]his is our truth about rights, now tell us yours.'[75] Three difficulties will be identified. The first is that neither government nor Parliament appears to regard the courts as merely making helpful suggestions about what the Convention may require. Instead, the democratic branches appear to adhere to the irritatingly old-fashioned view that the role of the courts is to declare what the law is. The second is that, far from regarding s.3 reinterpretations as a judicial usurpation, governments appear to prefer them to declarations of incompatibility under s.4. The third point (discussed in the next section) is that responses to s.4 declarations can be so disingenuous as to preclude the possibility of honest dialogue about the rights issue in question. All three of these points cast serious doubt on the applicability of 'weak form' dialogic theory to actual constitutional practice.

The first point is straightforward, and emerges from all the analysis below. As Young has pointed out, even in relation to the three declarations that she dubs 'contestable'—in other words, where the result was not clearly apparent from settled case-law:

[71] T. Hickman, "The Courts and Politics after the Human Rights Act: A Comment" [2008] P.L. 84, at 86.

[72] Hickman, "Constitutional Dialogue, Constitutional Theories and the HRA 1998", at pp.309–10.

[73] Hickman, "Constitutional Dialogue, Constitutional Theories and the HRA 1998", at p.311.

[74] A. Young, "Is Dialogue Working under the Human Rights Act?"; and see also *Parliamentary Sovereignty and the Human Rights Act* (Oxford: Hart, 2009), ch.5.

[75] Nicol, "Law and Politics", at p.745.

> [T]here is little, if any, evidence of discussion as to the definition or scope of the right in Parliament. Rather, Parliament appears to accept the conclusion of the court that the legislation in question contravenes Convention rights and seeks to amend the legislation accordingly.[76]

Young instances the response to the decision in *International Transport Roth Gmbh v Secretary of State for the Home Department*,[77] in which the Court of Appeal was split 2:1 in finding a breach of the Convention and recognised the necessity of deferring to the democratic branches on the difficult issue of balancing due process rights with important issues of social policy—an issue that it thought required close consideration by the legislature. Despite these implicit invitations from the Court for real legislative consideration of these difficult issues, there was little substantive discussion of them in Parliament.[78]

As for the second point, there appear to be a number of reasons for governments' seeming preference for uses of s.3, rather than s.4. The most mundane is simply that s.3 reinterpretations do not *require* a government response. The government does not have to do anything further: the courts have, in a practical sense, 'solved' the human rights problem by dealing with the statutory provision in question. In contrast, a s.4 declaration can become a major governmental headache: legislation has been very publicly declared in violation of human rights—something that a government may find embarrassing and/or politically inconvenient, a point developed further below in the context of anti-terrorism legislation. More prosaically, a s.4 declaration means that *something has to be done*: either the government has to incur at least some controversy by publicly refusing to act on the declaration, or it has to bring forward remedial legislation, as of course it has done in nearly every case. Both actions carry political costs. Remedial action is time-consuming and may involve re-jigging the parliamentary timetable, and thus delaying other legislation rather dearer to the government's heart. Moreover, remedial measures may open a can of worms: MPs, pressure groups, the Joint Committee on Human Rights (JCHR) and others may take the opportunity to lobby for more extensive changes to the legislative scheme in question than the government proposes—or for less. Restive backbenchers, aggrieved at yet another 'barmy' human rights ruling dictating change to Parliament, may kick up a stink in the House or in the media. The *Daily Mail* will doubtless be outraged; the *Daily Telegraph* will pontificate; the *Sun* may start a petition. Dealing with all this takes time and uses up government energy. In short a declaration is an 'event, dear boy' of the sort that can help knock a govern-

[76] Young, "Is Dialogue Working under the Human Rights Act?", at p.786.
[77] [2002] EWCA Civ 158; [2003] Q.B. 728.
[78] Young, "Is Dialogue Working under the Human Rights Act?", at pp.787–88.

ment off course, bog it down in reacting to, rather than driving, events. All of the above provide reasons why governments may not perceive a declaration of incompatibility as an earnest attempt to start a constitutional conversation about the proper interpretation of fundamental rights, but rather as a profound nuisance, considerably less desirable than use of the relatively unobtrusive and tidy s.3.

A further reason why governments may prefer s.3 to s.4 lies in the difference between what I have elsewhere termed the differing 'rhetorical power' each carries.[79] This point is best illustrated by the last government's response to the radical rewriting of the fair hearing provisions of the Prevention of Terrorism Act 2005 (PTA) governing Control Orders, undertaken by the House of Lords in *AF (No.3)*.[80] The Convention problem in this area arose because of the provisions of the 2005 Act concerning the procedure by which the imposition of Control Orders could be challenged by the controlee in the High Court. Any evidence against the suspect that the government considered sensitive could be classified as 'closed material'—which was not then disclosed to the suspect or the suspect's lawyer. Indeed the statutory rules provided that the court *could not* allow disclosure of material to the suspect (even redacted summaries) that it considered would be 'contrary to the public interest'.[81] Thus, as Baroness Hale put it, '[T]he [court] is *precluded* from ordering disclosure even where [it] considers that this is *essential* in order to give the controlled person a fair hearing.'[82] The rules themselves thus provided for no irreducible minimum of disclosure, and hence in this respect, as in others, subordinated fair trial rights to the public interest. In order to adduce some level of protection for the suspect, the evidence in the closed case was subject to a species of adversarial challenge—but only by special security-cleared counsel (termed 'special advocates').[83] The inherent weakness of the scheme was that the special advocates could not take any instructions from the suspect after they had seen the closed material[84] and so could not challenge the material on the basis of those instructions.

This problem was exacerbated by a further factor, which applied in a number of cases, in which, as one judge remarked:

> The basis for the Security Service's confidence is wholly contained within the closed material. Without access to that material it is difficult to see how, in

[79] See below at p.45. Part of the analysis that follows is drawn from H. Fenwick and G. Phillipson, "Covert Derogations and Judicial Deference: Redefining Liberty and Due Process Rights in Counter-terrorism Law and Beyond" (2011) 56 McGill L.J. 864.

[80] *Secretary of State for the Home Department v AF (No.3)* [2009] 3 W.L.R. 74.

[81] PTA 2005, Schedule, para.4(3)(d)–(f); Civil Procedure Rules (CPR), rr. 76.2(2), 76.29(8).

[82] *Secretary of State for the Home Department v MB* [2007] UKHL 46, at [69] (emphasis added).

[83] CPR, rr. 76.23, 76.24.

[84] CPR, rr. 76.25, 76.28(2).

> reality, the [suspect] could make any effective challenge to what is, on the open case before him, no more than a bare assertion.[85]

In the same case, Lord Bingham in the House of Lords agreed that in such cases the suspect 'was confronted by a bare, unsubstantiated assertion which he could do no more than deny'.[86] In other words, the special advocates were often left to tackle, not simply a few particularly sensitive pieces of evidence, but *the whole substantive case* against the suspect. These provisions created obvious potential tensions with the right in art.6 ECHR to a fair hearing,[87] which, as a starting point, requires proper disclosure to the accused,[88] and allows restrictions on the normal ingredients of a fair trial only when absolutely necessary.

Following a complex and unsatisfactory set of domestic cases on this issue,[89] Strasbourg eventually intervened decisively in the case of *A v United Kingdom*.[90] In that judgment, which concerned the previous pre-emptive system of detention without trial under Part 4 of the Anti-Terrorism, Crime and Security Act 2001, the Court made some clear findings of principle about what art.6 required in such hearings, which were clearly applicable to the almost identical procedures used under the PTA. The Grand Chamber found that, where a case against a suspect was based mainly on the open evidence, or even where it was not, if the allegations in the open material were sufficiently specific—for example, that the controlee had visited a specific training camp during particular dates—the proceedings could be fair. In either case, suspects would have a reasonable opportunity to challenge the case against them. However, the court, in a decisive passage, stated that procedural fairness could *not* be achieved when 'the open material consisted purely of general assertions and [the court's] decision ... was based solely or to a decisive degree on closed material'. In such instances the role of the special advocates, unable to take instructions on the secret evidence, was rendered nugatory—they 'could not perform [their] function in any useful way' and thus could not render the system art.6-compliant.[91]

[85] *Secretary of State for the Home Department v MB* [2006] E.W.H.C. 1000 (Admin), at [67].
[86] *MB*, at [41].
[87] Art.6(1) provides as relevant: 'In the determination of any criminal charge against him, or of his rights and obligations in a suit at law, everyone shall be entitled to a fair and public hearing by a competent, independent and impartial tribunal established by law.'
[88] *Rowe v United Kingdom* [GC], Application no.28901/95; [2000] ECHR 91.
[89] On which, see E. Bates, "Anti-terrorism Control Orders: Liberty and Security Still in the Balance" (2009) 29(1) L.S. 99; Fenwick and Phillipson, "Covert Derogations and Judicial Deference: Redefining Liberty and Due Process Rights in Counter-terrorism Law and Beyond", at 896–901.
[90] Application no.3455/05; [2009] ECHR 301; 49 E.H.R.R. 29.
[91] *A v United Kingdom*, at [220].

The House of Lords then had the opportunity to apply this judgment to the Control Orders context in *Secretary of State for the Home Department v AF (No.3)*.[92] Given that to apply it properly would require a clear departure from the PTA rules described above, one might have expected the House to issue a declaration of incompatibility in relation to the closed evidence provisions and art.6. Instead, the House used s.3(1) HRA to 'read into' the procedural rules a requirement that enough of the gist of the allegations must be disclosed to the suspect to enable the procedure overall to be fair. As Lord Phillips put it:

> [T]he controlee must be given sufficient information about the allegations against him to enable him to give effective instructions in relation to those allegations. Provided that this requirement is satisfied there can be a fair trial notwithstanding that the controlee is not provided with the detail or the sources of the evidence forming the basis of the allegations.[93]

It is important to note that, using s.3 to read this principle into the legislation, the House of Lords was reversing what was arguably a 'fundamental feature'—a fundamental principle even—of the legislation: the principle that the suspect's rights of disclosure were to be subordinated to the public interest, with (the government claimed) the ultimate aim of upholding national security in combating the terrorist threat. This might fairly be said to be a key feature of the legislation, since the whole raison d'être of 'pre-emptive' measures like Control Orders is precisely to avoid the disclosure of evidence to suspects that criminal prosecution in open court would require. Hence the continuation of 'control measures' in the recently passed Terrorism Prevention and Investigation Measures Act 2012, which contains provisions governing hearings that are substantively identical to those reinterpreted in *AF (No.3*). Moreover, this basic non-disclosure principle was made crystal clear by the relevant provisions of the PTA discussed above, which *precluded* the judge from allowing evidence to go into the open case that would be 'contrary to the public interest', *regardless* of the impact on procedural fairness. It is strongly arguable that *AF (No.3)* was, for this reason, the most radical use of s.3 yet. The principle of privileging the public interest over disclosure of evidence could persuasively be said to be fundamental to the whole scheme of Control Orders under the 2005 Act—far more so than the privileging of heterosexual over homosexual relationships in the Rent Act 1977 (reread in *Ghaidan*) or the particular 'rape shield' provisions in the Youth Justice and Criminal Evidence Act 1999 so radically reread in *R. v A (No.2)*.

How, then, could it be argued that the government preferred the use of s.3 in this case even though it effectively overturned this key feature of the

[92] [2009] UKHL 28; [2010] 2 A.C. 269.
[93] *AF (No.3)*, at [59].

legislation? The first indication was that government counsel made no attempt to argue before their Lordships that the House should instead make a s.4 declaration.[94] But the real answer lies in the way the government 'spun' this episode in Parliament and beyond. During the House of Lords debate on the annual renewal of the Control Orders legislation in 2010, Lord West, for the government, to the astonishment of the more well-informed parliamentarian members of the JCHR, said:

> The judgment [in *AF (No.3* (HL))] should also finally put to bed the argument ... that control orders are in some way an affront to human rights. That is clearly not the case. ... We remain firmly of the view that the legislation and the order before us today are fully compliant with the European Convention.[95]

Such a statement, to human rights lawyers, was simply disingenuous. But it could be made. And perhaps it gave the government—and some parliamentarians—enough of a fig leaf to procure the renewal of Control Orders for yet another year. Nor was this an isolated example. The JCHR had previously pointed out that one Home Office memorandum to a parliamentary committee had stated that 'various House of Lords judgments have confirmed the way in which the 2005 Act operates in a manner fully compliant with the ECHR'.[96] The JCHR vigorously objected to this 'mischaracterisation' of important court judgments, which, it said, was positively misleading.[97]

It is here, then, that the difference between the legal and rhetorical force of s.4 becomes apparent.[98] In terms of law and remedy, s.3(1) represents the desired outcome from the claimant's point of view. It gets something done—immediately: it changes the law and thus vindicates his or her rights. But, as the Control Orders saga reveals, it allows the government to say to Parliament, media and the public that the relevant scheme is compliant with human rights principles—hoping the important detail that *it was not so but for the s.3 HRA reinterpretation*, will be lost in the gulf between lawyer and layperson. Conversely, while a s.4 HRA declaration leaves the claimant languishing in a prison cell (as in *Belmarsh*),[99] or the wrong gender identity (as in *Ghaidan*) it has tremendous rhetorical force as a speech-act: it presents a simple and compelling narrative for the media to follow and hence for public discourse. My argument is that it is for this reason that governments, at least in some instances, appear to regard s.3 reinterpretations as less intrusive in political

[94] As noted by Lord Philips, *AF (No.3)*, at [68].
[95] See HL Debs, vol.717, no.49, col.1521, 3 March 2010.
[96] *Annual Renewal of Control Orders Legislation 2010* (Ninth Report of Session 2009–10, HL 64, HC 395, at para.81.
[97] JCHR, report at para.85.
[98] This paragraph draws briefly on Fenwick and Phillipson, "Covert Derogations and Judicial Deference", p.903.
[99] As in *A and others v Secretary of State for the Home Department* [2005] 2 A.C. 68.

terms than s.4 declarations, since they allow them to uphold the stance that their legislative scheme as a whole is compliant with the United Kingdom's human rights obligations.

'Let's Misuse Your Truth about Rights'

The above, then, provides some reasons why governments may generally prefer s.3 rereadings of legislation to declarations; it thus casts doubt on the notion that governments welcome 'honest dialogue' as in the principle-proposing model. But the recent saga over the Sex Offender Register judgment[100] opens up a fresh perspective—one that in a different way must make us even more doubtful about the prospects of such dialogue. It is a commonplace that, as Hickman has complained, the reactions of ministers to judicial decisions, far from being the calm, reflective response that 'principle-proposing' theories would envisage, are often rushed, intemperate and prone to grossly misrepresent the decision with which the government is now supposedly engaging in 'dialogue'.[101] Clearly one must not be too precious about these things—one does not expect or necessarily *want* government ministers or MPs to debate human rights law like barristers in court or academics at conferences. However, what we see in this incident goes, I contend, far beyond the ordinary 'rough and tumble' of politics. So striking was the misrepresentation by senior members of the government not only of the Supreme Court judgment itself, but of its status under the HRA, that I believe it is only explicable by a rather startling thesis: that what we saw in this incident was what I will term the tendency to 'weaponise' a declaration of incompatibility. My argument is that the effect sought is to turn a short-term political defeat over the Sex Offender Register into a move towards victory in a much longer-term campaign—that against the HRA itself.

In the case in question, the House of Lords considered a challenge to the requirement that those convicted of sexual offences and receiving a sentence of more than 30 months must be placed on the Sex Offender Register for life, with no possibility of review.[102] The House of Lords found that the lack of any provision for review was a disproportionate breach of the right to respect for private life under art.8 HRA. The argument was fairly clear: a person who

[100] *R. (on the application of F) v Secretary of State for the Home Department* [2010] UKSC 17; [2011] 1 A.C. 331.
[101] Hickman, "The Courts and Politics after the Human Rights Act: A Comment", at p.95.
[102] Found in ss.82–86 of the Sexual Offences Act. Being placed on the 'Register' in fact means being subject to an indefinite requirement to report regularly various personal details to the police, including one's address and, in particular, overseas travel plans.

had committed an offence at a very young age[103] might live the next 30–40 years quite blamelessly, but would nevertheless have no means of challenging the fact of remaining on the Register for life—have no means, in other words, of asking anyone to determine whether they still merited labouring under this restrictive and stigmatic regime. Now the government was no doubt irritated by this judgment. It provoked fury from both Conservative backbenchers and the right-wing media, in the face of which the government was in danger of being seen as cravenly bending the knee to 'barmy' liberal judges, rather than standing up for the rights of the 'law-abiding majority'. Its response appears to represent a political calculation as to how it could wrest some advantage from this difficult situation—snatch a bigger victory from the jaws of this specific defeat. The strategy that emerged to achieve this was a three-pronged one, consisting of the following elements: (a) grossly misrepresenting and attacking the judgment of the Supreme Court; while (b) pretending that it was binding on the government, in order (c) to generate hostility to the HRA and the senior judiciary in general.

The first main response came from David Cameron, when asked about the judgment at Prime Minister's Questions in February 2011:

> My hon. Friend speaks for many people in saying how completely offensive it is, once again, to have a ruling by a court that flies in the face of common sense. Requiring serious sexual offenders to sign the register for life, as they now do, has broad support across this House and across the country. I am appalled by the Supreme Court ruling. We will take the minimum possible approach to this ruling and use the opportunity to close some loopholes in the sex offenders register … I can also tell my hon. Friend that a Commission will be established imminently to look at a British Bill of Rights, because it is about time we ensured that decisions are made in this Parliament rather than in the courts.[104]

The way in which the attack on the judgment is immediately used as impetus for the setting up of the Commission is significant, and rather gives the game away.[105]

It may be presumed that the specific calculation in pretending that the government had to comply with the ruling was that, had the government instead said, 'Don't worry, the whole point of the HRA is that, where we disagree

[103] One of the challenges that led to the Supreme Court ruling had been brought by a person, known only as 'F', who had committed a serious sexual offence at the age of 11, and hence was faced with being on the register for his entire adult life.

[104] HC Debs, col.955, 16 February 2011, Q9.

[105] Of course, since it was clear already that Parliament is not legally obliged to respond to declarations of incompatibility, the proposal the Prime Minister made was a non-sequiter. The whole setting up of the Bill of Rights Commission seemed premised on a simple contradiction: replacing the HRA—which gives Parliament the final say on rights issues—with a British Bill of Rights that would give Parliament the final say on rights issues.

with the judges on a rights issue, we are not bound to follow their view, so we can simply decline to legislate in accordance with this judgment', the anti-HRA fury—and hence the case for replacing it—would have been somewhat diminished. Instead the government appeared to pretend that it was *forced* to put women and children at risk by 'barmy' judges. The breathtaking cynicism of this stance can hardly be exaggerated; nor the extent to which it breached the principle of comity between the different branches of government, and deliberately sought to undermine public confidence in both the judges and the rule of law. However its aim of stoking more fury against the HRA from Conservative backbenchers and—importantly—the right-wing media certainly appeared to work: the *Daily Mail* carried the headline 'End this Human Rights Insanity', over an article reporting that, 'David Cameron declared war on unelected judges yesterday after they put the human rights of paedophiles and rapists before public safety.'[106] Meanwhile one Conservative MP alleged that the 'out of touch' Supreme Court judges were 'now openly, proudly and provocatively saying that a paedophile's right to privacy is more important than children's protection from those who have committed evil sexual acts'.[107]

The formal debate on the declaration, led by the Home Secretary—who must be presumed to know the law—reveals exactly the same tendencies. Theresa May started by saying:

> The Government are disappointed and appalled by that ruling. It places the rights of sex offenders above the right of the public to be protected from the risk of their reoffending, but there is no possibility of further appeal.[108]

In response to the misleading suggesting that 'there was no appeal' from this judgment, Jack Straw felt obliged to point out to the Home Secretary a basic truth about the design of the HRA:

> Will she confirm that under section 4 of the Human Rights Act 1998 there is absolutely no obligation on her or the House to change the law one bit? All the Court did was to issue a declaration of incompatibility and section 4 makes it absolutely clear that any decision following that is a matter for the sovereign Parliament. It would be entirely lawful for the House and her to say that the existing regime will continue without any amendment.[109]

[106] 17 February 2011, http://www.dailymail.co.uk/news/article-1357472/Sex-offenders-register-Paedophiles-rapists-apply-remove-name.html#ixzz1kaM9abjY (accessed 14 May 2012).
[107] HC Debs, vol.523, col.965, 16 February 2011 (Adrian Burley).
[108] HC Debs, vol.531, col.959, 16 February 2011.
[109] HC Debs, vol.531, col.960, 16 February 2011.

The Home Secretary in response simply avoided the point[110] and the whole debate continued on the basis that the government was obliged to implement the dreadful judgment, with all energy concentrated upon how it would and should do so in the most minimal way possible.

One possible explanation of the above is that the Home Secretary and the Prime Minister were referring to the fact that the government saw itself as 'de facto' bound to implement the judgment. It has often been argued that s.4 declarations are rendered de facto binding because they can be eventually 'enforced' by a concurring Strasbourg judgment, which *is* binding, at least at the level of international law. But this argument has been substantially weakened by the recent House of Commons 'push-back' in the prisoners' voting rights saga.[111] It now appears that at least Conservative governments unwilling to pay the political cost of complying with rights judgments can use House of Commons votes by viscerally anti-European backbench MPs in order to demonstrate to the Council of Europe the practical impossibility of compliance. At the very least, the continuing lack of a legislative response to the *Hirst* case, some seven years after it was delivered, shows that governments can at the least delay compliance with even Strasbourg rulings for more than a Parliament—this is an age in political terms, and considerably longer than most post-war governments have lasted.[112] The government's outrage over the ruling appears even more phony in light of the fact that not only did it agree to act promptly by a remedial order—thus hastening the time at which women and children were to be put at risk from sex offenders (on its own account of the effect of the ruling)—but it also substantially liberalised its originally planned measure[113] in response to the recommendations of the JCHR.[114]

[110] 'The right hon. Gentleman makes a point about the application of the Human Rights Act and the European Convention on Human Rights and about Parliament having the final decision about what should happen. In this case, Parliament will have the final decision on what happens.'

[111] The saga originated with the Strasbourg decision in *Hirst v United Kingdom (No.2)* no.74025/01, 6 October 2005, which decided that the United Kingdom's blanket prohibition on prisoners' voting was a disproportionate interference with the right to vote (guaranteed under art.3 of Protocol 1 to the Convention). The Court did not require specific action by way of a remedy but said that the details of the response required were up to the United Kingdom and should be considered by its Parliament. There was then a series of delays in responding to this judgment, which led to a domestic challenge in *Smith v Scott* [2007] SC 345, resulting in a declaration of incompatibility. Further delays of several years followed (during which another domestic challenge led to a further DoI in *R. (on the application of Chester) v Secretary of State for Justice* [2010] EWCA Civ 1439; [2010] All E.R. (D.) 219 (Dec)), until, in 2011, the House of Commons had a backbench debate on the issue, which resulted in an overwhelming vote to reject the Strasbourg ruling and maintain the blanket ban: see HC Debs, cols.493–584, 10 February 2011.

[112] Only the Blair and Thatcher governments have lasted seven years or longer in the post-war era.

[113] See the final version of the Sexual Offences Act 2003 (Remedial) Order 2012, laid before both Houses on 5 March 2012.

[114] See Government Response to the Nineteenth Report of the JCHR, 2010–12, HC 1549. The two most important changes the government agreed to were as follows: the first allowed an appeal

What would have been the proper ‘dialogic’ response? The government would have said something like:

> We respectfully disagree with this judgment. While it does not mean that a single person will necessarily come off the Register, we believe so passionately that it is right to keep people on the register for life with no possibility of review, that we are going to maintain the system as it is and thus decline to implement this judgment.

The Home Secretary would then have gone on to explain in detail her *reasoned* disagreement with the Supreme Court’s findings on the balance between the privacy interests of sex offenders and public safety. Such a hypothetical response needs only to be stated to show how yawning is the gap between this idealised possibility and the political reality.

To sum up a long argument, we have seen two recent responses to judicial uses of ss. 3 and 4 of the Human Rights Act 1998, neither of which conforms to the ‘open debate about rights’ model argued for by political constitutionalists. The first response sees the government actively seeking to avoid a s.4 declaration, so that it can (disingenuously) maintain in public that it is both protecting the public *and* upholding human rights (the Control Orders issue). The second sees a government response to a declaration which, rather than honestly taking issue with the arguments made by the judges, grossly misrepresents both the judgment and its legal consequences in order to generate public hostility against the ECHR, the HRA and the judges—a response that seeks to weaponise a declaration of incompatibility.

To be clear, the above examples are not presented in order to contend that the notion of ‘principle-proposing’ dialogue is wrong or that successful dialogue never happens[115]; the argument is simply that such conceptions of dialogue have been stated in an idealised form that seems to comport very ill to at least the current political realities. A rethink on ‘dialogic’ theories grounded more in political reality seems to be called for.

---

to a magistrate’s court following a decision made by the police about whether someone should remain on the Register; the other was to make ‘express provision in the remedial order for the test to be applied by the police in determining a review’, namely one that involved ‘balancing the risk posed by the offender against the extent of the interference caused to that offender by a continuation of the notification requirements’ (para.24).

[115] One could argue that the *substantive outcome* of the Sex Offender Register case was, ironically, one example; Young also instances the response to *Bellinger v Bellinger* [2003] UKHL 21; [2003] 2 A.C. 467 (resulting in the Gender Recognition Act 2004) and *R. (on the application of M) v Secretary of State for Health* [2003] EWHC 1094 (Admin); [2003] 3 All E.R. 672 (resulting in the Mental Health Act 2007) as successful dialogic episodes.

3

The Continuation of Politics, by Other Means: Judicial Dialogue under the Human Rights Act 1998

C. R. G. MURRAY

The Rise of the New Judiciary

THE HUMAN RIGHTS ACT 1998 (HRA) has expanded the judiciary's role within the political constitution. The courts now regard themselves as 'the guardian of human rights'.[1] Prior to the enactment of the HRA, judges like Sir John Laws did not consider that this responsibility would politicise their role:

> [The courts'] interest and obligation ... is to protect values which no democratic politicians could honestly contest: values which, therefore, may be described as apolitical, since they stand altogether above the rancourous but vital dissensions of party politicians.[2]

Democracy as a vehicle enabling the collective pursuit of justice[3] would thrive, Laws hoped, over and above the floor of rights protections introduced by the HRA. This optimism has not been borne out by the first decade of the HRA's operation. As John Griffith famously warned, the loosely defined rights contained within the European Convention on Human Rights (ECHR) did not transform political disputes into legal ones but simply transferred them into the legal sphere.[4] As a consequence, in the HRA era 'distinctions between the business of judging and the pursuit of politics have diminished, and this has served to expose the contestability of judicial activity'.[5]

A wealth of scholarship on the concept of 'judicial dialogue' with the other branches of government has endeavoured to compensate for these

[1] *International Transport Roth GmbH v Secretary of State for the Home Department* [2002] EWCA Civ 158; [2003] Q.B. 728, at [27] (Simon Brown LJ).
[2] J. Laws, "Law and Democracy" [1995] P.L. 72, 93.
[3] See J. Rawls, *Political Liberalism* (New York: Columbia University Press, 1993).
[4] See J. Griffith, "The Political Constitution" (1979) 42 M.L.R. 1, 16.
[5] D. Nicol, "Law and Politics after the Human Rights Act" [2006] P.L. 722, 741.

Proceedings of the British Academy, **183**, 51–79.

thwarted expectations.[6] These contributions require us to reconceive the constitution as a 'multi-actor network' in which the judiciary 'can act as a facilitator and catalyst for change, but ... is unable to effect change single-handedly'.[7] Luc Tremblay provides a tantalising glimpse of the potential of dialogue theory:

> [T]he courts and the legislatures participate in a dialogue regarding the determination of the proper balance between constitutional principles and public policies, and, this being the case, there is good reason to think of judicial review as democratically legitimate. It is an ongoing dialogue because the judiciary does not necessarily have the last word with respect to constitutional matters and policies ...[8]

In other words, dialogue theory offers the promise of circumventing age-old arguments between political and legal constitutionalists[9] by recognising the important role of the courts within a constitutional system which nevertheless gives the last word on issues of rights compliance to an elected legislature.

The sudden upsurge in interest in dialogue theory, however, implies that the process of judicial interaction with the other branches of government started with the HRA. The emphasis on the HRA is heightened by some efforts to explain dialogue, with Alison Young, for example, confining the concept to exchanges between the courts and Parliament initiated by judicial decisions which are 'open to legislature reversal, modification or avoidance'.[10] This framing of the issue encourages a focus upon the powers of the courts under the HRA to re-interpret legislation to conform to human rights standards[11] and to issue declarations of incompatibility where such re-interpretation is impossible.[12] Whilst exercises of either power can draw out a

[6] See, for example, F. Klug, "Judicial Deference under the Human Rights Act" [2003] E.H.R.L.R. 125; R. Clayton, "Judicial Deference and 'Democratic Dialogue': The Legitimacy of Judicial Intervention under the Human Rights Act 1998" [2004] P.L. 33; T. Hickman, "Constitutional Dialogue, Constitutional Theories and the Human Rights Act 1998" [2005] P.L. 306; T. Hickman "The Courts and Politics after the Human Rights Act: A Comment" [2008] P.L. 84; P. Sales and R. Ekins, "Rights-consistent Interpretation and the Human Rights Act 1998" (2011) 127 L.Q.R. 217.

[7] M. Cohn, "Judicial Activism in the House of Lords: A Composite Constitutionalist Approach" [2007] P.L. 95, 105.

[8] L. Tremblay, "The Legitimacy of Judicial Review: The Limits of Dialogue between Courts and Legislatures" [2005] I.J.C.L. 617, 617.

[9] See A. Tomkins, "The Role of the Courts in the Political Constitution" (2010) 60 U.T.L.J. 1, 2.

[10] A. Young, *Parliamentary Sovereignty and the Human Rights Act* (Oxford: Hart Publishing, 2009), p.116. In this approach, Young is building upon the work of Peter Hogg and Allison Bushell, "The Charter Dialogue between Courts and Legislators (Or Perhaps the Charter of Rights Isn't a Bad Thing after All)" (1997) 35 *Osgoode Hall L.R.* 75, 79.

[11] HRA 1998, s.3(1).

[12] HRA 1998, s.4(2).

legislative response (and generate furious debate on the appropriate relationship between the powers),[13] declarations have captured the imagination of commentators, as they trigger the HRA's formal response mechanism of fast-track legislative amendment.[14] Even Sir John Laws has recognised that UK public law is in the process of evolving into 'a strategic partnership between the branches of government'.[15]

Whilst the HRA undoubtedly provided the judiciary with 'novel and powerful tools for participation in social decision-making' when human rights are at issue,[16] the first section of this essay places these developments in historical context. Rather than instituting a process of inter-institutional dialogue, the HRA's enactment is better understood as streamlining the judiciary's interaction with the other branches of government. The HRA's dialogue mechanisms build upon the myriad of calls for legislation, dissenting judgments and judicial comments on whether government policy is satisfactory which arguably once provided for a nascent form of constitutional dialogue. This analysis of pre-1998 interactions between the judiciary and legislature does not threaten to expand dialogue theory to the point where it becomes 'unstable and meaningless',[17] but rather seeks to place post-1998 developments in context. In relation to rights-based claims, the second and third sections of this essay assess how the HRA has not only raised the profile of judicial interventions but increased the volume of cases in which the courts are called upon to make politically sensitive decisions.

Many commentators laud these developments. Stephen Gardbaum, for example, argues that such 'Socratic dialogue' allows for 'the possibility of further deliberation by a now-alerted citizenry and political opposition'.[18] Nonetheless, simply because the judiciary's interventions on public policy are more high-profile and more frequent in the HRA era, it does not necessarily follow that the impact of such interventions has substantially increased. Indeed, declarations of incompatibility may be better characterised as supplanting, rather than supplementing, many of the modes of judicial interaction employed prior to the HRA. This process may have strengthened the

[13] See, for example, C. Gearty, "Reconciling Parliamentary Democracy and Human Rights" (2002) 118 L.Q.R. 248; M. Arden, "The Interpretation of UK Domestic Legislation in the Light of European Convention on Human Rights Jurisprudence" (2004) 25 *Stat. L.R.* 165; A. Kavanagh, "The Elusive Divide between Interpretation and Legislation under the Human Rights Act 1998" (2004) 24 O.J.L.S. 259; T. Allan, "Parliament's Will and the Justice of the Common Law: The Human Rights Act in Constitutional Perspective" (2006) 59 C.L.P. 27.

[14] HRA 1998, s.10(2).

[15] *R. (Chester) v Secretary of State for Justice* [2010] EWCA Civ 1439, at [31].

[16] Cohn, "Judicial Activism", 95.

[17] A. L. Young, "Is Dialogue Working under the Human Rights Act 1998?" [2011] P.L. 773, 774.

[18] S. Gardbaum, "Reassessing the New Commonwealth Model of Constitutionalism" [2010] I.J.C.L. 167, 172.

judicial voice in some cases but weakened it to a murmur in others. Moreover, the HRA's dialogue-facilitating features have drawn the judiciary onto uncertain ground. As Lord Scott has openly acknowledged, declarations of incompatibility are 'essentially political in character rather than legal'.[19] When individuals (frequently supported by pressure groups) pursue a rights-based claim they often do so not with the expectation that the courts will uphold their claim, but in the hope that judges will issue a declaration with which they can influence political debate. This essay examines judicial efforts to constrain these 'protest' cases, and the consequent instances when judges have failed to recognise the legal merit in a case because of the belief that the claimants are only interested in generating publicity.

The Development of Judicial Dialogue with Parliament

Historically, constitutional theorists have recognised the potential of judicial decisions to foment political debate. Long before the present popularity of dialogue theory, Lon Fuller saw that the process of statutory interpretation reveals the essentially 'cooperative nature of the task of maintaining legality'.[20] For much of the 20th century, however, the UK courts conceived of their role as distinct and indeed autonomous from the other branches of government. Judging was conceived as a 'technical enterprise'[21] concerned with statutory interpretation and the development of the remaining realms of common law, all the while acknowledging that Parliament had the capacity to codify or undo any aspect of such judge-made law and to recast important constitutional documents. To maintain these autonomous spheres of competence all that was necessary, in the words of Sir John Donaldson MR, was for judges and the other branches of government to respect each other's purview.[22]

The judiciary zealously guards its independent interpretation function to this day, with Baroness Hale recently remarking that 'it is not for government and official bodies to interpret the meaning of the words which Parliament has used'.[23] In dismissing claims that the decisions of the Upper Tribunal were not amenable to judicial review in *Cart*,[24] Laws LJ elaborated on the constitutional importance of this judicial function:

[19] *A v Secretary of State for the Home Department* [2004] UKHL 56; [2005] 2 A.C. 68, at [145] (Lord Scott).

[20] L. Fuller, *The Morality of Law* (New Haven, CT: Yale University Press, 1969), p.91.

[21] Nicol, "Law and Politics", 723.

[22] *R. v HM Treasury Ex p. Smedley* [1985] Q.B. 657, 666.

[23] *Yemshaw v Hounslow LBC* [2011] UKSC 3, at [25] (Baroness Hale).

[24] *R. (Cart) v Upper Tribunal* [2009] EWHC 3052 (Admin).

> [T]exts cannot speak for themselves. Unless their meaning is mediated to the public, they are only letters on a page. They have to be interpreted. The interpreter's role cannot be filled by the legislature or the executive: for in that case they or either of them would be judge in their own cause, with the ills of arbitrary government which that would entail.[25]

In performing this function, from the 1970s onwards, judges gradually abandoned the pretence that the common law's development does not involve a degree of law-making competence, declaring it to be a 'fairy tale'[26] and, eventually, a 'discredited myth'.[27] Beyond cases resolvable by technical application of legal rules there remain politically or morally controversial 'hard cases' which require judges to fill in the lacuna in the common law.[28] Today's widespread judicial acceptance of this positivist proposition[29] requires some explanation of why the judiciary sought for so long to eschew any form of inter institutional dialogue.

The Formalist Consensus

Public law's 'long sleep' in UK jurisdictions was the product of a culmination of factors in the late 19th and early 20th centuries. During his terms as Lord Chancellor, Lord Halsbury wielded his control over a highly politicised judiciary to stifle judge-made developments in the legal system. He denied that the House of Lords could depart from its previous decisions,[30] insisted that judgments should not extend beyond the facts of the case[31] and maintained that the alteration of established common law rules was a task for the legislature.[32] In short, 'Halsbury at every opportunity sought to put the brakes on judicial activism.'[33] This effort to purge the creative capacity of judges, of itself, would hardly have curtailed judicial engagement with issues of public law, for under 19th-century case law judicial review already required public

[25] *R. (Cart) v Upper Tribunal* [2009] EWHC 3052(Admin), at [37]. Baroness Hale would subsequently declare that any claim that the Tribunals, Courts and Enforcement Act 2007 ousted judicial review of the Upper Tribunal's decisions had been 'killed stone dead by Laws LJ', *R. (Cart) v Upper Tribunal* [2011] UKSC 28, at [37].

[26] J. Reid, "The Judge as Lawmaker" (1972) 12 *Jnl Soc Public Teachers of Law* 22, 22.

[27] *Kleinwort Benson Ltd v Lincoln City Council* [1999] 2 A.C. 349.

[28] See D. Dyzenhaus, *Hard Cases in Wicked Legal Systems: Pathologies of Legality* (Oxford: Oxford University Press, 2010), pp.1–33.

[29] T. Bingham, "The Judges: Active or Passive", 2005 British Maccabaean Lecture at Cardiff Law School, http://www.law.cf.ac.uk/publiclecture/transcripts (accessed 21 February 2012), 11–12.

[30] *London Street Tramways Co Ltd v London County Council* [1898] A.C. 375, 379.

[31] *Quinn v Leathem* [1901] A.C. 495, 506.

[32] *London Street Tramways Co Ltd v London County Council* [1898] A.C. 375, 381 and *Earldom of Norfolk Peerage Claim* [1907] A.C. 10, 12.

[33] R. Stevens, "Government and the Judiciary", in V. Bogdanor (ed.), *The British Constitution in the Twentieth Century* (Oxford: Oxford University Press, 2003), p.337.

bodies to respect the principles of natural justice.[34] However, Lord Halsbury was succeeded in office by a series of Liberal Lord Chancellors (together with Liberal-appointed Law Lords). With a universal franchise on the horizon, and eager to protect the government's social-reform programme, these judges denied their capacity to challenge administrative decisions by elected policy makers on any basis other than acting in excess of powers.[35]

These approaches were hardly set in stone. Lord Halsbury was prepared to ignore his own strictures when the opportunity arose to develop common law causes of action to allow companies to claim against trade unions for revenue losses resultant from strikes.[36] Nonetheless, they became fused together in the crucible of the First World War. By 1918, Scrutton LJ felt prepared to cast the judicial role in the most limited terms:

> Complaints have been sometimes made of the action of the judges or their failure to interfere with the action of officials. The answer is that Parliament has allowed certain action, and has laid down certain rules in statutes. The only duty of judges is to enforce and administer those statutes.[37]

With the acceptance of these restrictions on the judiciary's public-law role as orthodoxy, the courts developed other rules to enable them to steer clear of politically controversial spheres. For example, Lord Wilberforce accepted it as 'inherent in the very nature of the judicial process'[38] that the domestic courts would not rule upon the legality of a foreign state's actions as this issue lay within the realm of international relations and therefore within the bailiwick of the executive.

This suppression of the judiciary's role does not, however, undermine the thesis that the judiciary contributed to the political constitution throughout the 20th century. As Griffith cryptically declared, in the United Kingdom 'everything that happens is constitutional. And if nothing happened, that would be constitutional also.'[39] Ironically, Griffith's statement is best translated to the position of the judiciary by his adversary Lord Hailsham, speaking in parliamentary debates on the introduction of a Bill of Rights just months before Griffith's famous lecture was published:

> Judges cannot choose the work they do; they have to come to a decision one way or another on all litigation which is brought before them. If they assume

[34] See, for example, *Cooper v Wandsworth Board of Works* (1863) 143 E.R. 414.

[35] See *Board of Education v Rice* [1911] A.C. 179, 182 (Lord Loreburn LC) and *Local Government Board v Arlidge* [1915] A.C. 120, 132 (Lord Haldane LC). See J. Allison, "The Procedural Reason for Judicial Restraint" [1999] P.L. 452.

[36] *Taff Vale Railway Co v Amalgamated Society of Railway Servants* [1901] A.C. 426.

[37] T. Scrutton, "The Law and the War" (1918) 34 L.Q.R. 116, 119.

[38] *Buttes Gas and Oil v Hammer* [1982] A.C. 888, 932.

[39] Griffith, "The Political Constitution", 19.

> jurisdiction they are in politics; if they decline jurisdiction they are in politics. All they can hope to be is impartial ...[40]

The judiciary's creative capacity in the realm of public law existed throughout this period of judicial self-abnegation. Its suppression might be characterised as a 'noble lie', intended to protect judicial independence.[41] Decisions such as *Wednesbury*[42] and *Carltona*[43] warned off litigants in politically contentious cases, 'compelling them to seek solutions through political channels'.[44] Occasionally, however, *active* inter-institutional dialogue burst forth.

The best remembered example of such interaction came in *Liversidge v Anderson*,[45] concerning detention without trial of an individual during the Second World War. The majority in the House of Lords, led by Viscount Maugham, ruled that the power to detain an individual 'whose detention appears to the Secretary of State to be expedient in the interests of the public safety'[46] did not allow the courts to require the Home Secretary to establish some reasonable basis for his decision to detain.[47] By contrast, Lord Atkin noted that Regulation 18B, which was created under this power, stated in narrower terms that the Home Secretary must have 'reasonable cause to believe any person to be of hostile origin or associations'.[48] In refusing to require that the Home Secretary explain the basis for Liversidge's detention, Lord Atkin declared that the majority had effectively granted the government a power that it had not sought under Regulation 18B, and that, in his famous repost, his colleagues had shown themselves to be 'more executive minded than the executive'.[49]

Although, on its own terms, Lord Atkin's dissent has been criticised as less well-argued than Lord Shaw's similar dissent over First World War detention powers in *Ex p. Zadig*,[50] his strident refusal to conform to the normally 'restrained' nature of dissents in English courts,[51] and the boldness of his

[40] Lord Hailsham, HL Debs, vol.396, col.1384, 29 November 1978. See also J. Laws, "Law and Democracy" [1995] P.L. 72, 74.
[41] See *Duport Steel v Sirs* [1980] 1 W.L.R. 142, 169 (Lord Diplock). See also P. Devlin, "Judges and Lawmakers" (1976) 39 M.L.R. 1, 8.
[42] See *Associated Provincial Picture Houses v Wednesbury Corporation* [1948] 1 K.B. 223, 233 (Lord Greene MR).
[43] See *Carltona Ltd v Commissioner of Works* [1943] 2 All E.R. 560, 563 (Lord Greene MR).
[44] Nicol, "Law and Politics", 732.
[45] *Liversidge v Anderson* [1942] A.C. 206.
[46] Emergency Powers (Defence) Act 1939, s.1(2).
[47] *Liversidge v Anderson* [1942] A.C. 206, 219.
[48] Regulation 18B, Defence (General) Regulations, 1939.
[49] *Liversidge v Anderson* [1942] A.C. 206, 244.
[50] *R. v Halliday Ex p. Zadig* [1917] A.C. 260. See D. Foxton, "*R v Halliday Ex p. Zadig* in Retrospect" (2003) 119 L.Q.R. 455, 494.
[51] J. Alder, "Dissents in Courts of Last Resort: Tragic Choices?" (2000) 20 O.J.L.S. 221, 239.

challenge after several decades of judicial quiescence, combine to feed the perception of him 'as a sort of legal saint in a profession which is rather light on sanctity'.[52] Even if Brian Simpson, in his seminal review of the wartime detention powers, showed that Lord Atkin's concern was not with the liberty of the individual but with 'the relative status in the scheme of government of judges on the one hand and officials and ministers on the other',[53] this analysis only intensifies this dissent's relevance in terms of inter-institutional dialogue. As Simpson acknowledges, several parliamentarians took up the torch from Lord Atkin. If the Regulation itself survived this Commons debate unscathed, the Home Secretary did at least have to make great play of the fact that the advisory committee on detentions was, in the aftermath of *Liversidge*, chaired by a High Court judge.[54]

Judicial Re-engagement with Public Law

The 1960s and 1970s saw a gradual abandonment of legal formalism. Alan Paterson recognised three elements inherent in this shift: 'the relaxing of the chains of precedent, the hardening of the attitude of the courts to the executive, and the increased awareness and acknowledgement of the judges of the policy choices they are called upon to make'.[55] The first of these elements involved the rejection of Lord Halsbury's restriction on the House of Lords' ability to reconsider its own precedents,[56] opening up the possibility of the common law developing to reflect societal change (a development welcomed by even the most ardent legal formalists).[57] The hardening of judicial attitudes to the executive was much more gradual, building into a realisation that Parliament could not be relied upon to hold the executive to account in all cases, because '[s]ome cases are more likely to attract Parliamentary attention than others',[58] and that judicial review would have to rectify these gaps in political protections against maladministration. The third factor that Paterson identifies, judges' acceptance of the 'policy choices' inherent in their decisions, began with decisions such as *Padfield v Minister of Agriculture*,[59] where Lord Reid led the House of Lords in quashing a ministerial decision on the basis

[52] A. W. B. Simpson, *In the Highest Degree Odious: Detention Without Trial in Wartime Britain* (Oxford: Oxford University Press, 1992), p.407.
[53] Simpson, *In the Highest Degree Odious*, p.363.
[54] H. Morrison MP, HC Debs, vol.376, col.852, 26 November 1941. See Simpson, *In the Highest Degree Odious*, p.379.
[55] A. Paterson, "Judges: A Political Elite" (1974) 1 *Brit. J.L. & Soc'y* 118, 118.
[56] *Practice Statement (Judicial Precedent)* [1966] 1 W.L.R. 1234.
[57] See Devlin, "Judges and Lawmakers", 13.
[58] *R. v Secretary of State for the Home Dept. Ex p. Fire Brigades Union* [1995] 2 A.C. 513, 572 (Lord Lloyd).
[59] *Padfield v Minister of Agriculture, Fisheries and Food* [1968] A.C. 997.

that it conflicted with the purpose behind statutory safeguards.[60] As Lord Diplock would remark thereafter:

> To find out the meaning of particular provisions in social legislation of this character calls, in the first instance, for a purposive approach to the Act as a whole to ascertain the social ends it was intended to achieve and the practical means by which it was expected to achieve them. Meticulous linguistic analysis of words and phrases used in different contexts in particular sections of the Act should be subordinate to this purposive approach.[61]

Judicial interpretation was freed from the shackles of applying the literal wording of Parliament's enactments, 'enabling courts on occasion to construe legislation to mean precisely the opposite of the plain meaning of Parliament's words'.[62]

Unsurprisingly, this burgeoning judicial engagement with public policy-making in the decades before the HRA's enactment came as a shock to the other branches of government. These developments obliged public authorities to start assessing 'the range of signals' contained within judgments.[63] In other words, they forged an interaction between the courts and policy-makers. Ironically, however, it took a much more formalist search for the meaning of ageing statutory provisions to awaken the judiciary to the potential for such dialogue. In *Rookes v Barnard*,[64] the House of Lords accepted that industrial relations legislation did not give trade unions the ability to threaten a strike to maintain 'closed-shop' arrangements, and that such threats amounted to a tortious intimidation. The Labour Government under Harold Wilson responded immediately with legislation,[65] with the intention of 'putting right that aspect of the law which was never thought to have been in doubt 60 years ago'.[66] Arguably, this effort at 'putting right' legal arrangements by reversing a judicial decision, repeated in the same government's approach to the decision in *Burmah Oil v Lord Advocate*,[67] mollified judicial concerns over abandoning formalism. After all, as these examples of inter-institutional dialogue indicated, Parliament could swiftly reject any judicial developments with which it was unsatisfied.

The first flourishing of judgments which specifically sought a dialogue with Parliament over law reform saw some particularly far-sighted

[60] *Padfield v Minister of Agriculture, Fisheries and Food* [1968] A.C. 997, 1030.

[61] *Jones v Secretary of State for Social Services* [1972] A.C. 944, 1005.

[62] Nicol, "Law and Politics", 729. See also T. Allan, "Constitutional Dialogue and the Justification of Judicial Review" (2003) 23 O.J.L.S. 563, 574.

[63] R. Cranston, "Reviewing Judicial Review", in G. Richardson and H. Genn (eds), *Administrative Law and Government Action* (Oxford: Oxford University Press, 1994), p.74.

[64] *Rookes v Barnard* [1964] A.C. 1129.

[65] Trade Disputes Act 1965.

[66] H. Wilson MP, HC Debs, vol.702, col.192, 17 November 1964.

[67] *Burmah Oil v Lord Advocate* [1965] A.C. 75, countered by the War Damages Act 1965.

interventions. In *Harman v Home Office*,[68] for example, Lord Scarman was unable to persuade the majority of his colleagues to interpret provisions of the Contempt of Court Act 1981 (CCA) in light of the ECHR. Nonetheless, he used his dissent to warn Parliament in terms closely akin to a declaration of incompatibility:

> It can hardly be argued that there is a pressing social need to exclude the litigant and his solicitor from the right available to everyone else to treat as public knowledge documents which have been produced and made part and parcel of public legal proceedings. If English law should recognise this exclusion, it might well be inconsistent with the requirements of the European Convention.[69]

Increasingly, the judiciary tested the freedom granted in its status as Parliament's junior law-making partner. In *Duport Steel*,[70] the House of Lords may have upbraided Lord Denning's effort to provide his 'own preferred amendments'[71] to the Trade Union and Labour Relations Act 1974, but Lord Scarman was not slow to advise Parliament on a suitable model for statutory reform:

> If the law is unacceptable, the remedy lies with Parliament, not the judges. And if Parliament is minded to amend the statute … the draftsman should be bold and tackle his problems head-on. If he is to put a limitation on the [Trade Union] immunities … let him do so by limiting the heads of tortious liability where immunity is conferred: if he is to strengthen the availability of interlocutory relief in industrial relations, let him include clear guidelines in the statute. And, if he is to limit secondary or tertiary 'blacking' or picketing, the statute must declare whose premises may, or may not, be picketed and how far the 'blacking' or picketing may extend.[72]

Ultimately, judges such as Lord Goff—in Lord Bingham's opinion 'a wisely creative judge'[73]—moved beyond merely suggesting to Parliament that an area of law was ripe for reconsideration. Instead, in *Woolwich Building Society*,[74] he was willing to reform areas of law as he saw necessary and trust that if Parliament did not reverse his reforms that this amounted to tacit assent to them. Indeed, he considered that the judiciary had the capacity to clear parliamentary roadblocks; 'however compelling the principle of justice may be [in this case], it would never be sufficient to persuade a government to propose its legislative recognition by Parliament; caution, otherwise known as the Treasury, would never allow this to happen'.[75]

[68] *Harman v Secretary of State for the Home Department* [1983] 1 A.C. 280.
[69] *Harman v Secretary of State for the Home Department* [1983] 1 A.C. 280, 317 (Lord Scarman).
[70] *Duport Steel v Sirs* [1980] 1 W.L.R. 142.
[71] *Duport Steel v Sirs* [1980] 1 W.L.R. 142, 157 (Lord Diplock).
[72] *Duport Steel v Sirs* [1980] 1 W.L.R. 142, 171–72.
[73] Bingham, "The Judges: Active or Passive", 12.
[74] *Woolwich Building Society v Inland Revenue Commissioners (No.2)* [1993] A.C. 70.
[75] *Woolwich Building Society v Inland Revenue Commissioners (No.2)* [1993] A.C. 70, 176.

The Foundations of Inter-institutional Dialogue

Throughout the 1980s and early 1990s, however, such attempts to promote a robust dialogue between the courts and Parliament met with resistance from judges unwilling to be drawn beyond their traditional sphere. In *Duport Steels v Sirs*,[76] Lord Diplock famously rejected what he described as judicial 'amendments to statutes'[77] by way of non-literal interpretation, cautioning the courts to leave such reforms to Parliament:

> [A]t a time when more and more cases involve the application of legislation which gives effect to policies that are the subject of bitter public and parliamentary controversy, it cannot be too strongly emphasised that the British constitution, though largely unwritten, is firmly based upon the separation of powers; Parliament makes the laws, the judiciary interpret them.[78]

Three years later, Lord Diplock led the majority of the House of Lords in *Harman*, reducing the case to a technical exercise in statutory interpretation:

> It is not about freedom of speech, freedom of the press, openness of justice or documents coming into 'the public domain'; nor ... does it in my opinion call for consideration of any of those human rights and fundamental freedoms ... What this case is about is an aspect of the law of discovery of documents in civil actions in the High Court.[79]

And again, in *Secretary of State for Defence v Guardian Newspapers*,[80] he was on hand to corral a majority of Law Lords into rejecting the efforts of Lord Fraser and Lord Scarman to interpret the CCA's provisions protecting journalistic sources in light of the ECHR.[81] Lord Diplock was far from alone in his efforts to maintain the traditional role of the judiciary and, in fairness to him, his comments on proportionality in *GCHQ*[82] may have amounted to a recognition that the tide of public law was against him, but his approach would be loyally followed years after his death in cases such as *Ex p. Brind*.[83]

The movement towards increased engagement between the courts and Parliament over public-law issues would not be thwarted for long. Indeed, as

[76] *Duport Steel v Sirs* [1980] 1 W.L.R. 142.
[77] *Duport Steel v Sirs* [1980] 1 W.L.R. 142, 157.
[78] *Duport Steel v Sirs* [1980] 1 W.L.R. 142, 157. This statement can, of course, be contrasted with Lord Diplock's willingness to read requirements of business-like operation of public transport into the Transport (London) Act 1969 in *Bromley London Borough Council v Greater London Council* [1983] 1 A.C. 768.
[79] *Harman v Secretary of State for the Home Department* [1983] 1 A.C. 280, 299 (Lord Diplock).
[80] *Harman v Secretary of State for the Home Department* [1983] 1 A.C. 280.
[81] See *Harman v Secretary of State for the Home Department* [1983] 1 A.C. 280, 359 (Lord Fraser) and 361 (Lord Scarman).
[82] *Council of Civil Service Unions v Minister for the Civil Service* [1985] A.C. 374, 410.
[83] *R. v Secretary of State for the Home Department Ex p. Brind* [1991] 1 A.C. 696.

early as 1987 the then Home Secretary Douglas Hurd had to make a statement to Parliament restricting the use of his statutory discretion to adjust the sentences of life prisoners[84] and establishing a review of these powers[85] in response to the decision in *Ex p. Handscomb*.[86] A new generation of judges took up Lord Scarman's invocation of 'constitutional rights' in *Harman*,[87] with Steyn LJ recognising in *Ex p. Leech*[88] that '[e]ven in our unwritten constitution' a prisoner's interest in access to legal advice 'must rank as a constitutional right'[89] which justified a re-interpretation of the Prison Rules. By the end of the 1990s the House of Lords recognised the principle of legality under which '[f]undamental rights cannot be overridden by general or ambiguous words [in an Act of Parliament]'.[90] Furthermore, even if David Jenkins notes that '[u]ntil the Human Rights Act, no court had ever declared formally, as a remedy, that an Act of Parliament violated individual rights',[91] case law from the 1990s indicates that the courts were alive to the potential of declaratory remedies. In *Ex p. Doody*,[92] the House of Lords decided that the Home Secretary's failure to explain his setting of a mandatory life sentence's tariff element breached the requirements of procedural justice, in the face of the broad wording of this statutory power.[93] Nonetheless, Lord Mustill was willing to recognise the interest of such prisoners in being able to address the Home Secretary over their sentences as an 'obvious right', and was even willing to make a declaration that it must be respected with regard to tariff adjustments, on the basis that '[i]n a rapidly developing area of the law I think it useful for each new area to be formally marked-out'.[94]

The change in judicial interpretative approaches in the late 20th century was in large part the product of a new judicial attitude towards dialogue with the other branches of government. The courts adopted a mantle once rejected by Lord Devlin:

> I appreciate that radical reformers may take a fundamentally different view from mine about the function of the judiciary. They may see it not as arbitrating

[84] D. Hurd MP, HC Debs, vol.120, cols.347–49W, 23 July 1987.

[85] Lord Carlisle, *The Parole System in England and Wales*, Cm. 532 (31 December 1988).

[86] *R. v Secretary of State for the Home Department Ex p. Handscomb* (1987) 86 Cr.App.R. 59.

[87] *Harman v Secretary of State for the Home Department* [1983] 1 A.C. 280, 317.

[88] *R. v Secretary of State for the Home Department Ex p. Leech* [1994] Q.B. 198.

[89] *R. v Secretary of State for the Home Department Ex p. Leech* [1994] Q.B. 198, 210.

[90] *R. v Secretary of State for the Home Department Ex p. Simms* [1999] A.C. 115, 131 (Lord Hoffmann).

[91] D. Jenkins, "Common Law Declarations of Unconstitutionality" [2009] I.J.C.L. 183, 210.

[92] *R. v Secretary of State for the Home Department Ex p. Doody* [1994] 1 A.C. 531.

[93] Criminal Justice Act 1991, s.35(2).

[94] *R. v Secretary of State for the Home Department Ex p. Doody* [1994] 1 A.C. 531, 563. The Home Secretary responded to this decision by accepting the Court's restrictions upon his statutory discretion. M. Howard MP, HC Debs, vol.229, cols.861–64W, 27 July 1993.

> between citizens and as holding the balance between the state and the individual but as one of the three branches of the government.[95]

Lord Devlin believed that conceptualising the courts as one branch of government, 'networking' with the others, would lead, inevitably, to the judiciary marching in step with the other branches. What the majority of the judiciary recognised, according to Trevor Allan, was that such a role would instead free the courts to enforce underlying constitutional principles against the other branches. Rather than adhering to the literal will of Parliament, such a role provided the basis for a dialogue through a cycle of interpretation and legislative amendment in which '[t]here is always something more to be said'.[96]

The Increased Prominence and Volume of Judicial Dialogue

If the HRA does not mark the start of judicial dialogue with Parliament, it certainly raised the prominence of judicial interventions. Gardbaum has gone so far as to view the HRA as providing for a 'new model' of constitutionalism, characterised not only by a statement of rights but also by 'some form of enhanced judicial power to enforce these rights by assessing legislation (as well as other governmental acts) for consistency with them that goes beyond traditional presumptions and ordinary modes of statutory interpretation'.[97] Such ordinary modes of statutory interpretation were already under strain as a result of the development of common law fundamental rights, but the HRA's enactment presaged a 'structural change'[98] in public law, freeing the new jurisprudence from the vestiges of formalist opposition. This new model, however, also recognised the dangers inherent in giving the courts the ability to invalidate legislation, not least amongst these being that judges can be 'reluctant' to employ such a power.[99] Under the HRA the judiciary shares the task of rights deliberation with 'both the political branches and the citizenry'.[100]

[95] Devlin, "Judges and Lawmakers", 16.
[96] Allan, "Constitutional Dialogue", 571.
[97] Gardbaum, "Reassessing the New Commonwealth Model", 169.
[98] T. Poole, "Between the Devil and the Deep Blue Sea: Administrative Law in an Age of Rights", in L. Pearson, C. Harlow and M. Taggart (eds), *Administrative Law in a Changing State* (Oxford: Hart, 2008), p.19.
[99] C. Sunstein, *Designing Democracy: What Constitutions Do* (New York: Oxford University Press, 2001), p.62.
[100] Gardbaum, "Reassessing the New Commonwealth Model", 173.

Formal Inter-institutional Dialogue under the HRA

Much of the attention devoted to the concept of inter-institutional dialogue under the HRA has focused upon the capacity of declarations of incompatibility for promoting rights dialogue. They function as a lightning rod, attracting public and parliamentary attention to an issue and thereby promoting 'fruitful political dialogue between courts as primarily monitors and parliaments as the primary legislators on human rights'.[101] This relationship is highlighted by decisions such as *Belmarsh Detainees*,[102] in which the House of Lords declared incompatible the Anti-Terrorism, Crime and Security Act 2001's regime of detention without trial for suspected international terrorists, precipitating Parliament's hurried enactment of the Prevention of Terrorism Act 2005.

Ian Leigh and Roger Masterman caution, however, that '[i]f this is a dialogue at all, it is one in which the judicial voice is beginning to be heard the loudest'.[103] The HRA's purpose was always, in part, to enable the judiciary to identify inadequacies of domestic law against the standards set by the ECHR. Prior to the HRA's enactment Strasbourg's judgments were much more likely to prompt legislative change than complaints by domestic judges regarding fundamental rights. Whereas domestic judgments raising rights-based concerns regarding the Home Secretary's sentencing powers were 'bought off' with ministerial statements on the use of statutory discretion or with pledges to consider reform, adverse Strasbourg decisions drew legislative reform. The Carlisle Report's reform proposals on sentencing powers following *Ex p. Handscomb* were enacted, three years later,[104] only in response to Strasbourg's decision in *Thynne, Wilson and Gunnell*.[105] Parliament clearly vested a Strasbourg ruling on the breach of a Convention right with greater significance than the domestic courts' warnings of the likelihood of such breaches. Declarations of incompatibility allow the domestic courts to 'destabilise' existing legislative arrangements to a similar degree to a Strasbourg decision,[106] even if they do not call the legality of legislation into question.[107]

As an avowedly political remedy, declarations of incompatibility do not need to be followed by Parliament. As such, they defy traditional efforts to explain judicial independence as the product of 'respect' across the different

[101] T. Campbell, "Human Rights: A Culture of Controversy" (1999) 26 J.L.S. 6, 7.
[102] *Belmarsh Detainees* [2004] UKHL 56.
[103] I. Leigh and R. Masterman, *Making Rights Real: The Human Rights Act in Its First Decade* (Oxford: Hart, 2008), p.118.
[104] Criminal Justice Act 1991, Pt II.
[105] *Thynne, Wilson and Gunnell v United Kingdom* (1990) 13 E.H.R.R. 666.
[106] S. Wheatley, "Minorities under the ECHR and the Construction of a 'Democratic Society'" [2007] P.L. 770, 791.
[107] HRA 1998, s.4(6).

branches of government[108]; after all, Parliament can hardly be said to respect a declaration of incompatibility which it ignores. Similarly, much as the judges remain obliged to uphold statutes which they believe to be incompatible with human rights norms, declarations can hardly be described as respectful of Parliament's legislative choices, especially where ministers have certified to Parliament that legislation is ECHR compatible and that certification has been considered by the Joint Committee on Human Rights (JCHR).[109] Instead, declarations support a much more flexible vision of inter-institutional 'comity'[110] or 'respectful friendship' between the branches of government.[111] This relationship is built upon the expectations which each branch places upon the others,[112] with judges emphasising, from the earliest days of the HRA, that it did not transform them into 'substitute lawmakers'.[113] Despite such protestations, many politicians have failed to come to terms with this new relationship between the courts and Parliament. After the terrorist attacks of 7 July 2005 on London's transport network, for example, the then Conservative Party leader Michael Howard described the declaration issued in *Belmarsh Detainees* as exemplifying 'aggressive judicial activism'.[114] By contrast, Labour Home Secretary David Blunkett, when faced with an adverse judicial review ruling curtailing the operation of immigration legislation,[115] seemed to question why the Court had not instead issued a declaration, writing that '[l]ike most people, I respond better to an honest dialogue than to being shouted at'.[116]

Gardbaum agrees, in more prosaic terms, that 'the balance of power has ... gone a little too far in the judicial direction'[117] as a result of the courts' under-reliance upon declarations of incompatibility. For this reason, we must consider the interpretative duty as a mechanism for dialogue. The HRA not

[108] See *R. v HM Treasury Ex p. Smedley* [1985] Q.B. 657, 666. See, more recently, *In re McFarland* [2004] UKHL 17; [2004] 1 W.L.R. 1289, [7] (Lord Bingham).
[109] HRA 1998, s.19(1).
[110] Young, *Parliamentary Sovereignty*, p.172.
[111] A. Kavanagh, "Judicial Restraint in the Pursuit of Justice" (2010) 60 U.T.L.J. 23, 37–38.
[112] *Secretary of State for the Home Department v Pankina* [2010] EWCA Civ 719; [2011] Q.B. 376, at [35] (Sedley LJ).
[113] *R. (Rottman) v Commissioner of Police of the Metropolis* [2001] EWHC Admin 576; [2002] Crim L.R. 501, at [52] (Brooke LJ).
[114] M. Howard MP, "Judges Must Bow to the Will of Parliament", *Daily Telegraph*, 10 August 2005, http://www.telegraph.co.uk/comment/personal-view/3618954/Judges-must-bow-to-the-will-of-Parliament.html.
[115] *R. (Q) v Secretary of State for the Home Department* [2004] Q.B. 36; [2003] EWCA Civ 364.
[116] D. Blunkett MP, "I Won't Give in to the Judges", *Evening Standard*, 12 May 2003, http://www.thisislondon.co.uk/news/article-4780814-blunkett-i-wont-give-in.do.
[117] S. Gardbaum, "How Successful and Distinctive is the Human Rights Act? An Expatriate Comparatist's Assessment" (2011) 74 M.L.R. 195, 215.

only encouraged the courts to attempt to produce rights-respecting interpretations of statutory provisions, but obliged them to do so where possible, even if that led to a court departing from the 'legislative intention of Parliament'.[118] The theory behind this duty, together with the requirement to consider Strasbourg case law,[119] was that it would allow the United Kingdom to 'benefit more in the future from th[e] margin of appreciation than we could have in the past'.[120] In actually remedying the claimant's complaint, the interpretive duty has become the first recourse for the courts in addressing human rights claims against legislation.

The duty's importance was fully appreciated during the HRA's progression through Parliament, with Jack Straw claiming that 'in almost all cases, the courts will be able to interpret the legislation compatibly with the Convention'.[121] Moreover, judicial interpretation under the HRA, even if it amounts to 'reform by the judiciary',[122] was never intended to constitute the final word on an issue, but remains a platform for dialogue, with the potential for Parliament to respond to interpretations it does not approve of as decisively as it responded to *Rookes v Barnard*. As Lord Steyn concluded, having re-interpreted the Rent Act 1977 in *Ghaidan v Godin-Mendoza*,[123] the process of dialogue can continue after such a ruling; '[i]f Parliament disagrees with an interpretation by the courts under section 3(1), it is free to override it by amending the legislation and expressly reinstating the incompatibility'.[124] Admittedly, however, Parliament is yet to respond to any reinterpretation under the HRA in this manner.

Informal Inter-institutional Dialogue after the HRA

Beyond the mechanisms set out in the HRA, more traditional approaches to dialogue remain open in human rights decisions. First, judges can, dependent upon the circumstances of the case, remark upon the wider context of the action in a manner intended to feed into political discourse. The Court of Appeal's description of the US detention regime for suspected terrorists at Guantánamo Bay as 'a legal black hole'[125] resounded throughout parliamen-

[118] *Sheldrake v Director of Public Prosecutions* [2004] UKHL 43; [2005] 1 A.C. 264, at [28] (Lord Bingham).

[119] HRA, s.2.

[120] J. Straw MP, HC Debs, vol.346, cols.27–28, 13 March 2000.

[121] HC Debs, col.778, 16 February 1998.

[122] *R. v Director of Public Prosecutions Ex p. Kebilene* [2000] 2 A.C. 326, 375 (Lord Hope).

[123] *Ghaidan v Godin-Mendoza* [2004] 2 A.C. 557; [2004] UKHL 30.

[124] *Ghaidan v Godin-Mendoza* [2004] 2 A.C. 557; [2004] UKHL 30, at [43]. See also Gardbaum, "Reassessing the New Commonwealth Model", 194.

[125] *R. (Abbasi) v Secretary of State for Foreign and Commonwealth Affairs* [2002] EWCA Civ 1598, at [22] (Lord Phillips MR).

tary debates on Guantánamo,[126] especially after it was forcefully repeated by Lord Steyn in his 2003 Mann Lecture.[127]

Secondly, Parliament can follow up on judicial dissents in its discussions of an area of law. Dissents in the Supreme Court in particular, as the highest domestic court, are likely, as John Alder notes, to 'reveal disagreement in its most intractable form',[128] thereby identifying issues on which parliamentary debate may be desirable. In *Munjaz*,[129] the House of Lords was divided over the lawfulness of a hospital's policy covering the seclusion of individuals suffering from mental disorders which departed from the government's Code of Practice under the Mental Health Act 1983. Lord Steyn, in a powerful dissent, considered that policy-based departures from this Code amounted to a 'free-for-all',[130] conflicting with arts 3, 5 and 8 ECHR and risking 'lowering of the protection offered by the law to mentally disordered patients'.[131] His concerns featured prominently during parliamentary debate into the Mental Health Act 2007[132] and thereafter a new Code of Practice was promulgated in 2008.[133]

Thirdly, judges still occasionally find it necessary to call for Parliament to undertake law reform, even when human rights are at issue. In *Smith*,[134] a nine-judge panel of the Supreme Court considered whether the investigative obligation imposed by art.2 ECHR (where it was suspected that the authorities had breached the right to life) applied to the death of Private Smith, a solder serving in Iraq. The Court accepted that in this case, where Smith died of heat stroke on a military base in Iraq, the obligation was engaged, although Lord Hope considered that such a case-by-case approach to the issue should give way to parliamentary reform of the Coroners and Justice Act 2009:

> The solution to this highly unsatisfactory situation lies in a reform of the law which restricts inquiries in England and Wales ... to cases where there are grounds for thinking that the substantive obligation under article 2 has been violated.[135]

[126] See, for example, Baroness Williams, HL Debs, vol.646, col.847, 26 March 2003; and Lord Lester, HL Debs, vol.657, col.680, 15 January 2004.
[127] J. Steyn, "Guantánamo Bay: The Legal Black Hole" (2004) 53 I.C.L.Q. 1, 1.
[128] Alder, "Dissents in Courts of Last Resort", 226.
[129] *R. (Munjaz) v Mersey Care NHS Trust and others* [2005] UKHL 58; [2006] 2 A.C. 148.
[130] *R. (Munjaz) v Mersey Care NHS Trust and others* [2005] UKHL 58; [2006] 2 A.C. 148, at [44].
[131] *R. (Munjaz) v Mersey Care NHS Trust and others* [2005] UKHL 58; [2006] 2 A.C. 148, at [48].
[132] See Lord Patel, HL Debs, col.1474, 26 February 2007.
[133] See P. Bartlett, "The Code of Practice and the Ambiguities of 'Guidance'" (2009) 19 *Criminal Behaviour and Mental Health* 157.
[134] *R. (Smith) v Secretary of State for Defence* [2010] UKSC 29.
[135] *R. (Smith) v Secretary of State for Defence* [2010] UKSC 29, at [107]. See also *Gow v Grant* [2012] UKSC 29, at [44]–[56] (Baroness Hale).

The Changing Nature of Judicial Interventions

Once upon a time, Lord Halsbury could claim that 'a case is only an authority for what it actually decides'.[136] Declarations of incompatibility, however, effectively sideline the provision of a remedy to the instant claimant.[137] By opening such avenues for dialogue between the courts and the other branches of government the HRA has encouraged a growth in 'test cases' seeking broad judicial interventions into the policy-making process. Some litigation seems to go even further, with claimants 'not necessarily seeking a court decision but the publicity or public awareness generated by proceedings'.[138]

Despite the HRA's effect on public expectations regarding the role of the courts, the judiciary has remained wary of encouraging cases which appear to involve 'the continuation of protest by other means'.[139] 'Lawfare'[140]—the process by which campaigners seek to advance their policy objectives through litigation—has been a by-product of the advances in administrative law over the last half century. One of the most egregious of these attempts came in *Smeaton*,[141] in which the Society for the Protection of Unborn Children (SPUC) argued that issuing the morning-after pill constituted a criminal offence. Having rejected this claim out of hand, Munby J also rejected the SPUC's efforts to avoid having to pay costs as a result of its defeat:

> [T]his was a manufactured dispute—and a dispute manufactured by SPUC … in the humdrum world of everyday life, so far as I can see, this was simply not a matter of genuine public concern at all … at least not until SPUC commenced these proceedings.[142]

The outset of the HRA era, however, enhanced the desire amongst campaigners to transpose the marketplace of ideas 'into a courtroom'.[143] The House of Lords responded in *Rusbridger*,[144] which involved an effort by the *Guardian*'s editor to persuade the courts to recognise that the Treason Felony Act 1848 was incompatible with freedom of expression. Lord Hutton fulminated that the courts would not become a forum for tendentious claims

[136] *Quinn v Leathem* [1901] A.C. 495, at 506.
[137] Nicol, "Law and Politics", 728.
[138] J. Lewis, "Winning the Campaign or Winning the Case?" (2007) 12 *Jud. Rev.* 107, 108.
[139] *R. (Bancoult) v Secretary of State for Foreign and Commonwealth Affairs* [2008] UKHL 61; [2009] 1 A.C. 453, at [53].
[140] M. Pinto-Duschinsky, *Bringing Rights Back Home: Making Human Rights Compatible with Parliamentary Democracy in the UK* (London: Policy Exchange, 2011), p.17.
[141] *R. (Smeaton) v Secretary of State for Health* [2002] EWHC 610(Admin); [2002] 2 F.L.R. 146.
[142] *R. (Smeaton) v Secretary of State for Health* [2002] EWHC 886(Admin); [2002] 2 F.L.R. 146, at [22].
[143] *R. (Smeaton) v Secretary of State for Health* [2002] EWHC 886(Admin); [2002] 2 F.L.R. 146, at [20].
[144] *R (Rusbridger) v Attorney General* [2003] UKHL 38; [2004] 1 A.C. 357.

under the HRA, which was 'not intended to be an instrument by which the courts can chivvy Parliament into spring-cleaning the statute book'.[145]

It has proven increasingly difficult, however, for the courts in the HRA era to separate 'genuine' disputes, arising in the context of wider political campaigns, from 'protest' cases. In *Bancoult*, for example, which concerned the lawfulness of the United Kingdom's mandatory relocation of the Chagos Islanders in the 1960s to enable the USA to construct a base on Diego Garcia, the majority of the House of Lords were fearful that the claim was subordinate to wider political campaign and that, in the words of Lord Carswell, 'they could very easily get into the area of challenging what is essentially a political judgment, which is not for courts of law'.[146] The Court's rejection of the claim was criticised for effectively hiding behind 'the now discredited theory that certain matters can for all purposes be deemed to be non-justiciable'.[147] By contrast, the unsuccessful attempts by the Countryside Alliance to argue that the Hunting Act 2004 infringed the right of private and family life could not simply be dismissed at the claim stage.[148] Even though the latter case appeared largely to constitute an effort by the Countryside Alliance to keep the hunting ban in the public eye (or even an attempt by 'opponents of the Act to achieve through the courts what they could not achieve in Parliament'),[149] where a rights-based claim concerns legislation the ability to seek the re-interpretation of provisions or a declaration of incompatibility makes it very difficult for courts to exclude a case until the relevant rights have been considered in context.

Such cases also risk drawing the courts into ruling upon hypothetical issues rather than applying the law as necessary to the case at hand. In *Weaver*,[150] an exasperated Lord Collins complained that the efforts of claimants and interveners to press the Court of Appeal into deciding upon whether a housing trust amounted to a public body for the purposes of the HRA, when the issue was not live in the case, amounted to asking it 'to determine the question of principle divorced from any plausible factual scenario in which the question might arise'.[151] Moreover, whilst media attention swirled around the question of whether UK armed forces on operation overseas were

[145] *R. (Rusbridger) v Attorney General* [2003] UKHL 38; [2004] 1 A.C. 357, at [36].

[146] *Bancoult (No.2)* [2008] UKHL 61; [2009] 1 A.C. 453, at [130].

[147] M. Elliot and A. Perreau-Saussine, "Pyrrhic Public Law: *Bancoult* and the Sources, Status and Content of Common Law Limitations on Prerogative Power" [2009] P.L. 697, 710.

[148] *R. (Countryside Alliance) v Attorney-General* [2007] UKHL 52; [2008] 1 A.C. 719.

[149] *R. (Countryside Alliance) v Attorney-General* [2007] UKHL 52; [2008] 1 A.C. 719, at [45] (Baroness Hale).

[150] *R. (Weaver) v London and Quadrant Housing Trust* [2009] EWCA Civ 587; [2010] 1 W.L.R. 363.

[151] *R. (Weaver) v London and Quadrant Housing Trust* [2009] EWCA Civ 587; [2010] 1 W.L.R. 363, at [90] (Lord Collins).

subject to the HRA in *Smith*, Baroness Hale pointed out that this question did not need to be answered to address the appeal in question.[152] Lord Walker complained that the majority of the Supreme Court were making an advisory opinion, despite the judiciary's long-standing rejection of such a function:

> It is not the function of this Court to deliver advisory opinions, and in this case we may be going some way beyond what would be regarded as a proper exercise of judicial power in a country with a written constitution providing for the separation of powers.[153]

Other judges, however, have not been so quick to decry such developments under the HRA. In *Chester*,[154] Laws LJ considered the failure of successive governments to respond to the declaration of incompatibility issued with regard to the United Kingdom's blanket ban on prisoner voting. The claimants attempted to persuade the Court of Appeal to explain what reforms were necessary to resolve this incompatibility. Whilst Laws LJ refused to be tempted down this road in the instant case, he did recognise that other cases may warrant just such advice:

> The grant of an advisory opinion as to the legality of forthcoming legislation would have been a step too far for our predecessors in the common law no more than a generation or so ago. An advisory opinion as to what legislation, as yet undrafted, might properly contain or omit would have been quite beyond the pale. As it happens I can see a possible utility in such a jurisdiction in very carefully controlled circumstances …[155]

Even though this view can be regarded as an extension upon Laws LJ's earlier writings on the value of a system of pre-legislative advisory pronouncements by the courts,[156] it nonetheless indicates that the HRA may yet require an even more profound change in the judiciary's constitutional role. Such a leap into the unknown, however, is arguably unnecessary whilst existing modes of inter-institutional dialogue have yet to be developed to their full potential.

[152] *R. (Smith) v Secretary of State for Defence* [2010] UKSC 29, at [134].
[153] *R. (Smith) v Secretary of State for Defence* [2010] UKSC 29, at [129].
[154] *R. (Chester) v Secretary of State for Justice* [2010] EWCA Civ 1439.
[155] *R. (Chester) v Secretary of State for Justice* [2010] EWCA Civ 1439, at [31].
[156] See J. Laws, "Is the High Court the Guardian of Fundamental Human Rights?" [1993] P.L. 59 and J. Laws, "Judicial Remedies and the Constitution" (1994) 57 M.L.R. 213.

Dialogue under the HRA: Intermittent Transmission and Reception

The increasing *volume* of judicial dialogue under the HRA does not necessarily mean that the last decade has seen a consistently higher *quality* of judicial interaction with the other branches of government. Neither judicial nor parliamentary processes have yet been updated to the degree necessary to enable both branches to participate in the sort of fully-fledged dialogue which would embed human rights within the United Kingdom's political constitution.[157]

Impediments to Dialogue within and beyond the HRA

When looking ahead to the operation of the HRA, Ian Leigh and Laurence Lustgarten noted how the government had restricted standing provisions to confine pressure groups to either 'assisting a victim or submitting an amicus brief at the indulgence of the court'.[158] The HRA therefore tied the courts' hands against considering public-interest claims, a restriction that pressure groups and official human-rights-protection bodies have been eager to loosen. To do so, these bodies have extensively intervened in cases brought by other litigants.

Few such interventions have met with approval from the courts. In *Smith*, for example, Lord Collins highlighted the role of the Equality and Human Rights Commission in drawing the High Court and the Court of Appeal into ruling upon the broad issue of the application of the HRA for the purposes of international deployments of UK armed forces.[159] By contrast, in the highly charged *Holy Cross Primary School* litigation,[160] relating to the adequacy of police protection for the nationalist pupils of a school in north Belfast who endured sustained attacks from a loyalist mob, Lord Hoffmann criticised the intervention of the Northern Ireland Human Rights Commission on the basis that its arguments 'only repeated in rather more emphatic terms the points which had already been quite adequately argued by counsel for the appellant'.[161] In effect, in spite of a growing number of such interventions in the last decade, the HRA scheme leaves interveners in an irreducible bind. Either they become cheerleaders for one side, in which case they add nothing to the

[157] See C. Palley, *The United Kingdom and Human Rights* (London: Sweet & Maxwell, 1991), p.38.

[158] I. Leigh and L. Lustgarten, "Making Rights Real: The Courts, Remedies, and the Human Rights Act" (1999) 58 C.L.J. 509, 521.

[159] *R. (Smith) v Secretary of State for Defence* [2010] UKSC 29, at [223].

[160] *In re E (a child)* [2009] 1 A.C. 536; [2008] UKHL 66.

[161] *In re E (a child)* [2009] 1 A.C. 536; [2008] UKHL 66, at [3].

already adversarial nature of the court process,[162] or they draw in wider public-interest concerns and risk judges declaring that their interventions are 'not appropriately justiciable on the facts of the case'.[163]

This reluctance of the courts to engage with interventions which require the consideration of issues beyond the facts of the case has, to date, maintained the traditional focus of court proceedings. The approach has also prevented the HRA's restrictions upon public-interest claims from being circumvented 'by the back door'. Nonetheless, in restricting the scope of judicial engagement with human rights issues to the facts of cases at hand, any efforts towards a broad dialogue on an issue are curtailed, requiring the courts to respond to contentious human rights claims on a case-by-case basis. The narrow focus of dialogue under the HRA is, moreover, exacerbated by the restrictions upon the ability of the courts to 'question' proceedings in Parliament under the Bill of Rights.[164] Before the 1990s the courts interpreted this requirement as 'drawing a veil' over anything said in Parliament,[165] preventing the use of such material in the hunt for illusive (and, in any event, 'metaphorical')[166] parliamentary intention. In *Pepper v Hart*,[167] however, the House of Lords accepted that in 'very rare cases' the courts can draw upon clear statements by the promoter of legislation to resolve difficulties with interpretation.[168] Nonetheless, this approach remains strictly limited and does not, as Tom Lewis notes, allow the courts to assess 'the adequacy of reasons given by the legislature for measures interfering with fundamental rights'.[169] Such a restriction again weakens the judicial voice in any putative dialogue, potentially preventing assessment of the adequacy of Parliament's consideration of rights.

This restriction is significant because Strasbourg has long linked the margin of appreciation applicable to restrictions to qualified rights to the quality of legislative debate on such restrictions. Such linking can be seen, for example, in the recent decision in *A, B and C v Ireland*,[170] addressing whether Ireland's prohibition of abortion, even when pregnancy threatened the health and well-being of the mother, violated art.8 ECHR. Despite the gulf between

[162] T. Poole, "Questioning Common Law Constitutionalism" (2005) 25 L.S. 142, 156.

[163] *R. (Burke) v General Medical Council* [2005] EWCA Civ 1003; [2006] Q.B. 273, at [82] (Lord Phillips MR).

[164] The Bill of Rights 1689, art.9.

[165] See *Wilson v First County Trust Limited (No. 2)* [2003] UKHL 40; [2004] 1 A.C. 816, at [57] (Lord Nicholls).

[166] *Fothergill v Monarch Airlines Limited* [1981] A.C. 251, 279 (Lord Diplock).

[167] *Pepper v Hart* [1993] A.C. 593.

[168] *Pepper v Hart* [1993] A.C. 593, 616 (Lord Bridge).

[169] T. Lewis, "'Difficult and Slippery Terrain': Hansard, Human Rights and *Hirst v UK*" [2006] P.L. 209, 218.

[170] *A, B and C v Ireland* (2011) 53 E.H.R.R. 13.

Ireland's arrangements and the European consensus,[171] Strasbourg concluded that Ireland's 'lengthy, complex and sensitive debate' upon the issue of abortion sufficed to maintain the margin of appreciation.[172] Whilst Lord Nicholls may have maintained, in the early HRA case law, that '[l]ack of cogent justification in the course of parliamentary debate is not a matter which "counts against" the legislation on issues of proportionality',[173] it can very much count against legislation in terms of the margin of appreciation recognised by Strasbourg.[174]

This situation, whereby judicial evaluation of the adequacy of legislative debate is a commonplace practice in Strasbourg and 'constitutional anathema in the domestic context',[175] appears unsustainable. Indeed, some domestic judges appear increasingly willing to make normative evaluations of Parliament's intention based upon sweeping reviews of Hansard.[176] In *Hurley and Moore*,[177] a challenge to the legality of the Coalition Government's increase in student tuition fees, Elias LJ drew upon the 'extensive debate which took place inside and outside Parliament'[178] over the plans in rejecting suggestions that there had been insufficient analysis of the impact on the right to education of future students. Until domestic judges consistently display such willingness to reflect upon the adequacy of Parliament's discussion of human rights, it seems unlikely that their decisions will regularly foster a meaningful rights debate in Parliament.

Parliament: A Willing Partner in Dialogue?

Even if the court processes were honed to enable the judiciary to better engage with the policy concerns, this would not necessarily mean that Parliament would become any more receptive to dialogue. For all the myriad engagement strategies considered above it is difficult to shake the conclusion that Parliament becomes exercised by domestic human rights issues only when declarations of incompatibility are made or significant re-interpretations of

[171] *A, B and C v Ireland* (2011) 53 E.H.R.R. 13.
[172] *A, B and C v Ireland* (2011) 53 E.H.R.R. 13.
[173] *Wilson v First County Trust Limited (No.2)* [2003] UKHL 40; [2004] 1 A.C. 816, at [67].
[174] See *Hirst v UK (No.2)* (2006) 42 E.H.R.R. 41, at [79].
[175] S. Briant, "Dialogue, Diplomacy and Defiance: Prisoners' Voting Rights at Home and in Strasbourg" [2011] E.H.R.L.R. 243, 248.
[176] See, for example, *Ahmed v HM Treasury* [2010] 2 A.C. 534; [2010] UKSC 2, at [153] (Lord Phillips).
[177] *R. (Hurley and Moore) v Secretary of State for Business, Innovation and Skills* [2012] EWHC 201 (Admin).
[178] *R. (Hurley and Moore) v Secretary of State for Business, Innovation and Skills* [2012] EWHC 201 (Admin), at [61].

legislation occur under the HRA. Often, if a decision under the HRA does not involve a significant reverse for the government it is unlikely to reach the radar of many parliamentarians, with the exception of the ongoing and diligent analysis of human rights cases by the JCHR.[179]

For example, when the Court of Appeal decided in *Smith*[180] that the HRA extended to cover the general operations of UK armed forces on overseas deployment, the judgment resulted in questions before both Houses of Parliament.[181] The matter was even raised the day the case came before the Supreme Court.[182] Subsequent to the Supreme Court's rejection of claims that the HRA covered off-base UK military operations overseas, however, the case has not been raised again on the floor of either house, save for a question as to the litigation costs.[183] By contrast, when Yasmin Qureshi MP sought to question statements by Lord Hoffmann, in which he criticised the position of the European Court of Human Rights,[184] which had been heavily quoted by opponents of prisoner voting rights in the course of the Commons debate on the issue, she was prevented from pursuing her argument by a Deputy Speaker's ruling against any discussion of the 'background' of the House of Lords' members.[185] Whilst such rulings have historically restricted the potential for politically motivated attacks on judges, they also risk stifling parliamentary debate on human rights rulings. Such a deep-rooted respect for the judiciary as 'the sole authoritative voice of the law's meaning'[186] is, as Danny Nicol asserts, at odds with the co-operative nature of the judicial function where broadly worded and contestable Convention rights are at issue.[187]

If the potential of inter-institutional dialogue for developing domestic human rights law is to be realised, then Parliament as a whole will have to shoulder some of the burden of engaging with human rights jurisprudence which now falls almost exclusively on the JCHR.[188] The present reliance on the JCHR as a forum for collaboration between the three branches of government on human rights has allowed ministers to delay or sideline its reports

[179] See, for example, F. Klug and H. Wildbore, "Breaking New Ground: The Joint Committee on Human Rights and the Role of Parliament in Human Rights Compliance" [2007] E.H.R.L.R. 231.

[180] *R. (Smith) v Oxfordshire Assistant Deputy Coroner* [2009] EWCA Civ 441; [2009] 3 W.L.R. 1099.

[181] See HC Debs, vol.493, cols.1–4, 1 June 2009; HL Debs, vol.711, cols.837–39, 15 June 2009.

[182] M. Moon MP, HC Debs, vol.507, col.657, 15 March 2010.

[183] N. Harvey MP, HC Debs, vol.531, col.583W, 18 July 2011.

[184] L. Hoffmann, "The Universality of Human Rights" (2009) 125 L.Q.R. 416, 424.

[185] L. Hoyle MP, HC Debs, vol.523, col.535, 10 February 2010.

[186] Nicol, "Law and Politics", 742.

[187] See also, for analysis of the reaction of Parliament to judicial decisions regarding contestable rights, Young, "Is Dialogue Working?", 786–89.

[188] See A. Kavanagh, *Constitutional Review under the UK Human Rights Act* (Cambridge: Cambridge University Press, 2009), p.399.

where an issue is politically controversial, as evidenced by the delayed executive response to prisoner voting rights.[189] By the time the issue was substantively debated on the floor of the House of Commons in February 2011 over five years had elapsed since the United Kingdom had been found in breach of its ECHR obligations in *Hirst*.[190] This delay, in spite of a declaration of incompatibility being issued by the domestic courts[191] and numerous JCHR reports critical of the government's response in the intervening years, indicates the ongoing lack of human rights awareness in Parliament. When Sir Malcolm Rifkind recently responded to criticisms of the judicial role under the HRA and the European Communities Act 1972, he did so with a rhetorical question: '[I]s not the ultimate test of the sovereignty of Parliament whether Parliament can amend the law ... when the courts have interpreted the law to our dissatisfaction[?]'[192] Instead of engaging with particular human rights issues in this manner, however, much of the parliamentary debate around the HRA focuses instead on its repeal.[193] Meaningful dialogue has yet to be realised.

The 'Double-edged' Nature of Inter-institutional Dialogue

For all the supposed advantages of the willingness of the courts to engage in inter-institutional dialogue where human rights are at issue, less attention has been paid to the risks inherent in this process. Leaving aside Lord Devlin's apocalyptic concerns that ending the judiciary's constitutional isolationism and accepting its role as a third branch of government would inevitably stifle judicial constraint of the executive and lead, inexorably, to a 'totalitarian state',[194] the United Kingdom's experience under the HRA indicates that not all dialogue enhances rights protection. Mark Tushnet's thoughts on the double-edged nature of constitutional dialogue, in particular the readiness of governments to seize upon favourable judgments to stifle debate, are particularly insightful:

> [I]f courts purport to police the policymaking process but actually supervise it with an extremely loose hand, the negative case asserts that the judicial-review mechanism might *worsen* the political branches' performance because their members might mistakenly believe that the courts will bail the people out of whatever trouble the political branches make.[195]

[189] See C. Murray, "We Need to Talk: 'Democratic Dialogue' and the Ongoing Saga of Prisoner Disenfranchisement" (2011) 62 N.I.L.Q. 57, 74.
[190] *Hirst v United Kingdom (No.2)* (2006) 42 E.H.R.R. 41.
[191] *Smith v Scott* [2007] C.S.I.H. 9.
[192] HC Debs, vol.521, col.177, 11 January 2011.
[193] See C. Harvey, "Taking the Next Step? Achieving Another Bill of Rights" [2011] E.H.R.L.R. 24.
[194] Devlin, "Judges and Lawmakers", 16.
[195] M. Tushnet, "Controlling Executive Power in the War on Terrorism" (2005) 118 *Harv L Rev* 2673, 2680.

Similarly, against a background of regular signals from senior politicians to the effect that the courts are pursuing an overly activist approach to human rights law, ministers have been able to harness the resultant perception amongst parliamentarians to deflect criticism of government policy. On 23 October 2006, less than two weeks after the Court of Appeal's *Al Rawi* decision on whether UK residents detained in Guantánamo could seek diplomatic protection,[196] members of the House of Lords questioned the scope of the United Kingdom's obligations towards long-term residents, only for the Under-Secretary of State at the Foreign and Commonwealth Office, Lord Triesman, to respond that he considered that the judicial ruling had closed the matter: '[T]here are no obligations under international or domestic law. That was precisely the point that was put to the High Court and to the Court of Appeal ... and the matter was resolved unequivocally in those courts.'[197] This conclusion neglects the evident concern of the judges hearing these cases for the detainees' 'plight', and the fact that Laws LJ had limited his decision to marking out the 'legal edge between the executive and judicial functions'.[198] Beyond the limited legal obligations the courts were prepared to recognise,[199] the Divisional Court expressly stated that the claimants had advanced 'strong arguments in the context of political debate',[200] which could have been used by parliamentarians to push the government towards extending informal diplomatic protection towards the claimants. Indeed, despite Lord Triesman's insistence that there was nothing more the United Kingdom could do, the United Kingdom would eventually seek the return of the claimant on this basis in August 2007.[201]

One novel form of HRA engagement is the 'advisory' pronouncement within decisions challenging government policies regarding the steps which might be necessary to bring the law into line with minimum ECHR standards. These can be characterised as informal versions of fully-fledged advisory opinions.[202] For example, in the course of his *Belmarsh* speech, Lord Bingham emphasised that restrictions such as tagging of individuals and restricting or monitoring their access to communications equipment or other people would 'effectively inhibit terrorist activity'[203] without the need to resort to indefinite

[196] *R. (Al Rawi and others) v Secretary of State for Foreign and Commonwealth Affairs* [2006] EWCA Civ 1279; [2008] Q.B. 289.

[197] HL Debs, vol.685, col.992, 23 October 2006.

[198] *R. (Al Rawi and others) v Secretary of State for Foreign and Commonwealth Affairs* [2006] EWCA Civ 1279; [2008] Q.B. 289, at [148].

[199] For a criticism of this approach, see C. Murray, "In the Shadow of Lord Haw Haw: Guantánamo Bay, Diplomatic Protection and Allegiance" [2011] P.L. 115.

[200] *Al Rawi* [2006] EWHC 972 (Admin); [2006] HRLR 30, at [89] (Latham LJ).

[201] See M. Tran, "Britain Seeks Guantánamo Releases", *Guardian*, 7 August 2007, http://www.guardian.co.uk/uk/2007/aug/07/cuba.usa.

[202] See above, p.70.

[203] *Belmarsh Detainees* [2004] UKHL 56, at [35].

detention. As Nicol concludes, 'it is difficult to resist the conclusion that his Lordship was hinting that non-discriminatory house arrest could be lawful',[204] encouraging the government's subsequent development of Control Orders. Similarly, when the House of Lords ruled two years later that some Control Orders were so severe as to breach the right to liberty, Lord Brown effectively endorsed a limit of 16 hours on curfews imposed under Control Orders,[205] a standard that the government moved swiftly to adopt.[206]

This process was repeated in the *Ahmed* case,[207] in which the Supreme Court ruled that Orders in Council did not provide an adequate basis for terrorist asset-freezing orders. Despite acknowledging that it was not necessary to do so for the purpose of the case, Lord Mance made it clear that he was 'unpersuaded that the content of the Orders could be challenged on grounds of lack of proportionality',[208] encouraging the government to re-establish a very similar scheme on a statutory footing.[209] The expectation amongst judges providing such advice seems to be that it will limit litigation on reformed provisions. The danger, however, remains that by offering such advice under judicial imprimatur, government will willingly pursue these minimum standards, whereas had the courts remained silent on required reforms, Parliament may have actively pursued higher standards.

Judicial Dialogue: Dancing without a Partner?

Over a decade into the operational history of the HRA, neither transmission of judicial signals regarding legislative compliance with human rights nor parliamentary reception mechanisms for those signals have yet developed to their full potential. Judicial engagement with legislation in light of human rights concerns may be mandated under the HRA, but the adversarial nature of the courtroom process can undermine the judiciary's grasp of the wider implications of its decisions for public policy, whilst art.9 of the Bill of Rights restricts the judiciary's assessment of the adequacy of parliamentary consideration of rights concerns in legislative drafting. If, as Gardbaum

[204] Nicol, "Law and Politics", 735.

[205] *Secretary of State for the Home Department v JJ* [2007] UKHL 45, at [105].

[206] For criticism, see K. D. Ewing, *Bonfire of the Liberties* (Oxford: Oxford University Press, 2010), p.247.

[207] *Ahmed v HM Treasury* [2010] 2 A.C. 534; [2010] UKSC 2.

[208] *Ahmed v HM Treasury* [2010] 2 A.C. 534; [2010] UKSC 2, at [235]. See also [143] (Lord Phillips).

[209] Terrorist Asset-freezing (Temporary Provisions) Act 2010; Terrorist Asset-freezing etc. Act 2010.

argues, the 'deliberative process' between the courts and Parliament is the most important feature of the HRA model of rights protection,[210] some fine-tuning of the judicial contribution to dialogue remains necessary. These concerns, however, pale before the more serious issue of the lack of parliamentary engagement over specific decisions, as opposed to the currently stalemated debate over the very existence of the HRA.

Adam Tomkins has cautioned that 'we need to view the courts as an instrument of the political constitution' if the United Kingdom is to avoid the road leading to judicial supremacy.[211] If anything, however, members of the judiciary are by-and-large well aware of their constitutional role under the HRA. Perhaps because the United Kingdom has never maintained a functioning *conseil d'état*,[212] it is the elected branches of government which have been slower to appreciate the changed nature of the judiciary's constitutional role. Judicial decisions are all-too-often treated as definitive and not open to legislative challenge. Finding themselves dancing without a partner for much of the HRA's first decade, some judges have even resorted to offering advisory comment on potential rights compatibility of future enactments, with impact far beyond traditional obiter dicta. Only with the prisoner voting rights debate did parliamentarians show themselves capable of offering a substantive response to a judgment (admittedly from Strasbourg), as opposed to dutiful compliance.

Justice Secretary Ken Clarke responded to parliamentarians who objected to prisoner enfranchisement by insisting that the Coalition Government would do no more than 'necessary' to respond to the minimum standards of the right to vote.[213] Soon after that debate, David Cameron informed Parliament that he would take 'the minimum possible approach'[214] to comply with the Supreme Court's ruling that the notification requirements imposed under the Sexual Offences Act 2003 were incompatible with art.8 ECHR.[215] The HRA clearly allows for Parliament to seek minimum compliance, accepting the risk of further adverse judgments if it misjudges the basic standard of rights protection, as evidenced by the Control Order cases. Perhaps this focus on minimum compliance marks the start of an era in which Parliament will show a greater willingness to test the limits of the 'advice' it receives from judges on

[210] Gardbaum, "Reassessing the New Commonwealth Model", 193.

[211] Tomkins, "The Role of the Courts", 3.

[212] See, however, the almost unused Privy Council advisory facility contained within the Judicial Committee Act 1833, s.4.

[213] K. Clarke, Interview with BBC Radio 4's Today Programme, 9 February 2011, http://news.bbc.co.uk/today/hi/today/newsid_9391000/9391865.stm (accessed 21 February 2012).

[214] D. Cameron MP, HC Debs, vol.523, col.955, 16 February 2011.

[215] *R. (F) v Secretary of State for the Home Department* [2011] A.C. 331; [2010] UKSC 17.

the compatibility of legislation with rights standards under the Human Rights Act. Let dialogue commence?

Note. My thanks to Roger Masterman and Aoife O'Donoghue (both at Durham University) for their advice and comments upon earlier drafts of this article. Any errors remain my own.

4

Back to the Future? Judges, Politicians and the Constitution in the New Scotland

AIDAN O'NEILL

The Depoliticising Union of 1707

THE HISTORIAN CONRAD RUSSELL ONCE OBSERVED that the essential problem for any union between Scotland and England 'could be defined by saying that England could brook no equal and Scotland no superior'.[1] Various schemes for a wholly incorporating 'perfect' Union of Scotland and England had unsuccessfully been proposed to the English Parliament by James VI after he had acceded to the English throne in 1603 (and—in the face of opposition in the English Parliament to any change of name of the realm of England—proclaimed himself to be James I, King of Great Britain).[2] The 1707 Union

[1] See C. Russell, *James VI and I and His English Parliaments* (Oxford: Oxford University Press, 2011), p.124. See further p.138: 'The Union with Scotland presented England with a fundamental challenge to its intellectual world of a sort which was never offered by the relationship with Wales or even by the relationship with Ireland. This was for two inter-related reasons. One was the fundamental inconvenient fact of Scottish sovereignty. It was only in their relations with Scotland that the English had to share their king with an independent sovereign state with no dependence on the English political system, law, parliament or church. The other, which was in large measure a cause of the first, was that it was the king of Scots who had become king of England, not the king of England who had become king of Scots. The English had to share power within their king's dominions with an equal. It was that fact which shook them in a way which perhaps only the Chinese among the world's great powers would have understood.'

[2] See, for example, James VI and I in Speech before his first English Parliament (31 March 1607), reprinted in C. Mcllwain (ed.), *The Political Works of James I* (1918), pp.292–93: 'I desire a perfect union of laws and persons and such a naturalising as may make one body of both Kingdom under me your King ... And as for Scotland I avow such an Union as if you have got it by conquest but such a conquest as may be cemented by love, the only sure bond of subjection or friendship that as there is over both but one King so there may be in both but one flock and one law ... But I mean of such a general union of laws as may reduce the whole island, that as they live already under one monarch, so they may be all governed by one law: for I must confess that in my little experience since my coming hither, and I think I am able to procure it, that the grounds of the common law of England are the best in the world, either civil or municipal, and

Proceedings of the British Academy, **183**, 81–108.

differed from these earlier schemes in that, while ensuring the depoliticisation of Scotland, it put into place measures intended to protect—and indeed to strengthen—other aspects of Scotland's distinctive continuing nationhood. Russell puts it thus:

> In 1707 the English got the unitary sovereign power which they wanted and got it in the form based upon the existing English parliament, with an English majority within it. The Scots got their recognition as a separate sovereign State, both from the form of the Union of 1707 as an international treaty, and from the survival of Scots law and the Scottish church. It is that claim that Scotland is a sovereign nation state which is reasserted whenever the English forget that 1707 was not a 'perfect union' ... Scotland in accepting the Union in 1707 remained a nation and as a result any sovereignty in the British parliament could not be national sovereignty. This has always been hard for the English to understand
>
> ...
>
> If the question is whether the state *ought* to be unitary or plural, the range of consequential questions which may require to be addressed is almost infinite. This was not the way English lawyers posed the questions. To them it was tautological that the state *was* unitary, and that a union necessarily involved a full union of laws, religion, parliaments and the lot. The Act of Union of 1707 still shows an uneasy balance between these English and Scottish ideals of union.[3]

While the Scottish Parliament—the *Thrie Estaits* of nobles, senior clerics and burgesses—was abolished under the terms of the 1707 Union, the interests of the Scottish governing classes were preserved by:

1. England paying off the Scottish national debt which had resulted from the collapse of the Bank of Scotland after the failure of the Darien scheme seeking to establish a Scottish colony and trading post in Panama;
2. imposing a common currency, and providing for a single British internal market and customs union allowing for the free movement of goods, services and people between Scotland and England,[4] and for Scotland's free access to and trade with England's overseas empire;

---

the fittest for this people ... And now may you have fair occasion for amending and polishing your laws when Scotland is to be united with you under them: for who can blame Scotland to say if you take away our own laws I pray you give us better and clearer in place thereof.'

[3] See Russell, *James VI and I and His English Parliaments*, pp.126–27, 132.

[4] Article III of the Treaty of Union specified: 'that all the Subjects of the United Kingdom of Great Britain shall from and after the Union *have full freedom and Intercourse of Trade and Navigation to and from any port or place within the said United Kingdom and the Dominions and Plantations thereunto belonging*.'

3. creating a common (British) nationality;[5]
4. putting in place constitutional barriers preventing English law and English lawyers from practising in Scotland, and thereby preserve Scots law and pander to the interests of Edinburgh lawyers;
5. confirming and supporting Presbyterianism as the state-sponsored reformed national church in Scotland;
6. allowing the Scottish peers to elect a proportion of their number to sit in the House of Lords (this practice of elected Scottish peers continued until the early 1960s when all those with Scottish peerages were given UK titles to allow them to sit, as of right, in the House of Lords).

The long-term result of these measures in 1707 was that, in exchange for the effective depoliticisation of Scotland, the constituencies making up the former ruling classes of Scotland could comfortably commit to *political Unionism* while maintaining those other forms of (depoliticised) nationalism which the Union expressly protected and preserved, namely: *legal* nationalism (in the case of Scots lawyers); *ecclesiastical* nationalism (in the case of Scots Presbyterian clerics); and, ultimately, under the influence of the works of Sir Walter Scott, a *romantic* nationalism expressed (in the case of post-Union Scottish military, drawn in the main from the Scottish landed and gentry class) in tartan and bagpipes. The genius of the 1707 Union was that it allowed (Scottish) nationalism to continue to be experienced and expressed—and indeed to flourish—in these various constituencies without this nationalism spilling over to, and becoming expressed through, demands for radical political reforms (such as so many other European polities experienced in the year of revolutions of 1848).

For almost 300 years after the Union real politics went on elsewhere. Scottish internal affairs were managed by, in effect, a viceroy (originally in the form of the Lord Advocate and latterly with the Secretary of State for Scotland running the shop). Able Scottish politicians went to Westminster and thrived there. But this depoliticisation of Scotland for 300 years meant that the professional classes who stayed on in Scotland (the lawyers, the landed, the journalists, the academics, the bankers and the clergy) simply lost the *habitus* of direct engagement with political power, since politics was something that happened, not in Edinburgh, but in London.

As a result of the 1707 Union compromises, there developed in Scotland a public culture where there was no strong tradition of any active political

[5] See 'Calvin's Case': *Calvin v Smith*, 77 Eng. Rep. 377 (K.B. 1608) which addressed the question of whether Scots would, after the accession of James VI to the English Crown, be considered 'subjects' or aliens in English law.

involvement or engagement in Scotland by the lawyers, clerics or lairds. Perhaps, most worryingly of all for the health of the nation, there was no proper development in Scotland of public law to ensure that political power be kept within legal bounds.

The Decline of Public Law in Scotland

Insofar as the law in Scotland developed after the 1707 Union—or, as some would have it, declined from a mythic Golden Age of 17th-century pre-Union Roman–Dutch-based Scots law scholarship enthroned in Viscount Stair's *Institute of the Law of Scotland* (2nd edn, 1691)—it did so in a manner relatively undisturbed by politics and politicians.[6] In the course of the 18th and 19th centuries there was little, if any, litigation relative to public law issues, and such distinctive Scottish republican tradition in the law that there might have been,[7] withered on the vine. Indeed the very idea of 'public law' in Scotland itself fell into desuetude.[8] This is notwithstanding that the Acts of

[6] See J. R. Philip, "The Crown as Litigant in Scotland" (1928) 40 *Juridical Review* 238, 239–40: 'Stair and other institutional writers following his example refused to deal with constitutional law; and because the Crown as litigant is on the border lines of constitutional and private law, they avoid treating it, except incidentally under other topics... Again, in examining the early position of the Crown as litigant in Scotland, it seems dangerous to expect too strict an application of legal theory... Further, even if one hopes for a strict application of legal theory, it is a mistake to expect that the theory applied is always consistent. There are many illustrations of the truth that the history of Scots law is a mirror of the vicissitudes of Scottish history; that when the Scots Crown was weak, its immunity at law was weak, and that the habitual weakness of the Scots Crown account for the narrower limits of immunity.'

[7] See *Edwards v Cruickshank* (1840) 3 D 282, 306–07 (Lord President Hope): 'With regard to our jurisdiction [in Scotland], and the jurisdiction of the supreme courts in every civilized country with which I am acquainted, I have no doubt. They have power to compel every person to perform their duty—persons whether single or corporate; and, in our noble constitution, I maintain—though at first sight it may appear to be a startling proposition—the law can compel the Sovereign himself to do his duty, ay, or restrain him from exceeding his duty. Your Lordships know that the Sovereign never acts by himself, but only through the medium of his ministers or executive servants; and if any duty is refused to be done by any minister in the department over which he presides, or if he exceed his duty to the injury of the subjects, the law gives redress. ... In this country a person would proceed by action or by petition; and, if he was right, a decree would be passed and would be enforced by ordinary process of law.'

[8] See *Davidson v Scottish Ministers* (2006) S.C. (HL) 42, at [77] (Lord Rodger): 'Before going any further, I must say a word about the sense in which I have used the expression "private law". As my noble and learned friend, Lord Hope of Craighead, has recalled, until recently practitioners of both Scots law and English law had comparatively little use for the categories of "public law" and "private law". The categories had been of more service to authors of legal textbooks. Significantly enough, it was in an elementary work that Ulpian contrasted *publicum jus* and *privatum jus* (*Institutionum*, D.1.1.1.2). Justinian incorporated part of the passage into his own elementary work, *Institutes* (1.1.4). From there, despite the difficulties in defining their exact scope ("There is no need to pause on this," said Birks in his "Introduction" to *English Private*

Union had made specific reference to a difference of treatment as between matters concerning 'public right' and those dealing with private rights between subjects. Or that one of the first acts of the Union Government, in a scheme intended to render unnecessary the practice of Scots lawyers to travel abroad to the Low Countries to complete their education in the Roman–Dutch legal tradition, was to found and fund in 1707 the Regius Chair of Public Law and the Law of Nature and Nations at Edinburgh University. 'Scots law', instead, became synonymous with Scots private law, with rich men's disputes over land issues and wills and trusts predominating in the case law of the Court of Session of the 18th, 19th and, indeed, early 20th century. But, as was observed of the Scotland of this period, 'the poor had no lawyers'.[9]

Law, p xxxvi), the terms went on to find a place in many general accounts of the law—though not, for example, in Blackstone. Holland, *Jurisprudence* (p 128), said that, when rights subsist "between subject and subject", they are regulated by private law, when "between State and subject" by public law. According to Stair, *Institutions of the Laws of Scotland* (1.1.23), public rights are those which concern the state of the commonwealth; private rights are the rights of persons and particular incorporations. The terminology was sufficiently understood to be adopted in art XVIII of the Treaty of Union. Bankton also sees positive law as relating to public or private right (*An Institute of the Laws of Scotland*, 1.1.54). Erskine (*An Institute of the Laws of Scotland*, 1.1.29) says that private law "is that which is chiefly intended for ascertaining the civil rights of individuals." In the opening paragraph of his *Principles of Scottish Private Law* Prof Walker summarises the position in this way:

> The private law is the branch of the municipal law of Scotland comprising the principles and rules applied in defining and determining the rights and duties of ordinary private persons in their relations with one another, and of the State, and of public and governmental agencies and persons, in their relations with persons, in respects in which they do not enjoy any special position, right, or immunity, by virtue of any rule of public law. The division between private and public law is not clear or rigid nor is it so familiar as in continental legal systems.

The core idea is that private law regulates relations between individuals. I therefore use the expression "private law" simply as a convenient label for that branch of the law. But the Crown can, for example, own property and enter into leases and other types of contract with its subjects. It can also commit torts or delicts against them. When it does these things, unless statute provides otherwise, the same private law applies as between two subjects. Part II of the 1947 Act gives the procedure to be used when a subject sues the Crown in relation to such a private law matter in the English courts.'

[9] Professor Cosmo Innes (1798–1874), Professor of Universal History and Greek and Roman Antiquities (a Chair that was later named Constitutional Law and History) at the University of Edinburgh in his *Lectures on Scotch Legal Antiquities* (1872), pp.154–55: 'I do not suppose that any cruelty or injustice was ever premeditated by the legislature or the Government; that there was ever any intention to favour the rich at the expense of the poor, but *there are things in the history of our law that I cannot help censuring the more because I believe the evil was for the most part attributable to the straining of the law by lawyers* ... [O]ur lawyers lent themselves to appropriate the poor man's grazing to the neighbouring baron. They pointed to his charter with its clause of parts and pertinents, with its general clause of mosses and moors—clauses taken from the style book, not with any reference to the territory conveyed in that charter; and although the charter was hundreds of years old, and the lord had never possessed any of the common, when it came to be divided, the lord got the whole that was allocated to the estate, and the poor cottar none. The poor had no lawyer.'

On some accounts the ideals of a radical Scottish republican tradition (which had been given particular voice in the 16th-century Reformation and the 17th-century struggles to reject any royal authority over the Reformed Scottish church) were exported and flourished across the Atlantic once the Scots were given free access to England's North American colonies.[10] Indeed these ideals may ultimately have been realised in the 1776 American Declaration of Independence and in the terms of the 1789 US Constitution.[11]

But in 18th-century Scotland itself the depoliticisation of the ruling elites of Scottish society brought about by the 1707 Union of Parliaments—a process accelerated by the failure of the 1715 and 1745 Jacobite uprisings—meant that that pre-Union radical tradition of accountability of government to the law and to the people fell into abeyance. A Victorian popular commitment to the success of the unitary British state and the expansion of its empire in the course of the 19th century led to a certain downplaying in the courts of the continued existence of any distinctive Scottish public law constitutional tradition surviving the Acts of Unions. Thus, it came to pass that by 1866 one Scottish legal practitioner, J. F. Macqueen QC, could describe the situation in Scotland thus:

> The blessings of the English Constitution … were not extended to Scotland [at the Union in 1707]. The Scotch consequently have no Magna Charta, no Bill of Rights, no *Habeas Corpus*. … Personal freedom depends on the temper of the existing government, or rather on the discretion—peradventure the caprice—of the Lord Advocate. When that high functionary incarcerated a gentleman supposed to entertain dangerous political opinions, the Lord Advocate justified himself in the House of Commons by the proud boast that he represented the Scottish Privy Council, and that his powers were unlimited. Under the sway of a benignant sovereign Caledonian grievances have practically disappeared. But the grave question remains whether it is consistent with the dignity of an intellectual people that their political rights should depend on the clemency of the government.[12]

[10] See I. McLean, "The Eighteenth Century Revolution in Social Science and the Dawn of Political Science in America" (2006) 5 *European Political Science* 112: 'Scottish social and political science reached America through her fledgling universities, including The College of New Jersey (later Princeton) and the College of William and Mary in Williamsburg, VA: respectively the *almae matres* of Madison and of Jefferson. In the eighteenth century, the Scottish universities were at an intellectual peak; the only English ones, Oxford and Cambridge, in an intellectual trough of which both Smith and his friend Edward Gibbon wrote eloquently and sarcastically.'

[11] See A. O'Neill, "Limited Government, Fundamental Rights and the Scottish Constitutional Tradition" (2009) *Juridical Review* 85.

[12] J. F. Macqueen QC, paper read at the Manchester Congress of Social Science on 8 October 1866 (Lord Brougham presiding) cited by Hemming QC at 59–60 in *Mackintosh v Lord Advocate* (1876) 2 App Cas 41, HL (Sc).

The Post-1707 Continued Isolation of Scots Criminal Law

While the House of Lords exercised an appellate jurisdiction from decisions of the Inner House of the Court of Session in civil matters for over 300 years, there was and is no general right of appeal from decisions of the High Court of Justiciary (whether for the accused or the Crown) in Scottish criminal cases.[13] The result has been that the Scottish criminal justice system developed in a wholly home-grown manner, quite isolated from legislative or jurisprudential developments taking place south of Scotland. Thus the criminal law in Scotland was, in effect, made by the High Court of Justiciary in Edinburgh, in the absence of any interest in this issue from the UK legislature and untainted by any southern or other external influence. As Lord Bingham noted:

> When Scotland was united with England and Wales in 1707 it was clearly implicit in the Act of Union that there was no criminal appeal from Scotland to London … There was originally a doubt as to whether there was even a civil appeal from Edinburgh to London, but it was very quickly established that there was and indeed extensive use of it was made to such an extent that there was very little time to hear English appeals! But what is important is that *the Scots criminal system has always been self-contained and has had no English input at all.*[14]

And Lord Hope of Craighead observed:

> [T]he High Court of Justiciary, which is the supreme criminal court in Scotland, is unique among the superior courts of the United Kingdom in that its decisions are not subject to appeal to this House … In the result the system of criminal law which operates in Scotland has remained entirely separate from that of England. Prior to the coming into force of the Scotland Act 1998 on 1 July 1999 legislation relating to Scottish criminal law and procedure was dealt with by the United Kingdom Parliament. But even that matter has now been devolved to the Scottish Parliament. Thus, although there is now much common ground between England and Scotland in the field of civil law, their systems of criminal law are as distinct from each other as if they were two foreign countries.[15]

[13] See *Mackintosh v Lord Advocate* (1876) 2 App Cas 41, HL (Sc).
[14] Lord Bingham of Cornhill, evidence to the Parliamentary Joint Committee on Human Rights, 26 March 2001.
[15] *R. v Manchester Stipendiary Magistrate Ex p. Granada Television Ltd* [2001] 1 A.C. 300, 304 (Lord Hope of Craighead).

The Legal Constitution v the Political Constitution

The 1707 Union settlement expressly prohibited English courts from purporting to exercise any jurisdiction in Scotland. This prohibition is contained in Article XIX of the Acts of Union which provides that

> no Causes in Scotland be cognoscible by the Courts of Chancery, Queens-Bench, Common-Pleas, or any other Court in Westminster-hall; and that the said Courts, or any other of the like Nature, after the Union, shall have no Power to cognosce, review, or alter the Acts or Sentences of the Judicatures within Scotland, or stop the Execution of the same.

Accordingly, for any English court to purport to exercise jurisdiction within the realm of Scotland would be contrary to fundamental provisions of the Acts of Union between the two countries. Thus, when ruling that

> to foreign dominions, which belong to a prince who succeeds to the throne of England, this Court has no power to send any writ of any kind. We cannot send a *habeas corpus* to Scotland …[16]

Lord Mansfield was speaking against the background of those provisions of the Acts of Union of which he would have been well aware and to which he would have been particularly sensitive, being himself a Scot.

The paradox of the 1707 Union was that Scotland and England remained for legal purposes foreign countries in relation to one another, while being politically united. From a *constitutional* perspective this leads to a constant unresolved and irresoluble tension—indeed a classic Caledonian antisyzygy—between a legal-constitutionalist analysis and political-constitutionalist understanding of the Union. Influenced, perhaps, by the terms of Article XVIII of the Treaty of Union which provides that 'the laws concerning public right, policy and civil government may be made the same throughout the whole United Kingdom' there remained a strong tendency for the courts in Scotland to seek to align Scots law with English law in constitutional and public law issues generally such that, as was submitted on behalf of the appellant to the House of Lords in 1876 in *Mackintosh v Lord Advocate*:

> [T]he meaning of that Treaty [of 1707] was that the whole political and judicial constitution of Scotland was swept away, and that the political and judicial constitution of England was substituted for it in every particular not mentioned in the Treaty itself.[17]

By the early 20th century a Court of Session judge could say that

[16] *King v Cowle* 2 Burr. 834, 855–56; 97 Eng. Rep. 587, 599 (K.B. 1759).
[17] *Mackintosh v Lord Advocate* (1876) 2 App Cas 41, HL (Sc), 58 (Mr Hemming QC).

> the constitution of Scotland has been the same as that of England since 1707 [and] there is a presumption that the same constitutional principles apply in both countries.[18]

In the atmosphere of silent revolution associated with the social, economic and political reconstruction of Britain in the immediate aftermath of the Second World War such past constitutional certainties began to be questioned. Indeed by 1953 a new post-imperial constitutional tradition could be invented (or rediscovered) when Lord President Cooper made the following claims to a separate continuing Scottish constitutional tradition within the Union:

> The principle of the unlimited sovereignty of Parliament is a distinctively English principle which has no counterpart in Scottish constitutional law. It derives its origin from Coke and Blackstone, and was widely popularised during the nineteenth century by Bagehot and Dicey, the latter having stated the doctrine in its classic form in his *Law of the Constitution*. *Considering that the Union legislation extinguished the Parliaments of Scotland and England and replaced them by a new Parliament, I have difficulty in seeing why it should have been supposed that the new Parliament of Great Britain must inherit all the peculiar characteristics of the English Parliament but none of the Scottish Parliament, as if all that happened in 1707 was that Scottish representatives were admitted to the Parliament of England. That is not what was done.*
>
> Further, the Treaty and the associated legislation, by which the Parliament of Great Britain was brought into being as the successor of the separate Parliaments of Scotland and England, contain some clauses which expressly reserve to the Parliament of Great Britain powers of subsequent modification, and other clauses which either contain no such power or emphatically exclude subsequent alteration by declarations that the provision shall be fundamental and unalterable in all time coming, or declarations of a like effect. *I have never been able to understand how it is possible to reconcile with elementary canons of construction the adoption by the English constitutional theorists of the same attitude to these markedly different types of provisions.*
>
> The Lord Advocate conceded this point by admitting that the Parliament of Great Britain 'could not' repeal or alter such 'fundamental and essential' conditions. He was doubtless influenced in making this concession by the modified views expressed by Dicey in his later work entitled *Thoughts on the Scottish Union*, from which I take this passage (pp.252–253):
>
> > The statesmen of 1707, though giving full sovereign power to the Parliament of Great Britain, clearly believed in the possibility of creating an absolutely sovereign Legislature which should yet be bound by unalterable laws.
>
> After instancing the provisions as to Presbyterian Church government in Scotland with their emphatic prohibition against alteration, the author proceeds:

[18] *Macgregor v Lord Advocate* 1921 SC 847, 848 (the Lord Ordinary (Lord Anderson)).

> It represents the conviction of the Parliament which passed the Act of Union that the Act for the security of the Church of Scotland ought to be morally or constitutionally unchangeable, even by the British Parliament. A sovereign Parliament, in short, though it cannot be logically bound to abstain from changing any given law, may, by the fact that an Act when it was passed had been declared to be unchangeable, receive a warning that it cannot be changed without grave danger to the Constitution of the country.

I have not found in the Union legislation any provision that the Parliament of Great Britain should be 'absolutely sovereign' in the sense that that Parliament should be free to alter the Treaty at will. However that may be, these passages provide a necessary corrective to the extreme formulations adopted by the Lord Ordinary,[19] and not now supported.[20]

Lord Cooper's words—though oft-cited by Scottish legal nationalists—have never in the 60 years or so since they were written resulted in the courts accepting the validity of any challenge to any provision of an Act of (the Union) Parliament for its incompatibility with the requirements of the 1707 Union.[21]

[19] See *MacCormick v Lord Advocate* 1953 SC 396, OH, 403 (Lord Guthrie): 'In my opinion, the appellants' propositions in law are unsound and indeed extravagant. No Scottish Court has ever held an Act of Parliament to be *ultra vires*, and it has never been suggested that it could do so. I do not require to examine the contention that the Scottish Parliament was not sovereign, but there could not be a more remarkable exercise of sovereign power than the abolition of the separate Kingdom of Scotland by the Act of Union. The propositions of the appellants are based upon a challenge of the sovereignty of the Parliament of the United Kingdom, which, in the words of Professor Dicey, is, from a legal point of view, the dominant characteristic of our political institutions *Law of the Constitution* (9th ed.), p.39. The appellants urged that Professor Dicey's work was an English book, based on English law, and should not be accepted in Scotland. It is sufficient to say that his *Law of the Constitution* has been for generations accepted in the schools of law in our Scottish Universities as an authoritative exposition of the constitution of the United Kingdom. The doctrine of the sovereignty of Parliament is recognised in Scotland as a basic principle of constitutional law. It is expounded by Mr. W. I. R. Fraser, a Scottish writer, in his *Outline of Constitutional Law*, pp.12 *et seq*. It follows from that doctrine that 'any Act of Parliament, or any part of an Act of Parliament, which makes a new law, or repeals or modifies an existing law, will be obeyed by the Courts' Dicey, p.40. In later passages (pp. 889–1) the same author states three traits of Parliamentary sovereignty; first, the power of the Legislature to alter any law, fundamental or otherwise, as freely and in the same manner as other laws; *secondly, the absence of any legal distinction between constitutional and other laws*; thirdly, *the non-existence of any judicial or other authority having the right to nullify an Act of Parliament, or to treat it as void or unconstitutional*. As I regard these statements as an accurate exposition of the law, it follows that, in my opinion, this Court is bound to obey the will of Parliament as expressed in the Royal Titles Act, 1953.'

[20] *MacCormick v Lord Advocate* 1953 SC 396, IH, 407–08 (Lord President Cooper).

[21] See, for example, *Laughland v Wansborough Paper Co Ltd* 1921 1 SLT 341, OH, 345 (Lord Ashmore): 'A provision of the Treaty of Union is specially founded on. It is contained in the 18th article, which makes it a condition of legislation by the United Parliament that no alteration be made in laws which concern private right "except for the evident utility of the subjects within

It may be better therefore to regard these remarks as a form of poetic or romantic licence: fine rhetoric which is and never was descriptive of the post-1707 constitution as this had been understood and given effect to by any legal officials operating under and in terms of the relevant Hartian 'rule of recognition'.[22]

Devolution and the Repoliticisation of Scotland

The Scotland Act 1998 (SA) was passed by the new Labour government in the first wave of its constitutional reforms. It was enacted in the same parliamentary session that passed the Human Rights Act 1998 (HRA). Both statutes brought Convention rights into domestic law, albeit by quite different mechanisms. The HRA incorporated a 'lawfulness control' in s.6 which preserved the sovereignty of the UK Parliament to legislate in a manner incompatible with Convention rights (s.4 HRA) and authorised public authorities to implement and give effect to such Convention-incompatible legislation (s.6(2) HRA). By contrast, the SA made compatibility with Convention rights a condition of the legislative competence of the Scottish Parliament (s.29) and

---

Scotland" ... In spite of the difficulty and delicacy attending the exercise of the discretion committed to the English Court by the statute of 1875 and the relative statutory rules, however, it is apparent that the scheme of the legislation is intended to facilitate the administration of justice and to reduce the cost, and to meet the convenience of litigants in the different parts of the United Kingdom. Individual cases of hardship are not inconsistent with the general benefit. ... I am of opinion that no sufficient ground has been shewn by the complainer to justify the conclusion that the procedure embodied in the new sub rule "is not for the evident utility of the subjects within Scotland," and is not calculated on the whole to meet the convenience of the people at both ends of the island.' Compare with *Gibson v Lord Advocate*, 1975 SC 136, OH, 144 (Lord Keith): 'The making of decisions upon what must essentially be a political matter is no part of the function of the court, and it is highly undesirable that it should be. The function of the court is to adjudicate upon the particular rights and obligations of individual persons, natural or corporate, in relation to other persons or, in certain instances, to the state. *A general inquiry into the utility of certain legislative measures as regards the population generally is quite outside its competence.*'

[22] Compare *Jackson v Attorney General* [2006] 1 A.C. 262, at [126] (Lord Hope): 'There is a strong case for saying that the rule of recognition, which gives way to what people are prepared to recognise as law, is itself worth calling "law" and for applying it accordingly. It must never be forgotten that this rule, which is underpinned by what others have referred to as political reality, depends upon the legislature maintaining the trust of the electorate. In a democracy the need of the elected members to maintain this trust is a vitally important safeguard. The principle of parliamentary sovereignty which in the absence of higher authority, has been created by the common law is built upon the assumption that Parliament represents the people whom it exists to serve.'

of the *vires* of the Scottish government (s.57(2) SA), with no possibility of any member of the Scottish administration—other than the Lord Advocate prosecuting a criminal offence on the basis of a Convention-incompatible provision of UK legislation (s.57(3) SA)—acting in a manner contrary to Convention rights. There appears to have been little thought given in Parliament as to how these two statutes might interrelate with one another.[23]

In any event the SA brought politics back to Scotland after 300 years of Scottish political quietism. In so doing it unavoidably called into question the accepted wisdom and conventional pieties on the proper relationship between Scotland and England (and the proper relationship between law and politics within Scotland) which had grown up under, and since, their 1707 Union.

The Post-devolution Juridicalisation of Scottish Politics

In its devolution of political power to Scotland, the UK Parliament deliberately created devolved institutions of government in Scotland that were not

[23] See *Somerville v Scottish Ministers* 2008 SC (HL) 45, at [115]–[117] (Lord Rodger): '[I] in enacting the two statutes, Parliament has not imposed the same time-limit on proceedings by reference to the Scotland Act as on proceedings under the HRA … [I]t is not for the courts to second-guess Parliament's quite deliberate decision to frame the two statutes differently in this respect. The First Division came to a very different conclusion. On the basis that the HRA and the Scotland Act are to be regarded as closely interdependent, they held that (2007 SC 140, para 55):

> [I]t is right and proper to conclude that Parliament, in the absence of some compelling reason to the contrary, intended that sec 7(5) HRA should apply to limit in terms of time proceedings where a devolution issue arose as well as those where none arose.

As they went on to make clear, what they meant was that Parliament intended sec 7(5) HRA to apply to limit the time for bringing proceedings with reference to the vires limits in the Scotland Act as well as proceedings under the HRA. I cannot agree. Contrary to what their Lordships say, nothing in the relationship between the two Acts would make it "right" or "proper" to conclude that sec 7(5) HRA should apply to limit any proceedings other than the proceedings which Parliament has chosen, very deliberately, to make it limit. The First Division's construction flies in the face of the words which Parliament used in enacting sec 7(5) HRA. By its express terms, sec 7(5) HRA applies only to the proceedings "under this Act" specified in subsec (1)(a)—not even to the other cases described in subsec (1)(b). Given its express terms, sec 7(5) cannot possibly apply by implication to other proceedings—least of all, to proceedings brought by reference to a vires limit contained in another Act. In short, there is absolutely nothing in sec 7(5) or any other provision of the HRA, or in any provision of the Scotland Act, which applies the time-limit in sec 7(5) to proceedings brought against the Scottish Ministers by reference to the Convention right vires limit in the Scotland Act. The point does not bear elaboration.'

But compare and contrast the views of Lord Hope and Lord Rodger in this decision (in the majority overruling the decision of the First Division below) with the strongly dissenting views of Lord Scott (at [68]–[79]) and Lord Mance (at [179]–[194]).

'sovereign' in the classic Diceyan sense, but instead were to be limited by law and by the courts. The SA is premised on a unitary constitutional model (the United Kingdom as a 'nation state' rather than a 'state of nations'). Under this model legal power is devolved to Holyrood, but not divested from Westminster. On this constitutional analysis, s.1(1) SA provides that 'there shall be a Scottish Parliament' because the Crown, acting on the advice of the Westminster Parliament, so wills it; not because the 'Scottish people' has brought it into being.[24] The SA modifies the terms, but maintains the fact, of Union between Scotland and England: s.37 states that 'The Union with Scotland Act 1706 and the Union with England Act 1707 have effect subject to this Act.' The Westminster Parliament has set legally enforceable limits on the power of the Scottish Parliament by providing in s.29 SA as follows:

> 29.— Legislative competence
>
> (1) An Act of the Scottish Parliament is not law so far as any provision of the Act is outside the legislative competence of the Parliament.
> (2) A provision is outside that competence so far as any of the following paragraphs apply—
>   (a) it would form part of the law of a country or territory other than Scotland, or confer or remove functions exercisable otherwise than in or as regards Scotland,
>   (b) it relates to reserved matters,[25]

[24] See *AXA General Insurance Ltd v The Lord Advocate* [2012] 1 A.C. 868, at [46] (Lord Hope): 'The Scottish Parliament takes its place under our constitutional arrangements as a self-standing democratically elected legislature. Its democratic mandate to make laws for the people of Scotland is beyond question. Acts that the Scottish Parliament enacts which are within its legislative competence enjoy, in that respect, the highest legal authority. The United Kingdom Parliament has vested in the Scottish Parliament the authority to make laws that are within its devolved competence. It is nevertheless a body to which decision making powers have been delegated. And it does not enjoy the sovereignty of the Crown in Parliament ... Sovereignty remains with the United Kingdom Parliament. The Scottish Parliament's power to legislate is not unconstrained. It cannot make or unmake any law it wishes.'

[25] See *Martin v Most* 2010 SC (UKSC) 40, at [44], [49] (Lord Walker): 'The Scotland Act 1998 is on any view a monumental piece of constitutional legislation. Parliament established the Scottish Parliament and the Scottish Executive and undertook the challenging task of defining the legislative competence of the Scottish Parliament, while itself continuing as the sovereign legislature of the United Kingdom. That task is different from defining the division of legislative power between one federal legislature and several provincial or state legislatures (as in Canada or Australia, whose constitutional difficulties the Judicial Committee of the Privy Council used to wrestle with, often to the dissatisfaction of those dominions). The doctrine of "pith and substance" ... is probably more apt to apply to the construction of constitutions of that type. But both have to face the difficulty of defining (necessarily in fairly general and abstract terms) permitted or prohibited areas of legislative activity. ... Section 29(2)(b) prohibits legislation by the Scottish Parliament which "relates to" reserved matters. That is an expression which is familiar in this sort of context, indicating more than a loose or consequential connection, and the language of sec 29(3), referring to a provision's purpose and effect, reinforces that.'

(c) it is in breach of the restrictions in Schedule 4,
(d) it is incompatible with any of the Convention rights or with EU law,
(e) it would remove the Lord Advocate from his position as head of the systems of criminal prosecution and investigation of deaths in Scotland.[26]

Section 54(3) SA provides that it is outside the 'devolved competence' of the Scottish Ministers to exercise any of their functions in any way which would be outside the legislative competence of the Scottish Parliament and, as we have noted, s.57(2) SA states that '[a] member of the Scottish Executive has no power to make any subordinate legislation, or to do any other act, so far as the legislation or act is incompatible with any of the Convention rights or with EU law'.

These provisions of the SA allow challenges to be made before the court as to the validity of all legislation passed by the Scottish Parliament or made by the Scottish Ministers (and indeed any acts having legal effect). But as a legacy, perhaps, of the political quietism which the pre-devolution 1707 Union engendered in Scotland, there have been surprisingly few challenges to the validity of provisions of Acts of the Scottish Parliament (despite its prodigious output of legislation since it opened for business in 1999), and until very recently[27] none of these challenges had met with any success.

Clearly the direct judicial review of primary legislation which the SA provides for raises interesting but difficult questions regarding the proper relationship of the courts to the democratically elected legislature. It is essential to develop new principles of legitimacy which can justify the priority of the individual's fundamental rights over the claims of the legislature and the executive to protect the general public interest in a democracy as well as

[26] *Imperial Tobacco v Scottish Ministers* [2012] CSIH 9, at 164 (Lord Brodie): 'Section 29 [SA] defines the scope of the devolved power. It does so by identifying the characteristics of a provision which place it outside the legislative competence of the [Scottish] Parliament. The scheme whereby legislative competence is conferred on the Scottish Parliament is one where what is not specifically identified as being outside competence is devolved, albeit that in terms of section 28(7), the Parliament of the United Kingdom, consistent with its sovereign character, retains all of its pre-Act power to make law for Scotland (this is qualified in practice by the "Sewel Convention" in terms of which the Parliament of the United Kingdom will not legislate with regard to devolved matters without the consent of the Scottish Parliament).'

[27] See now *Cameron v Cottam* 2012 SLT 173, HCJ (AC) in which the criminal appeal court pronounced a declarator to the effect that the statutory bail conditions imposed by s.58 of the Criminal Justice and Licensing (Scotland) Act 2010 were 'not law' because incompatible with art.5 of the European Convention on Human Rights (ECHR). And see *Salvesen v Riddell* [2012] CSIH 26 where the Second Division ruled that s.72 of the Agricultural Holdings (Scotland) Act 2003 which imposed restrictions on a landlord's right to terminate an agricultural lease and recover possession could not be read in a manner that was compatible with the landlord's right to property protected by ECHR, art.1, Protocol 1 and was therefore outwith the legislative competence of the Scottish Parliament.

principles for determining the legitimate relationships among the Scottish, UK and European legislatures and executives governing the land. The courts in Scotland are still finding their way in this regard. Initially, it appeared that the Scottish Parliament would be regarded as just another statutory body, unproblematically subject to scrutiny by the courts. Lord President Lord Rodger of Earslferry made certain robust remarks apparently to this effect in his decision in *Whaley v Lord Watson*, in declaring that the Scottish Parliament would be regarded as 'any other litigant' in challenges to its acts before the courts.[28] But these remarks must be seen in context. They may now be read as no more than an assertion that the internal workings and privileges of the Scottish Parliament are not to be regarded as immune from judicial scrutiny. However, once the Scottish Parliament has duly acted in a legislative capacity, the court has to recognise the legitimacy that inheres to the substance of the resulting statute, by virtue of its being produced by a democratically mandated assembly. Consider, for example, *A v Scottish Ministers* which was a challenge to the Convention compatibility of the first ever Act of the Scottish Parliament, emergency legislation which had been passed by the Scottish Parliament with retrospective effect and with targeted and specific intent to close a perceived loop-hole in the law whereby persons who had been sentenced after trial to be detained indefinitely in a secure hospital were able to secure their release on the grounds that they were not now held to be suffering from any treatable mental illness. This challenge was unsuccessful in both the Inner House and on appeal to the Privy Council.[29] Both the First Division

[28] *Whaley and others v Lord Watson of Invergowrie and The Scottish Parliament*, 2000 SC 340, IH, 348H, 349D–E, 350B–C (Lord Rodger): '[T]he [Scottish] Parliament [i]s a body which—however important its role—has been created by statute and derives its powers from statute. As such, it is a body which, like any other statutory body, must work within the scope of those powers. If it does not do so, then in an appropriate case the court may be asked to intervene and will require to do so, in a manner permitted by the legislation. *In principle, therefore, the Parliament like any other body set up by law is subject to the law and to the courts which exist to uphold that law* ... [I]n many democracies throughout the Commonwealth, for example, even where the parliaments have been modelled in some respects on Westminster, they owe their existence and powers to statute and are in various ways subject to the law and to the courts which uphold the law. The Scottish Parliament has simply joined that wider family of parliaments. Indeed, I find it almost paradoxical that counsel for a member of a body which exists to create laws and to impose them on others should contend that a legally enforceable framework is somehow less than appropriate for that body itself. ... *While all United Kingdom courts which may have occasion to deal with proceedings involving the Scottish Parliament can, of course, be expected to accord all due respect to the Parliament as to any other litigant, they must equally be aware that they are not dealing with a Parliament which is sovereign: on the contrary, it is subject to the laws and hence to the courts*. For that reason, I see no basis upon which this court can properly adopt a "self-denying ordinance" which would consist in exercising some kind of discretion to refuse to enforce the law against the Parliament or its members. To do so would be to fail to uphold the rights of other parties under the law.'

[29] *A v Scottish Ministers*, 2002 SC (PC), 63.

and the Privy Council held that the Scottish Parliament's legislation was justified by considerations of continued safety of the general public as well as the staff and inmates of ordinary prisons all of which could properly be used to justify the continued detention of restricted patients in hospital, whether or not their mental disorder was treatable, notwithstanding that medical opinion had shifted since these individuals had been sentenced such that their condition—psychopathic disorder manifested by abnormally aggressive or seriously irresponsible conduct—was not now regarded as being capable of receiving treatment likely to alleviate or prevent a deterioration in their condition. In granting the legislature a degree of deference as regards its judgment on these issues, Lord Rodger of Earlsferry noted:

> One might envisage situations in which it was far from clear whether the minister concerned or the legislature had applied their minds to the balance which the Convention requires a State to hold between the community interest and the rights of individuals. But this is not such a situation. It is indeed plain from the report of the proceedings in the Scottish Parliament not only that ministers and members were aware of the Convention hovering above the debate, but also, more specifically, that they were conscious of the need to hold just that very balance …
>
> What we must therefore decide is whether, even though the members were conscious of the need to have regard to the human rights of the patients, the Parliament none the less failed to maintain the necessary fair balance by giving too much weight to the perceived danger to members of the public and, thereby, giving too little weight to the requirements of the protection of the patients' right to freedom and in particular their rights under art 5(1)(e) and (4). *In determining that issue, as the authorities show, it is right that the court should give due deference to the assessment which the democratically elected legislature has made of the policy issues involved.*[30]

The fact that the courts have been accorded by statute the power to rule, inter alia, upon the Convention compatibility of Acts of the Scottish Parliament and to suspend or disapply these provisions does not mean that the judges are now to be regarded as having untrammelled power or discretion over the democratic legislature. The judges' powers are circumscribed by the very statute which accords them this role and by broader constitutional considerations, for example the doctrine of proportionality should be applied in a careful and nuanced way, with the court not rushing in to substitute its assessment of policy matters for that of the legislature. This is certainly the approach taken by the courts in *AXA General Insurance v Lord Advocate*,[31] the unsuccessful judicial review taken by various companies providing employer's

[30] *A v Scottish Ministers*, 2001 SC 1, IH, 20–21 (Lord Rodger of Earlsferry, emphasis added).

[31] *AXA General Insurance v Lord Advocate* [2012] 1 A.C. 868, UKSC; 2011 SLT 439, IH; 2010 SLT 179, OH.

liability insurance challenging the validity and Convention compatibility of the Damages (Asbestos-related Conditions) (Scotland) Act 2009 which declared (for the avoidance of doubt engendered by the decision of the House of Lords to the contrary effect in the English test litigation *Rothwell*)[32] that asymptomatic plural plaques (and other related conditions) constituted actionable personal injury under the law of Scotland, in which Lord Hope in the Supreme Court of the United Kingdom (UKSC) observed as follows:

> The dominant characteristic of the Scottish Parliament is its firm rooting in the traditions of a universal democracy. It draws its strength from the electorate. While the judges, who are not elected, are best placed to protect the rights of the individual, including those who are ignored or despised by the majority, the elected members of a legislature of this kind are best placed to judge what is in the country's best interests as a whole. A sovereign Parliament is, according to the traditional view, immune from judicial scrutiny because it is protected by the principle of sovereignty. But it shares with the devolved legislatures, which are not sovereign, the advantages that flow from the depth and width of the experience of its elected members and the mandate that has been given to them by the electorate. This suggests that the judges should intervene, if at all, only in the most exceptional circumstances. As Lord Bingham of Cornhill said in *R. (on the application of Countryside Alliance) v Attorney General*, at [2008] 1 A.C., p.755, para.45, the democratic process is liable to be subverted if, on a question of political or moral judgment, opponents of an Act achieve through the courts what they could not achieve through Parliament.[33]

But, as the First Division noted in *Imperial Tobacco v Scottish Ministers* (which concerned the issue as to whether ss. 1 and 9 of the Tobacco and Primary Medical Services (Scotland) Act 2010, banning retail display of tobacco products and outlawing tobacco vending machines, was outside the legislative competence of the Scottish Parliament and accordingly not law), even if one were to characterise the SA as a 'constitutional statute', that did not mean that there was any legal presumption in favour of the validity of the acts of the devolved authorities under the statute. Lord Reed said this:

> The Scotland Act is not a constitution, but an Act of Parliament. There are material differences. The context of the devolution of legislative and executive power within the United Kingdom is evidently different from that of establishing a constitution for an independent state such as Jamaica or Barbados, or a British overseas territory such as Bermuda. In form, the Scotland Act does not resemble the fundamental rights provisions of a constitution: its provisions are dense and detailed. The Scotland Act can also be amended more easily than a constitution: a factor which is relevant, since the difficulty of amending a constitution is often a reason for concluding that it was intended to be given a

[32] *Rothwell v Chemical & Insulating Co Ltd* [2008] 1 A.C. 281.
[33] *AXA General Insurance v Lord Advocate* [2012] 1 A.C. 868, at [49] (Lord Hope).

> flexible interpretation. Although the UK Government's stated policy on legislation concerning devolved matters,[34] known colloquially as the Sewel Convention, may impose a political restriction upon Parliament's ability to amend the Scotland Act unilaterally, there have nevertheless been many amendments made to the Act. They include amendments to Schedules 4 and 5, which can be effected under section 30 by Order in Council.

And:

> [T]he power of the Scottish Parliament to legislate is limited by the Act of Parliament which established it. It is the function of the courts to interpret and apply those limits, when called upon to do so, so as to give effect to the intention of Parliament. In performing that function, the courts do not undermine democracy but protect it. As Lord Bridge of Harwich observed in *X Ltd v Morgan-Grampian (Publishers) Ltd* [1991] 1 A.C. 1, 48:
>
> > The maintenance of the rule of law is in every way as important in a free society as the democratic franchise. In our society the rule of law rests upon twin foundations: the sovereignty of the Queen in Parliament in making the law and the sovereignty of the Queen's courts in interpreting and applying the law.[35]

It remains the case, however, that any 'interested party'[36] or Convention rights 'victim' (see s.100(3) SA) may bring a challenge before the courts as to the compatibility of any Act of the Scottish Parliament (or action or inaction on the part of the Scottish Ministers) with the limitations on their powers as laid down in the SA. In essence what the SA has done is to ensure the juridicalisation of politics in Scotland, on a constitutional model reminiscent of the judicial constitutional primacy seen in the United States. It remains to be seen where this will lead us.

The Post-devolution Politicisation of Scots Law

At the same time as devolving political power to Scotland, the SA sought to achieve greater legal integration between Scotland and England, by giving final constitutional oversight of how the devolutionary settlement should work in Scotland, in the fields of both criminal and civil law, to a London-based court, initially the Judicial Committee of the Privy Council and, since the transfer of jurisdiction effected by s.40 of the Constitutional Reform Act

[34] Currently embodied in the *Memorandum of Understanding and Supplementary Agreements Between the United Kingdom Government, the Scottish Ministers, the Welsh Ministers, and the Northern Ireland Executive Committee*, Cm 7864 (2010), at [14].

[35] *Imperial Tobacco v Scottish Ministers* [2012] CSIH 9, at [58] (Lord Reed).

[36] *AXA General Insurance Ltd v The Lord Advocate* [2012] 1 A.C. 868, at [169]–[170] (Lord Reed).

2005, by the UKSC. Section 41(1) of the 2005 Act also affirms that 'nothing in this … is to affect the distinctions between the separate legal systems of the parts of the United Kingdom'. But it does seem clear that the UKSC is understood to be a new *constitutional* court, intended in its upholding of the post-1707 constitution further to bind the Union. The Court's very iconography—with an official emblem depicting an entwined wreath of plants creating a unity from its four jurisdictions—seems to lend some support to this view. And precisely because of this perception and presentation of it as a 'unionist institution', the UKSC has become the focus of continuing attacks in the new Scottish politics. In response to devolution juridicalisation of Scottish politics, what has emerged is the increasing politicisation of Scots law particularly in relation to criminal law in Scotland which, as we have seen, had previously been untouched by the fact of the Union.

Part of the constitutional novelty of the SA was that it made express provision in para.13 of Sch.6 for the possibility of an appeal in Scottish criminal cases against a determination of a 'devolution issue' by a court of two or more judges of the High Court of Justiciary (whether in the ordinary course of proceedings or on a reference from a lower criminal court under para.9) to the Judicial Committee of the Privy Council (JCPC). Such appeals on devolution issues in Scottish criminal cases could only proceed by leave of the High Court of Justiciary, which failing by special leave of the JCPC (and now with permission of the UKSC). During the time of this devolution jurisdiction, the JCPC (and now the UKSC) has exercised its power to grant permission to appeal to it where leave to appeal has been refused by the High Court of Justiciary on only a handful of occasions. And it is not always the accused who has appealed to London in Scottish criminal cases. The Crown, too, has had occasion to appeal southwards from a decision of the Scottish criminal courts which the Lord Advocate has disagreed with. The cases mark the fact that the Scottish criminal justice system has been made subject—for the first time since the 1707 Union—to some degree of external scrutiny by other UK judges who are not trained and formed within the Scottish legal system. As such the issue has been a rallying point for Scottish *legal nationalists*—even those who might otherwise be thought to be of *unionist political* persuasion. The very fact that the decision of the Edinburgh court to refuse leave to appeal can, in effect, be overruled by a decision of a court based in London (albeit with Scottish judges among its number) has rankled with sections of the Scottish judiciary and has been taken up as a cause by Scottish nationalist politicians avowedly seeking to preserve the 'sanctity of Scots law'.[37]

[37] See Alex Salmond MSP, "Why the Sanctity of Scots Law Remains an Important Cause and One Worth Fighting For", *Scotsman*, 31 May 2011.

The judges of the Court of Session first made collective representations in relation to the operation of the legal framework allowing for decisions being able to be appealed from Edinburgh to London in October 2008 in written submissions to the Calman Commission, which had been charged by the Scottish Parliament to look into the operation of the devolution settlement in Scotland. The Calman Commission considered that the concerns of the judges fell outside its remit. In September 2010 an 'Expert Group' chaired by Sir David Edward, a retired judge of the Court of Justice of the European Union, and containing a former Lord Advocate, two silks practising at the Scottish criminal bar and one legal academic was convened by the United Kingdom's Scottish Law Officer to look into these issues. In a collective submission to the Expert Group, the judges of the Court of Session said this:

> In *McDonald* v *HM Advocate*, 2010 SC (PC) 1 Lord Hope of Craighead held that a decision by the High Court of Justiciary *not* to entertain and determine a devolution issue that had been intimated to it could be treated as a 'determination' of the issue for the purposes of paragraph 13 of Schedule 6 to the Scotland Act 1998; *this might be thought a somewhat Jesuitical position.*
>
> …
>
> *[B]y a series of incremental decisions, taken on the basis of the statutory provisions under discussion, a major constitutional change has already been brought about in relation to the existence of a right of appeal from a decision of the Criminal Appeal Court to the Supreme Court, and that without the public consultation and careful consideration that such a major constitutional change might have been expected to receive. We cannot regard that as a satisfactory situation*, or think that such a result was ever intended by those who drafted the Scotland Bill 1998 or the United Kingdom Parliament which passed it.[38]

And in its contribution to the Expert Group the Scottish Law Commission said this:

> Section 57(2) is, standing the other provisions of the Scotland Act and of the Human Rights Act to which we refer below, an unnecessary provision. *Like all unnecessary provisions, it has a tendency to go septic.*
>
> …
>
> Scots criminal law is a jurisdiction which is not only constitutionally separate from English criminal law. Many of its practices and procedures differ substantially from those of English law. *There is no more reason why a particular feature of Scots criminal law need be the same as any feature of English criminal law in order to comply with the requirements of the Convention as there is that any feature of either system should be the same as a feature of Russian law to achieve that purpose.*

[38] Available at http://www.oag.gov.uk/oag/225.html (emphasis added).

> ...
>
> *[T]he rationale for civil appeals to the House of Lords is shrouded in constitutional mystery, but it is an established historical fact*; and it is the case that, at least in some areas, the principles which inform civil law in the two jurisdictions are similar ... But there is no such historical precedent or similarity of (some) principle in relation to criminal matters. The result is that *careful decisions of a large bench of the judges of the High Court of Justiciary, taken after a thorough consideration of the history and background of Scots criminal law, can be overruled by a bench, a majority of which comprises judges with no experience in that system.*[39]

And in his submission to the Edward Expert Group the Scottish Cabinet Secretary for Justice, paradoxically, called for (at least a partial) return to the state of the Union as it was before devolution, stating:

> [W]e believe that it is wrong in principle that the decisions of the High Court of Justiciary should be challengeable in a way *which was not possible before devolution*, and we are concerned about the problems this process of challenge is creating for the Scottish courts. The Scottish Government therefore wishes *to restore the position in criminal cases prior to devolution* and to stem the flow of criminal cases raising devolution issues to the Supreme Court. As the First Minister indicated, the High Court should be the highest criminal authority in Scotland, *as it was prior to devolution.*[40]

Clearly the collective constitutional/psychological impact of even the two or three decisions a year in Scottish criminal appeals to London has been of immense significance. What is perhaps of even more interest in these submissions is the language in which the authors couch their critiques. Their references to statutory provisions which have gone 'septic', or to judicial decisions from the court in London resting on 'Jesuitical' distinctions, and which effect the 'dilution of distinctive elements' of the Scottish legal system seem to speak more of the language of ritual (im)purity, of contagion and pollution, rather than of law and justice. The primary concern expressed in these (and other) submissions—which agitated, in effect, for the abolition of the possibility of Scottish criminal appeals ever going to London—appears to be one of the paramount need to preserve the integrity of the Scottish criminal justice system from the threat of external (English or indeed European) influence. Great concern is shown in these submissions for the preservation—or restoration—of the presumed integrity of the Scottish criminal justice system but little, if any, mention is made in these particular submissions as to what that system is *for*. And no consideration is given as to whether justice is, or is not, being done, or furthered, by the individual decisions complained of.

[39] Available at http://www.oag.gov.uk/oag/225.html (emphasis added).
[40] Available at http://www.oag.gov.uk/oag/225.html (emphasis added).

For example, is it a good or bad thing for the doing of justice in Scotland that, since the decision of the UKSC in *Cadder v HMA*,[41] persons detained by the police in Scotland have a right of access to a solicitor before they can be questioned? Is it a good or bad thing that, as a result of the decision of the JCPC in *Sinclair v HM Advocate*,[42] the prosecution has positive duties of disclosure to the defence of all relevant inculpatory and exculpatory information in the hands of the Crown? Is it a good or bad thing that, as a result of the Privy Council's reversal of the decision of the criminal appeal court in *McIntosh v HM Advocate*,[43] the authorities in Scotland can continue to operate the statutory regime for drug confiscation orders?

What is never examined or discussed is the culture of hostility and resistance evinced by the Scottish bench in criminal cases to any raising of Convention rights-based arguments. Innovation of any kind is resisted as a matter of principle in a legal system which is characterised by its institutional conservatism and always backward-looking stance in which the older a case or authority is, the more authoritative it is regarded, so that the writings of Baron David Hume on 18th-century criminal law are preferred over the pronouncements from Strasbourg in the latest decision of the European Court of Human Rights.

Following the May 2011 elections in Scotland which gave the newly elected Scottish National Party (SNP) government, for the first time, an absolute majority of the seats in the Scottish Parliament, the Scottish Ministers decided to heighten and personalise their attacks on the UKSC, seeking to portray it, for their own political purposes, as a foreign court foisted on Scotland and which, contrary to the compact set out in the 1707 Union, was intent on destroying the distinctiveness of Scots law. Thus, on 31 May 2011 the Minister for Justice, Kenny MacAskill MSP (who is also a legally qualified Scottish solicitor), is reported to have made the following remarks in a speech to Scottish police officers:

> We just want to be treated the same as other legal systems—we're not, because we're undermined routinely by a court that sits in another country and is presided over by a majority of judges who have no knowledge of Scots law, never mind Scotland.
>
> …
>
> Only in Scotland did we see a decision taken in London by a court that was not meant to deal with criminal matters result in a situation where we had to have emergency legislation through the Scottish Parliament and turn Scottish criminal law on its head.

[41] *Cadder v HM Advocate* [2010] W.L.R. 2601; 2011 SC (UKSC) 13.
[42] *Sinclair v HM Advocate*, 2005 SC (PC) 28.
[43] *McIntosh v HM Advocate*, 2001 SC (PC) 89.

...

We'll do so through our own courts at our own pace in our own way, not have it imposed by a court in London that is made up of a majority of judges who do not know Scots Law, who may have visited here for the Edinburgh Festival.[44]

On 1 June 2011 the Scottish Minister for Justice then announced that he had ordered his civil servants to investigate whether the Scottish government could pull out of funding the UKSC, and made the following public remarks:

> When I go to the Law Society I say that I will not routinely fund ambulance-chasing lawyers. It should be said that I am not going to pay for ambulance-chasing courts. As a Government we have to pay for the Supreme Court of the UK and I think they should recognise that we'll pay for our fair share of what goes there. But I am not paying money that would come out of the police budget, or prison budget or community payback budget because they are routinely taking cases that we as a country do not think should be going there. He who pays the piper, as they say, calls the tune.[45]

One might have thought that the Minister of Justice would be called in and rebuked—or perhaps indeed asked to resign—by the First Minister for these, surely somewhat intemperate and tendentious, remarks which are perhaps rather difficult to square with the Scottish Ministers' statutory duty to uphold the independence of the judiciary, including that of the UKSC.[46] But, instead, the next development in the saga was a magazine interview with the First Minister in the course of which he not only defended the remarks made by his Justice Secretary, but added more of his own in the same vein and, if anything, in a stronger tenor, noting:

> [T]he Supreme Court, like any other body that is set up, seeks to accrue authority to itself and is now doing things that it was never intended to do. Just as the Privy Council threw up unintended consequences, so too is the Supreme Court. I also think it is possible that you need a succession of incidences of things that are happening before the extent of the encroachment and the vulnerability of the Parliament really hits home.
>
> ...

[44] http://www.heraldscotland.com/mobile/news/politics/macaskill-in-new-attack-on-supreme-court-rulings-1.1104396.

[45] http://www.heraldscotland.com/news/crime-courts/macaskill-threat-to-end-supreme-court-funding-1.1104601?localLinksEnabled=false. This, strangely, echoes a remark of James VI and I quoted by Russell, *James VI and I and His English Parliaments*, p.73: 'In 1621, when opening his first Parliament for seven years James I complained that "I have often piped unto you, and you have not danced". If nothing else suggested it, that very Scottish image would suggest that the hurt of 1607 [the English Parliament's rejection of a scheme for Union with Scotland] was one of those on his mind.'

[46] See Judiciary and Courts (Scotland) Act 2008, s.1; Constitutional Reform Act 2005, s.3.

> [I]f we are to be scrutinised in terms of the overall scrutiny then let it be by the [European] court [of Human Rights] that scrutinises another 47 jurisdictions and not by the Supreme Court in England which in criminal matters can only do one of two things and that is: the judges can either all take their own independent view (and if that is the case then the majority will be of people that do not have an exact knowledge of Scots law); or secondly, they can follow the judgement of the two Scots judges in any case concerning Scotland (and if that is the case then you have a court being led by one or two judges). And I see no reason to believe why Lord Hope is any wiser than the seven judges who unanimously found for the Crown in the *Cadder* issue. And why did they find for the Crown, because they knew the checks and balances that exist here. Lord Hope said in his judgement that this issue should have been evident years ago … yeah, when he was Lord President?
>
> …
>
> [T]he present situation is unsupportable, untenable and cannot stand because if a legal system allows itself to get into a situation of confusion and second guessing then it undermines confidence in the law.[47]

Despite this concerted political pressure from the variety of legal, judicial and political constituencies in Scotland, in passing the Scotland Act 2012 the UK Parliament insisted on retaining the possibility of appeals from Edinburgh to London in criminal cases, turning down the request[48] from the Lord President of the Court of Session and Lord Justice-General for Scotland, Lord Hamilton, that such appeals to the UKSC be allowed only if certified by the High Court of Justiciary as being in the public interest (in effect seeking to make such appeals subject to a veto by the lower court).[49]

[47] http://www.holyrood.com/index.php?option=com_holyrood&func=article&artid=5140&edition=257&brick=3.

[48] See the letter dated 16 January 2012 to the 'Clerk of the Parliaments' from the Lord President of the Court of Session, Lord Hamilton, setting out his observations to Parliament regarding the Scotland Bill which was then before the House of Lords. The Lord President's observations are submitted by him under reference to s.5 of the Constitutional Reform Act 2005 which provides so far as relevant as follows:

(1) The chief justice of any part of the United Kingdom may lay before Parliament written representations on matters that appear to him to be matters of importance relating to the judiciary, or otherwise to the administration of justice, in that part of the United Kingdom.

(2) In relation to Scotland those matters do not include matters within the legislative competence of the Scottish Parliament, unless they are matters to which a Bill for an Act of Parliament relates.

…

(5) In this section 'chief justice' means–

  (a) …

  (b) in relation to Scotland, the Lord President of the Court of Session.

[49] But see (the face-saving) s.38 of the Scotland Act 2012 which requires the Secretary of State to arrange for a review, after three years, of the operation of the 2012 Act's provisions for appeals

Conclusion: Back to the Future—Reviving the Union of 1603?

There is within the United States—seen most notably in the reaction and response to the 5:4 decision of the US Supreme Court in *Bush v Gore*[50] to strike down a decision of the Florida Supreme Court to order a recount in the presidential election of 2000, thereby awarding victory to the Republican Party candidate, George W. Bush—a very strong tradition of acceptance of the lawfulness of the decisions emanating from the US Supreme Court, even where one strongly disagrees and is critical of their reasoning. Going by the above noted remarks of the Scottish First Minister and the Scottish Minister for Justice, there would appear to be no such tradition in Scottish society, nor any desire among the current ruling politicians to cultivate or foster such a tradition. How has the situation arisen in Scotland where political leaders—charged with upholding the rule of law and the independence of the judiciary—are so ready to disregard these strictures and launch such highly personalised attacks on individual judges and lawyers who practise before the courts? Why is such a tradition of acceptance of contrary judicial decision apparently lacking among the current political class now governing in Scotland? And why do calls to respect the rule of law apparently fail to resonate within the current Scottish political culture?

As we have noted, the end of the British empire appeared to call into question some of the previous economic justification given for the 1707 Union, and the consequent post-Second World War rise in Scottish political nationalism has been able to tap into the other forms of professional nationalism which have been maintained by those Scottish constituencies in the 300 years of the Union.

Devolution has brought politics back to Edinburgh, and in so doing has called into question the previously apparently happy 300-year marriage of political unionism with a depoliticised legal, ecclesiastical and tartan nationalism. Now Scottish political nationalism can ally itself with claims of Scottish legal nationalism and this makes for a heady and volatile mix.

Scotland's grumbling nationalism (whether legal, political or cultural) too often remains one of reaction against perceived English slights and insults. Thus readiness to blame the English for their woes allows political nationalist

---

from Edinburgh (either with the permission of the High Court or, failing that permission, with the permission of the Supreme Court) on Convention issues or matters of EU law in Scottish criminal cases to the UKSC. Section 38(3)(c) of the 2012 Act provides that this review must 'consider (in particular) whether an appeal to the Supreme Court on a compatibility issue should lie only if the High Court of Justiciary certifies that the issue raises a point of law of general public importance'. A report of the conclusions of the review is to be made to the Secretary of State, and a copy of the report given to the Scottish Ministers.

[50] *Bush v Gore* 513 U.S. 98 (2000) (00–949).

politicians to wrap themselves in the mantle of a proclaimed legal nationalism. Thus cloaked, they appear to feel able and justified to make attacks on the integrity of judges within the system because they can mis-characterise these judges as operating from and for an English (dominated) court. It should be noted that it is not a generalised xenophobia which is being tapped into by the politicians with these remarks—since they seem wholly unconcerned by the Scottish legal and criminal justice system being found wanting by the European Court of Human Rights in Strasbourg (which has no judges trained in Scots law). These politicians appear to be giving vent to their Anglophobia, feeling free to attack the decisions and judges of the UKSC because it is based in London and is, they would say, dominated by English-trained lawyers, with those Scots-trained judges who serve on it being dismissed or explained away as having gone (Anglo-)native or turned Quisling.

This is extraordinary stuff, and must not be dismissed as mere knockabout politics which one might expect from a northern Ruritania, a faraway country of which we know little and need care about less. It is a far more serious problem than that. Respect for the independence of the judiciary (and of the lawyers who practise before the courts, particularly in cases taken against the government) is an issue which is the foundation of the rule of law and respect for fundamental rights. The remarks of Scotland's First Minister and Justice Minister betray a constitutional hollowness within Scotland and show that the mutuality of respect and restraint upon which the concept of the rule of law—of a government of laws, not of men—rests, can so readily be shattered.

In their attacks on the judges, these SNP politicians are expressing views which run wholly contrary to the pre-Union Scottish republican tradition, which had so bedevilled James VI in his relations with his northern kingdom.[51] Interestingly the constitutional model for independence now favoured by the SNP is one which would seek to revoke the 1707 Union of Parliaments while leaving intact the post-1603 Union of Crowns, in which two independent countries with distinct foreign and domestic policies (and currencies)

[51] Its most notable exponent being George Buchanan (tutor to James VI) who wrote in his *De iure regni apud Scotos: On Constitutional Government in Scotland* (written 1567, published in 1579)—translated and edited by Roger Mason and Martin Smith as *A Dialogue on the Law of Kingship among the Scots: A Critical Edition and Translation of George Buchanan's De iure regni apud Scotos dialogus* (Ashgate: Aldershot, 2004), pp.33, 55, 133, 143—as follows: '[T]he law should be yoked to the king to show him the way when he does not know it or lead him back to it when he wanders from it. … I want the people, who have granted the king authority over themselves, to be allowed to dictate to him the extent of his authority; and I require him to exercise as a king only such right as the people have granted him over them … [T]he power received by our kings from our ancestors was not unbounded but was limited and restricted within fixed boundaries … There is no justification either for the complaint and protest of those who argue that it is neither

nonetheless shared the same monarch.[52] Perhaps Salmond is (unconsciously) drawing on the constitutional tradition which James VI and I sought to develop once he had left Scotland, in order to expand his (kingly) office against the trammelling of the law.[53] The constitutional tradition of 'divine right'—forged in 17th-century Jacobean power politics and subsequently forming the basis for 18th-century Jacobite counter-Revolution—was summarised thus by Conrad Russell:

> The biggest allergy of James I was based on the experience of James VI: it was to any claim to possess an authority independent of his own … So long as his bishops were 'my bishops', his judges were 'my judges' and his parliament was 'my parliament', he would debate with them until the cows came home. Once they claimed any independent authority they became Andrew Melville, Guy Fawkes and the Pope all rolled into one. That was the shock James experienced when he encountered a precedent-based system of law. Because it was precedent based, it was not *his* law.
>
> …

proper or just that a verdict on a king should be delivered by a man of lower rank … For no one who comes before a judge comes before an inferior, especially since God himself pays so much honour to the judicial order that He calls them not only judges but gods and, so far as this is possible, imparts to them His own dignity. … The verdicts of judges are valid when pronounced in accordance with law, otherwise they are rescinded. … The judge has his authority from the law, not the law from the judge … and the lowly rank of the person pronouncing the verdict does not diminish the dignity of the law, but the dignity of the laws is always the same, whether it is a king, or a judge or a herald who pronounces the verdict.'

[52] James Wilson (a Scots-born and Scottish university-educated signatory of the 1776 American Declaration of Independence, who was influential in the drafting of the 1789 US Constitution and went on to become one of the first Justices of the US Supreme Court) observed in his *Lectures on Law: Volume I* (Philadelphia, IL: Bronson & Chauncey, 1804), ch.9, "Of Man, as a Member of the Great Commonwealth of Nations": 'Two sovereign states may employ the same executive magistrate, or bear allegiance to the same prince, without any dependence on each other; and each may retain all its national rights, free and undiminished. This last, under the house of Stuart, was the case of England and Scotland, before the nation of Great Britain was formed by their union. This last, also, as shall be hereafter shown at large, was the case of Great Britain and the American colonies, before the political connexion between them was declared to be dissolved.'

[53] See, for example, King James VI and I, *Political Writings*, ed J. P. Somerville (Cambridge: Cambridge University Press, 1994), p.75, "The Trew Law of Free Monarchies or The Reciprock and Mutuall Duetie betwixt a Free King and his Naturall Subjects": 'The King is above the law, as both the author and giver of strength thereto.' This sentiment favouring the Divine Right of Kings may be starkly contrasted with the words of the leading second-generation Scottish Protestant reformer, Andrew Melville, in 1596, who proclaimed before the General Assembly of the Reformed Church of Scotland that this same king 'was God's silly vassal and that there are two kings and two kingdoms in Scotland. There is Christ Jesus the King, and His kingdom the Kirk, whose subject King James VI is—and of whose kingdom, not a king, nor a lord, nor a head, but a member he was.'

> *The key political theory issue of James' reign was nothing to do with the House of Commons: it was the independence of the judiciary. As tends to happen in periods of parliamentary weakness the king received challenge after challenge from a judiciary which showed increasing signs of confidence.* Behind the judiciary's sense of independence there was more than the considerable vanity of Sir Edward Coke. There was also an issue of genuinely Melvillian proportions: the relationship between the king and the common law. Was the common law 'his' law in the same way as the parliament was 'his' parliament, or did it have an authority and legitimacy entirely independent of James's own will?
>
> …
>
> *James never thought legally and had never much sense of judicial independence* … He attacked the notion of precedent based law … It was this sort of thing which helped to give James an intense allergy to the notion of judge-made law. It is no coincidence that it is in his speech on the dismissal of Coke CJ that he spelt this out most clearly. He told the judges:
>
>> you are no makers of law, but interpreters of law, according to the true sense thereof: for your office is *ius dicere* rather than *ius dare*. And you are so far from making law that even in the higher house of Parliament you have no voice in the making of a law, but only to give your advice when you are required …
>
> *When he added that he would never trust any interpretation which did not agree with his own common sense and reason, we begin to recognise an anti-professionalism which our own profession now must find painfully familiar. This was a man who simply did not understand what trying a legal case was all about.*[54]

Readers may draw their own conclusions on what relevance, if any, this tradition may yet have for, and in, contemporary Scotland.

[54] Russell, *James VI and I and His English Parliaments*, pp.142, 143, 150, 151–52 (emphasis added).

Part II

Domestic Protections within a European Framework

5

Deconstructing the Mirror Principle

ROGER MASTERMAN

Introduction

DESPITE LACKING A CLEAR HERITAGE in the provisions of the Human Rights Act 1998 (hereafter HRA),[1] the 'mirror principle'—the broad notion that domestic human rights protections under the HRA should replicate the protections afforded to those same rights by the European Court of Human Rights—has been a pervasive influence on the judicial interpretation, and application, of the Act.[2] The mirror metaphor captures a number of distinct strands of judicial reasoning in rights cases. First, it speaks to the approach taken by courts seeking to determine how the Strasbourg jurisprudence should be 'taken into account' and thereby translated into domestic law under the 'flexible' terminology of s.2(1) HRA[3]; with the judicial suggestion that 'clear and constant' jurisprudence of the Strasbourg organs should generally be 'followed'[4] bringing a degree of predictability to the broad discretion available to courts under that provision. Secondly, the mirror principle concerns

[1] HRA, s.2(1) provides: 'A court or tribunal determining a question which has arisen in connection with a Convention right must take into account any—(a) judgment, decision, declaration or advisory opinion of the European Court of Human Rights, (b) opinion of the Commission given in a report adopted under Article 31 of the Convention, (c) decision of the Commission in connection with Article 26 or 27(2) of the Convention, or (d) decision of the Committee of Ministers taken under Article 46 of the Convention, whenever made or given, so far as, in the opinion of the court or tribunal, it is relevant to the proceedings in which that question has arisen.'

[2] The phrase 'mirror principle' is from J. Lewis, "The European Ceiling on Rights" [2007] P.L. 720. See also R. Masterman, "Aspiration or Foundation? The Status of the Strasbourg Jurisprudence and the 'Convention Rights' in Domestic Law", in H. Fenwick, G. Phillipson and R. Masterman (eds), *Judicial Reasoning under the UK Human Rights Act* (Cambridge: Cambridge University Press, 2007); J. Beatson, S. Grosz, T. Hickman, R. Singh and S. Palmer, *Human Rights: Judicial Protection in the United Kingdom* (London: Sweet & Maxwell, 2008), pp.40–45.

[3] S. Tierney, "Devolution Issues and s.2(1) of the Human Rights Act 1998" [2000] E.H.R.L.R. 380, 392.

[4] *R. (on the application of Alconbury Developments Ltd) v Secretary of State for the Environment, Transport and the Regions* [2003] 2 A.C. 295, at [26] (Lord Slynn); *R. (on the application of Anderson) v Secretary of State for the Home Department* [2003] 1 A.C. 836, at [10] (Lord Bingham).

Proceedings of the British Academy, **183**, 111–137. © The British Academy 2013.

the range and scope of the rights protected under the HRA,[5] with the injunction that domestic courts seek to provide 'no more, but certainly no less'[6] protection than would be provided by the Strasbourg court itself seeming to curb the ability of domestic courts to extend (or reduce) the scope of the protections provided by the Convention rights beyond that countenanced by the European Court of Human Rights. Finally, the mirror model of interpretation provides a lens through which the entire remedial structure of the HRA can be viewed, giving rise to the suggestion that the Act is no more than a cipher through which the rights and remedies which would otherwise be available only at Strasbourg are duplicated in domestic law.[7]

At the level of individual decision-making the mirror principle holds the potential to wield a regulating influence over the exercise of judicial discretion in HRA adjudication, limiting the scope for domestic courts to depart from Strasbourg authority and the breadth of those rights afforded protection. At the constitutional level, the principle facilitates access to the Strasbourg level of protection in domestic courts, but—through the denial of a distinctly domestic content to rights protections under the HRA—impedes the ability of the HRA to operate as a proto-Bill of Rights for the United Kingdom.[8] The mirror principle aspires to both descriptive and normative characteristics; it is at once an encapsulation of what many courts *have* done in seeking to reconcile domestic law with the demands of the Convention rights under s.2(1), and for many—in the wider debate over the constitutional purpose of the HRA—a prescription of what the courts *should* do in order to give effect to the Act as a whole.

Yet, in reality, the inflexible relationship between the Convention rights as given effect under the HRA and those rights as policed by the European Court of Human Rights that is at the heart of the mirror principle—strictly construed—is neither a requirement of the HRA itself, nor of the Convention: s.2(1) HRA requires only that domestic courts 'take into account' relevant Strasbourg authority in determining questions relating to the Convention rights,[9] while the application of the margin of appreciation by the Strasbourg court ensures that the uniform application of the Convention throughout the

[5] HRA, s.1(1).

[6] *R. (on the application of Ullah) v Special Adjudicator; Do v Immigration Appeal Tribunal* [2004] UKHL 26; [2004] 2 A.C. 323, at [20] (Lord Bingham).

[7] *R. (on the application of Al-Jedda) v Secretary of State for Defence* [2007] UKHL 58; [2008] 1 A.C. 332, at [55] (Lord Rodger); *R. (on the application of Begum) v Headteacher and Governors of Denbigh High School* [2006] UKHL 15; [2007] 1 A.C. 100, at [29] (Lord Bingham).

[8] F. Klug, "A Bill of Rights: Do We Need One or Do We Already Have One?" [2007] P.L. 701, 706–08.

[9] An amendment which would have seen courts bound to adhere to Strasbourg decisions was tabled, and rejected, during the parliamentary progress of the Human Rights Bill: HL Debs, vol.583, col.514, 18 November 1997.

Council of Europe is ultimately an impossibility.[10] In spite of the linguistic vagary of s.2(1),[11] and the difficulties associated with using the Strasbourg case law as a blueprint for a national rights jurisprudence,[12] the prevailing judicial approach to the interpretation of s.2(1) HRA during the first 10 years of its operation can be stated succinctly: '[f]ollowing Strasbourg will be the norm and departing from it will be the exception'.[13]

In the early years of the HRA's operation, indications were given that domestic courts might depart from potentially applicable Strasbourg authority where it could be shown that the European Court had 'misunderstood' the relevant domestic law,[14] where the Strasbourg organs had received insufficient guidance on the point in question to form a conclusion[15] or where application of the relevant authority would 'compel a conclusion fundamentally at odds with the distribution of powers under the British constitution'.[16] Actual exceptions to the general presumption in favour of adherence to Strasbourg authority were more difficult to find[17]; at least one commentator was able to suggest, in research published in 2007, that so few were the occasions on which the courts had distinguished or departed from relevant Strasbourg authority the supposed exceptions to the mirror principle existed in theory alone.[18]

The weight of evidence in favour of a dilution of the mirror principle has since steadily grown. In a series of cases concerning the impact of art.8 on possession proceedings, the ability of domestic courts to engage in a 'creative dialogue'[19] with the European Court on the meanings of the rights protected by the HRA has been amply demonstrated.[20] The House of Lords decision in

[10] *Handyside v United Kingdom* (1979–80) 1 E.H.R.R. 737, at [48].

[11] Cf. Lord Irvine of Lairg, "A British Interpretation of Convention Rights" [2012] P.L. 237, 238–39: 'The terms of this provision are simple ... The meaning of the provision is clear.'

[12] On which, see R. Masterman, "Taking the Strasbourg Jurisprudence into Account: Developing a 'Municipal Law of Human Rights' under the Human Rights Act" (2005) 54 I.C.L.Q. 907, 915–18.

[13] A. Kavanagh, "Special Advocates, Control Orders and the Right to a Fair Trial" (2010) 73 M.L.R. 836, 845.

[14] *R. v Lyons (No.3)* [2002] UKHL 44; [2003] 1 A.C. 976, at [46] (Lord Hoffmann).

[15] *R. v Spear* [2002] UKHL 31; [2003] 1 A.C. 734, at [12] (Lord Bingham).

[16] *R. (on the application of Alconbury Developments Ltd) v Secretary of State for the Environment, Transport and the Regions* [2003] 2 A.C. 295, at [76] (Lord Hoffmann).

[17] R. Masterman, "Section 2(1) of the Human Rights Act 1998: Binding Domestic Courts to Strasbourg?" [2004] P.L. 725.

[18] Lewis, "The European Ceiling on Rights", 731.

[19] Lord Steyn, "2000–2005: Laying the Foundations of Human Rights Law in the United Kingdom" [2005] E.H.R.L.R. 349, 361. See also Chapter 6, this volume.

[20] The relevant domestic authorities are *Harrow LBC v Qazi* [2003] UKHL 43; [2004] 1 A.C. 983; *Kay v Lambeth LBC* [2006] UKHL 10; [2006] 2 A.C. 465; *Doherty v Birmingham CC* [2008] UKHL 57; [2009] 1 A.C. 367; *Manchester CC v Pinnock* [2010] UKSC 45. The relevant European Court of Human Rights decisions are *Connors v United Kingdom* (2004) 40 E.H.R.R. 189; *McCann v United Kingdom* (2008) 47 E.H.R.R. 913; *Kay v United Kingdom*, Application no.37341/06, 21 September 2010. For discussion, see I. Loveland, "The Shifting Sands of Article 8 Jurisprudence in English Housing Law" [2011] E.H.R.L.R. 151.

Re P demonstrates that in those areas in which the European Court has held the margin of appreciation to apply the mirror metaphor cannot coherently operate: 'the question is one for the national authorities to decide for themselves'[21] in accordance with the principles underpinning the relevant Convention right(s) and informed by what authority is discernable from the Strasbourg case law. Most strikingly, the decision of the UK Supreme Court in *R. v Horncastle* provides perhaps the most compelling authority to date for the suggestion that domestic courts will not simply apply even relevant and clear Strasbourg case law as a matter of course, and in so doing provides further implicit support for the suggestion that in their meaning and application, the domesticated Convention rights might well deviate from their Strasbourg cousins.[22]

But these decisions by no means mark the complete abandonment of the mirror principle as either a constraint on the scope of the rights protected under the HRA, or as a factor governing judicial interpretation of the overall HRA scheme.[23] The notion that the domestic court acting pursuant to the HRA does so as a local proxy for the European Court of Human Rights runs deep. As a result the presumption that the 'clear and constant' jurisprudence of the Strasbourg organs should ordinarily be followed continues to resonate in UK Supreme Court decisions.[24] So too does the suggestion that courts should not afford a more generous interpretation of the Convention rights domestically than that afforded by the European Court of Human Rights.[25] It follows that the sentiments expressed by Lord Rodger of Earlsferry in the House of Lords decision in *Secretary of State for the Home Department v AF*—'[e]ven though we are dealing with rights under a United Kingdom statute, in reality, we have no choice: *Argentoratum locutum, iudicium finitum*—

[21] *In Re P* [2008] UKHL 38; [2009] 1 A.C. 173, at [31] (Lord Hoffmann). On which, see J. Lewis, "*In Re P and others*: An Exception to the 'No More, Certainly No Less' Rule" [2009] P.L. 43.

[22] *R. v Horncastle* [2009] UKSC 14; [2010] 2 A.C. 373. See now *Al-Khawaja v United Kingdom* (2012) 54 E.H.R.R. 23.

[23] T. Cross and C. Knight, "Public Law in the Supreme Court 2009–2010" (2010) 15 J.R. 299, 301. Cf. J. Wright, "Interpreting Section 2 of the Human Rights Act 1998: Towards an Indigenous Jurisprudence of Human Rights" [2009] P.L. 595.

[24] *Manchester City Council v Pinnock* [2010] UKSC 45; [2010] 3 W.L.R. 1441, at [48] (Lord Neuberger MR): 'Where … there is a clear and constant line of decisions whose effect is not inconsistent with some fundamental substantive or procedural aspect of our law, and whose reasoning does not appear to overlook or misunderstand some argument or point of principle, we consider that it would be wrong for this court not to follow that line.' See also *Cadder v HM Advocate* [2010] UKSC 43; [2010] 1 W.L.R. 2601, at [45]–[51] (Lord Hope).

[25] *Ali v Birmingham City Council* [2010] UKSC 8; [2010] 2 A.C. 39, at [38] (Lord Hope); *HM Treasury v Ahmed* [2010] UKSC 5; [2010] 2 A.C. 534, at [74] (Lord Hope); *Ambrose v Harris* [2011] UKSC 43, at [17]–[20] (Lord Hope)—cf. at [126]–[130] (Lord Kerr).

Strasbourg has spoken, the case is closed'[26]—have by no means been erased from history.

This essay questions the continuing utility of the mirror principle as a guiding interpretative tool, arguing that it can increasingly be seen to provide an inadequate account of judicial practice under the HRA and, more fundamentally, that it provides an unstable normative foundation for the shape and content of the HRA's rights jurisprudence.

The Origins of the Mirror Principle

The origins of the mirror principle lie in the unclear status of the Convention rights as legal standards in the domestic context.[27] This uncertainty is traceable to the fact that while the HRA itself is a creation of the UK Parliament, its implications cannot be fully appreciated without reference to the international treaty (and its attendant case law) to which the Act was designed to give 'further effect'. As a result, the Convention standards enjoy a split personality: they are at once enforceable in domestic law under the provisions of the HRA, and standards of international law by which the conduct of the United Kingdom, as a state party to the European Convention on Human Rights, can be assessed.[28]

While s.2(1) of the Act directs that courts 'take into account' decisions of the Strasbourg organs when 'determining a question which has arisen in connection with a Convention right', it gives no guidance as to the weight—precedential, persuasive or otherwise—to be attributed to those decisions in HRA adjudication. The text of the HRA lends support to the view that the meanings given to the Convention rights in the domestic context cannot be *completely* divorced from the meanings attributed to those rights by the Strasbourg court—the Convention rights provide the legal standards against which statutes and public authority activities are to be tested[29]—but it by no means follows that the application of the HRA is inescapably and inflexibly tied to *only* the meanings of the Convention articulated by the Strasbourg bodies.[30]

[26] *Secretary of State for the Home Department v AF (No.3)* [2009] UKHL 28; [2010] 2 A.C. 269, at [98] (Lord Rodger). For a specific analysis of the role of s.2(1) HRA to this case, see Kavanagh, "Special Advocates, Control Orders and the Right to a Fair Trial", 843–47.

[27] For a detailed discussion of the uncertain constitutional status of the HRA itself, see T. Hickman, *Public Law after the Human Rights Act* (Oxford: Hart Publishing, 2010), pp.24–49.

[28] See A. Kavanagh, "Strasbourg, the House of Lords or Elected Politicians: Who Decides about Rights after *Re P*?" (2009) 72 M.L.R. 828, 834–36.

[29] HRA, ss. 3(1) and 6(1).

[30] As Lord Irvine argued during the parliamentary debates on the Human Rights Bill, 'our courts must be free to try to give a lead to Europe as well as to be led': HL Debs, vol.583, col.514, 18 November 1997.

The HRA clearly contains meaning that is—and should be—entirely independent of the requirements of the rights to which it gives further effect.

In giving effect to the Convention rights under the HRA, the interpretational difficulty faced by domestic courts therefore lies in the question of whether the nature of those rights as they apply in the domestic context differs in any way from those rights as enforced by the European Court of Human Rights. Do the Convention rights as applied under the Human Rights Act possess the exact same characteristics in domestic law as they would when applied by the Strasbourg court? Or has their transition into the domestic context—via the HRA—altered those characteristics in some way? Responses to these questions are central to understanding the HRA, and have manifested themselves across a spectrum of judicial opinion under which the HRA is variously viewed as a conduit through which those rights available to applicants at Strasbourg can be realised in domestic law,[31] as a mechanism which seeks to blend Convention and common law protections for rights[32] and as an instrument which has created anew a distinctly domestic species of legal rights.[33]

The dominant approach towards the construction and application of s.2(1) HRA has tended towards the conservative end of that spectrum, displaying a clear hesitance on the part of the courts to find meaning in the domesticated Convention rights that cannot be traced back to their Strasbourg counterparts. Domestic courts have—for the most part—taken their lead from, and have been reluctant to exceed, the protections afforded by the European Court of Human Rights. The origins of this incorporationist approach can be found in the speech of Lord Slynn in the House of Lords decision in *Alconbury*.[34] In that decision, Slynn indicated that 'in the absence

[31] For example, *R. (on the application of Al-Jedda) v Secretary of State for Defence* [2007] UKHL 58; [2008] 1 A.C. 332, at [55] (Lord Rodger); *R. (on the application of Begum) v Headteacher and Governors of Denbigh High School* [2006] UKHL 15; [2007] 1 A.C. 100, at [29] (Lord Bingham).

[32] For example, *Runa Begum v Tower Hamlets London Borough Council* [2002] 2 All E.R. 668, at [17] (Laws LJ): '[T]the court's task under the HRA … is not simply to add on the Strasbourg learning to the corpus of English law, as if it were a compulsory adjunct taken from an alien source, but to develop a municipal law of human rights by the incremental method of the common law, case by case, taking account of the Strasbourg jurisprudence as HRA s.2 enjoins us to do.'

[33] For example, *R. (Animal Defenders International) v Secretary of State for Culture, Media and Sport* [2008] UKHL 15; [2008] 1 A.C. 1312, at [44]–[45] (Lord Scott); *In Re McKerr* [2004] UKHL 12, at [65] (Lord Hoffmann): 'Although people sometimes speak of the Convention having been incorporated into domestic law, that is a misleading metaphor. What the Act has done is to create domestic rights in the same terms as those contained in the Convention. But they are domestic rights, not international rights. Their source is the statute, not the Convention … their meaning and application is a matter for domestic courts, not the court in Strasbourg.'

[34] *R. (on the application of Alconbury Developments and others) v Secretary of State for the Environment, Transport and the Regions* [2001] UKHL 23; [2003] 2 A.C. 295.

of some special circumstances … clear and constant jurisprudence of the European Court of Human Rights'[35] should be followed, and, in so doing, effectively established a rebuttable presumption in favour of applying relevant Strasbourg case law in HRA decision-making.[36]

If *Alconbury* confirmed that domestic case law should mirror its Strasbourg counterpart, then the decision of the House of Lords in *R. (on the application of Ullah) v Special Adjudicator* extended that approach to the scope of the substantive protections afforded under the HRA. While, in a now famous passage, Lord Bingham was prepared to countenance departure from Strasbourg jurisprudence, the end result of such a course of action should not, he stressed, result in the expansion (or indeed reduction) by the *courts* of protections afforded at the domestic level. Lord Bingham argued:

> … a national court subject to a duty such as that imposed by section 2 should not without strong reason dilute or weaken the effect of the Strasbourg case law. It is indeed unlawful under section 6 of the 1998 Act for a public authority, including a court, to act in a way which is incompatible with a Convention Right. It is of course open to member states to provide for rights more generous than those guaranteed by the Convention, but such provision should not be the product of interpretation of the Convention by national courts, since the meaning of the Convention should be uniform throughout the states party to it. The duty of national courts is to keep pace with the Strasbourg jurisprudence as it evolves over time: no more, but certainly no less.[37]

The cumulative effect of the 'clear and constant' and 'no more, but certainly no less' lines of reasoning is to attempt to provide structure to the discretion available to courts when considering the precedential force of Strasbourg decisions, and to place limitations on the scope of the protections that might be afforded to the Convention rights under the HRA. Both strands of reasoning—that domestic courts should generally apply both Strasbourg *case law* and Strasbourg *standards*—are consistent with a broader reading of the HRA which posits that the primary function of the Act is to make accessible in domestic courts only the rights and remedies which would otherwise be available to applicants at the Strasbourg level.[38]

[35] *R. (on the application of Alconbury Developments and others) v Secretary of State for the Environment, Transport and the Regions* [2001] UKHL 23; [2003] 2 A.C. 295, at [26] (Lord Slynn). See also *R. (on the application of Anderson) v Secretary of State for the Home Department* [2002] UKHL 46; [2003] 1 A.C. 837, at [18] (Lord Bingham); *R. (on the application of Amin) v Secretary of State for the Home Department* [2003] UKHL 51; [2004] 1 A.C. 653, at [44] (Lord Slynn).

[36] A. Kavanagh, *Constitutional Review under the UK Human Rights Act* (Cambridge: Cambridge University Press, 2009), p.146.

[37] *R. (on the application of Ullah) v Special Adjudicator; Do v Immigration Appeal Tribunal* [2004] UKHL 26; [2004] 2 A.C. 323, at [20] (Lord Bingham).

[38] *R. (on the application of Begum) v Headteacher and Governors of Denbigh High School* [2006] UKHL 15; [2007] 1 A.C. 100, at [29]. See also *R. v Secretary of State for the Home Department Ex p. Greenfield* [2005] UKHL 14; [2005] 1 W.L.R. 673, at [19] (Lord Bingham); *R. (on the*

In its 'wider application',[39] therefore, the mirror metaphor is argued to extend to the interpretation of the HRA as a whole. In *R. v Secretary of State for Foreign and Commonwealth Affairs Ex p. Quark Fishing*, Lord Nicholls suggested that the combined effect of ss. 6 and 7 HRA was to 'mirror in domestic law the treaty obligations of the United Kingdom in respect of the corresponding articles of the Convention and its protocols'.[40] Drawing support from the views of Lord Hope in *Wallbank*,[41] he continued:

> The [Human Rights] Act was intended to provide a domestic remedy where a remedy would have been available in Strasbourg. Conversely, the Act was not intended to provide a domestic remedy where a remedy would not have been available in Strasbourg.[42]

In *Al-Jedda*, Lord Rodger appeared to broadly agree, noting that the task of the domestic court operating under the HRA was to 'assess how a claim by the appellant … would fare before the European Court of Human Rights'.[43] Both perspectives arguably minimise the distinctively domestic aspects of the HRA, viewing the Act as an instrument enabling access to rights and remedies which would in its absence only be available through recourse to Strasbourg. In cases such as *Quark* and *Al-Jedda*, in which the territorial integrity of the Convention—a matter falling within the clear competence of the European Court of Human Rights—was at issue, such an approach is entirely defensible. But it by no means follows that the same considerations should apply in determining the reach of the Convention rights given specific domestic effect by the HRA. Extending the mirror metaphor so that it holds the potential to exert influence over the entire substantive and remedial structure put in place by the HRA elevates the principle to the status of a

---

application of Quark Fishing Ltd) v Secretary of State for Foreign and Commonwealth Affairs [2005] UKHL 57; [2006] 1 A.C. 529, at [24] (Lord Bingham); at [34] (Lord Nicholls); at [88] (Lord Hope); *Huang v Secretary of State for the Home Department* [2007] UKHL 11; [2007] 2 A.C. 167, at [8].

[39] *In Re P (Adoption: Unmarried Couple)* [2008] UKHL 38; [2009] 1 A.C. 173, at [79] (Lord Walker).

[40] *R. (on the application of Quark Fishing Ltd) v Secretary of State for Foreign and Commonwealth Affairs* [2005] UKHL 57; [2006] 1 A.C. 529, at [34] (Lord Nicholls).

[41] *Aston Cantlow and Wilmcote with Billesley Parochial Church Council v Wallbank* [2004] 1 A.C. 546, 564, [44]: '[The] purpose of … sections [6 and 7 HRA] is to provide a remedial structure in domestic law for the rights guaranteed in the Convention.'

[42] *R. (on the application of Quark Fishing Ltd) v Secretary of State for Foreign and Commonwealth Affairs* [2005] UKHL 57; [2006] 1 A.C. 529, at [34] (Lord Nicholls). Lord Bingham, at [25], advanced a similar perspective, suggesting that 'the purpose of the 1998 Act was not to enlarge the field of application of the Convention but to enable those subject to the jurisdiction of the United Kingdom and able to establish violations by United Kingdom public authorities to present their claims in the domestic courts of this country and not only in Strasbourg'.

[43] *R. (on the application of Al-Jedda) v Secretary of State for Defence* [2007] UKHL 58; [2008] 1 A.C. 332, at [55] (Lord Rodger).

virtual tenet of constitutional interpretation. On this reading, the HRA functions not as a proto-Bill of Rights, but simply to span the gap between national law and those rights and remedies which would otherwise be enforced by the European Court of Human Rights. Domestic courts, in turn, operate as local 'agents or delegates of the ECHR'[44] rather than autonomous constitutional actors charged with giving further effect to the Convention standards at the national level.

The Merits of Reflection

The mirror approach to the Strasbourg case law and meanings of the Convention rights under the HRA can be defended on both pragmatic and constitutional grounds. At a practical level, an adherence to the mirror principle brings clear benefits for litigants in HRA cases; the relatively stable relationship between the Strasbourg jurisprudence and domestic law that the mirror metaphor promotes not only displays respect for the findings of the Strasbourg court,[45] but also contributes to greater certainty for both victims of purported infringements and for public body respondents. The principle dictates that clear, constant and relevant Strasbourg reasoning will generally be adopted, and applied, by a domestic court, and holds that public bodies should not be expected to uphold standards of rights protection that exceed those countenanced by the European Court of Human Rights. The obligations to adhere to 'clear and constant' jurisprudence, and to provide no higher (or lower) standard of protection than would be afforded at Strasbourg, therefore promote legal certainty at the domestic level, and—in providing a protection which does not fall below the Strasbourg baseline—reduce the potential for an applicant to appeal successfully to the European Court of Human Rights.

The mirror principle might also be defended on constitutional grounds. From a judicial perspective, the arguments in favour of the mirror approach—given ongoing controversies over the counter-majoritarian nature of rights adjudication—are easily appreciated. First, an adherence to the principle can be argued to empower domestic courts. By tying the development of the Convention rights in national law as closely as possible to those rights as defined at Strasbourg, domestic courts legitimise their actions when, for instance, adopting 'strained' interpretations or reading in implied terms or

[44] Lord Irvine of Lairg, "A British Interpretation of Convention Rights" [2012] P.L. 237, 238.

[45] *R. (on the application of Ullah) v Special Adjudicator; Do v Immigration Appeal Tribunal* [2004] UKHL 26; [2004] 2 A.C. 323, at [20] (Lord Bingham); *Ahmed v HM Treasury* [2010] UKSC 5; [2010] 2 A.C. 534, at [74] (Lord Hope).

additional words under s.3(1),[46] or finding public body activity to have contravened the standards required by the HRA.[47] Relying on a variant of the doctrine of precedent, domestic courts are able to argue that utilising their powers to interpret legislation in such a way is effectively *compelled* by the findings of unequivocal Strasbourg authority.[48] On the basis of such an approach courts are able to avoid accusations that the content of domestic human rights law is a product of overly imaginative judicial engineering or, rather less favourably, that it has simply been 'made up'.[49] As a result, one of the dangers of rights adjudication—that judges will compromise their independence through overt law-making—is avoided: first by adopting a 'precedential' approach to the Convention jurisprudence,[50] secondly by displaying a reluctance to attribute meaning to the Convention rights which does not find clear support in existing Strasbourg case law.

The mirror model is also arguably partially congruous with the constitutional division of labour between the three branches of government. Consistent with the Labour government's intentions in implementing the HRA's distinctive model of rights protection,[51] the mirror model respects parliamentary sovereignty through recognising only those rights specified by Parliament in the HRA and, in turn, only to the extent clearly provided for by the European Court of Human Rights.[52] In its application, the mirror model therefore reflects the sovereignty-driven notion that Parliament—and not the courts—should be the appropriate author of legal frameworks of rights protection which extend, or are otherwise at variance with, the protections that would be

[46] See, for instance, *R. v A (No.2)* [2001] UKHL 25; [2002] 1 A.C. 45; *Ghaidan v Godin-Mendoza* [2004] UKHL 30; [2004] 2 A.C. 557.

[47] Take, for instance, the decision of Sullivan J in the Afghan Hijackers case (*R. (on the application of S) v Secretary of State for the Home Department* [2006] EWHC 1111). While the then Home Secretary, John Reid, was able to claim that Sullivan J's decision was 'bizarre and inexplicable' ('Ministers Accused of Fuelling Myths on Human Rights', *Guardian*, 14 November 2006) the Court of Appeal commented that, 'we commend the judge for an impeccable judgment. This history of this case … has attracted a degree of opprobrium for those carrying out judicial functions. Judges and adjudicators have to apply the law as they find it, and not as they might wish it to be' (*R. (on the application of S) v Secretary of State for the Home Department* [2006] EWCA Civ 1157).

[48] On which, see the comments of Baroness Hale in *Re P (Adoption: Unmarried Couple)* [2008] UKHL 38; [2009] 1 A.C. 173, at [116]: '[I]n all the cases in which either the interpretative duty in section 3 has been used, or a declaration of incompatibility made under section 4, it has been reasonably clear that the Strasbourg court would hold that United Kingdom law was incompatible with the Convention.'

[49] As suggested in I. Loveland, "Making It Up As They Go Along? The Court of Appeal on Same-sex Spouses and Succession Rights to Tenancies" [2003] P.L. 222.

[50] Masterman, "Section 2(1) of the Human Rights Act 1998".

[51] HL Debs, vol.582, col.1228, 3 November 1997 (Lord Irvine); HC Debs, vol.306, col.772, 16 February 1998 (Jack Straw MP).

[52] *Brown v Stott* [2003] 1 A.C. 681, 703 (Lord Bingham).

afforded by the Strasbourg court.[53] Yet it is at this point that the weaknesses of the mirror model begin to become apparent; the uncodified constitution has long recognised the limited law-making role of the judiciary.[54] The complete denial of even an incremental judicial law-making function (in the context of the meaning of the Convention rights under the HRA) which would be the consequence of a rigid adherence to the mirror model is therefore difficult, if not impossible, to reconcile with the common law dimensions of the United Kingdom's constitutional order.

The Constitutional Deficiencies of the Mirror Model

It is undoubted that the role of the domestic court under the HRA was, in part, to operate as a local proxy for the European Court of Human Rights, reducing the potential cost and delay associated with pursuing Convention-based litigation as far as Strasbourg.[55] But to suggest that the role of the court was *only* to so act reflects an incomplete understanding of the intentions behind the HRA: indications were also given in *Rights Brought Home* that the purpose of the HRA would permit the Convention rights to be 'subtly and powerfully woven into our law' (rather than to supplant it) and would enable the judiciary to 'make a distinctively British contribution to the development of the jurisprudence of human rights in Europe' (rather than to passively reflect it).[56] In practice, the mirror model of interpretation oversimplifies the requirements of the both the Convention—a point that is explored in more detail below—and of the HRA itself. Three constitutional difficulties can be identified: the first relates to the structural requirements of HRA adjudication, the second to the dynamic relationship between national authorities and the European Convention organs, and the third to the judicial obligation to consider each case on its merits.

As to the first of these, reasoning of the type seen in the House of Lords decisions in *Quark* and *Al-Jedda*—when deployed as a general principle applicable to the interpretation of the HRA[57]—gives insufficient recognition to the fact that the HRA creates a remedial structure which cannot be coherently explained by reference to the Convention alone. Elements of this structure

[53] *R. (on the application of Ullah) v Special Adjudicator; Do v Immigration Appeal Tribunal* [2004] UKHL 26; [2004] 2 A.C. 323, at [20] (Lord Bingham).

[54] Lord Reid, "The Judge as Law Maker" (1972–73) 12 *Journal of the Society of the Public Teachers of Law* 22.

[55] *Rights Brought Home* (1997), Cm.3782, at [1.14].

[56] *Rights Brought Home* (1997), Cm.3782, at [1.14].

[57] As in *R. (on the application of Begum) v Headteacher and Governors of Denbigh High School* [2006] UKHL 15; [2007] 1 A.C. 100, at [29] (Lord Bingham).

have no heritage in either the Convention itself or its case law; the notion of hybrid public authorities[58] and the declaration of incompatibility,[59] for instance, are purely domestic concepts that go directly to the scope and extent of the protections afforded by the HRA. The remedial capacity of the HRA is therefore as much a matter for domestic law as it is the Strasbourg jurisprudence: the approach of domestic courts to the boundary between legitimate statutory interpretation and impermissible amendment in the use of s.3(1) HRA, for instance, owes as much, or more, to local constitutional influences—the continuing relevance of the sovereignty doctrine and the fluctuating contours of the relationship between courts and Parliament—as it does to the strict requirements of the Convention as articulated by the Strasbourg court. Interpretations of where the line between permissible interpretation and illegitimate legislative amendment lie, will of course differ. For the purposes of this particular argument, the precise point at which this line might be drawn is irrelevant; it is sufficient to acknowledge that concerns *other than those* originating in the Convention are material. In short, determining the specific requirements of the HRA in the context of a particular case is an analytical exercise that is linked to—but distinctive from—a court's assessment of the perceived requirements of the Convention. The latter is relevant to the former, but only insofar as determining the meaning to be afforded to the Convention rights in the domestic context. The mirror model of interpretation conflates these two levels of analysis, treating the requirements of the Convention as being synonymous with those of the HRA itself.

A further concern over the adoption by national courts of the mirror model of interpretation relates to the symbiotic relationship between national authorities and the Convention organs that is an expectation of the European Court of Human Rights. While the mirror model may—in part at least—be premised on the assumption that Parliament, and not the courts, should be the ultimate guarantor of human rights standards in the domestic context, this distinction is, from the perspective of the Convention bodies, largely irrelevant[60]; the Convention is binding on *the state*. As a result, it is at least arguable that 'the ECHR's injunction to further realise human rights and fundamental freedoms ... is addressed to domestic courts' as well as legislatures.[61] The tendency of national courts to mirror the findings of the European

[58] HRA, s.6(3)(b). See *YL v Birmingham City Council* [2007] UKHL 27; [2008] 1 A.C. 95, at [4] (Lord Bingham).

[59] HRA, s.4.

[60] *In Re P (Adoption: Unmarried Couple)* [2008] UKHL 38; [2009] 1 A.C. 173, at [32] (Lord Hoffmann): 'Like all international tribunals, [the European Court of Human Rights] is not concerned with the separation of powers within the member state.' See also *R. (on the application of Countryside Alliance) v Attorney-General* [2007] UKHL 52; [2008] 1 A.C. 719, at [125] (Baroness Hale).

[61] Judge S. K. Martens, "Incorporating the European Convention: The Role of the Judiciary" [1998] E.H.R.L.R. 5, 14.

Court of Human Rights deprives the latter court of one of the key indicators of emerging consensus (or otherwise) among Convention signatories[62] and is inconsistent with the fact that 'the machinery of protection established by the Convention is subsidiary to [the protections afforded within] national systems'.[63] A rigid adherence to the mirror approach to the application of the Convention jurisprudence therefore has the unintended consequence of distorting the dynamic nature of the relationship between the United Kingdom as a state party to the Convention and its governing court. This danger has been recognised by the Supreme Court in *Pinnock v Manchester City Council*:

> This court is not bound to follow every decision of the European Court. Not only would it be impractical to do so: it would sometimes be inappropriate, as it would destroy the ability of the court to engage in the constructive dialogue with the European Court which is of value to the development of the Convention law ...[64]

A precedent-like approach to the Strasbourg case law undermines the upward influence of national courts in this dialogue, and gives credence to the suggestion that the Convention standards are European impositions—rather than the product of a collaborative exercise between national and supra national institutions—in so doing.

Finally, the application of any overriding principle which seeks to mirror liability under the Convention in the domestic context—that is, an approach which holds the potential to displace context-specific analysis of the relevancy and applicability of the available Strasbourg case law—will be susceptible to the same arguments that have been levelled against the perceived operation of a doctrine of deference in HRA adjudication. The accusation that courts might allow their judgment on human rights issues to be displaced by the generation of a doctrinal approach to deference—under which the independent decision-making capability of the courts is surrendered in acknowledgment of the supposedly superior credentials of the primary decision-maker[65]—finds a parallel in the suggestion that the purpose of the HRA is to replicate protections that would otherwise be enforced by the European Court of Human Rights. The effect of the mirror principle is that

[62] On which, see K. Dzehtsiarou, "Does Consensus Matter? Legitimacy of European Consensus in the Case Law of the European Court of Human Rights" [2011] P.L. 534.

[63] *Handyside v United Kingdom* (1979–80) 1 E.H.R.R. 737, at [48].

[64] *Manchester CC v Pinnock* [2010] UKSC 45, at [48]. See also Chapter 6, this volume.

[65] For perhaps the most forceful rejection of such a doctrine, see: T. R. S. Allan, "Human Rights and Judicial Review: A Critique of Due Deference" [2006] C.L.J. 671. Cf. M. Hunt, "Sovereignty's Blight: Why Contemporary Public Law Needs the Concept of 'Due Deference'", in N. Bamforth and P. Leyland (eds), *Public Law in a Multi-layered Constitution* (Oxford: Hart Publishing, 2003).

the obligation of the court to consider the case before it, and available authority, on its merits is constrained by the overriding concern to mimic the Strasbourg standards in the domestic context. As Lord Irvine has argued, '[s]ection 2 of the HRA means that it is our judges' duty to decide the cases for themselves'[66] rather than to defer to the expertise, or authority, of a supposedly superior decision-maker. The exceptions that exist to the requirements imposed by the mirror principle may weaken this particular line of attack, but only insofar as the mirror metaphor extends to questions of the precedential force of Strasbourg authority. The restraints placed on the scope of the protections afforded under the HRA, and the extension of the mirror metaphor to the interpretation of the HRA scheme as a whole, both continue to operate as external constraints on the discretion of courts that find little—at best only partial—support in the text of the HRA itself.

As Tom Hickman has observed, the mirror model of interpreting the HRA has 'crystallised into a powerful principle of purposive construction that has greatly influenced the Act's interpretation and effect'.[67] Yet, the overarching approach advocated by the mirror model is based on but one of the motivating factors behind the enactment of the HRA. It can offer only an inadequate account of the overall constitutional purpose of the Act, and is therefore of dubious authority when (occasionally) presented as an authoritative statement of the Act's objectives. In addition, it holds the potential to upset the relationship between national courts and the European Court of Human Rights and to present an obstacle to the effective discharge of the courts' obligations under the HRA. In short, the deficiencies of this overarching construction of the HRA are significant.

The Practical Inadequacy of the Mirror Model

In the context of *individual* judicial decisions, there may well be salient reasons underpinning reliance on a relevant Strasbourg decision or decisions and/or the endorsement by a domestic court that the standard of protection afforded by the European Court of Human Rights should be co-terminus with the level of protections afforded under the HRA. The utility of this presumption should not, however, be stretched unduly. During the parliamentary debates on the Human Rights Bill—while acknowledging that relevant jurisprudence and principles would generally be applied by domestic courts[68]—Lord Irvine

[66] Lord Irvine of Lairg, "A British Interpretation of Convention Rights" [2012] P.L. 237, 252.
[67] Hickman, *Public Law after the Human Rights Act*, p.31.
[68] HL Debs, vol.583, cols.514–15, 18 November 1997 (Lord Irvine).

was careful to remind that Strasbourg authority could not be presumed to be directly applicable in the domestic context:

> Should a United Kingdom court ever have a case before it which is a precise mirror of one that has been previously considered by the European Court of Human Rights, which I doubt, it may be appropriate for it to apply the European Court's findings directly to that case; but in real life cases are rarely as neat and tidy.[69]

Lord Irvine's concern—subsequently reflected in the House of Lords decision in *Gillan*[70]—is revealing of a central weakness of the mirror metaphor; it relies on the false premise that Strasbourg jurisprudence is both suitable to be directly applied in a precedential manner and that it contains all the answers to the difficult questions that routinely arise at the domestic level. Each of these assumptions is open to question.

The Particular Characteristics of the Strasbourg Jurisprudence

Early in the life of the HRA, Laws LJ cautioned against the unquestioning adoption and application by domestic courts of the Strasbourg jurisprudence; the English court, he argued, should not be regarded as a 'Strasbourg surrogate'[71] whose job is simply to 'add on the Strasbourg learning to the corpus of English law'.[72] The distinctive characteristics of the Strasbourg case law present a range of difficulties for courts seeking to extract and apply Convention norms in the domestic context.[73] Three practical problems can be briefly highlighted.

First, the fact that the jurisprudence of the European Court is declaratory in nature—being indicative of a breach (or otherwise) of the Convention rather than specifying a particular course of remedial action—makes its application in the domestic context contingent on a degree of creativity on the part of national authorities, the courts included. As the Convention organs are 'not seeking to harmonise constitutional traditions'[74] member states are free to determine the method of achieving compatibility in accordance with the rules of their national legal system in response to a finding by the European Court of a breach.[75] It is not an objective of the Convention system to supplant

[69] HL Debs, vol.584, col.1270, 19 January 1998 (Lord Irvine).
[70] *R. (on the application of Gillan) v Commissioner of Police for the Metropolis* [2006] UKHL 11; [2006] 2 A.C. 307, at [23] (Lord Bingham).
[71] *R. (on the application of ProLife Alliance) v British Broadcasting Corporation* [2002] 2 All E.R. 756, at [33].
[72] *Runa Begum v Tower Hamlets London Borough Council* [2002] 2 All E.R. 668, at [17].
[73] Masterman, "Taking the Strasbourg Jurisprudence into Account", 915–18.
[74] A. Clapham, *Human Rights in the Private Sphere* (Oxford: Clarendon Press, 1992), p.181.
[75] *Vermeire* v *Belgium* (1993) 15 E.H.R.R. 488.

protections for legal rights already existent in the national system, but to re-enforce them. That the HRA was designed to be consistent with this notion is evident from the inclusion of s.11, which indicates that the rights available under the HRA should run in parallel with those already operative in domestic law.

Secondly, the promotion of a regimented relationship between domestic law, and the jurisprudence of the European Court of Human Rights—by definition a 'shifting'[76] body of law which feeds on developments at the national level[77]—is not without difficulty; decisions of the European Court of Human Rights might, over the course of time, be superseded by jurisprudential developments and therefore become inapt to be followed or applied in any way.[78] Finally, the fact that the jurisprudence of the European Court of Human Rights is directed towards multiple jurisdictions and, in turn, has given rise to the margin of appreciation, raises concerns relating to the transferability of findings of the Strasbourg court between member states. Decisions in which the European Court of Human Rights has invoked the margin of appreciation are, for instance, heavily conditioned by factors prevalent in the respondent state and should not be assumed to be directly applicable elsewhere.

Each of these distinctive characteristics of the Strasbourg case law points towards the conclusion that the processes of integrating the Convention jurisprudence into the existing body of domestic common and statute law is therefore—or should be—far from a straightforward task.[79] In addition to addressing questions of practical and temporal relevance and applicability, domestic courts should actively 'take into account' the jurisdictional, fact-sensitive and declaratory dimensions of potentially applicable European Court decisions in order to fashion a coherent reading of the requirements of the Convention. It is from this basis that a court's subsequent assessment of how, or whether, this reading can be given effect to—and set a domestic precedent—via the HRA should proceed. The central weakness of the mirror model of interpretation is that this complex process of reconciliation is distilled into a series of binary questions—of whether to straightforwardly follow or not, of how to provide 'no less' but 'no more' protection than Strasbourg—that cannot provide coherent responses to the more difficult questions posed by the courts' attempts to give effect to their obligations under the HRA. A series of examples will illustrate this point in practice.

[76] HL Debs, vol.584, col.1268, 19 January 1998 (Lord Browne-Wilkinson).

[77] *Stafford v United Kingdom* (2002) 35 E.H.R.R. 32, at [68].

[78] *R. (on the application of Quila) v Secretary of State for the Home Department* [2011] UKSC 45; [2011] 3 W.L.R. 836.

[79] C. A. Gearty, "Tort Law and the Human Rights Act", in T. Campbell, K. D. Ewing and A. Tomkins, *Sceptical Essays on Human Rights* (Oxford: Oxford University Press, 2001), pp.252–53.

Unclear Authority and the Mirror Model

While the mirror model might be argued to reinforce the reasoning of domestic courts where clear and constant authority can be relied upon, at the level of individual judicial decision-making an overly rigid adherence to the mirror ideal holds the potential to exercise a disempowering effect on the ability of courts to provide a remedy or adequate answer to the legal problem arising. The response of the House of Lords to those areas in which clear guiding authority at the Strasbourg level has been lacking demonstrates the inability of the mirror approach to provide an adequate framework from which judicial analysis can proceed. In the House of Lords decision in *N v Secretary of State for the Home Department*, for example, the Law Lords' survey of the Strasbourg jurisprudence concluded that the relevant authority was 'not in an altogether satisfactory state', lacked 'its customary clarity' and displayed evidence of reasoning that was not 'entirely convincing'.[80] Yet, as Lord Hope argued:

> Our task, then, is to analyse the jurisprudence of the Strasbourg court and, having done so and identified its limits, to apply it to the facts of this case ... It is not for us to search for a solution ... which is not to be found in the Strasbourg case law. It is for the Strasbourg court, not for us, to decide whether its case law is out of touch with modern conditions and to determine what further extensions, if any, are needed to the rights guaranteed by the Convention. We must take the case law as we find it, not as we would like it to be.[81]

The apparent consequence of this particular dynamic of the mirror model is to either require the perceived deficiencies of the Strasbourg case law to be replicated, or otherwise leave the domestic court powerless to take remedial action in translating the relevant authority into the domestic setting.

Where a domestic court is confronted with an issue on which *no* relevant Strasbourg jurisprudence is available, the House of Lords has indicated that a measure of 'self-restraint' is required, 'lest we stretch our own jurisprudence beyond that which is shared by all the states parties to the Convention'.[82] Such an approach is grounded in the view that the meaning of the Convention should be uniform throughout the Council of Europe, and that the HRA rights merely replicate those rights enforced by the European Court of Human Rights. While defended on grounds of respect for the European Court of

[80] *N v Secretary of State for the Home Department* [2005] UKHL 31; [2005] 2 A.C. 296, at [11], [14] (Lord Nicholls) and at [91] (Lord Browne).
[81] *N v Secretary of State for the Home Department* [2005] UKHL 31; [2005] 2 A.C. 296, at [25] (Lord Hope).
[82] *R. (Clift) v Secretary of State for the Home Department* [2006] UKHL 54; [2007]1 A.C. 484, at [49] (Lord Hope).

Human Rights as the ultimate interpreter of the Convention standards,[83] this particular aspect of the mirror model holds the potential to preclude domestic courts from providing adequate responses to the legal questions arising before them. The suggestion that the courts should approach those areas in which clear Strasbourg authority is lacking as 'no go areas'[84] tantamount to being non-justiciable has provoked Lord Kerr to lament the '*Ullah*-type reticence' under which 'it is not only considered wrong to attempt to anticipate developments at the supra national level of the Strasbourg court, but ... that we should not go where Strasbourg has not yet gone'.[85] In the Supreme Court decision in *Ambrose v Harris*, Lord Kerr argued:

> ... it is the duty of this and every court not only to ascertain 'where the jurisprudence of the Strasbourg court clearly shows that it currently stands' but to resolve the question of whether a claim to a Convention right is viable or not, even where the jurisprudence of the Strasbourg court does not disclose a clear current view.[86]

The HRA conclusively put paid to the suggestion that questions relating to the Convention rights fell outside the competence of the domestic judiciary[87]; it would be an unusual result of the implementation of the HRA if it were to perpetuate the argument that Convention rights issues are effectively non-justiciable in those areas where no directly applicable Strasbourg authority is available.

Conflicting Authority and the Mirror Model

Nor can the mirror model of interpretation provide an adequate explanation of how courts should respond to conflicting Strasbourg case law. In the case of *Animal Defenders International* the House of Lords was asked to adjudicate on the compatibility of the prohibition on political advertising in s.321(2) of the Communications Act 2003 with the art.10 right to freedom of expression. Two potentially applicable decisions of the European Court of Human Rights were raised in argument. The first of these—*VgT Verein gegen Tierfabricken v Switzerland*[88]—provided authority for the suggestion that a blanket ban on advertising for political ends would be a disproportionate

[83] *R. (on the application of Ullah) v Special Adjudicator; Do v Immigration Appeal Tribunal* [2004] UKHL 26; [2004] 2 A.C. 323, at [20] (Lord Bingham); *Ahmed v HM Treasury* [2010] UKSC 5; [2010] 2 A.C. 534, at [74] (Lord Hope).

[84] Lewis, "The European Ceiling on Rights", 732.

[85] *Ambrose v Harris* [2011] UKSC 3; [2011] 1 W.L.R. 2435, at [126]. See also Lord Kerr, "The UK Supreme Court—The Modest Underworker of Strasbourg?", Clifford Chance Lecture, 25 January 2012.

[86] *Ambrose v Harris* [2011] UKSC 3; [2011] 1 W.L.R. 2435, at [129]. Cf. at [18]–[20] (Lord Hope).

[87] *R. v Secretary of State for the Home Department Ex p. Brind* [1991] 1 A.C. 696.

[88] *VgT Verein gegen Tierfabricken v Switzerland* (2002) 34 E.H.R.R. 4.

interference with freedom of expression. The second—*Murphy v Ireland*[89]—suggested that a restriction on advertising for *religious* purposes would fall within the range of reasonable responses available to states under the margin of appreciation doctrine.

In declining to grant the declaration of incompatibility requested by the applicants, the House of Lords opted to place reliance on *Murphy v Ireland*, which—given that its subject matter was a prohibition on *religious* advertising—was arguably the less factually relevant of the two decisions. The Law Lords used *Murphy* to illustrate that a consensus amongst the contracting states was lacking, and that—as a result—a margin of appreciation would be afforded to the regulatory decisions of national authorities in this field. On the basis of this supposed margin of appreciation, the Law Lords were able to find that 'great weight'[90] should be attributed to Parliament's decision to ban political advertising in full knowledge of the potential inconsistency of the prohibition with at least one decision of the European Court of Human Rights. In this latter respect at least, the decision of the House of Lords is almost certainly correct; the HRA places no bar on Parliament legislating in a way which is potentially inconsistent with the Convention rights. Yet in order to reach this point—hamstrung by their own presumption in favour of the application of relevant and clear authority—the Law Lords' reasoning provides an unconvincing defence of why the clear and relevant decision in *VgT*—arising on facts which, as Lord Bingham acknowledged, were 'very similar to those in the present case'[91]—was not followed. On its face, s.2(1) provides courts with the flexibility needed to consider and weigh up the merits of potentially conflicting Strasbourg authority, permitting courts to assess the relevancy of potentially applicable—and potentially contradictory—decisions. The rudimentary questions posed by the mirror model of interpretation, in this instance, proved unable to underpin a coherent judicial response.

The Increasing Inaccuracy of the Mirror Metaphor

The case against the perpetuation of the mirror model becomes more compelling when account is taken of the increasing evidence illustrating further departures from the notion that the Strasbourg and domestic protections

[89] *Murphy v Ireland* (2004) 38 E.H.R.R. 13.

[90] *R. (on the application of Animal Defenders International) v Secretary of State for Culture, Media and Sport* [2008] UKHL 15; [2008] 1 A.C. 1312, at [33] (Lord Bingham).

[91] *R. (on the application of Animal Defenders International) v Secretary of State for Culture, Media and Sport* [2008] UKHL 15; [2008] 1 A.C. 1312, at [9] (Lord Bingham).

should mirror each other in both form and substance. That many of these departures cannot be explained by reference to the so-called exceptions to the principle indicates that to speak of domestic law as straightforwardly replicating the requirements of the Convention provides an inaccurate encapsulation of the processes of judicial reasoning—and their outcomes—in HRA adjudication. In this sense, the mirror principle unfairly implies an uncritical attitude to the Strasbourg authority that is largely absent from the recent record of the courts under the HRA. While *AF* demonstrates that the precedential weight of a decision of the Grand Chamber of the European Court of Human Rights remains considerable,[92] *Horncastle* confirms that such authority—even 'a clear statement of principle … in respect of the precise issue' before the domestic court—will not be regarded as being determinative as a matter of course.[93] But a focus on such cases—where the requirements of, and exceptions to, the presumption in favour of adherence to Strasbourg authority are explicit considerations—distracts from a crucial point; that the stated exceptions to the mirror model of interpretation are unequal to the task of facilitating the ordered reconciliation of domestic and Strasbourg authority.

Limited Authority and the Mirror Model

The impossibility of sustaining an adherence to the mirror principle becomes most obvious in those areas in which domestic courts are operating within a context where the relevant and applicable Convention jurisprudence provides only partial support for the decision eventually taken. While a strict adherence to the mirror model would not seem to sanction building on, or developing, nominally applicable—though insubstantial—authority,[94] notable examples exist of domestic courts pursuing exactly this type of creative reasoning. In the House of Lords decision in *Limbuela*,[95] the 'only approximately relevant authority'[96] at the Strasbourg level was the admissibility decision in *O'Rourke v United Kingdom*.[97] The treatment, by the European Court of Human Rights, of the relevant law in *O'Rourke* runs to a mere four paragraphs, yet on the basis of that slight authority the House of Lords was not only able to fashion a remedy, but was able to arguably extend the scope

[92] *Secretary of State for the Home Department v AF* [2009] UKHL 28; [2009] 3 W.L.R. 74.
[93] *R. v Horncastle* [2009] UKSC 14; [2010] 2 A.C. 373, at [11] (Lord Phillips).
[94] *N v Secretary of State for the Home Department* [2005] UKHL 31; [2005] 2 A.C. 296, at [25].
[95] *R. (Limbuela) v Secretary of State for the Home Department* [2005] UKHL 66; [2006] 1 A.C. 396.
[96] C. Warbrick, "The European Convention on Human Rights and the Human Rights Act: The View from the Outside", in Fenwick, Phillipson and Masterman, *Judicial Reasoning under the UK Human Rights Act*, p.48.
[97] *O'Rourke v United Kingdom* (2001) ECtHR no.39022/97.

of protection offered by Article 3 of the Convention in the domestic context in so doing.[98]

Campbell v Mirror Group Newspapers provides a further illustration of exactly the type of progressive judicial reasoning that a strictly construed mirror principle would apparently preclude. Prior to the decision in *Campbell*, the question of whether the Convention required member states to make available remedies for breaches of art.8 caused by private persons was a 'difficult question' to which 'Strasbourg case law provide[d] no definitive answer'.[99] While the decision of the European Court of Human Rights in *Peck v United Kingdom*[100] had concerned the interference with art.8 rights by the *state*, the only relevant decision on the particular *horizontal* application of art.8 was in the form of the admissibility decision of *Spencer v United Kingdom*.[101] Yet in *Campbell* the House of Lords was, by a majority, able to find that the requirements of the Convention rights were such that remedies should be made available, *in advance* of a conclusive decision on point from the European Court of Human Rights.[102]

In both *Limbuela* and *Campbell*, the available Strasbourg authority provided only limited support for the decision taken by the House of Lords; in both cases the Law Lords were able to resolve questions of law to which the Strasbourg jurisprudence provided no complete answer.[103] Such decisions are, of course, entirely consonant with the incrementally progressive approach of the common law court and serve to highlight the fact that ultimately the strict requirements of the mirror model of interpretation are inconsistent with the limited creative role that is afforded to courts by the constitution.[104]

The Integration of Convention and Common Law

In those areas in which the common law and the Convention run in train, the mirror metaphor again oversimplifies the processes of reconciling the demands

[98] Lewis, "The European Ceiling on Rights", 736.

[99] G. Phillipson, "Judicial Reasoning in Breach of Confidence Cases under the Human Rights Act: Not Taking Privacy Seriously?" [2003] E.H.R.L.R. *(Special Issue: Privacy 2003)* 54, 57.

[100] *Peck v United Kingdom* (2003) 36 E.H.R.R. 41.

[101] *Spencer v United Kingdom* (1998) 25 E.H.R.R. CD105.

[102] Such a decision did not come from the European Court of Human Rights until *Von Hannover v Germany* (2005) 40 E.H.R.R. 1, handed down a month after the decision of the House of Lords in *Campbell v Mirror Group Newspapers Ltd* [2004] UKHL 22; [2004] 2 A.C. 457.

[103] See also *EM (Lebanon) v Secretary of State for the Home Department* [2008] UKHL 64; [2009] 1 A.C. 1198.

[104] Tom Hickman has suggested that decisions such as these should not be regarded as a repudiation of the mirror model: '[S]uch departures are necessary incidents of domestic courts having a jurisdiction to remedy violations of the European Convention. They are consistent with the domestic courts seeking to provide a remedy which would be provided if the claimant were to go all the way to Strasbourg' (Hickman, *Public Law after the Human Rights Act*, p.39).

of the Convention rights with established doctrines, both as a matter of substance and of judicial technique. A strict adherence to the mirror principle would see established domestic principles overridden in the name of replicating the Strasbourg rights at the national level. Yet the character of the common law has, for the most part, been preserved rather than usurped by the application of the Convention rights.[105] Even in that area of the common law where the influence of the Convention has been most palpable—the protection of personal privacy—change has been both incremental and arguably not fully reflective of the protections offered by the European Court of Human Rights. The development of the action of breach of confidence has certainly been marked—and clearly driven by the perceived requirements of arts 8 and 10 of the Convention—but it is notable also for highlighting a series of inaccuracies relating to the so-called mirror principle.

While courts have sought to give effect to the requirements of art.8 (and indeed art.10) in the domestic context, domestic courts have consciously avoided declaring that the HRA requires the creation of a free-standing action for infringement of personal privacy.[106] Instead, a recalibrated breach of confidence doctrine has been the vehicle by which the Convention standards have been transferred into domestic law. This cause of action has, in the words of one commentator, developed to 'precisely mirror' the protections for personal information found in art.8 of the Convention.[107] Yet, on closer inspection, the relationship between domestic privacy protections and those provided by the Convention has not been as neat and tidy as this assessment would immediately suggest. In the first instance, early decisions on breach of confidence eschewed application of the art.8 case law and saw the adoption of a test of offensiveness originating in the Australian High Court decision of *Australian Broadcasting Corporation v Lenah Game Meats*.[108] Domestic courts 'took their lead' not from Strasbourg, but from a comparable common law jurisdiction. More recent decisions demonstrate an equally uneven record. We have already seen that in one sense the House of Lords decision in *Campbell v MGN* pre-empted the decision of the European Court of Human Rights in *Von Hannover v Germany*, yet it is also arguably the case that another aspect

[105] See J. Steele, "(Dis)owning the Convention in the Law of Tort", in J. Lee (ed.), *From House of Lords to Supreme Court: Judges, Jurists and the Process of Judging* (Oxford: Hart Publishing, 2010).

[106] *Wainwright v Home Office* [2003] UKHL 53; [2004] 2 A.C. 406.

[107] Hickman, *Public Law after the Human Rights Act*, p.55.

[108] *Australian Broadcasting Corporation v Lenah Game Meats* [2001] HCA 63. See, for instance, *A v B plc* [2002] EWCA Civ 337; [2003] Q.B. 195.

of that case—the expansive reading of art.8 adopted by the European Court—has not been fully embraced by domestic courts.[109]

The public law sphere provides further examples of the inability of the mirror metaphor to accurately encapsulate developments since the enactment of the HRA, with the integration of proportionality into English public law providing a useful illustration. Determining whether a given restriction on a qualified right satisfies the Convention requirements of necessity and proportionality cannot be coherently informed by the objective of mirroring the perceived requirements of the Strasbourg case law. In this regard the text of the Convention can at best provide a series of analytical questions from which domestic judicial inquiry can proceed. Is the contested limitation prescribed by law? Is it in pursuance of a legitimate aim? The Strasbourg case law cannot provide answers to these questions in the abstract. Instead domestic courts are required to make their own assessment of concepts such as whether the limitation answers a 'pressing social need' and whether it is 'necessary in a democratic society'.[110] Answers to these questions are, of course, heavily contextual. The Convention and its case law can only provide a framework around which a domestic court might structure its decision-making process. Yet, even in this role, the Convention jurisprudence has proved only to be of limited assistance.

As a result of the failure of the European Court of Human Rights to articulate a consistent, structured, approach to questions of proportionality,[111] domestic courts have sought guidance from elsewhere. The leading House of Lords case of *R. (on the application of Daly) v Secretary of State for the Home Department*[112] saw Convention authority rejected in favour of

[109] The formal obstacle to domestic courts adopting the reading of art.8 put forward in *Von Hannover* is, of course, the ruling of the House of Lords—in *Kay v Lambeth LBC* [2006] UKHL 10; [2006] 2 A.C. 465—that the domestic doctrine of precedent has not been altered by the enactment of the HRA. In the context of misuse of private information *Campbell* remains authoritative, as a matter of domestic law. This has not, however, prevented numerous lower courts from wrestling with the implications of *Von Hannover* for domestic privacy protection. See, for example, *Mosley v News Group Newspapers* [2008] EWHC 1777 (QB); [2008] E.M.L.R. 20; *Murray v Express Newspapers Plc* [2008] EWCA Civ 446; [2009] Ch. 481. On which, see G. Phillipson, "Privacy: The Development of Breach of Confidence—The Clearest Case of Horizontal Effect?", in D. Hoffman (ed.), *The Impact of the UK Human Rights Act on Private Law* (Cambridge: Cambridge University Press, 2011), pp.142–46.

[110] See, for example, *Handyside v United Kingdom* (1979–80) 1 E.H.R.R. 737, at [48], where—consistently with the position of the Strasbourg organs as a secondary layer of rights protection—the European Court conceded that 'it is for the national authorities to make the initial assessment of the reality of the pressing social need implied by the notion of "necessity" in this context'.

[111] See, for example, *R. v Shayler* [2002] UKHL 11; [2003] A.C. 247, at [60] (Lord Hope); R. Clayton, "Regaining a Sense of Proportion: The Human Rights Act and the Proportionality Principle" [2001] E.H.R.L.R. 504, 510–12.

[112] *R. (on the application of Daly) v Secretary of State for the Home Department* [2001] UKHL 26; [2001] 2 A.C. 532.

the test of proportionality adopted by the Judicial Committee of the Privy Council in *de Freitas*.[113] *Daly*—itself a case concerning rights existent at common law—saw the *de Freitas* test endorsed as the appropriate standard of review in adjudication concerning the Convention rights and has been endorsed as such in subsequent decisions.[114] While the post-HRA standard of review employed by domestic courts might well be broadly consistent with the expectations of the European Court,[115] the techniques employed to achieve this consistency—in particular in drawing on and incrementally refining Commonwealth and other jurisprudence from beyond the Convention system[116]—have more in common with the established techniques of common law development than with any attempted mirroring of Strasbourg case law in the domestic context.[117]

The Reasonably Foreseeable Development

While initial indications suggested that it was not for courts to 'pre-empt'[118] Strasbourg where a domestic court suspected that a European Court of Human Rights decision was outdated, out of line with the emerging European consensus, or failed to fully resolve the issue to be determined, recent cases have indicated a subtle change of direction. The possibility of the courts using their limited creative powers to engineer a 'reasonably foreseeable' development of the law in this regard was raised obliquely in the speech of Baroness Hale in *Gentle*:

> Parliament is free to go further than Strasbourg if it wishes, but we are not free to foist upon Parliament or upon public authorities an interpretation of a Convention right which goes way beyond anything which we can reasonably foresee that Strasbourg might do.[119]

[113] *de Freitas v Permanent Secretary of Ministry of Agriculture, Fisheries, Land and Housing* [1999] 1 A.C. 69, 80 (Lord Clyde): 'whether (i) the legislative objective is sufficiently important to justify limiting a fundamental right; (ii) the measures designed to meet the legislative objective are rationally connected to it; and (iii) the means used to impair the right or freedom are no more than is necessary to accomplish the objective'.
[114] See, for example, *Huang v Secretary of State for the Home Department* [2007] UKHL 11; [2007] 2 A.C. 167; *E v Chief Constable of the Royal Ulster Constabulary* [2008] UKHL 66; [2009] 1 A.C. 536.
[115] Though, in practice, see *S v United Kingdom* (2009) 48 E.H.R.R. 50; *Gillan and Quinton v United Kingdom* (2010) 50 E.H.R.R. 45.
[116] See, for example, *R. (on the application of Daly) v Secretary of State for the Home Department* [2001] UKHL 26; [2001] 2 A.C. 532, at [27]–[28]; *Huang v Secretary of State for the Home Department* [2007] UKHL 11; [2007] 2 A.C. 167, at [19]–[20].
[117] For a similar observation—made in the context of EU law—see *R. (on the application of Sinclair Collis Ltd) v Secretary of State for Health* [2011] EWCA Civ 437, at [82].
[118] *M v Secretary of State for Work and Pensions* [2006] UKHL 11, at [30] (Lord Nicholls).
[119] *R. (on the application of Gentle and another) v Prime Minister* [2008] UKHL 20; [2008] 1 A.C. 1356, at [56]. See also *R. (on the application of Countryside Alliance) v Attorney-General* [2007] UKHL 52; [2008] 1 A.C. 719, at [125] (Baroness Hale).

While at pains to stress the institutional competence issues in such a proposed development, Baroness Hale's careful use of hyperbole does appear to suggest that it may well be open to courts to put forward an interpretation of a Convention right which incrementally develops, in a reasonably foreseeable way, pre-existing Strasbourg case law.[120]

Predictive reasoning of this sort was in evidence in the decision of the House of Lords in *Re P*.[121] *Re P* has been hailed as confirming an exception to the mirror principle in those areas where the European Court has held that the margin of appreciation applies,[122] it also provides evidence of the highest court engaging in a degree of overt speculation over how—if confronted with a similar case—the European Court of Human Rights might respond.[123] While such decisions might be presented as a pragmatic domestic response to areas of uncertainty within the Convention jurisprudence consistent with the *general* principle in favour of applying relevant Strasbourg authority,[124] they appear to depart from the suggestion that it is not for domestic courts to provide answers to legal problems which cannot be found in the Strasbourg case law.[125] Questions of institutional competence are central to this particular inquiry, with the creative abilities of the courts—the power of the courts to generate outcomes that are respectful of, though not strictly mandated by, the Convention jurisprudence—arguably greater in those areas of domestic law where the common law applies or those areas where the influence of the Convention is conditioned by a margin of appreciation. So long as those creative powers are exercised compatibly with the tenor of the Strasbourg case law,[126] and with the incremental law-making powers bestowed upon judges by the constitution,[127] s.2(1) imposes no bar on their use.

[120] Incidentally, the legitimacy of 'reasonably foreseeable' development of the law (engineered by the courts) would also appear to gain support from the European Court of Human Rights: *SW v United Kingdom*; *CR v United Kingdom* (1996) 21 E.H.R.R. 363.

[121] *In Re P (Adoption: Unmarried Couple)* [2008] UKHL 38; [2009] 1 A.C. 173.

[122] Lewis, "*In Re P and others*: An Exception to the 'No More, Certainly No Less' Rule" [2009] P.L. 43.

[123] *In Re P (Adoption: Unmarried Couple)* [2008] UKHL 38; [2009] 1 A.C. 173, at [27] (Lord Hoffmann), [53] (Lord Hope). Cf. Lord Walker at [82].

[124] Hickman, *Public Law after the Human Rights Act*, p.39.

[125] *N v Secretary of State for the Home Department* [2005] UKHL 31; [2005] 2 A.C. 296, at [25] (Lord Hope).

[126] Masterman, "Taking the Strasbourg Jurisprudence into Account", 917–21.

[127] On which, see G. Phillipson and A. Williams, "Horizontal Effect and the Constitutional Constraint" (2011) 74 M.L.R. 878, 887–90.

Conclusion: The False Premise of the Bill of Rights Debate?

The mirror principle remains a paradox at the heart of the judicial approach to the interpretation and application of the HRA. The highest courts have consistently pronounced the HRA to be a constitutional measure, requiring 'generous and purposive interpretation'.[128] Simultaneously, the mirror metaphor—emerging out of a constraining reading of s.2(1) and of the HRA itself—has presented a quiet, formalist, obstacle to the effective realisation of this lofty ambition. As we have seen, however, the notion that domestic protections should mirror their Strasbourg counterparts is flawed, both constitutionally and practically; with the mirror metaphor reflecting an overly narrow interpretation of the HRA and proving in its implementation unequal to the task of permitting the orderly transition of Strasbourg authority into domestic law. The principles of interpretation associated with the mirror principle can, at best, provide only a basic explanation of the reasoning processes that have sought to give effect to the substantive protections afforded by the HRA. The binary distinctions that are at its core—to follow or not; to do no less, but no more, than the Convention jurisprudence requires—cannot provide adequate responses to the complex processes of reconciling the demands of the Convention rights with domestic statute and common law. Increasingly, signs are visible that the strictures imposed by the mirror model of interpretation are loosening, and that an approach to the meaning of the Convention rights which is consonant with the domestic separation of powers—and therefore recognises the legitimacy of the limited definitional role played courts in giving meaning to those rights—is beginning to gain credence. As a result, the evidence in favour of the slow emergence of a distinctly domestic body of human rights law is a more tenable suggestion than the straightforward reflection of the mirror metaphor would have us believe.

Yet the political currency of the mirror principle remains well-established. The perception that domestic courts are inflexibly bound to adhere to the rulings of the European Court of Human Rights continues to manifest itself in the debates on whether a national Bill of Rights might be more responsive to 'British' rights than the HRA,[129] and has undoubtedly fuelled calls for the United Kingdom to extract itself from the Convention system in order to escape what have been referred to by one former Law Lord as the 'occasional

[128] See, for example, *R. v DPP Ex p. Kebeline* [2000] 2 A.C. 326, 375 (Lord Hope); *Brown v Stott* [2003] 1 A.C. 681, 703 (Lord Bingham).
[129] "A Pincer Movement on No 10", *Independent on Sunday*, 20 February 2011.

extravagances of the Strasbourg Court'.[130] The Conservative drive to repeal the HRA, or to replace it with a more non-European rights instrument, is therefore premised in part on continued influence and acceptance of the mirror metaphor and the parallel suggestion that domestic institutions are rendered 'subservient'[131] to the European Court of Human Rights through the combined efforts of the Convention system and the HRA. It would be unfortunate, to say the least, if, in spite of the increasing evidence in favour of the dilution of the mirror principle, continued perceptions of rigidity and undue deference to Strasbourg contributed to the premature demise of the HRA.

Note. My thanks are due to Merris Amos, David Mead, Gavin Phillipson and Alison Young for their suggestions and comments on a draft. Any errors and omissions are, of course, my own.

[130] HL Debs, vol.721, col.709, 18 October 2010 (Lord Scott). See also Lord Hoffmann, "The Universality of Human Rights" (2009) 125 L.Q.R. 416; M. Pinto-Duschinsky, *Bringing Rights Back Home: Making Human Rights Compatible with Parliamentary Democracy in the UK* (London: Policy Exchange, 2011).
[131] Pinto-Duschinsky, *Bringing Rights Back Home*, p.17.

6

From Monologue to Dialogue: The Relationship between UK Courts and the European Court of Human Rights

MERRIS AMOS

Introduction

IN JUDICIAL, POLITICAL AND ACADEMIC CIRCLES, there is a growing interest in what has been labelled the 'dialogue' which takes place between UK courts and the European Court of Human Rights (ECtHR). The Supreme Court, for example, has recently observed that in some instances, it is appropriate to give the ECtHR the opportunity to reconsider a particular aspect of its jurisprudence and that this might inspire a 'valuable dialogue' between the two courts.[1] The desire for dialogue has been expressed extra-judicially by judges from UK courts and the ECtHR[2] and the metaphor has also been employed by the Department for Constitutional Affairs, now the Ministry of Justice, to support its claim that this kind of relationship, and exchange, ensures better results for the United Kingdom before the ECtHR.[3] But, although there is much willingness to label the interactions between these courts as a 'dialogue', there has been very little close analysis of what is actually taking place. As the relationship between the courts continues to grow and develop, it is important to consider what exactly is meant by the metaphor of dialogue and what opportunities there really are, at both the domestic and international levels, for it to take place. It is also important to consider what impact a relationship of dialogue between UK courts and a supranational court can have in practice, and to consider the consequences if dialogue were to increase and expand, as some have argued for.

[1] *R. v Horncastle* [2009] UKSC 14.
[2] See, for example, European Court of Human Rights, *Dialogue between Judges* (Council of Europe, 2010), www.echr.coe.int; and M. Arden, "The Changing Judicial Role: Human Rights, Community Law and the Intention of Parliament (2008) 67 C.L.J. 487, 499.
[3] *Review of the Implementation of the Human Rights Act*, DCA 38/06 (2006).

Proceedings of the British Academy, **183**, 139–159.

Opportunities for Dialogue

To describe an exchange between two courts as a 'dialogue' implies that there is 'communication between two courts that is effectively initiated by one and responded to by the other' and accompanied by an 'awareness on the part of both participants of whom they are talking to and a corresponding willingness to take account of the response'.[4] Considering the existing relationship between UK courts and the ECtHR, in theory there are considerable possibilities for dialogue, as defined, to take place. As discussed by Masterman in his essay in this volume,[5] the Human Rights Act 1998 (HRA) has, in a sense, been designed to 'mirror' for claimants before UK courts the treatment an applicant would receive before the ECtHR. UK courts are interpreting and applying exactly the same Convention rights as the ECtHR. They are also prompted by s.2 HRA to 'take into account' relevant Strasbourg jurisprudence when determining claims under the HRA. The United Kingdom has remained a Contracting State to the European Convention on Human Rights (ECHR); therefore it remains possible for an individual who has exhausted remedies under the HRA, without success, to make an application to the ECtHR.[6] In determining the application, the ECtHR now has the benefit of the prior consideration of Convention rights issues by the UK courts. In some instances a claim under the HRA may have been considered by three different UK courts, all the way up to the Supreme Court. At each level there is the opportunity for the UK courts to initiate a dialogue with the ECtHR on a particular Convention rights issue. They can do this explicitly, or, as explained in the following paragraphs, implicitly, and it is no secret for UK judges that their judgments under the HRA might eventually be considered by the ECtHR.

On the other side of the equation, the ECtHR has made it very clear that it is open to the possibility of dialogue with national courts. It has held on numerous occasions that the machinery of protection established by the Convention 'is subsidiary to the national systems safeguarding human rights',[7] and in its view:

> [N]ational courts should initially have the opportunity to determine questions of the compatibility of domestic law with the Convention and that, if an application is nonetheless subsequently brought before the Court, it should have the benefit of the views of the national courts, as being in direct and continuous contact with the forces of their countries.[8]

[4] A. M. Slaughter, "A Typology of Transjudicial Communication" (1994) 29 *University of Richmond Law Review* 99, 113.

[5] See Chapter 5, this volume.

[6] European Convention on Human Rights, art.35. If a claimant has succeeded before a UK court, he or she no longer has victim status before the ECtHR.

[7] *Seal v United Kingdom*, Application no.50330/07, 7 December 2010, at [53].

[8] *A v United Kingdom*, Application no.3455/05, 19 February 2009, at [154].

Furthermore, for it to correctly apply the margin of appreciation 'limiting the spectrum of the ECtHR's interference in certain matters to an "external" review of the compatibility of domestic acts with the Convention',[9] the ECtHR must take account of the perspective of the national court. The desire for dialogue has also been expressed extra-judicially by judges of the ECtHR. In 2010, Jean-Paul Costa, president of the ECtHR, stated that it was essential that 'domestic judicial authorities assume ownership of the Convention; that there should be, so to speak, a distribution of responsibilities in the field of human rights protection between the national authorities and the Court'.[10]

Clearly therefore, at least in theory, there is scope for communication between UK courts and the ECtHR, initiated by one, responded to by the other, with a willingness on the part of both to change position as a result. However, in practice use of the metaphor of dialogue to describe the interaction between the courts is not so straightforward. First, despite its best efforts to improve, the ECHR system is breaking down under the strain of too many applications, and lengthy delay plagues still the system. If the metaphor of dialogue implies a quick exchange on the interpretation and application of Convention rights, this does not happen in practice and, unless the matter is expedited, an applicant can wait on average five years for their application to be determined by the ECtHR. One example is the litigation which took place to challenge the indefinite retention of DNA samples and profiles by police in the United Kingdom. The first judgment of a UK court, finding the practice compatible with Convention rights, was given on 22 March 2002.[11] An appeal was dismissed by the Court of Appeal[12] and an appeal from that judgment dismissed by the House of Lords on 22 July 2004.[13] The unsuccessful claimants then lodged an application with the ECtHR and, on 4 December 2008, the Grand Chamber unanimously found a violation of art.8 of the ECHR. The dialogue then continued back to the UK level and, taking into account the interpretation and application of Convention rights on this issue by the ECtHR, the Supreme Court overturned the judgment of the House of Lords and found the practice incompatible with art.8 in relation to a different claimant on 18 May 2011.[14] This particular dialogue between the courts, eventually resulting in a consensus on the legal position, took more than nine years. A successful claimant must then wait even longer for a change in the law as a

[9] C. L. Rozakis, "The European Judge as Comparatist" (2005) 80 *Tulane Law Review* 257, 272–73.
[10] European Court of Human Rights, *Dialogue between Judges*, 5.
[11] *R. v Chief Constable of South Yorkshire, Ex p. S; R. v Chief Constable of South Yorkshire Ex p. Marper* [2002] EWHC 478 (Admin).
[12] [2002] EWCA Civ 1275.
[13] [2004] UKHL 39.
[14] *R. (GC) v The Commissioner of Police of the Metropolis* [2011] UKSC 21.

result of a judgment of the ECtHR or declaration of incompatibility. As the Joint Committee on Human Rights has noted, the United Kingdom's generally good record on implementation 'is undermined to a considerable extent by the very lengthy delays in implementation in those cases where the political will to make the necessary changes is lacking'.[15] Many would argue that it is stretching the meaning of dialogue quite a bit by using it to describe an exchange of views, and eventual change in the law, over such a lengthy period.

A second problem is that it is still possible for the ECtHR to be considering applications against the United Kingdom where the Convention rights issue has not actually been considered already by UK courts. Whilst this can also be attributed to delay in some instances, there are those applications where, due to the design of the HRA, it has not been possible to bring the Convention rights argument before the courts at the UK level. In particular, the ECtHR does not regard the declaration of incompatibility, available under s.4 HRA, as an effective remedy which must be sought prior to an application being brought.[16] Therefore, an applicant whose argument is essentially that a provision of primary legislation is incompatible with Convention rights need not bring proceedings under the HRA first. This was the position in *Greens and MT v UK*,[17] where the applicant prisoners brought a further application concerning the ban on prisoner voting. As the ban was contained in primary legislation[18] the ECtHR concluded that there was no effective remedy available to them utilising either s.3 or s.4 HRA, and it therefore did not matter that they had not brought domestic proceedings first.[19] In other applications to the ECtHR there has been no prior consideration of Convention rights issues by a UK court as the claim is simply not possible under UK law. One example was the application of Max Mosley, whose argument was that the United Kingdom had violated its positive obligation under art.8 by failing to impose a legal duty on the *News of the World* to notify him in advance of its intention to publish material invasive of his private life and thereby enable him to seek an injunction.[20] It is not possible under the HRA to bring a claim in relation to a failure to legislate[21] and therefore it was not considered by the ECtHR to be a barrier to this part of his application that he had not raised it before the UK courts first.

[15] Joint Committee on Human Rights, *Enhancing Parliament's Role in Relation to Human Rights Judgments 2009–2010*, HL Paper 85, HC 455, p.59.

[16] *Burden v United Kingdom*, Application no.13378/05, 29 April 2008.

[17] Application nos 60041/08 and 60054/08, 23 November 2010.

[18] Representation of the People Act 1983.

[19] Application nos 60041/08 and 60054/08, 23 November 2010, at [66]–[72].

[20] *Mosley v UK* Application no.48009/08, 10 May 2011.

[21] HRA, s.6(6).

But the most serious obstacle to dialogue between the courts is the fact that, in most HRA claims, UK courts, particularly courts lower than the Supreme Court, are content to simply apply Convention jurisprudence and not enter into a protracted and conscious dialogue with the ECtHR. In his essay, Masterman has examined the impact of s.2 HRA and the fact that UK courts almost always consider themselves bound by this case law, as made clear by Lord Bingham in his judgment in *Ullah* in 2004.[22] Recently the Supreme Court confirmed:

> [where] there is a clear and constant line or decisions whose effect is not inconsistent with some fundamental or procedural aspect of our law, and whose reasoning does not appear to overlook or misunderstand some argument or point of principle, we consider that it would be wrong for this Court not to follow that line.[23]

Following Strasbourg case law in this way makes it quite difficult for the courts to communicate with the ECtHR, respond to its judgments or change position as a result of feedback on an interpretation of Convention case law. The exchange is better described as a monologue or a matter of prior consensus. If a UK court, applying settled Convention law, finds against a claimant and that claimant makes an application to the ECtHR, the claim will usually be found to be inadmissible by the ECtHR.

Government lawyers now regularly rely upon domestic jurisprudence to support their argument that an application is inadmissible, and the ECtHR is not reluctant to rely upon the decisions of UK courts either. For example, in *Abu Hamza v United Kingdom*[24] the applicant claimed that his trial had been unfair. The ECtHR stated that it agreed with the trial judge and the Court of Appeal that nothing that had been done by the authorities could be treated as an assurance that the applicant would not be prosecuted.[25] In relation to the issues of delay and adverse publicity, it adopted the approach of the UK courts generally, noting:

[22] See Chapter 5, this volume. *R. v Special Adjudicator Ex p. Ullah* [2004] UKHL 26; [2004] 2 A.C. 323, at [20].

[23] *Manchester City Council v Pinnock* [2010] UKSC 45, at [48] (Lord Neuberger giving the judgment of the Court). See also *Cadder v Her Majesty's Advocate* [2010] UKSC 43. This confirmed the position previously adopted in *R. v Special Adjudicator Ex p. Ullah* [2004] UKHL 26; [2004] 2 A.C. 323, at [20] (Lord Bingham). See further R. Masterman, "Section 2(1) of the Human Rights Act 1998: Binding Domestic Courts to Strasbourg" [2004] P.L. 725; M. Amos, "The Principle of Comity and the Relationship between British Courts and the European Court of Human Rights", in P. Eeckhout and T. Tridimas (eds), *Yearbook of European Law 2009* (Oxford: Oxford University Press, 2010); and R. Masterman, "Interpretations, Declarations and Dialogue: Rights Protection under the Human Rights Act and Victorian Charter of Human Rights and Responsibilities" [2009] P.L. 112.

[24] Application no.31411/07, 18 January 2011.

[25] Application no.31411/07, 18 January 2011, at [35].

> the United Kingdom courts are well aware of that risk ... The Court shares their view that a fair trial can be held after intensive adverse publicity ... As Lord Hope stated in *Montgomery* ... it is not the purpose of Article 6 to make it impracticable to bring those who are accused of crime to justice.[26]

In the present case it shared the view of the Court of Appeal that there was no violation of art.6.[27] His application was rejected as manifestly ill-founded. This clearly cannot be described as an example of dialogue. All of the courts are applying the same law in what is more accurately described as a monologue followed by eventual confirmation of the legal position.

Dialogue in Practice

At this point it is tempting to conclude that whilst in theory there is scope for it, in practice there is in fact very little dialogue between UK courts and the ECtHR; and, when it does occur, it is extraordinarily protracted, in one instance taking more than nine years to reach a consensus. However, that would be unduly pessimistic and not entirely accurate. It is important to remember that given the delays in the Convention system, and the fact that the HRA has only been in force since 2 October 2000, it is only in the last few years that real dialogue between the courts has started to emerge. It is true that in the majority of HRA claims, the clear and constant jurisprudence of the ECtHR is simply applied by UK courts and that is the end of the matter. If an applicant in such an instance has been unsuccessful at the national level and applies to the ECtHR, the most likely outcome will be that his or her application will be found inadmissible as manifestly ill-founded, the ECtHR applying its own jurisprudence in full agreement with the UK court.[28] However, it is clear that as the higher courts, in particular the Supreme Court, gain in confidence with their role under the HRA, the exchange between the courts is moving from one of monologue and consensus to one where, in certain defined instances, dialogue is sought, and eventually does take place.

At present, three paths to dialogue can be identified from the case law. The first is where a UK court considers that a relevant judgment of the ECtHR is wrong. This possibility has been present in UK law for some time and was first mentioned by Lord Hoffmann in his judgment in *Alconbury*,[29] where he stated that the UK courts were not bound by a decision of the ECtHR which

[26] Application no.31411/07, 18 January 2011, at [39].
[27] Application no.31411/07, 18 January 2011, at [40].
[28] See, for example, *PF and EF v United Kingdom*, Application no.28326/09, 23 November 2010.
[29] *R. v Secretary of State for Environment, Transport and the Regions Ex p. Alconbury Developments Ltd* [2001] UKHL 23; [2001] 2 W.L.R. 1389.

compelled a conclusion 'fundamentally at odds with the distribution of powers under the British constitution'.[30] However, there are very few examples and almost all concern art.6 and are judgments of the Supreme Court, Privy Council or House of Lords.[31] A high-profile example was the judgment of the Supreme Court in *R. v Horncastle*,[32] where it held that it was not going to follow the decision of the ECtHR in *Al-Khawaja and Tahery v United Kingdom*.[33] It explained its decision as follows:

> There will, however, be rare occasions where this court has concerns as to whether a decision of the Strasbourg Court sufficiently appreciates or accommodates particular aspects of our domestic process. In such circumstances it is open to this court to decline to follow the Strasbourg decision, giving reasons for adopting this course. This is likely to give the Strasbourg Court the opportunity to reconsider the particular aspect of the decision that is in issue, so that there takes place what may prove to be a valuable dialogue between this court and the Strasbourg Court. This is such a case.[34]

The second path to dialogue opens when a UK court considers that the subject matter of the claim comes within the United Kingdom's margin of appreciation. However, this particular opportunity for dialogue occurs very rarely in practice and the possibility was not confirmed by the House of Lords until 2008 in the case of *In re P*.[35] Here the claimants argued that it was not compatible with arts 8 and 14 for a couple to be excluded from consideration as the adoptive parents of a child on the ground only that they were not married to each other. ECtHR jurisprudence on the question was fairly conservative and Lord Hoffmann explained that the House of Lords might be going further than the ECtHR had ever gone were it to find a breach of art.14.[36] Nevertheless, he concluded that this was an issue within the national margin of appreciation and therefore:

> [I]t is for the court in the United Kingdom to interpret articles 8 and 14 and to apply the division between the decision-making powers of courts and Parliament in the way which appears appropriate for the United Kingdom.[37]

[30] *R. v Secretary of State for Environment, Transport and the Regions Ex p. Alconbury Developments Ltd* [2001] UKHL 23; [2001] 2 W.L.R. 1389, at [76].

[31] See, for example, *Brown v Stott* [2003] 1 A.C. 681 and *Boyd v The Army Prosecuting Authority* [2002] UKHL 31.

[32] [2009] UKSC 14.

[33] (2009) 49 E.H.R.R. 1.

[34] [2009] UKSC 14, at [11] (Lord Phillips, giving the judgment of the Court).

[35] [2008] UKHL 38; [2008] 3 W.L.R. 76.

[36] [2008] UKHL 38; [2008] 3 W.L.R. 76, at [29]

[37] [2008] UKHL 38; [2008] 3 W.L.R. 76, at [37]–[38]. See also the observations of Lord Hope at [50], Baroness Hale at [120] and Lord Mance at [129].

But to date this is the only firm example. Whilst both Baroness Hale and Lord Brown referred to the margin of appreciation in the context of the ban on hunting which was subject to challenge in the *Countryside Alliance* case,[38] neither was prepared to hold that this meant the UK courts were entirely free to make up their own minds on the question of compatibility, free from the influence of the ECtHR.

The third path by which UK courts engage in a dialogue with the ECtHR is less straightforward, but far more common than the previous two. This path to dialogue arises from the nature of ECtHR jurisprudence itself. It is frequently stated that the decisions of the ECtHR can lack clarity,[39] are not 'entirely convincing'[40] and 'do not speak with one voice'.[41] In his judgment in *McCaughey*,[42] which concerned the circumstances in which the procedural duty to investigate a death under art.2 arose, Lord Phillips stated that he was not alone in 'having difficulty in identifying the precise circumstances in which the procedural obligation attaches'[43] from his reading of the Grand Chamber's judgment in *Šilih v Slovenia*.[44] Lord Hope observed that only the 'most starry-eyed admirer of the Strasbourg court could describe the guidance that the Grand Chamber offered ... as clear'.[45] Given the confusion which can be present in Convention jurisprudence, in determining a claim under the HRA often a UK court is placing its own interpretation on unclear and contradictory jurisprudence in order to reach a decision. Usually the court will make its confusion over the case law clear, but guidance and eventual confirmation from the ECtHR is usually not expressly sought, despite comments such as those made by the judges in *McCaughey*. Nevertheless, where Convention case law is not in a satisfactory state, this is exactly the type of application which is found to be admissible by the ECtHR, resulting in a dialogue which has not been explicitly sought by UK courts. Whilst it could be argued that this type of case should not be included within the examples of dialogue, by making it clear that they are struggling with the intended meaning

[38] *R. (Countryside Alliance) v Her Majesty's Attorney General* [2007] UKHL 52, at [124]–[132] (Baroness Hale) and at [141] (Lord Brown).

[39] *N v Secretary of State for the Home Deparmtnet* [2005] UKHL 31; [2005] 2 A.C. 296, at [11] and [14] (Lord Nicholls).

[40] *N v Secretary of State for the Home Deparmtnet* [2005] UKHL 31; [2005] 2 A.C. 296, at [91] (Lord Brown).

[41] *R. (Al-Skeini) v Secretary of State for Defence* [2007] UKHL 26, at [67] (Lord Rodger).

[42] *In the matter of an application by Brigid McCaughey and another for Judicial Review (Northern Ireland)* [2011] UKSC 20.

[43] *In the matter of an application by Brigid McCaughey and another for Judicial Review (Northern Ireland)* [2011] UKSC 20, at [46] (Lord Phillips).

[44] (2009) 49 E.H.R.R. 996.

[45] *In the matter of an application by Brigid McCaughey and another for Judicial Review (Northern Ireland)* [2011] UKSC 20, at [73]. Similar struggles with Convention case law are evident in *R. (G) v The Governors of X School* [2011] UKSC 30 *and E (Children)* [2011] UKSC 27.

of the ECtHR, UK courts are implicitly seeking a dialogue and possible confirmation from the ECtHR, particularly if there are dissenting judgments on the correct interpretation. Even if an interaction with the ECtHR is not expressly sought, there remains an awareness on the part of the UK court, particularly if it finds against a claimant, that the matter could end up before the ECtHR where it will give its response.

Often the outcome for the UK court in those instances where it is not entirely sure of the correct interpretation of Convention case law is a good one. An example is *Carson v United Kingdom*,[46] where the Grand Chamber expressly agreed with the decision of the majority of the House of Lords that the failure to up-rate the pensions of certain UK pensioners living abroad was in violation of art.1 of Protocol No. 1 in conjunction with art.14. But on other occasions the dialogue implicitly sought does not go so well. An example is the litigation to challenge the indefinite retention of fingerprints, DNA samples and profiles by the police. This was obviously a difficult case for the House of Lords with little directly relevant ECtHR authority to draw upon; Lord Steyn noting that what authorities there were 'are relevant but far from conclusive'.[47] Baroness Hale, not looking for directly relevant authority, dissented from the majority opinion that art.8(1) was not engaged, observing that the 'general tenor of the jurisprudence of the European Court and Commission of Human Rights is that the retention, keeping or storage or private information by state institutions is an interference with article 8(1) rights'.[48] However, the House of Lords concluded unanimously, on the assumption that art.8(1) was engaged, that the interference was justified under art.8(2). With a dissenting judgment and observations that Strasbourg case law was not clear on this particular point, whilst the House of Lords was not consciously entering into a dialogue with the ECtHR, implicitly this was what was being sought. Relying upon its own jurisprudence, and the judgment of Baroness Hale, the ECtHR held that the retention of fingerprints, cellular samples and DNA profiles was an interference with private life.[49] Obviously unimpressed by the judgment of the House of Lords, it did not refer to it at all when considering the question of justification and afforded a very narrow margin of appreciation to the United Kingdom. Finding that there was a very clear violation of art.8 it stated:

> [T]he blanket and indiscriminate nature of the powers of retention of the fingerprints, cellular samples and DNA profiles of persons suspected but not

[46] Application no.42184/05, 16 March 2010.
[47] *R. v Chief Constable of South Yorkshire Police Ex p. S; R. v Chief Constable of South Yorkshire Police Ex p. Marper* [2004] UKHL 39, at [26].
[48] *R. v Chief Constable of South Yorkshire Police Ex p. S; R. v Chief Constable of South Yorkshire Police Ex p. Marper* [2004] UKHL 39, at [76].
[49] Applications nos 30562/04 and 30566/04, 4 December 2008, at [86].

> convicted of offences ... fails to strike a fair balance between the competing public and private interests ... the respondent State has overstepped any acceptable margin of appreciation in this regard.[50]

In these three types of case, and ignoring for the moment the problem of delay, it is clear that UK courts are entering into a dialogue with the ECtHR. These interactions really do constitute communication between two courts: initiated by one, responded to by another with 'awareness on the part of both participants of whom they are talking to and a corresponding willingness to take account of the response' as defined by Slaughter. But it is important to note that this is not the position in every HRA claim. As previously discussed, the most usual outcome is that the UK court will apply ECtHR jurisprudence and the exchange between the courts is more accurately described as a monologue from the ECtHR to the UK courts, the interpretation and application of Convention rights a matter of consensus. But the conditions under which dialogue takes place are becoming much clearer and, as the judicial and political appetite for dialogue with the ECtHR continues to grow, it is next important to consider the impact of dialogue between a national and a supranational court.

Outcomes from Dialogue

In 2006 the Department for Constitutional Affairs maintained that dialogue between the courts in part accounted for the significant reduction in the number of adverse decisions against the United Kingdom.[51] It is true that since the ECtHR has started to consider applications where Convention rights arguments had already been considered by a UK court, there has been a consistent decrease in the number of violations on the part of the United Kingdom found by the ECtHR. In 2009 and 2010 only 14 violations were found.[52] But this decrease cannot be attributed to dialogue between the courts. What has really resulted in fewer violations has been the UK courts applying the clear and constant jurisprudence of the ECtHR, rather than seeking clarification of a difficult point of law, submitting that the ECtHR jurisprudence was wrong or seeking to fit a particular issue within the United Kingdom's margin of appreciation. In fact it is often in those instances where the UK courts have implicitly sought dialogue with the ECtHR that it is more likely to find a

[50] Applications nos 30562/04 and 30566/04, 4 December 2008, at [125].
[51] *Review of the Implementation of the Human Rights Act*, DCA 38/06 (2006), 4.
[52] European Court of Human Rights, *Annual Reports*, 2009 and 2010.

violation, such as in the series of judgments concerning the impact of art.8 on proceedings for possession.[53]

The United Kingdom gets better results than previously because, under the HRA, UK courts finally have the opportunity to consider Convention rights arguments for themselves before an application is made to the ECtHR. It is actually a monologue from the ECtHR to the UK courts, and consensus on the majority of Convention jurisprudence, which has produced this outcome. Where dialogue does take place, it has a different kind of impact. Commentators have identified three broad areas of impact which are reflected in the experience of UK courts with the ECtHR. The first is norm creation; the second the legitimacy of international and domestic human rights law; and the third the power of the judiciary.

The Creation of Human Rights Norms

In engaging in a dialogue about the interpretation and application of Convention rights UK courts and the ECtHR are making human rights norms which are different from those which would be made by a single court acting alone. Many commentators agree that the quality of decision-making is therefore better,[54] and the norms created by both enjoy greater protection from political interference. For example, Helfer and Slaughter state that the 'participants—both individuals and institutions—understand themselves to be linked through their participation in, comprehension of, and responsibility for legal discourse'. In their view this means that 'participants are perceived by non-participants—politicians and other domestic institutions—as engaged in activity that should ordinarily be protected from direct political interference'.[55] The ECtHR firmly believes that listening to national courts helps it to find the best and most acceptable solution for all Contracting States.[56]

The role played by the jurisprudence of the ECtHR in national immigration law is a good example and UK courts have played a particular role in its development. The first example is *Ullah*,[57] which had been a difficult judgment for the House of Lords as the claimants sought to push the boundaries of human rights protection on deportation, arguing that articles of the ECHR, in addition to art.3, could be engaged in relation to the removal of an individual from the United Kingdom where the anticipated treatment in the

[53] *McCann v United Kingdom*, Application no.19009/04, 13 May 2008, and *Kay v United Kingdom*, Application no.37341/06, 21 September 2010.

[54] Slaughter, "A Typology of Transjudicial Communication", 132.

[55] L. Helfer and A. M. Slaughter, "Toward a Theory of Effective Supranational Adjudication" (1997) 107 *Yale Law Journal* 273, 370.

[56] European Court of Human Rights *Dialogue between Judges*, 9.

[57] *R. (Ullah) v Special Adjudicator* [2004] UKHL 26; [2004] 2 A.C. 323.

receiving state would be in breach of the ECHR but would not meet the minimum requirements of art.3. The case was particularly difficult because there was no direct authority from the ECtHR on the question their Lordships were required to answer. As Lord Steyn noted in relation to arts 9, 10 and 11:

> The jurisprudence of the ECtHR does not provide much help. On the other hand, the possible engagement of these articles has not been ruled out. I would also not rule out their possible application in the field of immigration decisions.[58]

Their Lordships concluded that deportation would be incompatible with the Convention only where it was shown that there would be a flagrant denial or gross violation of the right whereby the right would be completely denied or nullified in the destination country.[59] Faced with almost the same facts in *Z and T*,[60] and with no Strasbourg case law directly on point, in determining admissibility the ECtHR adopted a test the same as that established by the House of Lords.[61]

The second example is *N v UK*,[62] where the Grand Chamber of the ECtHR adopted the conclusion of the House of Lords, in reliance upon ECHR jurisprudence—that it was only in the most exceptional circumstances, that an applicant suffering an illness could resist deportation on art.3 grounds. Their Lordships had surveyed relevant Convention jurisprudence, and formulated a test; whilst approval was not explicitly sought from the ECtHR, this was an instance where, at least implicitly, dialogue would be expected.[63] The ECtHR essentially adopted the test formulated by the House of Lords finding:

> The decision to remove an alien who is suffering from a serious mental or physical illness to a country where the facilities for the treatment of that illness are inferior to those available in the Contracting State may raise an issue under Article 3, but only in a very exceptional case, where the humanitarian grounds against the removal are compelling.[64]

[58] *R. (Ullah) v Special Adjudicator* [2004] UKHL 26; [2004] 2 A.C. 323, at [48].

[59] *R. (Ullah) v Special Adjudicator* [2004] UKHL 26; [2004] 2 A.C. 323, at [24] (Lord Bingham).

[60] *Z and T v UK*, Application no.27034/05, 28 February 2006.

[61] Other examples of the ECtHR explicitly relying upon or approving of UK case law include *Burke v United Kingdom* (dec.), Application no.19807/06, 11 July 2006; *Uttley v United Kingdom* (dec.), Application no.36946/03, 29 November 2005; *Coghlan v United Kingdom* (dec.), Application no.8535/02, 29 November 2005.

[62] Application no.26565/05, 27 May 2008.

[63] *N v SSHD* [2005] UKHL 31.

[64] Application no.26565/05, 27 May 2008, at [42]. See also *Saadi v UK*, Application no.13229/03, 29 January 2008 and *O'Halloran v UK*, Application nos 15809/02 and 25624/02, 29 June 2007.

The role played by the UK courts in these two immigration decisions of the ECtHR also demonstrates that dialogue can give national courts a voice in the creation of human rights norms and ensure that the ECtHR is aware of national concerns in making law for other Contracting States. As Waters has observed:

> Norm export occurs when domestic courts and other domestic law-declaring fora articulate or champion a particular domestic norm at the transnational level. The norm is then picked up by other transnational actors, thus being diffused around the world and becoming part of the international legal discourse. If the norm becomes sufficiently embedded in a large number of other domestic or international legal regimes, it becomes the dominant normative standard on a given issue.[65]

Finally, dialogue can help to ensure the maintenance of national differences particularly if the ECtHR has determined that subject matter of the claim engages a State's margin of appreciation. In such instances it is important for the ECtHR to have the perspective of the national court. The jurisprudence of the ECtHR over the years demonstrates that there is room for national differences in the creation of European human rights standards and judges have a crucial role in this process given the 'destiny of the national cultural traditions in Europe is in the first place entrusted to the constitutional courts, which express the voice of the national constitutions'.[66] The judgment of the House of Lords in *In re P*[67]—that it would adopt a different approach than the ECtHR in relation to discrimination against unmarried couples due to the national margin of appreciation—is a good example.

Obviously dialogue between a national court and a supranational court can have a positive impact on norm creation, but it is also important to appreciate the negative impact which is primarily generated from the uncertainty created in the national legal system about which court has the final word on the application and interpretation of Convention rights—a problem which is only exacerbated by the delays in the ECHR system. There are already a number of examples illustrating this difficulty—including the litigation concerning police retention of fingerprints, DNA samples and profiles—although one of the best illustrations is provided by the numerous decisions, both nationally and by the ECtHR, concerning the impact of art.8 of the ECHR on proceedings for possession. Since the judgment of the House of Lords in

[65] M. A. Waters, "Mediating Norms and Identity: The Role of Transnational Judicial Dialogue in Creating and Enforcing International Law" (2005) 93 *Georgetown Law Journal* 487, 503. See also the comments of M. Arden, European Court of Human Rights, *Dialogue between Judges*, 24–25.

[66] M. Cartabia, "Europe and Rights: Taking Dialogue Seriously" (2009) 5 *European Constitutional Law Review* 5, 23. See also Waters, "Mediating Norms and Identity".

[67] [2008] UKHL 38; [2008] 3 W.L.R. 76.

Qazi v London Borough of Harrow[68] in 2003, UK courts at all levels have struggled with the applicability of art.8, and the role of the courts, particularly the question of whether or not an individual faced with an order for possession, could raise a proportionality argument before a court. When the issue came before the ECtHR, in two key judgments[69] it expressly disagreed with the position which had been adopted by the UK courts. However, at the UK level clarity was still not really provided until 2010 when the Supreme Court gave its judgment in *Pinnock*,[70] where it followed Strasbourg jurisprudence and overruled three earlier decisions of the House of Lords in order to do so. But the matter was still not finally settled until 2011 by the Supreme Court in *Powell*,[71] when Lord Phillips confirmed that the ECtHR

> has made it plain that ousting the powers of the court to consider the proportionality of dispossessing a non-secure tenant is not compatible with the procedural requirements of article 8.[72]

Whilst this could be portrayed as an excellent example of dialogue, the UK courts putting their position on Convention law to the ECtHR for an answer, the real cost of the resulting uncertainty for claimants, their advisers and the legal system generally must also be recognised.

A further problem is that in some instances, the UK court may not feel sufficiently qualified to enter into dialogue with the ECtHR to create norms regarding the interpretation and application of Convention rights. The pattern of decision-making emerging demonstrates that whilst the Supreme Court is confident to enter into dialogue over the interpretation and application of art.6 (the right to a fair trial),[73] it is less confident in relation to other Convention rights such as art.8 (the right to respect for private life).[74] This is most likely explained by the fact that UK courts are far more comfortable with the right to a fair trial, which has been protected at common law for many hundreds of years, than with the right to privacy, which has never been

[68] [2003] UKHL 43.

[69] *McCann v UK*, Application no.19009/04, 13 May 2008; *Kay v UK*, Application no.37341/06, 21 September 2010.

[70] *Manchester City Council v Pinnock* [2010] UKSC 45.

[71] *Mayor and Burgesses of the London Borough of Hounslow v Powell* [2011] UKSC 8.

[72] *Mayor and Burgesses of the London Borough of Hounslow v Powell* [2011] UKSC 8, at [75]. See, further, I. Loveland, "A Tale of Two Trespassers: Reconsidering the Impact of the Human Rights Act on Rights of Residence in Rented Housing: Part 1" [2009] E.H.R.L.R. 148; I. Loveland, "A Tale of Two Trespassers: Reconsidering the Impact of the Human Rights Act on Rights of Residence in Rented Housing: Part 2" [2009] E.H.R.L.R. 495; A. Latham, "Talking Without Speaking, Hearing Without Listening? Evictions, the Law Lords and the European Court of Human Rights" [2011] P.L. 730.

[73] See, for example, *R. v Horncastle* [2009] UKSC 14.

[74] See, for example, *R. (Countryside Alliance) v Her Majesty's Attorney General* [2007] UKHL 52.

a right explicitly protected by the common law. In future years it may be that UK courts will become more confident with the interpretation and application of the 'newer' rights and there will not be the current unevenness between which rights are subject to dialogue and which rights are not.

The Legitimacy of National and International Human Rights Law

By engaging in dialogue, UK courts and the ECtHR are also having an impact on their own legitimacy and the legitimacy of both the ECHR and the HRA. As Tremblay has observed:

> A deliberative dialogue is a process that has a particular normative value, and, at least in certain contexts, it may have legitimating force. It may confer legitimacy on its outcomes, whatever the final action or decision.[75]

The ECtHR must engage in a dialogue with national courts to encourage compliance with its judgments.[76] To maintain respect as a supranational court it needs to demonstrate that it is actively listening to the national position and, in its eventual decision, that it has carefully considered what national courts have decided. But dialogue with the ECtHR can also help the HRA, and judgments interpreting and applying the HRA, to gain more legitimacy.

Essentially the HRA is a transplant of international law to the UK legal system. For UK courts to also transplant to the national legal system, without any question, the case law accompanying the ECHR does jeopardise the assimilation of the ECHR, via the HRA in the UK legal system, the legitimacy of the courts and the legitimacy of the HRA itself.[77] As already discussed, UK courts are more often than not eager to follow Strasbourg jurisprudence without any question of dialogue, and this has already done serious damage to the standing and legitimacy of the HRA in the UK legal system where it is generally perceived as a European instrument having little to do with national law. The HRA has not attained the status of a Bill of Rights in the national consciousness and there remains limited public knowledge of it and respect for it.[78] Although it has not been a failure, its position in UK law has always been insecure and it is currently under review by a Commission which is considering the creation of a British Bill of Rights.

[75] L. Tremblay, "The Legitimacy of Judicial Review: The Limits of Dialogue between Courts and Legislatures" (2005) I.J.C.L. 617, 632.
[76] N. Krisch, "The Open Architecture of European Human Rights Law" (2008) 71 M.L.R. 183, 206. See also Helfer and Slaughter, "Toward a Theory of Effective Supranational Adjudication", 285.
[77] Waters, "Mediating Norms and Identity", 559.
[78] See, further, M. Amos, "Problems with the Human Rights Act and How to Remedy Them: Is a Bill of Rights the Answer?" (2009) 72 M.L.R. 883.

More dialogue between UK courts and the ECtHR would improve the legitimacy of the HRA, at least in the eyes of the general public.[79] Politically there remains a desire to distance the UK legal system from Europe. Where UK courts question a particular judgment of the ECtHR and suggest that it is incorrect, or not in keeping with the UK approach to a particular issue (where there is room for the margin of appreciation), judges are effectively distancing the UK legal system from Europe. This is often perceived as 'standing up' to a European institution thereby meeting the political objective and increasing the legitimacy of the HRA. As a result, that particular judgment will be seen as more British and less European, therefore deserving of more respect.

However, whilst more dialogue would boost the legitimacy of the HRA there can also be a negative impact, particularly where dialogue between the courts results in the ECtHR finding that the UK courts have incorrectly interpreted and applied Convention rights. If what results is a prolonged debate between the two courts, government, Parliament, or all, it can result in a loss in legitimacy for the HRA, the ECHR, and the national and international court. The most recent illustration of this problem is the highly charged political issue of prisoner voting. UK prisoners are currently disqualified from voting in domestic elections and elections to the European Parliament.[80] In 2001 the Divisional Court found that the ban was not in violation of Convention rights, stating:

> [I]n deference to the legislature courts should not easily be persuaded to condemn what has been done, especially where it has been done in primary legislation after careful evaluation and against a background of increasing public concern about crime.[81]

In 2005 the Grand Chamber of the ECtHR held that the ban resulted in a clear violation of art.3 of Protocol No. 1 as there was no evidence that Parliament had ever sought to weigh the competing interests or to assess the proportionality of the blanket ban. Furthermore, in its view, it was evident from the judgment of the national court that the ban 'was in general seen as a matter for Parliament and not for the national courts ... [t]he court did not therefore undertake any assessment of proportionality of the measure itself'.[82]

The decision of the Grand Chamber was not well received by government and no change to the law resulted. The matter therefore was once again the

[79] The experience of the UK is not unique and similar problems arise in other Contracting States. See, further, Krisch, "The Open Architecture of European Human Rights Law", 191.
[80] Representation of the People Act 1983.
[81] *R. (Pearson) v Secretary of State for the Home Department; Hirst v Attorney-General* [2001] EWHC Admin (239); [2001] H.R.L.R. 39, at [20]. Leave to appeal was refused by the Court of Appeal [2001] EWCA Civ 927.
[82] *Hirst v United Kingdom (No.2)*, Application no.74025/01, 6 October 2005, at [79]–[80].

subject of litigation under the HRA. In 2007, implementing the decision of the Grand Chamber, the Scottish Registration Appeal Court found the disqualification incompatible with art.3 of Protocol No. 1 and made a declaration of incompatibility.[83] Other UK courts where similar claims were brought came to the same conclusion on lawfulness, but declined to make a declaration of incompatibility as one had already been made.[84] In 2010 the issue was again before the ECtHR in the case of *Greens and MT v UK*,[85] although the applicant prisoners had not sought a domestic remedy. The ECtHR, referring to its judgment in *Hirst*, again found a violation of art.3 of Protocol No. 1, stating that such a 'general, automatic and indiscriminate restriction on a vitally important Convention right must be seen as falling outside any acceptable margin of appreciation, however wide that margin might be'.[86] Again this decision was not well received by government and, in February 2011, 234 MPs voted to keep the ban in place. Whilst the dialogue between the courts eventually resulted in both assuming the same position on the violation of Convention rights, the fact that government and Parliament were not in agreement has had a negative impact on the legitimacy of the HRA, ECHR, UK courts and the ECtHR. Whilst it would obviously not have been the best result for prisoners, in the eyes of the general public at least, more legitimacy for the HRA would have been gained by the UK courts not changing from their original position as a result of the decision of the ECtHR. A very similar analysis could be made of the litigation over the retention of DNA samples and profiles.

The impact of dialogue on legitimacy of the HRA, ECHR and the national and supranational courts remains a double-edged sword. More dialogue, with the UK courts effectively seeking a different interpretation of Convention rights from the ECtHR, increases the legitimacy of the HRA and UK courts but undermines the legitimacy of the ECtHR and ECHR at the domestic level. Not engaging in dialogue and simply accepting the clear and constant jurisprudence of the ECtHR means that the HRA and UK judges suffer a loss in legitimacy. If the issue is politically charged and government and Parliament are not in agreement with the courts, all of the courts and the human rights instruments suffer, although it is important to remember that the stalemate now reached on prisoner voting is an isolated, nevertheless serious, example.

[83] *Smith v Scott* 2007 S.L.T. 137.

[84] *Traynor v Secretary of State for Scotland* [2007] C.S.O.H. 78; *R. v Secretary of State Ex p. Toner and Walsh* [2007] N.I.Q.B. 18; *Chester v Secretary of State for Justice* [2009] EWHC 2923 (Admin).

[85] Application nos 60041/08 and 60054/08, 23 November 2010.

[86] Application nos 60041/08 and 60054/08, 23 November 20, at [82].

Judicial Power

Although the example of prisoner voting discussed above illustrates a lack of real judicial power when it comes to difficult political issues, this situation is unusual and commentators have observed that dialogue between national and supranational courts more usually results in a dramatic increase in the power of the judiciary. Reference has already been made to the view that judges, via dialogue, are creating a 'community of law' which is 'at least partially protected from direct political interference'. By referring to and reinforcing one another 'they create a space that is insulated, but not isolated, from politics, economics and society'.[87] Putting to one side the example of prisoner voting, it is clear that by engaging in a dialogue with the ECtHR, UK judges have been able to take many decisions that they might not have been prepared to take without it. Waters has observed that 'a striking feature of transnational judicial dialogue is its transformative impact on domestic courts' roles within the domestic polity'. This means less deference to the executive branch, and also that courts

> are less likely to defer to domestic audiences on issues of individual human rights, and are more willing to import foreign and international norms into domestic law, even when those norms do not necessarily comport with majority views.[88]

Once again a good example is the litigation concerning the retention of fingerprints, samples and DNA profiles. Although a majority of the House of Lords had concluded in *Marper*[89] that the retention of fingerprints, samples and DNA profiles was not a violation of art.8, once the Grand Chamber of the ECtHR had determined that it was,[90] when the matter was considered again by the Supreme Court it found violation of art.8 and used s.3 of the HRA to fashion a remedy thereby bypassing Parliament and avoiding the protracted debates which have accompanied prisoner voting reform.[91] Parliament will also not be involved in the reception into UK law of the ECtHR's judgment in *Al-Skeini v UK*,[92] where it found, contrary to the conclusion of the House of Lords,[93] that, at the relevant time, the HRA applied to the activities of British armed forces in Iraq. However, the litigation over prisoner voting and the resulting political debates illustrate the problems an

[87] Helfer and Slaughter, "Toward a Theory of Effective Supranational Adjudication", 371.
[88] Waters, "Mediating Norms and Identity", 520.
[89] *R. v Chief Constable of South Yorkshire Police Ex p. S; R. v Chief Constable of South Yorkshire Police Ex p. Marper* [2004] UKHL 39.
[90] *S and Marper v United Kingdom*, Applications nos 30562/04 and 30566/04, 4 December 2008.
[91] *R. (GC) v Commissioner of Police of the Metropolis* [2011] UKSC 21.
[92] Application no.55721/07, 7 July 2001.
[93] *R. (Al-Skeini) v Secretary of State for Defence* [2007] UKHL 26.

increase in judicial power can bring. Whilst dialogue might confer legitimacy on the ECHR and HRA, this is clearly not democratic legitimacy. As McCrudden has observed, ignoring the problem of participation, whilst at the same time 'appearing to engage in a closed dialogue with other judges at the supranational level, may weaken the protection of human rights rather than reinforcing it'.[94] Although Parliament passed the HRA, containing s.2, and thereby formalised a relationship between UK courts and the ECtHR, seeking to confer democratic legitimacy on judge-made law in this way is notoriously difficult.[95]

The Future of Dialogue

There is now considerable interest in dialogue between UK courts and the ECtHR and there are those who maintain that it must continue and expand. Mary Arden, a judge of the Court of Appeal, has argued that the ECtHR must show more respect for the role of national institutions via the principle of subsidiarity and application of the doctrine of the margin of appreciation. She would like UK courts to be able

> to say to the Strasbourg Court that it has not made the principle clear, or that it has not applied the principle consistently, or that it has misunderstood national law or the impact of its decisions on the legal system in the relevant part of the United Kingdom.

However, she is clear to point out that she is not suggesting a 'free-for-all, or that domestic courts should be free to reinvent the wheel on human rights jurisprudence'. But she would like an approach more flexible than that presently adopted by UK courts in relation to s.2 HRA.[96] It is difficult to see how this would differ from the approach which has already been adopted by UK courts.

The bare bones of what it means for UK courts and the ECtHR to engage in dialogue have now emerged. What is clear is that dialogue is quite rare and is sought only when a higher court, usually the Supreme Court, believes that a judgment of the ECtHR is wrong or where the subject matter of the claim engages the United Kingdom's margin of appreciation. It is also implicitly sought, as has been argued in this essay, where UK courts are not really

[94] C. McCrudden, "A Common Law of Human Rights? Transnational Judicial Conversations on Constitutional Rights" (2000) O.J.L.S. 499, 531–32.

[95] See, for example, the debates over democratic justifications for judicial review such as T. R. S. Allan, "Constitutional Dialogue and the Justification of Judicial Review" (2003) 23 O.J.L.S. 563 and "Legislative Supremacy and Legislative Intent: A Reply to Professor Craig" (2004) O.J.L.S. 563.

[96] European Court of Human Rights, *Dialogue between Judges*, 25–26.

sure of the correct interpretation of a particular area of Convention jurisprudence. This latter path to dialogue is actually where the most expansion is likely because, increasingly, the claims before UK courts concern areas where the Convention jurisprudence is not settled. One recent example is *Home Office v Tariq*,[97] where the Supreme Court dealt with a difficult issue concerning the interpretation of art.6 and, having reviewed relevant ECtHR case law, determined that

> the demands of national security may necessitate and under European Convention law justify a system for handling and determining complaints under which an applicant is, for reasons of national security, unable to know the secret material by reference to which his or her complaint is determined.[98]

Therefore, the use of a statutory closed material procedure before the Employment Tribunal was lawful. It is almost certain that whilst it did not explicitly seek a dialogue with the ECtHR on this particular issue, a dialogue will eventually result with the ECtHR giving a further opinion on this difficult and developing area of law. This is made even more likely by the fact that Lord Kerr dissented from the opinion of the majority on one issue.

For dialogue to expand, it is important to appreciate that this would require UK courts to take a far bolder and perhaps less careful approach to Convention jurisprudence than has previously been the case. They would need to be more willing to find particular judgments to be incorrect or to assert the United Kingdom's margin of appreciation more often, although the approach presently taken when Convention jurisprudence is unclear would most likely continue with courts being more explicit that their interpretation should eventually be the one adopted by the ECtHR. But the difficulties in abandoning a careful and incremental approach would be numerous, and past experience demonstrates that where a UK court deviates from the general tenor of Strasbourg case law, as occurred in *Marper*, this almost always results in the ECtHR reaching the opposite conclusion, particularly if there are dissenting judgments and subsequent academic critique. Furthermore, setting out to identify more claims where the United Kingdom's margin of appreciation might be engaged is no simple task. The margin of appreciation utilised by the ECtHR remains inconsistent and occasionally incoherent.[99]

If carried out carefully, more dialogue can bring with it the benefits outlined above. The impact made by UK courts on the development of ECHR standards in national immigration law has already been discussed. But it also

[97] [2011] UKSC 35.

[98] 2011] UKSC 35, at [36] (Lord Mance). See also *Tomlinson v Birmingham City Council* [2010] UKSC 8.

[99] R. St J. MacDonald, "The Margin of Appreciation", in R. St J. MacDonald, F. Matscher and H. Petzold (eds), *The European System for the Protection of Human Rights* (London: Martinus Nijhoff, 1993), p.85.

must be appreciated that such opportunities do not often arise. An unchecked desire to be involved in norm creation at the ECtHR level on the part of a national court can simply result in the ECtHR reaching the opposite conclusion. Not only does this impact poorly on the United Kingdom's record before the ECtHR, but it creates confusion and uncertainty in the national legal system as well. Although a positive dialogue with the ECtHR can create legitimacy for both the HRA and the UK courts—particularly if the UK position on a difficult issue of Convention jurisprudence has been adopted—the ECtHR finding against the UK position can result in a serious loss in legitimacy for international law. Were the number of instances where a UK court and the ECtHR had diametrically opposed views to increase, with no subsequent consensus with the position of the ECtHR reached by UK courts, this could call into question the force and effect in the United Kingdom of international human rights law and the judgments of an international human rights court. Finally, it is important to remember that this is a dialogue between judges, and more dialogue on a wider range of Convention rights issues will further increase the power of the judiciary. Where the UK courts and the ECtHR reach agreement on a particular issue, this can be a fairly intractable force for change unless, as has occurred with prisoner voting, government and Parliament remain opposed.

Conclusion

Since October 2000, UK courts have moved in their relationship with the ECtHR from monologue to dialogue. There is now clear evidence of fruitful dialogue taking place between the courts even though it might take nine years or more to reach a consensus. Recent case law from the Supreme Court indicates that there is judicial willingness to go down the path of more dialogue, although very carefully and one step at a time. Whilst the HRA remains in force, it is likely that the paths to dialogue already established will continue to be utilised, but it is important that when dialogue is sought the UK court is sure of its particular interpretation and application of Convention rights. Working carefully and thoroughly, via dialogue with the ECtHR, UK courts can have a real impact on norm creation by the ECtHR, maintain national differences where these are warranted, champion the rights of unpopular groups and secure some much needed legitimacy for the HRA.

Part III

A Permanent Revolution in Legal Reasoning?

7

Human Rights and Judicial Technique

JACK BEATSON

Introduction

THE QUESTION WE HAVE BEEN ASKED TO ADDRESS is whether there has been a revolution in legal reasoning and, if so, whether it is a permanent one: these comments on judicial technique are set in that context. The changes in judicial style and approach since the enactment of the Human Rights Act (HRA) will be compared with those in the 21 years between 1963 and 1984 when modern public law was formed. Has the HRA led to changes which are (a) of a different order, and (b) irreversible? This essay suggests that the answer to the first question is 'yes', but that to the second, at this stage of the development of the law, is 'no'. The last part of the essay suggests that it is fundamentally important not to sideline or forget the potential of the common law.

The changes between 1963 and 1984 were indeed major: from *Ridge v Baldwin*,[1] through *Anisminic*[2] and *Padfield*,[3] to *GCHQ*.[4] The courts deployed powerful and restrictive principles of statutory construction limiting general words in statutes, and in doing so they relied on common law principles to accord special protection to certain interests, notably that of access to the court, which Laws LJ has described as a 'constitutional right',[5] and procedural fairness.

So, why is it correct to see the changes in judicial technique because of the HRA as of a different order? The Convention is concerned with rights and not, as some see the common law, with interests or misuses of public power.[6] Secondly, the Convention accords special protection to a wider range of rights than those accorded a 'constitutional' or 'fundamental' status at common law.

[1] [1964] A.C. 40.
[2] [1969] 2 A.C. 147.
[3] [1968] A.C. 997.
[4] [1985] A.C. 374.
[5] *R. v Lord Chancellor Ex p. Witham* [1998] Q.B. 575.
[6] See, for example, *R. v Somerset CC Ex p. Dixon* (1998) Env L.R. 111, 121 (Sedley LJ); *R. (Quila) v Secretary of State for the Home Department* [2010] EWCA Civ 1482, at [37].

Proceedings of the British Academy, **183**, 163–175.

It does so by bringing them within the scheme of protection of ss. 6 and 8 HRA. Thirdly, the requirements of 'legality' and 'justification' reverse the Diceyan principle (reflected in *Malone v Commissioner of Police of the Metropolis*)[7] that all that is not prohibited is permitted. Finally, and perhaps most importantly, both the 'unique interpretative technique'[8] of s.3 and the power in s.4 to declare primary legislation to be contrary to fundamental norms are step changes. As Tom Hickman has said, these factors show that the HRA 'reaches places that the common law cannot reach'.[9]

Concern with Rights and Whether They Have Been Breached Rather than Misuse and Abuse of Power

The fact that the Convention creates 'rights' means that the courts have had to refocus their inquiries. They must consider the existence and extent of the relevant right, and whether it has been breached. This has involved a greater concern with substance than our courts have been used to in the context of public law adjudication, particularly in the exercise of the judicial review jurisdiction. It has also led to less concern with whether the decision-maker took the Convention rights into account—i.e. with the decision-making process—and more concern with whether a Convention right has been breached.[10] It must be said that some cases do show a concern with process, and the approach eschewing such concern has been criticised.[11] It has been criticised, inter alia, on the ground that the court needs to see whether the decision-maker has taken into account relevant considerations and has excluded irrelevant ones, particularly where there may be issues of relative institutional competence as between the decision-maker and the court. It has also been criticised because the person affected is entitled to have a decision made or remade on a proper basis.

Moreover, in determining the outcome of a particular case, courts have taken into account whether the decision-maker has in fact exercised such relative institutional or factual expertise as it possesses in its decision-making procedure. So, for example, in *R. (on the application of Begum) v Denbigh*

[7] [1979] Ch. 344.

[8] *R. v J* [2004] UKHL 42; [2005] 1 A.C. 562, at [15].

[9] T. Hickman, *Public Law after the Human Rights Act* (Oxford: Hart Publishing, 2010), p.23.

[10] See *R. (SB) v Governors of Denbigh High School* [2006] UKHL 15, at [29]; *Belfast City Council v Miss Behavin' Ltd* [2007] UKHL 29; [2007] 1 W.L.R. 1420, at [13] and [31].

[11] In *Belfast City Council v Miss Behavin' Ltd* [2007] UKHL 29; [2007] 1 W.L.R. 1420. See J. Beatson, S. Grosz, T. Hickman, R. Singh with S. Palmer, *Human Rights: Judicial Protection in the United Kingdom* (London: Sweet & Maxwell, 2008), pp.3–120ff.

High School Governors,[12] the House of Lords took into account the fact that school governors consulted mainstream Muslim opinion before adopting a dress code permitting girls to wear the shalwar kameeze, which its consultees considered satisfied Islamic requirements, but not permitting a long coat-like garment known as a jilbab. Where the decision-maker has addressed the balance between the rights and interests affected it will be difficult for the court to upset its conclusion, but where it has not, its views will be entitled to less weight.[13]

In assessing whether there has been a breach of a Convention right the courts have also had to face up to the consequences of the fact that, as recognised in some cases,[14] the task for the court is to determine whether there has been a breach, and not to determine whether the decision-maker could have reasonably concluded that there was no breach. A comparison of the decisions of the Court of Appeal in *R. v Ministry of Defence Ex p. Smith*[15] and of the Strasbourg Court in *Smith & Grady v United Kingdom*[16] shows the problems of the latter. But the complicating factor in this context is that, while it is for the court to determine whether the applicable Convention right has been violated, and notwithstanding the greater concern with substance, on many aspects of a case the distinction between review and substitution of judgment remains not only relevant but important.

This is so for a number of reasons. First, the structure of most of the Convention rights means that the process of deciding whether they have been breached involves a balancing of interests. This is so even in the case of apparently unqualified rights such as those under art.6. Secondly, while the Convention creates a number of norms of general application, often it does not presume that there is only one legitimate outcome in a given situation. Neither does the Strasbourg Court. In the context of 'proportionality' the court decides only whether a given choice by the decision-maker is *dis*proportionate, not what the most proportionate option is. Thirdly, there are situations in which, for the reasons canvassed above, the court will not be as well placed to evaluate a consideration taken into account by the decision-maker in reaching its conclusion.

[12] [2006] UKHL 15; [2007] 1 A.C. 100, at [14]–[15], [33]–[34], [44], [88], [98].
[13] *Belfast City Council v Miss Behavin' Ltd* [2007] UKHL 29; [2007] 1 W.L.R. 1420, at [37] (Baroness Hale).
[14] *Huang v Secretary of State for the Home Department* [2007] UKHL 11; [2007] 2 A.C. 167; *Belfast City Council v Miss Behavin' Ltd* [2007] UKHL 29; [2007] 1 W.L.R. 1420.
[15] [1997] Q.B. 517.
[16] (1999) 29 E.H.R.R. 493.

The Language Used by Courts to Analyse an Issue

The second change concerns the language of the analysis. In assessing the respective roles of the primary decision-maker and the court the notions and concepts deployed by the courts are now articulated in the language of the European Convention on Human Rights (ECHR) rather than the classic language and terminology of common law public law. So, instead of 'ultra vires' there is 'legality', and instead of the melange of language brought together in and since the *Wednesbury* case[17]—'unreasonableness' and 'irrationality'—there is now 'proportionality', 'necessity' (art.8(2)), 'absolutely necessary' (art.2(2)) and 'strictly necessary' (art.6(1)). Decisions such as the *GCHQ*[18] case show that the first steps were in fact taken well before the enactment of the HRA. At the initial stage the process could be seen as a mere linguistic or terminological change. Later, as the decision in *R. v Secretary of State for the Home Department Ex p. Pierson*[19] shows, the pace of change increased and started to change in nature. This was particularly so in the period immediately prior to the introduction of the legislation that became the HRA. And, since the HRA, the language has had a more substantive meaning. The change of language has also led to a more open and direct discussion.

'Justiciability', 'Institutional Competence' and 'Weight'

One manifestation of the greater directness is that discussion in the older cases and literature in terms of 'justiciability' (which encompassed both what the courts *are able to do* and what they *should do*) has now largely been replaced and recast in wider and more nuanced (although no less controversial) terms: 'deference', 'respect', 'margin of discretion' or, as I would prefer, 'institutional capacity or competence' or 'weight'. The new language is no less controversial because, with regard to the respective roles of the court and elected bodies, while some judges[20] have considered the courts should accord significant 'weight' to the assessment of a primary decision-maker which is directly democratically accountable, others[21] have emphasised both the duty of the court

[17] *Associated Provincial Picture Houses Ltd v Wednesbury Corporation* [1948] 1 K.B. 223.

[18] [1985] A.C. 374.

[19] [1998] A.C. 539.

[20] See, for example, Lord Mance in *R. v Quayle* [2005] EWCA Crim 1415; [2005] 1 W.L.R. 3642, at [68]; *Belfast City Council v Miss Behavin' Ltd* [2007] UKHL 29; [2007] 1 W.L.R. 1420, at [46]; Lord Hoffmann in *Secretary of State for the Home Department v Rehman* [2001] UKHL 47; [2003] 1 A.C. 153, at [50]–[54]; and *R. (on the application of ProLife Alliance) v BBC* [2003] UKHL 23; [2004] 1 A.C. 185, at [76].

[21] See, for example, Lord Bingham in *A v Secretary of State for the Home Department (Belmarsh)* [2004] UKHL 56; [2005] 2 A.C. 68, at [42] and (extra-judicially) Lord Steyn, "Deference: A Tangled Story" [2005] P.L. 346.

not to accord 'deference' on this ground alone and the importance of a court deciding a matter which has been remitted to it provided it is institutionally capable of doing so.[22]

In assessing institutional capacity or competence, courts have taken into account a number of factors and have done so in a more open and direct way than was the case when the language used was of 'justiciability'. They have considered whether the determination requires an assessment of a question which the primary decision-maker is better equipped to make or whether it is a question of policy. The extent of a threat of terrorism or of public disorder[23] are examples of the first. They involve an element of prediction rather than ascertaining facts. Whether cannabis is a danger to the public,[24] the frequency of medical reviews of long-term detained persons,[25] and whether corporal punishment in schools should be banned[26] are examples of the second. The cases concerning cannabis and frequency of medical reviews show the overlap between the two categories.

The courts have also stated that they will be constrained where the form of an adversarial hearing means they cannot confidently draw general conclusions. The leading examples are *Re S (Care Order)* in 2002[27] and *Bellinger v Bellinger* in 2003.[28] In *Re S* the court had regard to the difficulty of assessing the far-reaching consequences for local authorities and the allocation of scarce resources if it used s.3 to read the Children Act as requiring a system of 'starred care plans' to ensure an effective remedy against defaulting local authorities. In *Bellinger v Bellinger* the need for extensive consultation and discussion of social policy and the administrative feasibility of extending the state of 'marriage' to post-operative transsexuals and the unsuitability of the courts for this were the reasons it was not possible to read the relevant statutory provision (Matrimonial Causes Act 1973, s.11(c)) in a Convention-compatible way.

The Material before the Court

Two aspects of this issue must be distinguished. The first is the question of the material that *is in fact* before the court. It is dealt with only briefly here,

[22] See also *RJR MacDonald v A-G Canada* [1995] 3 S.C.R. 199, at [136] (McLachlin J).
[23] *R. (on the application of Gillan) v Commissioner of Police of the Metropolis* [2006] UKHL 12; [2006] 2 A.C. 307, at [17], [64]; *R. (Laporte) v Chief Constable of Gloucester* [2006] UKHL 55; [2007] 2 A.C. 105, at [55] and [106].
[24] *R. v Quayle* [2005] EWCA Crim 1415; [2005] 1 W.L.R. 3642.
[25] *R. (Munjaz) v Mersey Care NHS Trust* [2005] UKHL 58; [2006] 2 A.C. 148.
[26] *R. (on the application of Williamson) v Secretary of State for Education and Employment* [2005] UKHL 15; [2005] 2 A.C. 246.
[27] [2002] UKHL 10; [2002] 2 A.C. 291, at [43].
[28] [2003] UKHL 21; [2003] 2 A.C. 467.

because the impact of the new jurisdiction on questions such as the extent of disclosure required, when there should be oral evidence and cross-examination, and the extent to which intervention by third parties—whether public interest groups or other public bodies—should be permitted and, if so, on what conditions, is dealt with in Rabinder Singh's essay in this volume.[29]

There is a related but narrower point which concerns *how the material is presented to the court*. This concerns the extent to which legal process has been changed to enable courts to deal with matters when the operation of classical notions of what the adjudicative process requires has prevented or inhibited them from doing so. I have in mind the extent to which the rights of the defence have been limited because of particular concerns. For example, there are now special procedures to protect vulnerable witnesses—in particular those who allege they have been raped or sexually assaulted—by limiting the right of the defence to confront and question the complainant. Also, arrangements have been made to enable courts to adjudicate in cases where the state does not wish to reveal the full case against a person in open court. The best known examples concern suspected terrorists where, for reasons of national security, special advocates—who have all the information but who are not allowed to communicate it to the defendant or his lawyers or to take instructions from them—make submissions to the court in a closed hearing. The initial arrangements in cases concerning suspected terrorists were the product of legislation ('encouraged' by the Strasbourg Court),[30] but their use in other contexts has been the product of judicial decisions.[31]

The second aspect is what material *should be* before the court and should be required by the court. How widely should a court range in considering an issue? Should it have before it all the material necessary for the resolution of an issue even if it is what Lon Fuller described as 'polycentric' and which has traditionally been regarded as non-justiciable? One response to the concerns expressed in *Re S* and *Bellinger v Bellinger* might be to widen the material before the courts, for instance by 'Brandeis briefs' of the sort used in United States public law litigation. But to go too far would further erode the line between adjudication and the sort of public inquiry which many appear to favour (particularly if chaired by a judge)[32] for solving broad problems or dealing with institutional failures. And as to what the court should see and take account of when the defendant does not see it, it has been recognised by the House of Lords (albeit, it would appear, only because of a judgment of

[29] Chapter 8.

[30] In *Chahal v United Kingdom* (1997) 23 E.H.R.R. 413, at [131].

[31] See *R. (Roberts) v Parole Board* [2005] UKHL 45; [2005] 2 A.C. 738l; *R. v H* [2004] UKHL 3; [2004] 2 A.C. 134.

[32] For the difficulties that may arise if a serving judge chairs, see J. Beatson, "Should Judges Conduct Public Inquiries?" (2005) 121 L.Q.R. 221.

the Strasbourg Court) that a defendant must have sufficient information about the case against him to mount a defence and that, where he does not, the use of the special advocate procedure will not enable the court to determine the matter.[33]

Sections 3 and 4 of the Human Rights Act

The third and fourth important changes are the powerful new interpretative tool afforded by s.3 HRA requiring the court to read a legislative provision in a Convention-compatible way where 'it is possible to do so' and the power in s.4 enabling it to make a declaration of incompatibility where it is not possible to do so. The obligation under s.3 has been described by Lord Hoffmann as 'a modified judicial review of statutes'.[34] Section 4 gave the court a new power to examine primary legislation and declare it to be contrary to fundamental norms.

The courts recognised the power of the tool contained in s.3 from the outset, although the earliest cases showed an understandable caution when describing its limits. Thus, in determining whether it was 'possible' to read a statutory provision compatibly with the Convention rights, they were initially concerned with 'linguistic' possibility.[35] But they have now set aside what might have become a 'translation exercise' with distinctions turning on a semantic lottery depending on the linguistic choices of the draftsman to concern with what is 'conceptually possible' and (as we have seen) the difficulties of courts ascribing a meaning which involves a conclusion on broad questions of social and economic policy.

It is clear that s.3 enables a meaning to be given which differs from what Parliament had in mind,[36] and to alter the meaning of a statute to make it conform to higher principle; that is to the Convention rights. What the courts can do is thus fundamentally different from what they can do by applying the 'ordinary' principles of statutory interpretation.[37] The breadth of the power is

[33] *AF (No.3) v Secretary of State for the Home Department* [2010] 2 A.C. 269; [2009] 3 W.L.R. 74 following *A v UK* (2009) 49 E.H.R.R. 29, at [220].

[34] *Matadeen v Pointu* [1999] 1 A.C. 98, at 110. See also *R. v Secretary of State for the Home Department Ex p. Simms & O'Brien* [2000] 2 A.C. 115, at 131.

[35] See *R. v Lambert* [2001] UKHL 37; [2002] 2 A.C. 545, at [80]; *Re S (Care Order)* [2002] UKHL 10; [2002] 2 A.C. 291, at [41].

[36] *Ghaidan v Godin-Mendoza* [2004] UKHL 30; [2004] 2 A.C. 557, at [105] (Lord Hope); *Sheldrake v DPP* [2004] UKHL 30; [2004] 2 A.C. 557, at [28] (Lord Bingham).

[37] *Wilson v First County Trust* [2003] UKHL 40; [2004]1 A.C. 816, at [61] (Lord Nicholls). On the difference between the sort of updating construction which can be given to a statute at common law and that which can be given using s.3, cf. *Fitzpatrick v Sterling Housing Association* [2001] 1 A.C. 27 with *Ghaidan v Godin Mendoza* [2004] UKHL 30; [2004] 2 A.C. 557.

shown by the decision of the Divisional Court in *R. (Hammond) v Home Secretary*.[38] The court read a statutory provision stating that the High Court was to determine certain minimum terms of imprisonment for those sentenced to life imprisonment 'without an oral hearing' as enabling an oral hearing in 'exceptional cases' where such a hearing was required to comply with a prisoner's art.6 rights. In the House of Lords neither party challenged this. Lord Bingham described what the Divisional Court had done as an 'interpolation'.[39] The effect appears to, or comes close to, being a contradiction of the statutory words. Nevertheless, it was relied on in a later House of Lords case.[40] It would thus appear that the only limit on what the court can do pursuant to s.3 is that set by constitutional propriety.

Notwithstanding the breadth of their approach when considering the compatibility of a statutory provision with the Convention, the courts have resisted the temptation to proceed straight to s.3. There are many examples of courts resolving a case without recourse to s.3 because the meaning of a provision construed according to the 'ordinary' principles of construction involves no apparent incompatibility with the Convention.[41] They have been right to do so. Not only was it the HRA's aim to preserve the sovereignty of the United Kingdom Parliament, but the 'ordinary' approach is more likely to promote clarity as to the meaning of the provision under examination and to preserve the integrity of our statute law.[42] This is because it does not alter the *meaning* of the statutory language, whereas, as is clear, if s.3 is applied the meaning of the statutory language is altered, for example by 'reading in' Convention rights to the provision. I return to this when considering the continuing importance of the common law.

The courts have also not succumbed to the temptation to escape from the hard choices they may have to make in considering the application of s.3 HRA by diluting the content of the Convention rights and thus finding that there is no apparent incompatibility with a Convention right.[43]

Turning to the relationship between ss. 3 and 4, although, in 2004, Lord Steyn in the *Ghaidan* case thought that the number of cases in which a

[38] *R. (on the application of Hammond) v Secretary of State for the Home Department* [2004] EWHC 2753 (Admin); [2005] 4 All E.R. 1127 (Div Ct); [2005] UKHL 69; [2006] 1 A.C. 603 (HL).

[39] *R. (on the application of Hammond) v Secretary of State for the Home Department* [2005] UKHL 69; [2006] 1 A.C. 603, at [17].

[40] *Secretary of State for the Home Department v MB* [2007] UKHL 46; [2008] 1 A.C. 440.

[41] Some are given in Beatson, Grosz, Hickman, Singh, with Palmer, *Human Rights: Judicial Protection in the United Kingdom*, pp.5–33, n.102.

[42] J. Beatson, "Common Law, Statute Law, and Constitutional Law" [2007] Stat. L. Rev. 1.

[43] See Beatson, Grosz, Hickman, Singh, with Palmer, *Human Rights: Judicial Protection in the United Kingdom*, pp.5–51.

declaration of incompatibility had been made indicated that a wrong turn had been taken, there was little agonising by the courts in determining that s.3 was to have primacy. But giving it such primacy could, as Francesca Klug has suggested,[44] be seen as a rebalancing away from the scheme promoted by the Labour government in 1997 and legislated in 1998. This is because parliamentary sovereignty and a role for Parliament were carefully preserved in both the proposals and the HRA. Despite the undoubted force of Klug's point, three powerful reasons for giving primacy to s.3 have prevailed.

First, if the purpose of the HRA was to 'bring rights home', giving s.3 primacy promoted and gave effect to that purpose because, where the court has to have recourse to s.4, no domestic remedy is given.[45] As Lord Scott said, making a declaration is not in any orthodox sense a judicial act and the effect of doing so is political not legal.[46] Secondly, the terms of s.4 expressly make the interpretation of legislation in accordance with s.3 an essential preliminary step to making a declaration of incompatibility. Thirdly, it is only when it is certain that it is not possible to read the legislation in a Convention-compatible way that it can be justifiable to invoke the fast-track parliamentary procedure to remove the incompatibility.[47]

Relationship with the Strasbourg Court and Its Decisions

What of the relationship between our courts and the Strasbourg Court? Our courts must, under s.2 HRA, 'take into account' the jurisprudence of the Strasbourg Court. Suggestions, notably by Laws LJ,[48] that a distinctly UK human rights law should be developed have not been taken up. The general approach is to mirror the Strasbourg jurisprudence as it evolves but not to stretch our jurisprudence beyond it. The approach of the courts is 'no less, but certainly no more' than Strasbourg.[49] The consequence is that UK courts can, in a case in which there is no relevant Strasbourg jurisprudence or where

[44] F. Klug, "The Human Rights Act—A 'Third Way' or 'Third Wave' Bill of Rights?" [2001] E.H.R.L.R. 361.

[45] See *Ghaidan v Godin Mendoza* [2004] UKHL 30; [2004] 2 A.C. 557, at [106] (Lord Rodger).

[46] *A v Secretary of State for the Home Department (Belmarsh)* [2004] UKHL 56; [2005] 2 A.C. 68, at [142]–[145].

[47] *A v Secretary of State for the Home Department (Belmarsh)* [2004] UKHL 56; [2005] 2 A.C. 68, at [15] (Lord Nicholls).

[48] See, for example, *R. (on the application of Pro Life Alliance) v BBC* [2002] EWCA Civ 297; [2002] 3 W.L.R. 1080, at [33]–[34].

[49] *R. (Ullah) v Special Adjudicator* [2004] UKHL 26; [2004] 2 A.C. 323, at [20] (Lord Bingham) modified by Lord Brown in *R. (Al Skeini) v Secretary of State for Defence* [2007] UKHL 26; [2008] 1 A.C. 153, at [106].

the case law is not clear, or in a state of development, spend many pages trying to predict what the Strasbourg Court would do if the matter came before it.[50] The approach and the consequent need for a predictive approach reflect the view that the purpose of the HRA is to provide a domestic remedy for breach of the United Kingdom's international obligations and remove the need to have recourse to Strasbourg. But, as I have said elsewhere,[51] the 'certainly no more' part of the approach also shows an acute sense by our judges of the limits of their constitutional role. The judgments rejecting the challenges to the statutory ban on hunting suggest that the approach is likely to be applied with particular firmness by courts when considering whether an Act of Parliament is compatible with Convention rights[52]; although Lord Scott's approach differed on this[53] and Baroness Hale stated that there is nothing to prevent the courts from developing the common law to give greater protection to human rights than Strasbourg.[54]

It is also important to note that while initially the view that a UK court should not give less protection than the Strasbourg Court appeared to be a rule, recent cases show this outcome is not invariable. Where the Strasbourg decision is by the Grand Chamber and is 'clear and authoritative' and 'expresses an entirely coherent view' it will generally be followed.[55] But where the decision is not by the Grand Chamber there is now more willingness to depart from decisions of the Strasbourg Court. So, the House of Lords and the Supreme Court have not followed decisions of the Strasbourg Court where they considered that Strasbourg had not been fully appraised of the legal position in this country, the reasons for that position, and the way in which the law sought to safeguard the position of the person whose Convention rights appeared to be infringed, or did not understand them.[56]

[50] See this volume, Chapter 5, pp.134–35.

[51] J. Beatson, "Reforming an Unwritten Constitution" (2010) 126 L.Q.R. 48, at 70.

[52] *R. (Countryside Alliance) v Attorney General* [2007] UKHL 52; [2008] 1 A.C. 719, at [126]; *R. (Animal Defenders International) v Secretary of State for Culture, Media and Sport* [2008] UKHL 15; [2008] 1 A.C. 1312.

[53] *R. (Animal Defenders International) v Secretary of State for Culture, Media and Sport* [2008] UKHL 15; [2008] 1 A.C. 1312, at [44]–[46].

[54] *R. (Animal Defenders International) v Secretary of State for Culture, Media and Sport* [2008] UKHL 15; [2008] 1 A.C. 1312, at [53].

[55] See *R. v Horncastle* [2009] UKSC 14; [2010] 2 A.C. 373, at [118] (Lord Brown), citing *AF (No.3) v Secretary of State for the Home Department* [2010] 2 A.C. 269; [2009] 3 W.L.R. 74, at [98] (Lord Rodger): "*Argentoratum locutum, iudicium finitum*—Strasbourg has spoken, the case is closed."

[56] *Doherty v Birmingham City Council* [2008] UKHL 57; [2009] 1 AC 367; *R. v Horncastle* [2009] UKSC 14; [2010] 2 A.C. 373, affirming [2009] EWCA Crim 964. See also *R. (GC) v Commissioner of Police of the Metropolis* [2011] UKSC 21; [2011] 1 W.L.R. 1230, a leapfrog appeal from the Divisional Court which held that, notwithstanding the Strasbourg decision in *Marper v United Kingdom* (2009) 48 E.H.R.R. 501, it was bound by *R(S) v Chief Constable of South Yorkshire* [2004] UKHL 39; [2004] 1 W.L.R. 2196.

Two observations can be made about the current position. First, in such cases (see especially *R. v Horncastle* on the use of hearsay evidence in criminal trials in the light of the Strasbourg decision in *Al Khawaja v United Kingdom*)[57] great care has been taken in explaining English law and why the Strasbourg authorities which had been relied on did not in fact compel a finding that English law did not meet Convention requirements. Secondly, the decision in *Horncastle* uses a novel way of presenting a judgment, in some ways akin to a collaborative piece of academic work. The main judgment, by Lord Phillips, with which the rest of the court agreed, contained four annexes, two prepared by other judges. Lord Mance analysed the position in other common law countries. Lord Judge CJ analysed the Strasbourg cases. He explained what would have happened on their facts had they come before an English court to show that English common law courts do not accord less protection than the civilian jurisdictions considered in the Strasbourg cases.

Finally, I observe that I consider criticisms that our courts have used their powers under the HRA and the Strasbourg jurisprudence improperly, for example to create a right to privacy, or to create rights for undeserving criminals and would-be immigrants, to be misplaced. An analysis of what courts have in fact done, as opposed to what it has been said they have done, makes this clear.

The Role of the Common Law

In a position where the common law is not compatible with a Convention right the courts will need to consider developing the common law to remove that incompatibility. Where the HRA and the Convention are given a 'horizontal effect', common law and equitable principles may require development, as has happened in the context of the protection of confidentiality and privacy. There is also some potential for this to happen in the context of contractual rights.[58] Before the HRA came into force there were signs[59] that in a situation in which the matter fell within the scope of a Convention right the common law would nevertheless be allowed to develop its capacity to afford protection to fundamental rights. Lester and Pannick argued this was needed to 'weave the Convention rights into the principles of the common law and equity so that they strengthen rather than undermine those

[57] (2009) 49 E.H.R.R. 2196.

[58] See Beatson, Grosz, Hickman, Singh, with Palmer, *Human Rights: Judicial Protection in the United Kingdom*, pp.4–242.

[59] See, for example, *Reynolds v Times Newspapers* [2001] 2 A.C. 127; *R. (on the application of Daly) v Secretary of State for the Home Department* [2001] UKHL 26; [2001] 2 A.C. 532; *Campbell v Mirror Group Newspapers* [2004] UKHL 22; [2004] 2 A.C. 457.

principles'.[60] Despite some judicial support[61] this has, however, not happened uniformly or consistently.

There are some signs of a tendency to sideline the common law in situations in which the Convention rights apply. See, for example, Lord Rodger in *Watkins v Home Office* who described the efforts of some judges in seeking to deploy the concept of constitutional rights in the law of tort as 'heroic'.[62] He stated that it was not worth doing, and that, if the matter fell within the scope of a Convention right, a claimant can be expected to invoke his remedy under the HRA rather than to seek to fashion a new common law right. Not all appellate judges take this view. So, in *R. (Animal Defenders) v Secretary of State for Culture, Media and Sport*, Baroness Hale considered in appropriate circumstances it is open to the courts to develop the common law to give greater protection to human rights than the Strasbourg jurisprudence.[63] In *JD v E Berkshire Community NHS Trust*, Lord Bingham, albeit in a dissenting judgment, considered that in such situations the common law should be allowed to develop analogically and incrementally rather than leaving difficult and important problems to be swept up by the Convention.[64] In the case of *Watkins* he said this could not be done where there was a settled principle pointing against such development, but that is simply a reflection of the nature of what is possible by incremental common law development and the limits of such development.[65]

If the fact that a matter falls within the scope of a Convention right is seen to have an inhibiting effect on the deployment and the development of the common law, that would be both unfortunate and distorting. It is unfortunate because it will lead to the fragmentation of the law and the possible atrophy of parts of the common law. It is distorting because the court is a public body with a duty to ensure compatibility where that is possible, and, as the confidence/privacy cases show, will do so. Sidelining the common law may also mean that where there is an overlap between issues concerning Convention rights and the principles upon which public authorities should exercise their discretion, familiar common law requirements (concerning the decision-making process, taking account only of relevant considerations, and acting for proper purposes) may be forgotten if the only question concerns the

[60] D. Pannick and A. Lester, "The Impact of the Human Rights Act on Private Law: The Knight's Move" (2000) 116 L.Q.R. 380, at 383.

[61] See *Doherty v Birmingham City Council* [2008] UKHL 57; [2009] 1 A.C. 367, at [109] (Lord Walker). See also *Smith v Chief Constable of Sussex* [2008] EWCA Civ 39.

[62] [2006] UKHL 17; [2006] 2 A.C. 395, at [64].

[63] *R. (Animal Defenders International) v Secretary of State for Culture, Media and Sport* [2008] UKHL 15; [2008] 1 A.C. 1312, at [53] (Baroness Hale).

[64] [2005] UKHL 23; [2005] 2 A.C. 373, at [50].

[65] [2006] UKHL 17; [2006] 2 A.C. 395, at [26].

decision itself. Finally, the common law is enduring and may in certain circumstances afford a remedy where the HRA does not, for example because of the statutory limitation on standing to victims and the one-year time limit for proceedings under s.6.

There is a reason of a different sort for not sidelining the common law. The HRA remains a controversial measure in the eyes of some important political and media interests. Sidelining the common law and basing decisions exclusively on the HRA and the Convention may have the effect of hiding what the common law is capable of in this context and possibly stoking hostility to the HRA. For that reason, it is important that cases should, where possible, be based on common law principles, and that the weaving process described by Lester and Pannick should take place. Additionally, even those who have argued that the doctrine of parliamentary sovereignty has been modified and qualified have not argued that it is beyond Parliament's power to repeal the HRA. Should the Act be repealed, it will be easier for public law to develop along a vibrant and vigorous common law-based trajectory without going through the wilderness years it experienced for the first half of the 20th century if it has not been sidelined in those areas in which the Convention rights apply.

Conclusion

The differences in the approach of different courts and different judges since the HRA has been in force in dealing with what on any view is a significant constitutional instrument are not surprising. Many of the differences (including the way account is taken of the Strasbourg jurisprudence and the role of the common law where a situation falls within the scope of a Convention right) may reflect the tension between the dominant view that the HRA simply provides a domestic remedy for breach of the United Kingdom's international obligations and the alternative (as yet minority) view[66] that it is a constitutionally significant measure creating a new domestic law of human rights.

Note. This is a lightly revised version of a paper presented at the Durham Human Rights Centre's conference in September 2010.

[66] Hickman, *Public Law after the Human Rights Act*, pp.24–49 finds it in *In Re McKerr* [2004] UKHL 12; [2004] 1 W.L.R. 807, at [63] (Lord Hoffmann) (and *quaere* at [75] (Lord Rodger)); *YL v Birmingham City Council* [2007] UKHL 27; [2008] 1 A.C. 95, at [4] (Lord Bingham) and [54] (Baroness Hale); *Re G (Adoption: Unmarried Couples)* [2008] UKHL 38; [2009] 1 A.C. 173, at [33]–[34] (Lord Hoffmann) and [129] (Lord Mance).

8

The Impact of the Human Rights Act on Advocacy

RABINDER SINGH

Introduction

I WRITE THIS ESSAY AT THE END of my career at the Bar. Doing so has given me the opportunity to reflect on the changes which have come about in the work of an advocate in this country as a result of the Human Rights Act 1998 (HRA). Inevitably these reflections are personal but I hope they are of some general interest too.

Before I make some specific observations it is worth noting one general point. In the years leading up to the coming into force of the HRA two different sorts of prediction tended to be made. Either it would make no difference at all or it would flood the courts with new claims, many of which it was thought would be unmeritorious. The truth is that neither prediction proved right. The HRA has bedded in surprisingly easily and quickly into the natural landscape of our existing legal system. It has not on the whole led to new procedures having to be devised. This is in part due to the all-pervasive nature of s.7(1) HRA, which allows the Convention[1] rights to be relied upon not only to found a cause of action but also in any legal proceedings, for example by way of defence. In practice, this has meant that the Convention rights tend to be relied upon not to launch an entirely new kind of claim but rather as an additional item in the toolkit of the practitioner, for example as a ground for judicial review, or to bolster an interpretation of legislation which is favourable to the claimant (pursuant to the strong interpretative obligation in s.3 of the HRA).

This tendency of the HRA to bed in naturally into our legal landscape has been reflected also in the context of procedure and evidence. The way in which courts and tribunals conduct proceedings has continued generally as before.

[1] In this essay I refer to the European Convention on Human Rights as the 'Convention' or the 'ECHR'.

Proceedings of the British Academy, **183**, 177–196.

So, if a point under the HRA is raised in criminal proceedings or ordinary civil proceedings, where live evidence and cross-examination are the norm, it will be possible to cross-examine a witness (for example a police officer) on factual matters which are relevant to the HRA issue in the case (was use of a certain policing technique proportionate?). However, in the type of proceedings where live evidence and cross-examination are far from the norm, points arising under the HRA will usually be dealt with in the same way as any other point, by way of written evidence and legal submission. This is typically how a claim for judicial review is conducted. This is significant in practice because experience suggests that the largest number of cases in which a point under the HRA is taken arise by way of judicial review. Nevertheless, it is notable that the HRA has had some impact on practice and procedure even in the context of judicial review proceedings.

Evidence

The first important impact of the HRA on advocacy has been on the kind of evidence which it is necessary and appropriate to deploy in litigation, whether an advocate is acting for the claimant or for the defendant. The court's role has changed as a result of the HRA, which often requires the court to assess the proportionality of a decision or measure, and may even require the court to adjudicate on the compatibility of primary legislation with the Convention rights. In particular, questions may arise as to the extent to which it is permissible to refer to statements made in Parliament in order to support or challenge the compatibility of primary legislation.

These issues were addressed by the House of Lords in *Wilson v First County Trust (No.2)*.[2] The opinion of Lord Nicholls of Birkenhead helpfully sets out the main points of principle as to the correct approach. Lord Nicholls observed:

> [The HRA] requires the court to exercise a new role in respect of primary legislation. This new role is fundamentally different from interpreting and applying legislation. The courts are now required to evaluate the effect of primary legislation in terms of Convention rights and, where appropriate, make a formal declaration of incompatibility.[3]

He went on to state that, in carrying out this exercise of evaluation, the court has to compare the effect of the legislation with the Convention right invoked and that the court must compare the policy objective of the legislation with

[2] [2003] UKHL 40; [2004] 1 A.C. 816.
[3] [2003] UKHL 40; [2004] 1 A.C. 816, at [61]–[67].

the policy objective which under the Convention may justify a prima facie infringement of that right. Moreover, when asking what is the policy objective of the legislation, the court must ask not, as it would when performing its traditional role of interpreting statutes, what is the objective of the legislation on its own terms but must instead look for 'the underlying social purpose'[4] which the legislation seeks to achieve.

Furthermore, as Lord Nicholls continued, the HRA requires the court to ask not only whether the legislation has a legitimate aim but also whether it satisfies the principle of proportionality:

> The court must decide whether the means employed by the statute to achieve the policy objective is appropriate and not disproportionate in its adverse effect. This involves a 'value judgment' by the court ...[5]

Although this function of performing a value judgment is not a new one for the courts of this country, it is relatively unusual in the context of primary legislation, leaving aside those areas which fall within the scope of directly effective European Union law. It requires courts, and therefore advocates appearing before them, to be comfortable when referring to, and analysing, data which may relate to policy justifications, including social and economic data. As Lord Nicholls put it, 'the court may need enlightenment on the nature and extent of the social problem'[6] at which the legislation is aimed. In assessing the proportionality of a measure, the court will necessarily have to evaluate the relative efficacy of possible alternative means to solve that social problem, an exercise which at one time would have been regarded in this country as raising policy questions which are traditionally unsuited to argument or resolution in a forensic context.

Lord Nicholls then drew a crucial distinction between (i) the permissible exercise of having regard to explanatory notes published with a Bill and even ministerial statements made in Parliament during the course of a Bill's passage—just as resort to other published material such as a White Paper is permissible, in order to understand the legislation and relevant background information, is 'constitutionally unexceptionable'[7] and indeed is mandated by the HRA; and (ii) the impermissible exercise of questioning or evaluating the cogency of what is said in Parliament:

> The proportionality of a statutory measure is not to be judged by the quality of the reasons advanced in support of it in the course of parliamentary debate, or by the subjective state of mind of individual ministers or other members ... Lack of cogent justification in the course of parliamentary debate is not a

[4] [2003] UKHL 40; [2004] 1 A.C. 816, at [61].
[5] [2003] UKHL 40; [2004] 1 A.C. 816, at [62].
[6] [2003] UKHL 40; [2004] 1 A.C. 816, at [63].
[7] [2003] UKHL 40; [2004] 1 A.C. 816, at [65].

> matter which 'counts against' the legislation on issues of proportionality. The court is called upon to evaluate the proportionality of the legislation, not the adequacy of the minister's explanation of the policy options or of his explanations to Parliament.[8]

He emphasised that this is not simply a matter of judicial diffidence but rather flows from constitutional principle, since to do the latter 'would contravene Article 9 of the Bill of Rights. The court would then be presuming to evaluate the sufficiency of the legislative process leading up to the enactment of the statute.'[9]

Such constitutional constraints do not apply to the European Court of Human Rights. When UK legislation is assessed by the Strasbourg Court for its compatibility with the Convention rights, the Court has no compunction about examining what, if anything, was said in Parliament to justify the measure and, where appropriate, will comment on the adequacy of parliamentary debate.

This is illustrated by the decision of the Grand Chamber in *Hirst v United Kingdom (No.2)*.[10] In this case the Court held that the United Kingdom's ban on all convicted prisoners from voting in elections while they are in prison violates art.3 of the First Protocol to the Convention. That ban is currently to be found in s.3 of the Representation of the People Act 2000 but has a long history going back to the Forfeiture Act 1870 and, before that, the common law, which regarded a convicted felon as having suffered a 'civic death' and, since the right to vote was in pre-democratic times viewed as being akin to a property right, it was forfeit along with other property. The Grand Chamber observed:

> [T]here is no evidence that Parliament has ever sought to weigh the competing interests or to assess the proportionality of a blanket ban on the right of a convicted prisoner to vote.[11]

The Court noted that the question had been considered in 1968 by a multi-party Speaker's Conference on Electoral Law, which unanimously recommended that a convicted prisoner should not be entitled to vote. It also noted that the working party which had made the recommendation, accepted by Parliament in 2000, that the legislation should be amended to allow unconvicted prisoners (i.e. those on remand) to vote, had recorded that successive British governments had taken the view that convicted prisoners had lost the moral authority to vote and did not argue for a change to this aspect of the legislation.

[8] [2003] UKHL 40; [2004] 1 A.C. 816, at [67].
[9] [2003] UKHL 40; [2004] 1 A.C. 816, at [67].
[10] (2006) 42 E.H.R.R. 41.
[11] (2006) 42 E.H.R.R. 41, at [79].

The Court was prepared to accept that it might be said that Parliament had 'implicitly'[12] affirmed the need for the restriction by passing the legislation it had in 2000. However, the Court was firmly of the view that

> it cannot be said that there was any substantive debate by members of the legislature on the continued justification in light of modern day penal policy and of current human rights standards for maintaining such a general restriction on the right of prisoners to vote.[13]

This aspect of the Court's reasoning would appear to require advocates appearing in Strasbourg to engage in an exercise of justifying the quality of the reasoning and debate in Parliament in a way which would not be permissible in a domestic court under the HRA in accordance with the approach endorsed by the House of Lords in *Wilson*.

Disclosure and Candour in Judicial Review Proceedings

Secondly, the HRA has had some impact on the rules of disclosure in judicial review proceedings, which has been required by the more searching scrutiny of public decision-making which is often called for under the HRA. The traditional rule that disclosure is not automatic in judicial review proceedings, in contrast to ordinary civil litigation, remains in place but has been modified in order to allow the court to perform its role under the HRA to decide questions of proportionality: *Tweed v Parades Commission for Northern Ireland*.[14] Although that case arose from Northern Ireland, the relevant rules on disclosure are the same in England and Wales and the reasoning of the House of Lords referred to both jurisdictions. Lord Bingham of Cornhill began with the starting-point that claims for judicial review 'characteristically, raise an issue of law, the facts being common ground or relevant only to show how the issue arises. So the disclosure of documents has usually been regarded as unnecessary, and that remains the position.'[15] However, Lord Bingham predicted that applications for disclosure are likely to increase in frequency, since human rights decisions under the Convention tend to be very fact-specific and any judgment on the proportionality of a public authority's interference with a Convention right 'is likely to call for a careful and accurate evaluation of the facts'.[16] Nevertheless, Lord Bingham was of the view that, even in such cases, orders for disclosure should not become automatic: 'The

[12] (2006) 42 E.H.R.R. 41, at [79].
[13] (2006) 42 E.H.R.R. 41, at [79].
[14] [2007] 1 A.C. 650.
[15] [2007] 1 A.C. 650, at [2].
[16] [2007] 1 A.C. 650, at [3].

test will always be whether, in the given case, disclosure appears to be necessary in order to resolve the matter fairly and justly.'[17]

Lord Brown of Eaton-under-Heywood agreed that proportionality challenges have brought 'a new dimension to judicial review' and, in certain cases at least, 'a more sophisticated and intensive process of review'.[18] He urged caution, nonetheless. He took the view that disclosure orders are likely to remain exceptional in judicial review proceedings, even in proportionality cases, and that the courts should guard against what appear to be 'fishing expeditions'.[19] Even Lord Brown accepted, however, that the courts may be expected to show a somewhat greater readiness than hitherto to order disclosure of the main documents underlying proportionality decisions, particularly in cases where a comparatively narrow margin of discretion falls to be accorded to the decision-maker. Lord Brown thought that this would be so a fortiori where the complaint was of a violation of an unqualified right in the Convention.[20]

One of the reasons why, as Lord Brown noted in *Tweed*, disclosure is often unnecessary in judicial review proceedings is that there is a special duty imposed by the law on public authorities which is not imposed on other litigants in ordinary civil proceedings, often referred to as the duty of candour. Lord Brown said:

> [I]t is a well-established principle that once permission to bring a claim for judicial review has been given public authorities are under a duty of candour to lay before the court all the relevant facts and reasoning underlying the decision under challenge.[21]

It was the application of that principle in practice which was found to be wanting in the next case which I address.

The Treasury Solicitor has issued new guidance to government lawyers on the obligation of candour and cooperation with the court as a result of unsatisfactory disclosure in *R. (Al-Sweady) v Secretary of State for Defence*.[22] Although this claim began as one for judicial review and in form remained as such, the Divisional Court recognised that in substance it had evolved for practical purposes into an ordinary Queen's Bench Division action. There was a great deal of factual dispute and this added to the Court's concern that there should be full disclosure in what was a very sensitive case raising allegations of serious human rights abuses, including possible homicide, by

[17] [2007] 1 A.C. 650, at [3].
[18] [2007] 1 A.C. 650, at [53].
[19] [2007] 1 A.C. 650, at [46].
[20] [2007] 1 A.C. 650, at [57].
[21] [2007] 1 A.C. 650, at [54].
[22] [2009] EWHC 2387 (Admin); [2010] H.R.L.R. 2.

British forces of Iraqi detainees which needed careful scrutiny in the public interest.

The Divisional Court, citing earlier authorities, emphasised that the duty of candour was 'a very high duty'[23] which falls upon a public authority to assist the court with full and accurate explanation of all the facts relevant to the issue the court must decide. Sadly, as the Court concluded, the defendant in that case consistently and repeatedly failed to comply with that obligation. In particular, the Court considered that there had been 'lamentable disclosure failures'[24] by the Royal Military Police. The Court went on to state that the duty of disclosure in a case such as that one is heightened by the fact that the allegations raised concerned some of the most important and basic rights in the Convention, in particular arts 2 and 3, which are unqualified rights. As we shall see later, one of the reasons why extensive disclosure was necessary in that case was that it had already been ordered by the Court that there should be cross-examination of witnesses because the Court would have to decide 'hard-edged' questions of fact.[25] This had an important consequence for the duty of disclosure in such a case. For there to be effective cross-examination, the Court considered that it was 'vital for full disclosure to occur'.[26] Putting the point in another way, the Court said:

> [W]here the court is involved in fact-finding on issues as crucial to the outcome of the case as they were in the present case, the approach to disclosure should be similar to that in an ordinary Queen's Bench action.[27]

At one time such cases might have been difficult to bring in the courts of this country, especially by way of judicial review. Under the HRA it has become clear that the courts will, where necessary and appropriate, modify their practices and procedures in order to do justice in the case. This is a welcome example of substance prevailing over form.

Cross-examination in Judicial Review Proceedings

The third impact on the work of an advocate is that there will be some cases under the HRA requiring live evidence and cross-examination where previously there would have been written evidence only. This is still not as common as it was thought at one time it would become but the courts will

[23] [2009] EWHC 2387 (Admin); [2010] H.R.L.R. 2, at [22].
[24] [2009] EWHC 2387 (Admin); [2010] H.R.L.R. 2, at [51].
[25] [2009] EWHC 2387 (Admin); [2010] H.R.L.R. 2, at [64].
[26] [2009] EWHC 2387 (Admin); [2010] H.R.L.R. 2, at [27].
[27] [2009] EWHC 2387 (Admin); [2010] H.R.L.R. 2, at [27].

order it when it is necessary to decide disputed facts, which is more likely to happen under the HRA.

In *R. (Wilkinson) v Broadmoor Special Authority*,[28] a mental health case which concerned allegations under art.3 of the Convention in relation to forcible treatment, it was significant in the view of the Court of Appeal that the proceedings could have been brought by way of an ordinary civil claim for a tort, e.g. battery. As Hale LJ explained:

> [I]t cannot and should not matter whether proceedings in respect of forcible treatment of detained patients are brought by way of an ordinary action in tort, an action under s.7(1) of the [HRA] or judicial review. If there are any relevant disputed issues of fact these will have to be determined, by cross-examination if necessary.[29]

This is another example of substance triumphing over form.

In *R. (N) v M* the Court of Appeal endorsed this approach but emphasised the words 'if necessary' in the above passage in the judgment of Hale LJ.[30] The Court did not feel that it would be necessary to order cross-examination in judicial review proceedings in every case raising an allegation under art.3 of the Convention even if it raised an issue of fact which had to be resolved by the court itself. This is because the court may be in a position where it has adequate evidence before it in order to make that decision of fact without the need for oral evidence. This may be because it is clear to the court on the written evidence alone that there will be a breach of art.3 or, conversely, that there will be no such breach.

These principles were applied, again with graphic effect, in *Al-Sweady*. In this last case, although not every witness was called or cross-examined, about 10 of the defendant's witnesses were required to give live evidence and were subjected to cross-examination. They included senior officers, including a captain who had been the intelligence officer in the regiment concerned, the commanding officer of the regiment, and the colonel who was deputy head of the Royal Military Police. The Divisional Court emphasised that the case turned on 'hard-edged' questions of fact.[31] Although the case was not a routine one—it involved difficult questions to do with extra-territorial jurisdiction under the Convention and allegations of serious abuses of human rights, including those under arts 2 and 3—the Court was far from wishing to discourage orders for cross-examination in those cases where it is necessary. The Court envisaged that such cross-examination 'might occur with increasing regularity in cases where there are crucial factual disputes between the

[28] [2001] EWCA Civ 1545; [2002] 1 W.L.R. 419.
[29] [2001] EWCA Civ 1545; [2002] 1 W.L.R. 419, at [62].
[30] [2002] EWCA Civ 1789; [2003] 1 W.L.R. 562, at [35].
[31] [2009] EWHC 2387 (Admin); [2010] H.R.L.R. 2, at [18].

parties relating to jurisdiction of the ECHR and the engagement of its articles.'[32] Later in its judgment the Court emphasised:

> [T]he court should always scrutinise with care the stance of parties to judicial review applications (and in particular those concerning human rights claims) to ascertain if there is any critical factual issue which requires orders for cross-examination ... or disclosure as being ... 'necessary in order to resolve the matter fairly and accurately'.[33]

Third-party Interventions

The fourth impact on the work of an advocate I would highlight is the increasing role played by third-party interveners, especially statutory bodies and NGOs, in proceedings under the HRA, and the special responsibilities that can fall upon advocates acting for such interveners. At one time, third-party interventions (similar to what has long been a feature of US litigation, the amicus brief)[34] were relatively unusual in this country. A well-known example of an important case which had an impact going far wider than the immediate parties but in which an NGO, the Children's Legal Centre, was refused leave to intervene was *Gillick v West Norfolk AHA*.[35]

In 1996 a working party established jointly by JUSTICE and the Public Law Project, chaired by Sir John Laws, recommended that a more benevolent attitude should be taken to giving third-party interveners access to the courts in public interest cases.[36] A cultural shift appeared to be underway by the turn of the century but, for a short while, it seemed that a more cautious approach might re-emerge as a result of the unfortunate experience in the *Pinochet* litigation, in which Amnesty International had been an intervener, giving rise to the problem of Lord Hoffmann's involvement as a judge in the first hearing in the House of Lords of that case because of his association with that NGO.[37] However, experience since then suggests that the courts, especially the appellate courts, are usually willing to permit third-party interventions, in particular by

[32] [2009] EWHC 2387 (Admin); [2010] H.R.L.R. 2, at [19].
[33] [2009] EWHC 2387 (Admin); [2010] H.R.L.R. 2, at [29].
[34] The term 'amicus curiae' was until recently used in this jurisdiction but not in the American sense: here it tended to refer to counsel appointed by the Attorney General (but independent of government) to assist the court, in particular in cases where one or more parties were unrepresented. Like most Latin phrases the term has now been replaced in this jurisdiction by an English one: advocate to the court.
[35] [1986] A.C. 112.
[36] Public Law Project/JUSTICE, *A Matter of Public Interest: Reforming the Law and Practice of Interventions in Public Interest Cases* (1996).
[37] *R. v Bow Street Metropolitan Stipendiary Magistrate Ex p. Pinochet (No.2)* [2000] 1 A.C. 119.

responsible NGOs such as Liberty and JUSTICE, which have become regular participants in human rights cases, and statutory bodies such as the Equality and Human Rights Commission. They may sometimes restrict the intervention to one in writing only and, where permission to intervene at an oral hearing is granted, as it often is, the court will usually impose a relatively short time limit, of an hour or even less, for the intervener's submissions; this is usually welcomed by all concerned, including the intervening organisation, as it tends to keep the impact on the length of the hearing to a minimum. This also tends to mean that usually interveners are not at risk of a costs order against them: while they usually cannot claim their costs against the losing party either, they tend to receive *pro bono* representation and so this does not cause problems in practice. Although third-party interventions are not confined to human rights cases, it is notable that they have become an established feature of procedure in the courts in this country since the HRA came into force.

Interveners often add value to a case but care needs to be taken that the intervener does not become 'an additional counsel for one of the parties'.[38] It should also be noted that, although usually interveners support the submissions of claimants in human rights claims, this will not invariably be so. A good example of a case where a well-known NGO, the Royal Society for the Prevention of Cruelty to Animals, intervened in support of the government in defending primary legislation which was challenged under the HRA is *R. (Countryside Alliance) v Attorney General*,[39] which concerned the compatibility of the Hunting Act 2004 with the Convention rights. The House of Lords by a majority rejected the challenge and a subsequent application to the European Court of Human Rights also failed.

Impact of International Law on HRA Cases

One particular development which I have observed in the first decade of the HRA's operation and in my own practice is the increasing importance of public international law in the domestic courts. To some extent this is a general phenomenon whose origins and full significance lie outside the scope of this essay. However, I would suggest that the nature of the HRA and the ECHR themselves have inevitably required the domestic courts to grapple with some questions of general international law. This in turn has had a significant impact on the kind of materials and arguments which advocates have to

[38] *E v Chief Constable of the RUC* [2008] UKHL 66; [2009] 1 A.C. 536, at [2]–[3] (Lord Hoffmann).

[39] [2007] UKHL 52; [2008] 1 A.C. 719.

deploy in legal proceedings in this country. I refer to three major cases to illustrate this point.

The first is the *Belmarsh* litigation, which concerned the compatibility of Part 4 of the Anti-terrorism, Crime and Security Act 2001: *A v Secretary of State for the Home Department*.[40] The second is the set of test cases in *R. (Al-Skeini) v Secretary of State for Defence*,[41] which concerned the extra-territorial exercise of jurisdiction by the United Kingdom. The third is *R. (Al-Jedda) v Secretary of State for Defence*,[42] which concerned (i) the attributability of military acts to a particular state such as the United Kingdom when it takes part in a multinational operation; and (ii) the relationship between human rights obligations, particularly those in the ECHR and the HRA, and binding resolutions of the United Nations (UN) Security Council.

A v Secretary of State for the Home Department, often referred to as the *Belmarsh* case,[43] is widely regarded as the most important case decided by the courts in this country under the HRA, and by some as the most important case to be decided since the Second World War. Unusually for its time, it was heard by a panel of nine judges sitting in the Appellate Committee of the House of Lords (the judicial body which preceded the Supreme Court of the United Kingdom, which tends to sit more frequently in panels of seven or nine judges). The main issue in the case concerned the compatibility of provisions in the Anti-terrorism, Crime and Security Act 2001, which permitted the Secretary of State to authorise the detention without charge of some suspected international terrorists. The legislation was passed quickly after the attacks by Al Qaida on New York and Washington DC on 11 September 2001 ('9/11' as that date has become known). What is of interest for present purposes is that the government of the United Kingdom sought to derogate from art.5 of the ECHR, which guarantees the right to personal liberty. As that request for derogation implicitly recognised, detention without charge authorised by the executive would ordinarily be incompatible with art.5. The derogation was made under art.15 of the ECHR and was sent, as required by the Convention system, to the Secretary-General of the Council of Europe. This was an act operating at the level of international law.

Article 15 is not part of domestic law: it has not been incorporated by statute, not even in the HRA itself. At first sight, therefore, it might have been thought that art.15 was simply irrelevant in domestic law. In fact, it assumed a critical importance in the *Belmarsh* case. This is because the government needed to give effect to the derogation in domestic law because, without such

[40] [2004] UKHL 56; [2005] 2 A.C. 68.
[41] [2007] UKHL 26; [2008] 1 A.C. 153.
[42] [2007] UKHL 58; [2008] 1 A.C. 332.
[43] [2004] UKHL 56; [2005] 2 A.C. 68.

domestic effect, art.5 would have operated with its full and unmodified force in domestic law. Accordingly, the Secretary of State made a designated derogation order, as he has power to do in principle under s.14 HRA. Since that was a piece of secondary, not primary, legislation, it was amenable to judicial review and could be quashed if necessary by the domestic courts (in fact Parliament conferred this jurisdiction of review on the Special Immigration Appeals Commission, which was chaired by a High Court judge). Whether it should be quashed depended on whether there were grounds for doing so which were justiciable in the domestic courts. In the litigation, the Attorney-General conceded, and the courts endorsed his concession, that it was in principle justiciable in the domestic courts. This was because the derogation order purported to give effect in domestic law to the derogation made at the international level: if that international derogation was unlawfully made under art.15 of the ECHR, it would follow that there was nothing for the domestic order to give effect to in domestic law.

There were ultimately three distinct grounds on which the majority of the House of Lords (the main opinion being that of Lord Bingham) held that the derogation was unlawful under the terms of art.15 and therefore invalid in domestic law too. The first was that, although the majority (apart from Lord Hoffmann) accepted that the government was entitled to conclude that there was, after the events of 9/11, a public emergency threatening the life of the nation, the measure adopted was not 'strictly required' to meet the exigencies of the situation. This required the principle of proportionality to be satisfied. It was not. In particular, the government had been unable to demonstrate that there was a rational connection between the asserted aim of the measure and the means used: the asserted aim was to prevent international terrorism but the means used would lead to the detention only of foreign nationals. This was not only discriminatory, it was irrational and therefore failed to meet one of the requirements of the doctrine of proportionality.

The second reason for the decision of the House of Lords was that the derogation did not comply with art.14 of the ECHR because it unjustifiably discriminated between British citizens and foreign nationals. There had been no derogation from art.14, which continued to have full effect in international law and is also one of the Convention rights in domestic law as it is set out in Sch.1 to the HRA. The obligations in art.14 constituted other international obligations within the meaning of art.15, and so breach of art.14 meant that there was also a breach of a condition precedent for a valid derogation under art.15.

Thirdly, the unjustified discrimination in the detention powers led to there being a further breach of another international obligation, namely the prohibition on discrimination in international law more generally, in particular in art.26 of the International Covenant on Civil and Political Rights (ICCPR).

This last point is significant because it would have sufficed by itself even if there had not also been a breach of art.14 of the ECHR. It should be noted that, although the ICCPR has been ratified by the United Kingdom, and is therefore binding on it in international law, it has not been incorporated into domestic law by Act of Parliament. This is of potential importance in the future, since the scope of art.26 is broader than art.14 of the ECHR. As is well-known, art.14 does not contain a 'freestanding' prohibition on discrimination but prohibits discrimination only in the enjoyment of other Convention rights. Although this does not require there to be a breach of another Convention right, it does require the case to fall within the ambit of such a right. There is no such limitation on the scope of art.26 of the ICCPR.

More generally, what this aspect of the reasoning in the *Belmarsh* case demonstrates is that, under the HRA, domestic courts are entitled and required to adjudicate on questions of compliance by the United Kingdom with its obligations under international law generally and not just under the ECHR, where a derogation is made. This is because the terms of art.15 of the ECHR, which the United Kingdom voluntarily accepted along with its other obligations in that Convention, expressly refer to such international law obligations. In this context it is simply irrelevant that those international obligations may otherwise be binding only as a matter of international law and have not been incorporated into domestic law by Parliament. The domestic courts can and must adjudicate on such questions: this is a powerful impact of the HRA and has changed the nature of the legal materials which an advocate in the domestic courts has to be able to deploy.

Turning to *R. (Al-Skeini) v Secretary of State for Defence*,[44] the main issue in this set of test cases turned on the meaning of 'jurisdiction' in art.1 of the ECHR. Again, it is striking that this is not reproduced in Sch.1 to the HRA and is not as such part of domestic law. Nevertheless it has proved to be of critical importance in practice. The domestic courts have taken the view that the geographical reach of the HRA should be construed to be the same as the reach of the ECHR. This is in conformity with a more general principle which is sometimes called the 'mirror principle': that the HRA should reflect what the position would be in Strasbourg, or, to put it another way, that the domestic courts should strive to avoid a result which would result in the United Kingdom being in breach of its obligations under the Convention in Strasbourg.[45] All of the courts in the domestic legal system reached that conclusion on the scope of the HRA. Lord Bingham dissented on this point in the House of Lords.

[44] [2007] UKHL 26; [2008] 1 A.C. 153.

[45] On which, see Chapter 5, this volume.

The meaning of 'jurisdiction' in art.1 therefore fell to be interpreted and applied by the domestic courts under the HRA. Again, as with art.15, the court could not avoid having to adjudicate on difficult questions of public international law. It was common ground in *Al-Skeini* that the concept of jurisdiction should be construed in a manner which is consistent with general principles of international law. It was also common ground that the concept goes beyond a state's territory: although the primary meaning of jurisdiction is territorial, there are well-established exceptions which are recognised in international law. Having said that, it is important to note one point at the outset about the meaning of jurisdiction in international law: in that context the concept is a permissive one, in other words it refers to the circumstances in which a state is *permitted* by international law to exercise jurisdiction. In contrast, the question under art.1 of the Convention is a *factual* one, whether a Contracting State in fact exercised jurisdiction over a person even if such exercise was not permitted by international law.

Although the territorial principle is the main basis for the permissible exercise of jurisdiction, it is well-established in international law that a state may exercise jurisdiction outside its own territory in certain limited circumstances, e.g. in relation to its own nationals (the nationality principle). By way of example, English criminal law extends to a British national who commits murder outside the territory. However, jurisdiction in the sense used by art.1 of the ECHR does not have quite the same meaning, since it refers to a factual question. Did a state party to the ECHR in fact exercise jurisdiction over a person so as to bring them within the protection of the ECHR? That exercise of jurisdiction may have been unlawful as a matter of international law, for example if it was in breach of the fundamental norm which prohibits the use of force against another state, to be found in art.2(4) of the UN Charter. An illegal occupation of the territory of another state will still constitute the exercise of jurisdiction as is demonstrated by the many cases that have followed the invasion of northern Cyprus by Turkey in 1974.

Jurisdiction in its original (etymological) sense means 'speaking the law'. I would suggest that it means, in the context of art.1 of the ECHR, the exercise or purported exercise of legal authority over persons or property. Such legal authority, or jurisdiction in international law, can consist of any or all of the three classic functions of a state: the legislative, the executive and the judicial.

It is clear that the concept of jurisdiction is primarily territorial. However, it is also clear that it is not exclusively territorial. There are well-established exceptions to the principle of territoriality in which the Strasbourg institutions have recognised that a Contracting State was exercising jurisdiction outside its territory. The case law contains examples of all of the three classic functions of a state being exercised outside its territory, e.g. legislation which applied in the territory of another state; courts that were sitting in another state; police officers who arrested a person or consular officials who exercised executive functions in another state.

In *Al-Skeini* the House of Lords was prepared to accept (as was conceded by that stage of the litigation) that one of the test cases before it did fall within the jurisdiction of the United Kingdom for the purposes of art.1 of the ECHR: that of Baha Mousa, who died in British custody in September 2003. However, it was prepared to do this only on a narrow basis, that detention in a British facility was analogous to places such as ships, aircraft, embassies and consulates, in which it had been recognised by the Strasbourg institutions that a state had exercised extra-territorial jurisdiction. This was because the House of Lords felt that, although the Strasbourg case law did not speak with one voice, it was constrained by the admissibility decision by the Grand Chamber in *Bankovic v France and others*[46] to hold that exceptions to the territorial principle of jurisdiction should be applied narrowly. In that case the European Court of Human Rights had held that civilians who had been killed in aerial bombing of Belgrade did not fall within the jurisdiction of states which were parties to the ECHR. It should be noted that the case did not concern either military occupation or the conduct of policing or other security operations.

The decision of the House of Lords in *Al-Skeini* left the law in an unsatisfactory state, even in the case of Baha Mousa and the others who were detained with him. As emerged at the Baha Mousa public inquiry, conducted by Sir William Gage, who published his report on 8 September 2011,[47] the detainees had been subjected to some ill-treatment at the hotel where they were arrested. On the reasoning of the House of Lords the detainees were at that stage outside the United Kingdom's jurisdiction despite being under arrest by British soldiers, since they had not yet been taken to a British detention facility.

The decision of the House of Lords also excluded from the jurisdiction of the United Kingdom many other Iraqi civilians who had died apparently at the hands of British forces. These included a person who had been arrested and allegedly thrown into a river; a person who had been shot in his house when it was the subject of a forcible entry and search; and a person who had been shot as he was said to be trying to escape from a compulsory checkpoint for cars. Moreover, all of the relevant deaths had occurred during the period of occupation, between about 1 May 2003 and 28 June 2004, a period when (it was accepted on behalf of the government) the United Kingdom was the occupying power in south-east Iraq, a region in which the largest city is Basra.

[46] (2001) 11 B.H.R.C. 435.
[47] *The Baha Mousa Public Inquiry Report*, HC 1452 (London: Stationery Office, 2011).

The European Court of Human Rights, sitting as a Grand Chamber, gave its judgment in *Al-Skeini v United Kingdom* on 8 July 2011.[48] It held that all of the cases before it fell within the jurisdiction of the United Kingdom and that there had been a violation of the obligation under art.2 of the ECHR to secure an independent and effective investigation into the deaths of those who had arguably died at the hands of British soldiers in Iraq during the occupation of 2003–04. The Court did not regard its earlier decision in *Bankovic* as standing in the way of that conclusion, unlike the House of Lords. The Court did not consider that the rights in the ECHR necessarily had to be conferred in an all or nothing manner: it was possible to divide and tailor the rights according to the particular exercise of jurisdiction in the case before it. Furthermore, the Court did not consider that the ECHR was confined to the geographical space (or *espace juridique*) of the Council of Europe as had been submitted for the government and appeared to have been stated by the Court in *Bankovic*. Rather the Court accepted a broader principle for the exercise of extra-territorial jurisdiction, based on the exercise of control and authority over a person abroad. In the cases before it the Court considered that there had been such exercise of control and authority flowing from the performance by British soldiers of security functions in Basra.

Finally, I turn to the case of *R. (Al-Jedda) v Secretary of State for Defence*.[49] The claimant in this case was a dual national of Iraq and the United Kingdom. He travelled to Iraq during the occupation of that country by the United Kingdom and was interned by British forces. He argued that his internment violated his right to personal liberty in art.5 of the ECHR. The first issue which arose before the House of Lords was whether the acts of the British forces in question were attributable to the United Kingdom or to the UN. This was an argument advanced on behalf of the government in reliance upon the decision of the European Court of Human Rights in *Behrami v France*.[50] That case had concerned the actions of an international peacekeeping force in Kosovo under the auspices of the UN. The majority of the House of Lords had little difficulty rejecting that argument. The main opinion was given by Lord Bingham, who concluded that the analogy with the *Behrami* case broke down 'at almost every point'.[51] In particular, the United Kingdom was an occupying power and not part of a UN peace-keeping force. For present purposes, what is significant is that the reasoning of the House of Lords, and the arguments of the advocates in the case, had to grapple in detail with intricate points of public international law and, in particular, the law

[48] (2011) 53 E.H.R.R. 18.
[49] [2007] UKHL 58; [2008] 1 A.C. 332.
[50] (2007) 45 E.H.R.R. SE10.
[51] [2007] UKHL 58; [2008] 1 A.C. 332, at [24].

relating to the respective responsibilities of states and international organisations. This again illustrates the changing character of the materials which an advocate may have to deploy in a domestic court under the HRA. When the case went to the European Court of Human Rights, the Grand Chamber agreed with the reasoning and conclusion of Lord Bingham on this first issue and also held that the acts of the British forces who detained the applicant were attributable to the United Kingdom and not to the UN.

I turn now to the second main issue in *Al-Jedda*: the relationship between the Convention rights and the obligations of a Member of the UN under art.103 of the UN Charter, which provides that:

> In the event of a conflict between the obligations of the Members of the United Nations under the present Charter and their obligations under any other international agreement, their obligations under the present Charter shall prevail.

The obligation which apparently arose under the Charter was the obligation in art.25 to 'accept and carry out the decisions of the Security Council in accordance with the present Charter'. It was argued on behalf of the government that, should that obligation conflict with an obligation under another international agreement—even a human rights treaty such as the ECHR—art.103 requires a Member of the United Nations to comply with its obligations under the Charter. In particular it was argued that Resolution 1546, passed by the UN Security Council on 8 June 2004, had authorised and indeed required internment in Iraq. The House of Lords accepted those arguments. In doing so it held that the right to personal liberty in art.5 of the ECHR had to be read in a way which was consistent with general international law, in particular the obligation in art.103 of the UN Charter. The effect was that an unincorporated international instrument, a resolution by the UN Security Council, could prevail over a norm of domestic law, namely the right in art.5(1) as set out in Sch.1 to the HRA.

In principle there ought not to be any conflict between these two sets of obligations. After all the UN arose from the same ashes as human rights treaties after the Second World War. One of the fundamental purposes of the UN is to promote human rights. It is also important to recall that it is open to Contracting States to derogate from their obligations under the Convention in time of war or public emergency where the strict requirements of art.15 permit. Whether or not that would have been permitted in the present case, the fact remains that the United Kingdom did not derogate from art.5 of the Convention. Accordingly, the rights in that Article had to be secured to everyone within its jurisdiction to the fullest extent. The applicant was within its jurisdiction and enjoyed the rights in the Convention to the same extent as anyone on its territory.

This leads to the next point which deserves emphasis. Nothing in the reasoning of the House of Lords turned on the point that the applicant was detained in Iraq. If the reasoning of the House of Lords is correct, it would apply equally to any person who is within the territory of the United Kingdom. Suppose a UN Security Council Resolution required Members of the UN to introduce internment for suspected terrorists or for some other group of people in society. The effect of the reasoning of the House of Lords would be that the United Kingdom would be able to introduce internment of British citizens on its own territory—without a derogation from art.5 and while continuing to maintain that it was in fact complying with the rights in that Article.

And the potential consequences do not stop there. If the logic of the House of Lords is to be applied consistently, it would mean that the UN Security Council could require not merely internment but the use of torture or inhuman or degrading treatment, contrary to art.3 of the Convention. Or even the imposition of the death penalty, in spite of the complete and categorical abolition of that penalty in Protocol 13, which the United Kingdom has ratified, and which prohibits the death penalty even in time of war.

It may be said that the example I have given of conduct which is contrary to art.3 would be prohibited in any event by norms of *ius cogens* (that is peremptory norms of international law which permit of no derogation). Even if that is true, and governments may not accept that it is true in the case of inhuman or degrading treatment short of torture, that would assume that the *ius cogens* operates as a limitation on the powers of the UN Security Council and, moreover, that the European Court of Human Rights or a domestic court (and not the International Court of Justice) has the jurisdiction to pronounce on the validity of resolutions passed by the Security Council. But there is a more fundamental problem if one takes the example of the death penalty. However great the abhorrence of the death penalty in the public policy of the Council of Europe, including the United Kingdom, it cannot be said that the prohibition of the death penalty is a norm of *ius cogens*. Many states, including many democratic states which have Bills of Rights, such as the USA, continue to permit the death penalty for certain offences. Yet, if the reasoning of the House of Lords in *Al-Jedda* is right, it is difficult to avoid the logical consequence that the UN Security Council could require a member of the Council of Europe which has accepted Protocol 13 to use the death penalty on its own soil against one of its own citizens. The same could be said of those members of the Council of Europe which have ratified Protocol 6 on the death penalty but not the Thirteenth.

I would suggest that that cannot be right and that guidance as to the correct approach can be found in the judgment of the European Court of

Justice in Cases C-402/05 and C-415/05, *Kadi v Council of the European Union.*[52] In that case the Grand Chamber held that:

> [T]he Community judicature must, in accordance with the powers conferred on it by the EC Treaty, ensure the review, in principle the full review, of the lawfulness of all Community acts in the light of the fundamental rights forming an integral part of the general principles of Community law, including review of Community measures which, like the contested regulation, are designed to give effect to the resolutions adopted by the Security Council under Chapter VII of the Charter of the United Nations.[53]

The Court went on to hold that the Regulation in that case was incompatible with those general principles of Community law, in particular the right to property, the right to a fair hearing and the right to effective judicial review.

The first reason why the judgment in *Kadi* is significant—even though it was not directly concerned with the Convention rights —is that it is well-established that the law of the European Union contains within it the principle of respect for human rights, and in particular the Court of Justice draws upon the Convention as a guide to what that principle entails.

But there is a more fundamental reason why it is relevant. It helps to understand that each court must apply the corpus of law which is relevant to its own functions and in accordance with the treaty which establishes it. The European Court of Justice applied principles of European Union law and held that organs of the Union could implement UN Security Council Resolutions only in a manner which is compatible with the fundamental principles of European Union law, in other words the autonomous legal order which that Court has a duty to uphold.

Similarly, the European Court of Human Rights has a duty to uphold and apply the Convention, and the domestic courts of this country have a duty to apply the HRA. While they will seek to interpret the Convention in a way which is in harmony with general international law, they will not do so in a way which conflicts with the fundamentals of the Convention itself. This is in no way to impugn the validity of the actions of the UN. The same was said by the European Court of Justice in *Kadi*. This may or may not lead to a breach of the United Kingdom's obligations under the UN Charter. But this is a consequence which international law has always contemplated as a possibility. For example, it is a fundamental principle of international law that a state may not invoke a provision of its own internal law, even a provision of its own constitution, in order to justify a breach of international law. The same may be true of its obligations under a regional treaty such as the Convention. But, when looked at from the perspective of that state's internal

[52] [2009] 1 A.C. 1235.
[53] [2009] 1 A.C. 1235, at [326].

law, or from the perspective of regional law, it is clear that the state must comply with its obligations under those legal orders and cannot rely on a provision of general international law in order to excuse itself from full compliance with those obligations. This simply flows from the fact that a state will often have undertaken different obligations under different treaties.

It is worth noting that the United Kingdom is a permanent member of the UN Security Council and can veto resolutions before that body. In 2004 it did not have to allow Resolution 1546 to be passed. In fact it supported it. Although it may be said that the obligations in the UN Charter were created in 1945, before the United Kingdom became a party to the Convention, that does not affect the fact that at the relevant time in 2004 the United Kingdom knew that it had the obligations which it does in the Convention and yet chose to allow Resolution 1546 to pass in the Security Council and indeed to support it. If the United Kingdom (or any other Contracting State) could rely on its own acts and omissions in the Security Council to avoid its obligations under the Convention, in circumstances where it has not sought to derogate from it, the guarantees of the Convention could be limited or excluded at will.

Conclusion

In this essay I have sought to suggest that the HRA has had an important, but not revolutionary, impact on the work done by advocates in domestic courts. This impact has been felt in four general areas: the type of evidence that can and should be adduced; the obligations on public authorities of disclosure and candour; the extent to which there may have to be live evidence and cross-examination, in particular in judicial review cases; and the role of third-party interveners. I have also looked at one particular context in which the HRA has had a profound impact: the changing character of the materials that an advocate has to be able to handle in order to deal with the interpretation and application of the ECHR against the backcloth of public international law generally.

Note. Although many of the cases to which I refer are ones in which I appeared as an advocate, the views expressed here are mine alone. This essay is based on my presentation at the conference which took place at Durham Law School in September 2010 and also on the Lord Irvine Human Rights Lecture given by me at the Law School in February 2011.

Part IV

The Human Rights Act on the International Plane

9

Human Rights and Legislative Supremacy

ANTHONY MASON

INTRODUCTION

THE PURPOSE OF THIS ESSAY IS TO:

- outline the steps taken to provide protection for human rights in New Zealand, Australia and Hong Kong;
- note the influence of the United Kingdom and European jurisprudence on these developments; and
- show how popular regard for the political process and the doctrines of legislative supremacy (parliamentary sovereignty) and separation of powers has affected the course of events in Australia, most notably, and New Zealand.

New Zealand

It is convenient to begin with New Zealand. The Bill of Rights Act 1990 (NZ) (the BORA) was enacted after an unsuccessful attempt to introduce an entrenched Bill of Rights which would have enabled the courts to declare non-complying legislation invalid. The BORA follows the 'interpretive' or 'dialogue' model and recognises a range of civil and political rights taken from the International Covenant on Civil and Political Rights (ICCPR). They include the right not to be tortured, the right to vote, freedom of thought, conscience and religion, freedom of association, freedom from discrimination, due process rights and rights of minorities to enjoy their culture, practise their religion and use their own language.

The BORA contains a general limitation clause (s.5) which provides that rights 'may be subject only to such reasonable limits prescribed by law as can be demonstrably justified in a free and democratic society'. Section 6 (the interpretive provision) provides that:

Proceedings of the British Academy, **183**, 199–219.

> wherever an enactment can be given a meaning that is consistent with the rights and freedoms [recognised by the BORA], that meaning shall be preferred to any other meaning.

There is, however, no provision which expressly enables a court to make a declaration of incompatibility (inconsistency) in the event that legislation cannot be interpreted consistently with the recognised human rights. Despite the absence of such a provision, there is some judicial support for the making of a formal declaration in appropriate cases.[1] The case for making a declaration is based on the view that holding that legislation intrudes on recognised rights is the initiation of a dialogue with Parliament which may cause it to amend the law.[2] Whether the BORA implicitly authorises the making of a declaration on incompatibility remains a matter of debate in New Zealand.

Australia—Victoria

One State, Victoria, and one Territory, the Australian Capital Territory (ACT), have introduced human rights legislation. In each case the legislation conforms to the interpretive model. Although there are some differences between them, the differences are not significant for present purposes. Of the two, the Victorian Charter of Human Rights and Responsibilities Act 2006 (the Charter) is the more significant. The Charter protects many of the civil and political rights identified in the ICCPR, including the right to equality before the law, the right to life, protection of the family and children, freedom of movement, freedom of expression, the right to participate in public life, the right to a fair trial and the rights of children in the criminal process. The Charter also protects the rights of a member of a religious, ethnic or religious minority to declare and practise his or her religion and to use his or her own language. The Act does not deal with specific indigenous rights and responsibilities.

The Charter contains a general limitation provision (s.7(2)) which provides that a human right may be subject only:

> ... to such reasonable limits as can be demonstrably justified in a free and democratic society based on human dignity, equality and freedom and taking into account all relevant factors, including

[1] See *Moonen v Film & Literature Board of Review* [2000] 2 N.Z.L.R. 9, at [20]; *R. v Poumako* [2000] 2 N.Z.L.R. 695, at [86]–[107].

[2] *Moonen v Film & Literature Board of Review* [2000] 2 N.Z.L.R. 9, at [20]; *R. v Poumako* [2000] 2 N.Z.L.R. 695, at [86]–[107].

(a) the nature of the right; and
(b) the importance of the purpose of the limitation; and
(c) the nature and extent of the limitation; and
(d) the relationship between the limitation and its purpose; and
(e) any less restrictive means reasonably available to achieve the purpose that the limitation seeks to achieve.

The Charter also includes specific limitations which apply to certain rights, such as freedom of expression. That freedom, it is provided:

> ... may be subject to lawful restrictions reasonably necessary
>
> (a) to respect the rights and reputation of other persons;
> (b) for the protection of national security, public order, public health or public morality.[3]

Section 32(1), the interpretive provision, requires that courts and decision-makers must interpret all statutory provisions in a way that is compatible with human rights 'so far as it is possible to do so consistently with' the purpose of the statutory provisions. The limiting reference to 'purpose' differentiates the Victorian statutory provision from the expression of the corresponding provision in New Zealand and the United Kingdom.[4] It appears from the Explanatory Memorandum which accompanied the Bill, before it was enacted as the Charter, and other aspects of the legislative history, that the origin of the limiting reference to 'purpose' was the House of Lords decision in *Ghaidan v Godin-Mendoza*[5] on s.3 of the UK Human Rights Act 1998 (the HRA), where it was said that s.3 does not authorise an interpretation which is inconsistent with a fundamental feature of the primary enactment. As will become clear, however, what is express in Victoria seems to be implied in New Zealand.[6]

Section 36 authorises the court to issue a 'declaration of inconsistent interpretation' if it concludes that a statutory provision cannot be interpreted consistently with a human right, but this declaration has no legal effect on the rights of the parties.[7] Before issuing such a declaration the court must give notice to the Attorney-General and the Victorian Equality Opportunity and Human Rights Commission. The court is to give a copy of the declaration to the Attorney-General, who is then to provide it to the responsible minister, who is to table it in Parliament together with his or her response within six months.

[3] Charter, s.15(3).
[4] HRA 1998, s.3.
[5] [2004] 2 A.C. 557.
[6] See pp.203–05.
[7] Charter, s.37.

An Australian Federal Bill of Rights?

On 10 December 2008, the Federal Government set up a Committee, the National Human Rights Consultation (NHRC), to inquire into and report on human rights protection in Australia. The NHRC, which consulted widely with community and interest groups, reported that there was community support, despite opposition, for increased human rights protection, and recommended the introduction of a statutory Bill of Rights along the lines of the Victorian model. The NHRC reported:

> The so-called dialogue model of a Human Rights Act would sit more comfortably with Australians than other models because, even when the courts have expressed a view about the limits on rights, most Australians would prefer Parliament to express the final view, once it had received a further opinion from the executive in response to an adverse court finding.[8]

The NHRC recommended that the obligation to comply with the recognised rights should be imposed only on federal authorities and that the rights recognised by a statutory Bill of Rights should be confined to civil and political rights taken from the ICCPR. Some of those rights should be non-derogable:

- the right to life;
- protection from torture and cruel, inhuman or degrading treatment;
- freedom from slavery or servitude;
- retrospective criminals laws;
- freedom from coercion or restraint in relation to religion and belief; and
- the right to a fair trial.

Other recognised human rights, according to the NHRC, should be subject to a general limitation similar to that prescribed by the Victorian Charter.

The NHRC considered that the power to make a declaration of incompatibility should be confined to the High Court of Australia (Australia's final court of appeal) and that, if there were difficulties in so confining the exercise of the power, then it would be preferable that there should be no power to make such a declaration. Public discussion of proposals for a federal Bill of Rights was confused by expressions of opinion by some legal experts that a

[8] National Human Rights Consultation, *National Human Rights Consultation Report*, 'NHRC Report' (Barton, ACT: Human Rights Branch, Attorney-General's Department, 2009), pp.363–64. This conclusion in effect endorsed the government decision to exclude an entrenched model from the NHRC's inquiry.

federal Bill would be unconstitutional.[9] In the event, the Solicitor-General advised that a statutory Bill along the lines of the Victorian model, subject to certain amendments, would be constitutionally valid.[10]

The NHRC also recommended that any federal Human Rights Act require statements of compatibility to be tabled for all Bills introduced into the Federal Parliament before the third reading (so as to allow scrutiny of amendments) and legislative instruments. The NHRC further recommended that such an Act empower a proposed Joint Committee (from both Houses of Parliament) on Human Rights to review all Bills and the relevant legislative instruments for compliance with, first, an interim list and, later, a definitive list of Australia's human rights obligations.

Following its consideration of the report, the Federal Government announced in 2010 that it would not implement the recommendation to enact a federal Human Rights Act. The Government indicated that it would take steps to implement other recommendations in the Report. But what the Commonwealth has decided to do falls short of implementing all the other recommendations. Although supporters of a federal Human Rights Act have predictably expressed their disappointment, opponents—most notably the Murdoch press which campaigned vigorously against such an Act while urging an expanded approach to freedom of information and freedom of expression—have applauded the Government's decision. Predictably Australian politicians were, for the most part, opposed to a Human Rights Act. Less predictably, perhaps, various judges and retired judges were outspoken in their opposition to such an Act, mainly on the ground that it would involve judges deciding questions of policy which are best left to the political process.

The Legal Effect of the New Zealand and Victorian Interpretive Provisions

The courts in both New Zealand and Victoria have allowed only a narrow operation to the respective interpretive provisions. Neither the Supreme Court of New Zealand nor the Victorian Court of Appeal was willing to adopt the wide-ranging interpretation given to s.3 of the Human Rights Act embraced by the House of Lords in *Ghaidan v Godin-Mendoza*.[11] Here their Lordships considered that s.3 enabled a court to place a strained interpretation on the language of the primary enactment so long as it did not depart from one of

[9] Assertions that proposals for federal legislative reform are unconstitutional are common elements in the strategy of those who oppose such reform in Australia; the strategy is designed to create a climate of doubt and delay while legal complexities are resolved.
[10] NHRC Report, Appendix E.
[11] [2004] 2 A.C. 557.

its fundamental features. This approach called to mind the common law principle of straining the literal language of a statute in order to give effect to its fundamental purpose.[12] In the context of s.3, *Ghaidan* seemed to introduce a limitation by reference to statutory purpose rather than legislative intention, a notion—useful though it is in the frame of a single statute—is more difficult once it is applied outside that frame. The difficulty is evident in *Ghaidan* and in other cases where a reverse onus imposed on a defendant by the primary enactment was transformed by s.3 'interpretation' into an evidential onus.[13] In *Sheldrake v Director of Public Prosecutions*,[14] the House of Lords expressly acknowledged that it was not the intention of Parliament that only an evidential onus be imposed.

The reasoning in the later decision in *R (Wilkinson) v IRC*[15] struck a very different note. Lord Hoffmann, who delivered the principal speech, denied that s.3 was intended to require 'courts to give the language of statutes acontextual meanings'.[16] His Lordship went on to say that although s.3 created a very strong presumption,

> the question is still one of interpretation i.e. the ascertainment of what, taking into account the presumption created by s.3, Parliament would reasonably understood to have meant by using the actual language of the statute.[17]

The focus here is not on reconciling the provisions of two differently expressed statutes but on giving effect to the legislative intention in the primary enactment. In the result, the House of Lords refused to interpret the word 'widow' in a taxing statute as if it referred to 'the more general concept of a surviving spouse'. In effect, their Lordships declined to give the statute a more extensive operation than its words justified; in *Ghaidan*, their Lordships had reconciled the HRA and the primary enactment by reading its operation down.

Lord Hoffmann seemingly affirmed the proposition that the legislative intention of the primary enactment, as ascertained by the process of interpretation, must be respected. His Lordship did not say whether the interpretive provision would achieve outcomes stronger than those achieved by the principle of legality in the cases in which it applied. He appears to have regarded the interpretive provision as creating a stronger presumption than does the principle of legality. If s.3 (which is expressed as a direction) is to be

[12] *Sutherland Publishing Co Ltd v Caxton Publishing Co Ltd* [1938] 1 Ch.174, 201 (Mackinnon LJ).
[13] *R. v Lambert* [2002] 2 A.C. 545; *Sheldrake v Director of Public Prosecutions* [2005] 1 A.C. 264.
[14] *Sheldrake v Director of Public Prosecutions* [2005] 1 A.C. 264, at [15] and [53]; see also *Ghaidan v Godin-Mendoza* [2004] 2 A.C. 557, at [30], [32] and [67].
[15] [2005] 1 W.L.R. 1718.
[16] [2005] 1 W.L.R. 1718, at 17.
[17] [2005] 1 W.L.R. 1718, at 17.

converted into a presumption, that may well be right, but at the end of the day we may ask the following question. How much is needed to displace the presumption?

In *R. v Hansen*,[18] the Supreme Court of New Zealand preferred the *Wilkinson* to the *Ghaidan* approach, though there was some suggestion—the soundness of which is questionable—that s.3 was stronger than s.6, its New Zealand counterpart. The majority in *Hansen* concluded that s.6 of the BORA authorised a rights-compliant interpretation of the primary enactment *which was reasonably or properly open*. In that case s.6(6) of the Misuse of Drugs Act 1975 (NZ) provided that a person found in possession of more than specified amounts of prescribed drugs was deemed to possess them for the purpose of supply or sale 'unless the contrary is proved'. The meaning of this expression, the majority held, was so well established as creating a legal or persuasive burden of proof that it could not be interpreted as creating merely an evidential burden.

In the leading Victorian case, *R. v Momcilovic*,[19] the Victorian Court of Appeal, after concluding that s.32(1) did no more than pick up the common law principle of legality, held that s.5 of the Drugs Poisons Controlled Substances Act 1981 (Vic), which provided that a person in whose apartment drugs were found was deemed to be in possession of the drugs unless 'she satisf[ied] the court to the contrary', could *not* be interpreted as imposing only an evidential onus. The Victorian Court of Appeal endorsed the approach taken in *Hansen.* The Court, like the NZ Supreme Court, was unwilling to follow the House of Lords decisions on reverse onus provisions.[20]

Discussion

From a purely United Kingdom perspective, there is much to be said for the view that the object of the interpretive model was to secure an interpretation of primary legislation which would result in compatibility with the recognised human rights, even if, as a matter of conventional statutory interpretation, the primary legislation could not be so construed. In other words, the object was to authorise an interpretation which is compliant with human rights recognised by the European Convention on Human Rights and Fundamental Freedoms (the Convention), although it put a 'strained interpretation' on the language of the primary enactment.

[18] [2007] 3 N.Z.L.R. 1.
[19] [2010] VSCA 50 (13 March 2010).
[20] The decision of the High Court of Australia in *Momcilovic* is addressed in Chapter 10, this volume.

The expected operation of s.3 was captured in the speech of Lord Bingham of Cornhill in *Sheldrake* when he stated the effect of the decision in *Ghaidan.* In concluding that it was possible to interpret a provision in the primary enactment imposing a legal burden of proof on a defendant as imposing only an evidential onus, his Lordship said:

> Such was not the intention of Parliament when enacting [the provision in the primary enactment], but it was the intention of Parliament when enacting section 3.[21]

He had earlier made the point that *Ghaidan* established that the s.3(1) interpretive obligation was 'a very strong and far-reaching one and [might] require the court to depart from the legislative intention of Parliament'.[22] *Ghaidan* therefore authorised both a departure from the text of, and the legislative intention exhibited by, the primary enactment.

Lord Bingham then went on to make two points. The first was that a Convention-compliant interpretation under s.3(1) was 'the primary remedial measure', while a declaration of incompatibility was 'an exceptional course'. The second point was that during the passage of the HRA through Parliament, the promoters of the legislation informed both Houses that the need for a declaration of incompatibility would rarely arise.

Whether *Wilkinson* marks a tectonic shift in the House of Lords' approach to s.3(1) is not a matter on which I can venture an opinion. For present purposes it is sufficient to say that, in New Zealand and Australia, the *Wilkinson* approach has been preferred. Although no mention of them was made in the two Australasian cases to which I have referred, it is very likely that the judges in these cases took account of the constitutional considerations which led the House of Lords to give an expansive operation to s.3(1). One was the object of achieving domestic compliance with the Convention in order to avoid a continuation of the proliferation of 'appeals' to the Strasbourg Court brought by unsuccessful litigants in the House of Lords before the HRA came into operation. Another was the willingness of the English judiciary to modify the doctrine of parliamentary sovereignty according to Sir William Wade in order to accommodate the United Kingdom's membership of the European Union.[23] These two considerations support a contextual background which is very different from the background in Australia and New Zealand.

In the light of the difference in contextual background it is natural that New Zealand and Victorian courts would regard *Wilkinson* as enunciating an approach which is more conducive to the relationship which exists between

[21] [2005] 1 A.C. 264, at [53].
[22] [2005] 1 A.C. 264, at [28].
[23] See *R. v Secretary of State for Transport Ex p. Factortame Ltd (No.2)* (1991) 1 A.C. 603.

the legislative and judicial branches of government in Australia and New Zealand than *Ghaidan*. It is true that Australia and New Zealand have ratified the ICCPR. But the possibility of a finding by the UN Human Rights Committee that domestic legislation breaches international human rights obligations is by no means as effective a deterrent as the prospect of such a finding by the Strasbourg Court.

The effect attributed to the interpretive provisions in *Hansen* and *Momcilovic* raises the question whether the 'presumption' created by the provisions is more effective in generating a rights-compliant interpretation than the common law principle of legality. The Victorian Court of Appeal seemingly was of the view that the interpretive provision was to be equated to the principle of legality, while the majority in *Hansen* did not express a definitive opinion on the question.

Before discussing this question, two points must be made. The interpretive model has greater strength than the common law principle in two important respects. First, it identifies the range of rights and freedoms which are recognised and protected. The rights and interests protected by the common law remain to be fully identified. Presently they may well be fewer in number than those recognised and protected by statute. On the other hand, they are capable of expanding and including rights and freedoms not recognised and protected by statute. Secondly, the interpretive model has an important legitimising effect. It gives statutory force to an interpretive principle which, without that backing, may be seen by some as an unauthorised usurpation of power by the judiciary designed to qualify the expression of the legislative will. Because the interpretive principle has statutory backing, judges may have greater confidence in applying it than they have in the case of the principle of legality viewed in isolation.

To return to the question of the effect of the interpretive provision. It has been said, in the context of the principle of legality, that general words are not enough and that specific words will be required to displace a common law rights-compliant construction of legislation. But this statement does not mean that there is no scope for necessary implication to yield a contrary intention. *Wilkinson*, *Hansen* and *Momcilovic* speak eloquently on this score. These decisions and, for that matter, *Ghaidan* itself proceeded on the footing that necessary implication remains as an element in the process of ascertaining the meaning of the primary enactment. So there is no strong basis for thinking, as some would hope, that a rights-compliant interpretation will prevail unless such an interpretation is expressly negated. The point is that no interpretive provision has provided that an express statement negating a rights-compliant interpretation of the primary enactment is necessary to achieve such an outcome. Whether such an approach would be constitutionally possible is another question.

It has been suggested that the interpretive provisions might authorise a stronger or broader interpretation than that justified by the principle of legality, yet narrower than *Ghaidan.* It is by no means clear what this suggestion amounts to unless it means no more than that judges will apply an interpretive provision with more confidence than they would apply the principle of legality and that, in so doing, they may give effect to the interpretive provision in some cases where they would be less confident in applying the principle of legality. If this be so, the suggestion does not contemplate a new principle of interpretation; it simply means at most that there is a stronger presumption, the greater strength of which is not readily measurable in the form of a proposition capable of general application.

Although necessary implication remains an element in ascertaining the legislative intention of the primary enactment, it is possible that, in some cases, what otherwise could qualify as necessary implication might not be enough to displace a rights-compliant interpretation. It is, however, difficult, if not impossible, to fit all conceivable questions relating to rights-compliant interpretation within orthodox categories of interpretation. All that can be said is that questions of rights-compliant interpretation have the potential to be so infinitely various that the interpretive provision may perhaps tip the balance in some cases in which a court would have been reluctant to apply the principle of legality. Perhaps one way of looking at the matter is to ask the following question. Is there an irreconcilable intention to displace a rights-compliant interpretation?[24]

In this respect, a central element of the principle of legality, noted by Lord Hoffmann in *R. v Secretary of State for the Home Department Ex p. Simms*, was that

> the principle ... means that Parliament must squarely confront what it is doing and accept the political cost. Fundamental rights cannot be overridden by general or ambiguous words. This is because there is too great a risk that the full implications of their unqualified meaning may have passed unnoticed in the democratic process. In the absence of express language or necessary implication to the contrary, the courts therefore presume that even the most general words were intended to be subject to the basic rights of the individual.[25]

The point here is that the principle of legality has a dual aspect.

Although the principle is one of construction which creates a presumption, it is also a principle which is founded on a political assumption or hypothesis that the legislature will address the relationship between its proposed legislation and the need to protect human rights. If it emerges that

[24] See below, p.211.

[25] [2002] 2 A.C. 115, at 131; see also *Coco v The Queen* (1994) 179 C.L.R. 427, at 437–38; *Electrolux Home Products Pty Ltd v Australian Workers Union* (2004) 221 C.L.R. 309, at 329.

the legislature, in compliance with statutory requirements, internal procedures or otherwise, has given its attention to the impact of the primary enactment on human rights, then that would seem to be a factor which would be relevant to a judicial determination whether the presumption has or has not been rebutted. Some allowance should be made for the legislative judgment so long as it is recognised that it is not for the courts to assess the rationality or soundness of the legislative judgment.

The co-existence of the common law principle of legality and the statutory interpretive provision generates an unnecessary degree of complexity and all the more so because there is some degree of uncertainty about the scope of the interpretive provision. A procedure which requires the application of the justification (proportionality) analysis to the common law interpretation of the primary enactment before the application of the interpretive provision is rather awkward. This was the subject of debate in *Hansen*. The majority[26] took the view that s.6 (the interpretive provision) was engaged only if the ordinary interpretation of the primary enactment resulted in a limitation that could not be demonstrably justified under s.5. The majority considered that the ordinary meaning was Parliament's intended meaning and that, if the court proceeded to the s.5 meaning before applying the justification test to the ordinary meaning, as Tipping J said:

> [T]here would be the potential for the potential for subversion of a deliberate policy choice by Parliament and its (at least implicit) view that the ensuing limitation of a right or freedom was justified.[27]

Elias CJ dissented on this point. The Chief Justice considered that, as a matter of interpretation of the provisions of the BORA, s.6 was to be applied before the court engaged in the s.5 justification (proportionality) of the analysis.[28] In *Momcilovic*, the Victorian Court of Appeal agreed with Elias CJ on this point, though the justification provision in the Charter is located in the consideration of rights in Part 2 of the Charter, unlike the NZ justification provision which is disconnected from the consideration of rights.[29]

The dispute between the Chief Justice and the majority on this point has an air of unreality about it if, as seems to be the case, there is little difference between the principle of legality and the interpretive approach mandated by the statute. If this hypothesis is correct, there is little to be gained by insisting on a separation of the two interpretive approaches. Indeed, one would expect that, at some time in the future, hopefully sooner rather than later, the two

[26] [2007] 3 N.Z.L.R. 37.
[27] [2007] 3 N.Z.L.R. 37.
[28] [2007] 3 N.Z.L.R. 37, at 12–16.
[29] See S. Evans and C. Evans, *Australian Bills of Rights* (Australia: LexisNexis Butterworths, Australia, 2008), 3.39, 3.45 and 3.63.

approaches will merge into one, at least so far as the recognised rights and freedoms are concerned.

Antipodean Traditionalism

Enough has been said already to indicate why Australia and New Zealand have declined to follow the broad *Ghaidan* approach to the interpretation of the interpretative Bill of Rights model. The expressed point of departure has been a conflict of opinion about the limits of common law interpretation. Other conceptions of interpretation are not so limited. This conflict of opinion has been equated to an argument about the location of the boundary line between interpreting and legislating, even if the identification of that location is notoriously problematic.

In Australia, more so than New Zealand, the separation of powers, which is constitutionally based and involves a strict separation of the judicial power, has had a dominating influence on the development of public law jurisprudence. The consequence is that the ordinary (common law) process of interpretation is a central element in maintaining and observing the constitutional relationship which exists between the legislative and judicial branches of government. In *Zheng v Cai*,[30] the High Court of Australia said:

> [J]udicial findings as to legislative intention are an expression of the constitutional relationship between the arms of government with respect to the making, interpretation and application of laws ... the preferred construction by the court of the statute in question is reached by the application of rules of interpretation accepted by all arms of government in the system of representative democracy.[31]

This statement is to be understood in a setting in which, in Australia, other authoritative judicial statements have drawn attention to the importance and grammatical sense of the words that Parliament has chosen[32] in maintaining the accessibility of the law to the public and the accountability of the Parliament to the electorate. It is, of course, recognised that context and purpose, even as disclosed by extrinsic materials, may be influential. And the ordinary process of interpretation does extend in some situations to placing a strained interpretation on the text, for example in order to give effect to the statutory purpose and, also, when two apparently inconsistent provisions occur in the one statute, 'to reconcile them by interpretation is the only course

[30] (2009) 261 A.L.R. 481.

[31] (2009) 261 A.L.R. 481, at 486; see also *Wilson v Anderson* (2002) 213 C.L.R. 401, at 418 (Gleeson CJ).

[32] *International Finance Trust Co Ltd v NSW Crime Commission* (2009) 261 A.L.R. 220, at 223 (Federal Court); *NAAV v Minister for Immigration* (2002) 123 F.C.R. 298, at 410 (Federal Court).

open', as Dixon J noted in *South-eastern Drainage Board (SA) v Savings Bank of South Australia*.[33] He went on to say:

> They cannot both receive their full meaning as it is expressed. In other words, no-one can say that two provisions cannot live together when the legislature which gave them life found room for them in the one enactment.[34]

In these cases the court gives effect to the legislative intention as it is divined from the single statute.

It is otherwise, however, in the case of apparently inconsistent provisions in two different statutes, as it is or may be with the interpretive model and the primary enactment. Then there are two different legislative intentions, each separately ascertainable. In this context, reconciliation is difficult because there is no single legislative intention. At best the possibility of reconciliation is a matter of degree. In such a case, unless the general statute (the interpretive model) has constitutional or quasi-constitutional status, the legislative intention exhibited in the specific statute (the primary enactment), if it is inconsistent with that of the general statute, will ordinarily prevail, certainly if it is the later of the two statutes. Even if it is the first of the two statutes, it may still prevail because there is a preference for the specific over the general.

Relevant to this discussion is the doctrine of implied repeal, a doctrine which is an aspect of legislative supremacy and is associated with necessary implication. The doctrine of implied repeal was not discussed in the cases which applied the *Ghaidan* interpretation; nor has it been discussed in *Wilkinson*, *Hansen* and *Momcilovic*. Yet the approach taken in these cases, because it treats the ascertainment of the legislative intention of the primary enactment (admittedly in the light of a presumption created by another statute) as something to be ascertained according to its context, seems implicitly to acknowledge that implied repeal has a role to play.

That cannot be said of the reasoning which underlies the *Ghaidan* interpretation. This reasoning attributes a superior value to the legislative intention exhibited in the general statute so that it may prevail, subject to the 'fundamental feature' limitation, over an inconsistent legislative intention in the primary enactment even if it be the later in time. The explanation for this must lie in the general statute (the interpretive model) having a constitutional or quasi-constitutional status which displaces the doctrine of implied repeal.

In the United Kingdom there is the argument that the HRA modifies the doctrines of legislative supremacy and implied repeal because the HRA is a constitutional statute. This argument is based on the well-known judgment of Laws LJ (with whom Crane J agreed) in *Thorburn v Sutherland City*

[33] (1939) 62 C.L.R. 603, at 626.
[34] (1939) 62 C.L.R. 603, at 626–27.

Council,[35] where his Lordship considered that although 'ordinary statutes may be impliedly repealed constitutional statutes may not'.[36] Laws LJ described a constitutional statute as one:

> which (a) conditions the legal relationship between citizen and the State in some general overarching manner, or (b) enlarges or diminishes the scope of what would now be regard[ed] as constitutional rights.[37]

He instanced the HRA as a constitutional statute.

So far there is no indication that the courts in Australia and New Zealand will take this step. In Australia, the decision of the High Court in *South-eastern Drainage Board*[38] still stands as authority for the existence of the doctrine of implied repeal. The Court held that the provisions of a subsequent Act impliedly repealed by implication provisions in an earlier Act which provided for the registration of estates and interests in Torrens system land, although the earlier Act provided that any inconsistent or future law should not 'apply' to land under that Act unless it expressly enacted that it would apply 'notwithstanding the provisions of' the earlier Act. In reaching this conclusion, Dixon J said that the question was whether in the later statute 'there is an *irreconcilable* intention to include land under the Act'.[39]

Of course, the statute in *South-eastern Drainage Board* could not conceivably be regarded as a constitutional statute. It is, however, significant that in the Australian and New Zealand cases on the interpretive model there has been no discussion of the doctrine of implied repeal, except to the extent that the courts have recognised that necessary implication is an integral element in the process of statutory interpretation and in the ascertainment of legislative intention. Certainly there has been no discussion of the suggestion that the interpretive model could be regarded as a 'constitutional statute' with adverse consequences for the doctrine of implied repeal in such a context.

It follows that neither in Australia nor New Zealand is there at this time judicial support for the notion that express words will be required to sustain a non-rights-compliant interpretation of a primary enactment.

In Australia the borderland between interpretation and legislation has been extensively discussed, as it has been in the United States. This discussion has taken place in Australia in the context of the application of statutory severance provisions which are designed to preserve the validity of the residue of a statute in the event that a provision or provisions in the statute are

[35] [2003] Q.B. 151.
[36] [2003] Q.B. 151, at 186.
[37] [2003] Q.B. 151, at 186.
[38] (1939) 62 C.L.R. 603. Similar issues have arisen in New Zealand: see *R. v Pora* [2001] 2 N.Z.L.R. 37.
[39] (1939) 62 C.L.R. 603, at 627 (emphasis added).

declared invalid as ultra vires the Australian Constitution. For example, s.15A of the Acts Interpretation Act 1901 (Cth) authorises a court to sever and read down provisions held to be invalid, so as to enable them to have a valid operation on the footing that the legislative intention is that the enactment is to have as an extensive an operation as is possible. The section establishes

> a presumption in favour of the independence, from one another, of the various provisions of an enactment, to which effect should be given unless some positive indication of interdependence appears from the text, context, content or subject matter of the provisions.[40]

But there are limits to what a court can achieve under a section such as s.15A. It cannot apply 'to divert legislation from one purpose to another'.[41] Nor can it apply so as to alter the substance or effect of the enactment. Within these limits, the courts can give effect to a section such as s.15A if there is a sufficiently clear indication of the legislative intention.[42] If, however, the enactment is complex and it is held to be invalid and the court is left with various alternatives from which it is possible that a valid statute could be constructed, such a section will not authorise the court to execute such an undertaking. To do so would not constitute interpretation; it would amount to an exercise of legislative power not judicial power. Nor can 'Parliament direct courts to reconstruct out of the views of one invalid law of general application a number of valid laws of particular application'.[43] That said, there is still scope for a court to apply an interpretation which is significantly different from the primary legislative intention if that different interpretation is clearly identified by the legislature and is the subject of a clear legislative direction.

The jurisprudence on severance clauses serves to emphasise the importance of the absence of a legislative intention in the primary enactment that is contrary to the legislative intention of the interpretive statute and the absence of any judicial function which can be classified as a legislative exercise. The problem is that, in a variety of situations, the recasting of a primary enactment to make it rights-compliant may involve either a departure from its legislative intention or a reconstruction which amounts to an exercise of legislative power.

The approach taken to the interpretive provisions in Australia and New Zealand reflects a traditional common law approach based on the doctrines of legislative supremacy and implied repeal, supported by the separation of powers and divorced from the constitutional imperatives to which the United Kingdom is subject, imperatives which have seen a dilution in the force of the

[40] *Fraser Henleius Pty Ltd v Cody* (1945) 70 C.L.R. 100, at 127 (Dixon J).
[41] *Australian Railways Union v Victorian Railway Commissioners* (1930) 44 C.L.R. 319, at 386 (Dixon J).
[42] *Pidoto v Victoria* (1943) 68 C.L.R. 87, at 108–10 (Latham CJ); *Bank of NSW v Commonwealth* (1948) 76 C.L.R. 1, at 368–72 (Dixon J).
[43] *Strickland v Rocla Concrete Pipes Ltd* (1971) 124 C.L.R. 468.

doctrines of legislative supremacy and implied repeal. The difference in the antipodean approach to the interpretive model is a particular manifestation of the difference which is emerging between the general or common law of the United Kingdom and that of Australia. This difference arises from the influence in the United Kingdom of European law, particularly in administrative law where a gulf has opened up between UK and Australian law.[44] Australian judges have always had a tendency to see themselves as the keepers of the pure flame of the common law, just as New South Wales (NSW) lawyers see themselves as the lantern-jawed custodians of equity by reason of the fact that NSW did not adopt the Judicature Acts until 1980. Now that English law is being influenced by European law, the tendency has strengthened.[45]

Hong Kong

Hong Kong presents a very different picture. Its human rights regime, unlike the 'weak' New Zealand and Victorian models, takes the form of a 'strong' constitutionally entrenched model. The capacity of the Hong Kong courts to grant relief is therefore greater than that of the Australasian courts. Hong Kong courts can declare statutory provisions invalid for contravention of protected rights and the capacity of the Hong Kong courts to re-interpret non-conforming legislation is greater than that of Australasian courts.

Constitutional Arrangements

Human rights and fundamental freedoms in Hong Kong are protected both by the Basic Law (BL)—Hong Kong's constitution—and by the Bill of Rights Ordinance which incorporates a Bill of Rights (BOR) based on the ICCPR. The Basic Law is an enactment of the National People's Congress (NPC), the supreme law-making body in the People's Republic of China (PRC), pursuant to arts 31 and 62 of the PRC Constitution. These articles enable the NPC to set up a Special Administrative Region (SAR) and enact a constitution for it. The BL is in a form agreed upon by the PRC and the UK governments as set out in their Joint Declaration signed in 1984.

The BL mandates the continuation in the Hong Kong SAR (HKSAR) of a legal system based on the common law,[46] in accordance with the theme 'one

[44] See *Re Minister for Immigration Multicultural & Indigenous Affairs Ex p. Lam* (2003) 214 C.L.R. 1, at [73]; *D'Orta-Ekenalke v Victoria Legal Aid* (2005) 223 C.L.R. 1, at [60].
[45] I doubt that Lord Hoffmann would accept this statement. See "The Influence of European Law on the Common Law in English Courts", Fifth John Lehane Memorial Lecture, Sydney, 18 August 2010.
[46] Articles 8 and 18.

country, two systems'. The BL confers wide-ranging legislative and executive powers on the HKSAR, withholding only powers with respect to foreign affairs (art.13) and defence (art.14). Legislative power is vested in the Legislative Council (Legco) and executive power in the Chief Executive. So far Hong Kong does not have a universal franchise. Although art.26 guarantees the right to vote, this right does not translate into a universal franchise or an entitlement to vote in a direct election of the Chief Executive. The voting system for Legco involves functional or occupational as well as geographical constituencies.

The BL makes provision, in conformity with Chinese tradition, for a strong executive and a relatively weak legislature. On the other hand, the exercise of the judicial power of the SAR is vested in its courts (art.80), the power of final adjudication being vested in the Court of Final Appeal (CFA) (art.82). Judicial independence is guaranteed (art.85). The exercise of judicial power by the Hong Kong courts is, however, subject to art.158. This article vests the interpretation of the BL in the Standing Committee of the NPC and delegates the exercise of that power to the courts of the SAR in the adjudication of cases but requires the courts to follow any interpretation of the BL issued by Standing Committee. Although in 1999 the Standing Committee issued an interpretation under art.158 which overruled two decisions of the CFA on the right of abode guaranteed by art.24, there has been no subsequent Standing Committee interpretation overruling a court decision.

The existence of a 'weak' unicameral legislature and a powerful executive gives the role of the courts in Hong Kong an added importance. The judicial interpretation and enforcement of guaranteed rights and freedoms by the courts in Hong Kong seems to have strong popular support. In Hong Kong, the echoes of Professor Dicey's old views on legislative supremacy do not resonate as they do in Australia.

The BL contains a series of guarantees of human rights (arts 24–37 and 87). The BOR, which was enacted before the resumption of sovereignty over Hong Kong by the PRC, also guarantees a series of human rights. The provisions of the BOR also have constitutional force by reason of art.39 of the BL. There are some differences in expression between the relevant provisions of the BL and the BOR. So far they have not proved to be significant. The CFA has adopted a generous approach in ascertaining the scope of the rights protected by the BL and the BOR while narrowly interpreting permissible restrictions to them.[47] So in *Gurung Kesh Bahadur v. Director of Immigration*,[48] the freedom conferred on Hong Kong residents by art.31 of

[47] *Gurung Kesh Bahadur v Director of Immigration* (2002) 5 H.K.C.F.A.R. 480, at 490, 491 (Li CJ).

the BL to travel and enter and leave the SAR received a broad interpretation, while art.39(2) dealing with restrictions received a narrow interpretation. This principle of construction is not, of course, an absolute. Much will depend upon the competing contentions.

Interpretation

Section 8 of the BL preserves the common law of Hong Kong and, with it, the common law principles of interpretation. Neither the BL nor the BOR contains an interpretive provision similar to those in New Zealand and Victoria. The CFA in *HKSAR v Lam Kwong Wai*[49] held, however, that there is to be implied in the BL a wide power to make a remedial interpretation to a statute in order to make it BL-compliant. In reaching this conclusion, the CFA pointed to the power as one which was necessary in the context of courts entrusted with the responsibility of interpreting and enforcing human rights. As the judgment pointed out:

> The justification for now engaging in remedial interpretation is that it enables the courts, in appropriate cases, to uphold the validity of legislation, albeit in an altered form, rather than strike it down. To this extent, the courts interfere less with the exercise of legislative power than they would if they could not engage in remedial interpretation. In that event, they would have no option but to declare the legislation unconstitutional and invalid. Indeed, it can be safely assumed that the legislature intends its legislative provisions to have a valid, even if reduced, operation than to have no operation at all, so long as the valid operation is not fundamentally different from what it enacted.[50]

In essence, this approach reflects the *Ghaidan* interpretive approach.

As a result, in Hong Kong, where the courts have not, so far at any rate, adopted the Australian view of separation of powers or the narrow view of judicial power, the courts will engage in the techniques of severance, reading down and reading in; in other words, do whatever may be necessary by way of remedial interpretation to make legislation BL-consistent. The qualification is, of course, that the legislative provision in its 'remedied' form is not essentially or fundamentally different from what was enacted. If the provision cannot be 'remedied' in this way and is non-compliant, the court may declare it invalid, this being relief not available to a court in New Zealand and Victoria or, for that matter, the United Kingdom.

[48] *Gurung Kesh Bahadur v Director of Immigration* (2002) 5 H.K.C.F.A.R. 480, at 490, 491 (Li CJ).

[49] (2006) 9 H.K.C.F.A.R. 574, at 606–11 (Mason NPJ).

[50] (2006) 9 H.K.C.F.A.R. 574, at 610 (Mason NPJ).

Restrictions on Rights and Freedoms

In cases involving the BL, and the BOR as well, the courts are concerned with whether the restrictions on rights provided for by laws enacted by the legislature are valid. The burden is on the state to justify the restriction.[51] Any restriction must satisfy two requirements. First, it must be 'prescribed by law'. Secondly, it must satisfy the proportionality test.

The Proportionality Test

Any restriction permitted by the BOR must satisfy the relevant provision in the BOR.[52] In relation to many rights, the BOR prescribes that restrictions are justified only if they are necessary for specified purposes. These purposes constitute the legitimate purposes for permissible restriction. The test is one of necessity (not pressing necessity as in the Strasbourg jurisprudence). It has to be shown that a restriction is necessary for a legitimate purpose.

The CFA has formulated the proportionality test in these terms: first, the restriction must be rationally connected with the legitimate purpose or purposes permitted by the relevant provision in the BOR; secondly, the means used to impair the right must be no more than is necessary to accomplish the legitimate purpose in question.[53] The test is based on the test formulated in *R. v Oakes*,[54] the well-known Canadian case.

As has been noted, the BOR sets out the legitimate purposes for permissible restriction of a number of rights. For example, in relation to the freedom of speech or expression which is guaranteed by both the BL and the BOR,[55] art.16(3) of the Bill provides that the exercise of this right:

> carries with it special duties and responsibilities. It may therefore be subject to certain restrictions, but these shall only be such as are provided by law and are necessary—
>
> a. For respect of the rights or reputations of others; or
> b. For the protection of national security or of public order (ordre public), or of public health or morals.

[51] *HKSAR v Lam Kwong Wai* (2006) 9 H.K.C.F.A.R. 574, at 600–01.
[52] Article 39 and *Gurung Kesh Bahadur v Director of Immigration* (2002) 5 H.K.C.F.A.R. 480 (where the Court held that when the right or freedom is guaranteed only by the BL, the question whether it could be restricted and, if so, the test for ascertaining permissible restrictions, depends on the nature and subject matter of the right or freedom in issue).
[53] *Leung Kwok Hung v HKSAR* (2005) 8 H.K.C.F.A.R. 229, at 253.
[54] [1986] 1 S.C.R. 103, at [69]–[71] (Dickson CJC).

The Use of Foreign Law

A prominent feature of Hong Kong rights jurisprudence has been the extensive use of comparative jurisprudence, including that of the Strasbourg Court. One advantage of the Strasbourg jurisprudence is that it is mediated through UK jurisprudence and, by this means, to a common law legal system. A second advantage is that the Strasbourg jurisprudence is a very extensive body of sophisticated law, comparing favourably with the more fragmented and less elaborated jurisprudence of the UN Human Rights Committee, the body which oversees the ICCPR. A third advantage, which follows from the second, is that the Strasbourg jurisprudence more often provides a persuasive answer, or a stepping-stone to an answer, than any other source of human rights jurisprudence, in the context of the common law, despite Lord Hoffmann's criticisms of the Strasbourg Court to be mentioned shortly.

On the other hand, the rulings of the UN Human Rights Committee and its General Comments are a more direct source of authority than the Strasbourg jurisprudence. In this respect, the CFA judgment in *Koon Wing Yee v Insider Dealing Tribunal*[56] is an illustration of how the Court uses both sources of authority. One of the many issues in that case was what is the criminal standard of proof mandated by art.14 of the ICCPR (art.11(1) of the BOR). The Court concluded that it was proof beyond reasonable doubt, after considering the Strasbourg jurisprudence on art.6(2) of the European Convention[57] and, more particularly, the Human Rights Committee's General Comments 13 and 32.[58] It was argued that the CFA should disregard the General Comments because they were not issued by a judicial body exercising judicial power. The CFA (of which I was a member) dismissed that argument, holding that the General Comments were a valuable jurisprudential resource.

Apart from the interpretation of national constitutions adopted in the era that antedated the Universal Declaration of Human Rights where different considerations may apply, it is obvious that foreign law is capable of offering assistance and insights in various ways.

In relation to the application of the permitted restrictions and limitations on declared rights, there is a case for saying that foreign decisions should not necessarily have the same persuasive value as foreign decisions on the scope of rights. The flagship cases in the United States,[59] Hong Kong[60] and New

[55] Article 27 of the BL and art.16(2) of the BOR.

[56] (2008) 11 H.K.C.F.A.R. 170.

[57] (2008) 11 H.K.C.F.A.R. 170, 203, at [91]–[95].

[58] (2008) 11 H.K.C.F.A.R. 170, 204–06, at [96]–[103].

[59] *Texas v Johnson* 491 U.S. 397 (1989); *US v Eichman* 496 U.S. 310 (1990).

[60] *HKSAR v Ng Kung Sui* (1999) 2 H.K.C.F.A.R. 442.

Zealand[61] with their different outcomes, where the legislation in the United States and New Zealand contravened the protected freedom of expression but not so in Hong Kong, illustrate point. The need to preserve national unity in the light of the recent resumption of sovereignty by the PRC over Hong Kong was the critical factor on which the legitimacy of the restriction was justified in that case.

There are, of course, those who argue that limits such as 'necessary in the interests of national security' or 'reasonable limits [such as] can be demonstrably justified in a democratic society' set a uniform standard based on the concept of what can demonstrably be justified in *any* democratic society. While there is much to commend this broad reading, it would involve a comprehensive inquiry into the way in which other democratic societies deal with the problem under consideration.

Adoption of the broad approach encounters the risk that it will generate a standard which does not take account of conditions and values in the jurisdiction in which the question arises. This is where Lord Hoffmann's criticisms of the Strasbourg Court begin to bite. His point is that communities have distinct cultural, social and moral values and that it is preferable that legal answers involve consideration of them and should be undertaken by national courts in the light of local legislative judgment.[62] This perspective may have attractions for Hong Kong.

Conclusion

In the final analysis, the difference in the legislative regimes in Australia, New Zealand and Hong Kong is the product of differing sets of political and constitutional values—in one jurisdiction (Hong Kong), they favour entrenchment of human rights, in the other two, they favour preserving the ultimate autonomy of the political process and the legislature to a greater or lesser degree. When it comes to judicial interpretation, the influence of the doctrines of legislative supremacy and the separation of powers seems to be stronger in Australia and to a lesser extent New Zealand, than it is either in the United Kingdom or Hong Kong.

[61] *Hopkinson v Police* (2004) 3 N.Z.L.R. 714; *The Queen v Morse* (2010) 2 N.Z.L.R. 625.

[62] Lord Hoffmann, "The Universality of Human Rights" (2009) 125 L.Q.R. 416.

10

Australian Bills of Rights and the 'New Commonwealth Model of Constitutionalism'

SIMON EVANS AND JULIA WATSON

Introduction

IN 2001, STEPHEN GARDBAUM PUBLISHED an important article in the *American Journal of Comparative Law*.[1] He identified, and presented a normative argument in support of, a new intermediate model of constitutionalism—the 'new Commonwealth model of constitutionalism'[2]—that was distinctively different from both the traditional Commonwealth model of parliamentary sovereignty and the established US model of judicial supremacy or strong-form judicial review. The new Commonwealth model involves a legalised Bill or Charter of Rights in which a particular set of rights is given positive canonical form; 'some form of judicial power to enforce these rights against legislation that goes beyond ordinary modes of statutory interpretation', either by way of a strengthened interpretive mandate or a power to issue declarations of incompatibility or both; and, 'most distinctively', 'a formal legislative power to have the final word on what the law of the land is'.[3] Enhanced parliamentary scrutiny of legislation for human rights consistency is frequently associated with this form of review[4] as part of its effort to rebalance democratic political decision-making and judicial rights protection. Ever since Gardbaum's paper was published, the distinctiveness, normative appeal and success of 'weak

[1] S. Gardbaum, "The New Commonwealth Model of Constitutionalism" (2001) 49 *American Journal of Comparative Law* 707.
[2] Gardbaum, "The New Commonwealth Model of Constitutionalism", at 710.
[3] S. Gardbaum, "Reassessing the New Commonwealth Model of Constitutionalism" (2011) 8 I.C.O.N. 167, at 169.
[4] See J. Hiebert, "Constitutional Experimentation: Rethinking How a Bill of Rights Functions", in T. Ginsburg and R. Dixon (eds), *Comparative Constitutional Law* (London: Edward Elgar, 2011), p.298.

form' judicial review have been a staple of the comparative public law literature.[5]

Even in 2001, differences were apparent between the various exemplars of the new Commonwealth model in Canada, New Zealand and the United Kingdom, the most striking being the near complete judicial supremacy in Canada. The new Commonwealth model now appears to have new exemplars, including the two statutory Bills of Rights in Australia, the Victorian Charter of Human Rights and Responsibilities Act 2006 (Vic) (the Charter) and the Australian Capital Territory Human Rights Act 2004 (the ACT HRA). Our aim in this essay is to examine the influence of the new Commonwealth model (and in particular the UK model) on the form of the two Australian Bills of Rights, and then to consider the impact of Australia's distinctive legal culture and constitutional structure on the operation of these instruments. In particular, we focus on how the Australian approach to the interpretive mandate and power to issue declarations of incompatibility has diverged from the dominant UK approach—a divergence so striking that it may no longer be possible to identify the Australian statutory Bills of Rights as exemplars of the new Commonwealth model.[6]

The New Commonwealth Model in Australia

The Human Rights Act 1998 (UK) (the UK HRA) has profoundly influenced the ongoing debate about protection of human rights in Australia. A political–legal tradition shaped by Westminster had meant that, prior to the 1990s, there was no broadly based Bill of Rights or Human Rights Act and little support for change. Rights-focused judicial review was alien to a system built on parliamentary supremacy (modified for the peculiarities of a federal system) that embedded positive assumptions about the capacity of responsible and representative government to restrain abuse of public power. There had been regular attempts to enact statutory Bills of Rights (and even to entrench some constitutional rights protections) but none had been successful. Leaders of the judiciary and legal profession were sceptical, perhaps even largely opposed.[7] And, in contrast to the United Kingdom, Australia lacked

[5] See M. Tushnet, "The Rise of Weak Form Judicial Review", in Ginsburg and Dixon, *Comparative Constitutional Law*, p.321.

[6] For a survey of other aspects of Australian statutory Bills of Rights, see the *Victorian Government Submission to the Scrutiny of Acts and Regulations Committee's Review of the Charter of Human Rights and Responsibilities Act 2006*, http://www.parliament.vic.gov.au/images/stories/committees/sarc/charter_review/submissions/324_-_Victorian_Government_Submission.pdf.

[7] See, generally, A. Byrnes, H. Charlesworth and G. McKinnon, *Bills of Rights in Australia: History, Politics and Law* (Sydney: University of New South Wales Press, 2009); J. Waghorne and

(and continues to lack) the immediate external stimulus of a regional human rights court regularly drawing attention to problems with domestic rights protection.

The Australian debate began to shift, however, as the Canadian Supreme Court's jurisprudence under the Canadian Charter of Rights and Freedoms (the Canadian Charter) developed and the United Kingdom moved towards enactment of the UK HRA. By the early 1990s, judicial leaders were beginning to speak in favour of statutory rights protections.[8]

The first jurisdiction to move was the Australian Capital Territory. Following a broadly based public consultation led by Professor Hilary Charlesworth,[9] It enacted the ACT HRA in 2004. Victoria followed suit, enacting the Charter in 2006 following a public consultation led this time by Professor George Williams.[10] The recommendations of both of these consultations and the legislation ultimately enacted were shaped by the UK HRA.[11]

The terms of reference for the ACT consultation were open-ended. After considering a range of models, the ACT Human Rights Consultative Committee settled on a statutory model based on the UK HRA. The Committee was influenced by the balance that the UK model embodied—without parliamentary, executive or judicial dominance—and the possibilities of dialogue that it offered.[12]

The Victorian state government was more prescriptive in setting out a Statement of Intent for its consultation. It indicated that it was attached to the traditions of parliamentary supremacy and that it was 'interested in' the UK model of statutory rights protection and the model adopted in New Zealand and the Australian Capital Territory.[13] It preferred the soft political

---

S. Macintyre, *Liberty: A History of Civil Liberties in Australia* (Sydney: University of New South Wales Press, 2011).

[8] Anthony Mason, "A Bill of Rights for Australia?", Address to the Australian Bar Association Bicentennial Conference (1988); John Toohey, "A Government of Laws, and Not of Men?" (1993) 4 *Public Law Review* 158; Gerard Brennan, "The Impact of a Bill of Rights on the Role of the Judiciary: An Australian Response", in Phillip Alston (ed.), *Towards an Australian Bill of Rights* (Canberra: Centre for International and Public Law, ANU, 1994), p.184.

[9] ACT Bill of Rights Consultative Committee, *Towards an ACT Human Rights Act: Report of the ACT Bill of Rights Consultative Committee* (2003) (hereafter 'ACT HRA Report').

[10] Human Rights Consultation Committee, *Rights, Responsibilities and Respect: Report of the Human Rights Consultation Committee* (2005) (hereafter 'Charter Report').

[11] More recently there have been consultations at the national level and in Tasmania and Western Australia that recommended variants on the new Commonwealth model. Human rights instruments have not been enacted in either state. At national level, the government elected not to pursue a statutory Bill of Rights, instead introducing the Human Rights (Parliamentary Scrutiny) Act 2011 which came into force in 2012.

[12] ACT HRA Report, at 54–55 and ch.4 passim.

[13] Charter Report, 162.

entrenchment of this model rather than the legal entrenchment of rights protection in the USA and Canada. The sovereignty of Parliament was to be preserved and government would still be accountable for policy decisions affecting human rights through the ballot box.[14] Finally, it was 'attracted to' the statement of compatibility and scrutiny procedures in the United Kingdom, New Zealand and the Australian Capital Territory as a mechanism for focusing government attention on the human rights implications of policy before it became law.[15] The Victorian Consultation Committee canvassed other models but ultimately recommended a statutory Charter that included most of the features of the UK HRA. In 2008, the ACT HRA was amended so that most of its operative provisions are now very closely modelled on the corresponding Charter provisions.[16]

Australian Bills of Rights thus incorporate the key features of the UK HRA including an obligation on the proponents of legislation to prepare statements of compatibility[17]; a parliamentary scrutiny committee[18]; an interpretive mandate for the courts;[19] a power to make declarations of incompatibility (but without fast-track procedures for amending incompatible legislation)[20]; and an obligation on public authorities to act consistently with human rights (and to give them proper consideration in decision-making).[21]

There are some significant differences, however, the most important of which for present purposes are as follows.[22] First, Australian Bills of Rights do not purport to give direct effect to international human rights. Indeed, they give effect to only a limited selection of Australia's international human

[14] Charter Report, 162.
[15] Charter Report, 162.
[16] Human Rights Amendment Act 2008 (ACT).
[17] ACT HRA, ss.37–39; Charter, ss.28–29, cf. UK HRA, s.19.
[18] ACT HRA, s.38; Charter, s.30.
[19] ACT HRA, s.30; Charter, s.32(1); cf. UK HRA, s.3.
[20] ACT HRA, ss.32–33; Charter, ss.36–37; cf. UK HRA, s.4.
[21] ACT HRA, s.40B; Charter, s.38; cf. UK HRA, s.6.
[22] Other differences include the following. First, there is an extended definition of 'public authority' that includes some entities that have 'functions of a public nature': ACT HRA, s.40; Charter, s.4; cf. UK HRA, s.46. The Charter definition sets out five factors that are relevant but non-conclusive as to whether a function is of a public nature: Charter, s.4(2)–(3). Secondly, Courts (and, in Victoria, tribunals) are not public authorities except when they are acting in an administrative capacity. As such they are not required to act compatibly with Charter rights when acting judicially, although they are required to interpret legislation compatibly with human rights in accordance with the interpretive mandate. See ACT HRA, s.40(2)(b); Charter, s.4(1)(a)(i); cf. UK HRA, s.6(3)(b). However, s.6(2)(b) of the Charter makes the rights in Pt2 directly applicable to courts and tribunals. Thirdly, the provisions on proceedings and remedies are much more limited—and, although opaquely expressed, are designed to exclude freestanding human rights actions and in particular damages for breaches of human rights. See ACT HRA, s.40C; Charter, s.39; cf. UK HRA, s.8.

rights obligations. For example, even though many rights provisions set out in the Bills of Rights are based on rights in the International Covenant on Civil and Political Rights (ICCPR), neither contains a right to a remedy (compare art.2 of the ICCPR) or an enforceable right to compensation for unlawful arrest or detention (compare art.9(5) of the ICCPR).[23] And only individuals have human rights.[24] Secondly, each contains an express limitation clause that provides that human rights may be subject only to 'such reasonable limits as can be demonstrably justified in a free and democratic society based on human dignity, equality and freedom', language modelled on s.1 of the Canadian Charter, 'and taking into account all relevant factors' including five factors modelled on s.36 of the South African Constitution.[25] The limitation clause thus evokes the proportionality analysis characteristic of rights jurisprudence in those jurisdictions. Thirdly, there is a statutory obligation to produce statements of compatibility and they must identify *how* (and not just whether) the legislation is, or is not, compatible with human rights.[26] Fourthly, the interpretive mandate includes a purpose proviso, requiring interpreters to adopt a human rights-consistent interpretation only '[s]o far as it is possible to do so consistently with [the] purpose' of the provision.[27] The purpose proviso was intended by the Victorian Consultation Committee to give effect to the limits of the *Ghaidan v Godin-Mendoza*[28] approach to interpretation

[23] ACT HRA, Pt3; Charter, Pt2; cf. UK HRA, s.1, Sch.1. Some rights are omitted because in practice the legislative responsibility for the subject matter of the right lies at national rather than state or territory level in Australia: for example, the right to enter one's country (art.12(4)) and rights related to marriage (art.23).

[24] ACT HRA, s.6; Charter, s.6(1).

[25] ACT HRA, s.28; Charter, s.7(2).

[26] ACT HRA, s.37; Charter, s.28; cf. UK HRA, s.19.

[27] Neither the interpretive mandate (in Victoria) nor the power to make declarations of incompatibility (in Victoria and the ACT) affects the validity of incompatible legislation: ACT HRA, s.32(3); Charter, ss. 32(3) and 36(5).

[28] [2004] 2 UKHL 30; [2004] 2 A.C. 557 (hereafter '*Ghaidan*'). In *Ghaidan*, the House of Lords considered a provision of the Rent Act 1977 (UK) that extended certain protections to the 'spouse' of deceased tenants, including where the survivor had not been married to the deceased but had been living with them 'as his or her wife or husband'. Relying on the interpretive provision in the UK HRA, a majority of the House of Lords read the provision as protecting persons who had been living 'as if' they were wife and husband, thereby extending the protections in the Rent Act 1977 (UK) to homosexual partners. Despite this departure from the meaning of the legislative text intended by the Parliament, this interpretation was considered to be consistent with the UK HRA and constitutional principle as it was 'compatible with the underlying thrust of the legislation being construed' and not 'against the grain' of the legislation (Lord Nicholls, at [33]). The Victorian Consultation Committee saw the '*Ghaidan* approach' as one that would allow courts significant scope to give effect to a human rights-compatible interpretation to legislation yet nonetheless accord with the principle of parliamentary sovereignty. On one reading of the extrinsic materials, this approach was intended to be encapsulated in s.32(1), with the purpose proviso apparently included to ensure that the limits of the approach outlined by Lord Nicholls would be respected by Victorian courts. See the Charter Report, 82–83.

which it saw as relatively constrained,[29] perhaps in contrast to *R. v A (No.2)*.[30] When the ACT HRA's interpretive mandate was amended so that its language more closely tracked the Charter's interpretive mandate, the Explanatory Statement noted that this change 'dr[ew] on jurisprudence from the United Kingdom such as the case of *Ghaidan v Godin-Mendoza*'.[31] Fifthly, the Charter contains an override provision, comparable in some ways to the Canadian Charter's 'notwithstanding clause'. Its function is manifestly different in the two systems, however, given that Victorian courts do not have the power that the Canadian courts have to strike down legislation on human rights grounds, but certainly constitutes 'a formal [if otiose] legislative power to have the final word on what the law of the land is'.[32]

In the next section of this essay we examine how the interpretive mandates in the Charter and the ACT HRA have operated in practice.

The Interpretive Mandate Applied

The interpretive mandates in the ACT HRA and the Charter are now in substantially identical terms.[33] The Charter provision, s.32, reads, '[s]o far as it is possible to do so consistently with their purpose, statutory provisions must be interpreted in a way that is compatible with human rights'. The early cases in the Australian Capital Territory adopted a narrow approach to the interpretive mandate, some assuming that uncertainty or ambiguity was required to bring it into play.[34] Later cases tended either to dismiss or to follow *Ghaidan*, in either case without explaining why the textual differences between the ACT HRA and the UK HRA interpretative mandates were, or were not, significant.[35]

R. v Fearnside provided a temporary resolution of the proper approach to the interpretive mandate.[36] A provision of the Supreme Court Act 1933 (ACT) provided a right for an accused to elect, within a specified time-frame, to undergo trial by judge alone. The interpretive issue was whether the vacation of a trial date reactivated the right to elect such a trial after the specified time-

[29] Charter Report, 82–83.
[30] [2001] UKHL 25; [2002] 1 A.C. 45.
[31] Notes to clause 5.
[32] Gardbaum, "Reassessing the New Commonwealth Model of Constitutionalism", at 169.
[33] ACT HRA, s.30; Charter, s.32(1).
[34] See the cases cited in C. Evans and S. Evans, *Australian Bills of Rights: The Law of the Victorian Charter and the ACT Human Rights Act* (Chatsworth, NSW: LexisNexis Butterworths, 2008), p.85.
[35] Evans and Evans, *Australian Bills of Rights: The Law of the Victorian Charter and the ACT Human Rights Act*, p.85.
[36] [2009] ACTCA 3; (2009) A.C.T.L.R. 25.

frame had run. Besanko J (with whom the other members of the court agreed) found that, on ordinary principles of statutory construction, it did not. He therefore turned to the ACT HRA's interpretive mandate. He adopted a modified three-step version of the five-step approach adopted by the majority in the New Zealand Supreme Court in *R. v Hansen*.[37] The appropriate approach was to ask, he concluded:

> (a) Does the legislative provision in question 'enliven' a human right?
> (b) If yes to (a), does the provision contain a limitation which is reasonable within [the limitation provision]?
> (c) If no to (b), how should the provision be interpreted in accordance with [the interpretive mandate]?[38]

If the court reached this final step, the interpretive mandate would allow the court

> to adopt an interpretation of a legislative provision compatible with human rights which did not necessarily best achieve the purpose of that provision or promote that purpose, providing the interpretation was consistent with that purpose.

However, it would not allow the court 'to take the type of approach taken by the House of Lords in *Ghaidan*', by which he understood an approach that allowed a court to depart from the unambiguous meaning of the legislation and read in words which changed the meaning of the legislation.[39] Besanko J held that, in this case, 'reliance on the ACT HRA failed at the first stage', as no right was enlivened by the relevant provision.[40]

The first cases under the Victorian Charter referenced Charter rights in a general way without engaging with the operative provisions.[41] Over time, a more systematic approach developed. However, even now there are only a handful of cases that have relied upon ss. 32(1) and 7(2) (the interpretive mandate and the reasonable limits provision) to shape the interpretation of legislation. Two are particularly notable: *RJE v Secretary to the Department of Justice*[42] and *Re an application under the Major Crimes (Investigative Powers) Act 2004*.[43]

[37] [2007] NZSC 7; [2007] 3 N.Z.L.R. 1.
[38] As summarised in *In the matter of an application for bail by Islam* [2010] ACTSC 147; (2010) 4 A.C.T.L.R. 235, an important decision about interpretive issues by a judge who had previously been Commonwealth First Parliamentary Counsel.
[39] [2009] ACTCA 3; (2009) A.C.T.L.R. 25, at [89] and [85]. On the rejection of this reading of *Ghaidan*, see further *In the matter of an application for bail by Islam* [2010] ACTSC 147; (2010) 4 A.C.T.L.R. 235.
[40] [2009] ACTCA 3; (2009) A.C.T.L.R. 25, at [98].
[41] See, for example, *R. v Williams* [2007] VSC 2; (2007) 16 V.R. 168; *R. v White* [2007] VSC 142; *Re Unumadu* [2007] VSC 258.
[42] [2008] VSCA 265; (2008) 21 V.R. 526 ('*RJE*').
[43] [2009] VSC 381; (2009) 24 V.R. 415 ('*DAS*').

RJE concerned a statutory power to place a convicted sex offender who had completed his or her sentence under an 'extended supervision order' if the court was satisfied 'to a high degree of probability, that the offender was *likely* to commit a relevant offence if released into the community' (emphasis added). In the Court of Appeal, all three judges concluded that an earlier Victorian decision, which held that 'likely' included a less than 50 per cent chance, unreasonably limited an offender's rights and freedoms and should not be followed. However, only Nettle JA relied on the Charter in reaching this conclusion; Maxwell P and Weinberg JA relied on 'the common law rule favouring that interpretation which least encroaches on individual freedom'.[44] Drawing on the decisions of Lord Woolf CJ in *Poplar Housing and Regeneration Community Association Ltd v Donaghue*[45] and Mason NPJ in *HKSAR v Lam Kwong Wai*,[46] Nettle JA concluded that s.32(1) was a special rule of interpretation that permitted a departure from the intention of the legislation-enacting Parliament to give effect to the intention of the Charter-enacting Parliament. However, he considered it unnecessary to determine whether s.32(1) also required the 'more far reaching scope [of] the notion of interpretation'[47] adopted in *Ghaidan* by Lord Nicholls[48] and rejected by Besanko J in *Fearnside*, allowing the court, as he saw it, to change the meaning of legislation. Adopting the *Fearnside/Hansen* three-step approach, Nettle JA held that the prior interpretation of 'likely' was not compatible with Charter rights; nor was it reasonably justified. Absent the Charter, he held that he would have been required to follow the earlier decision. However, s.32(1) now required him to give effect to the intention of the Charter-enacting Parliament, and so interpret 'likely' as requiring a more than 50 per cent chance. That interpretation would ensure that only reasonable limitations were placed on the offender's rights of liberty, privacy and freedom of movement.

The most linguistically far-reaching application of s.32 occurred in *Re an application under the Major Crimes (Investigative Powers) Act 2004*.[49] A provision allowed for persons to be compelled to give evidence in relation to organised crime offences, and provided direct immunity in relation to compelled evidence, but not derivative immunity.[50] Warren CJ held that this abrogation of the right to silence, without the provision of derivative immunity, was incompatible with the rights to a fair hearing and not to be compelled to

[44] [2009] VSC 381; (2009) 24 V.R. 415, at [54].
[45] [2001] EWCA Civ 595; [2002] Q.B. 48, 72, at [75].
[46] [2006] HKCFA 84, 29; (2006) 9 H.K.C.F.A.R. 574.
[47] [2008] VSCA 265; (2008) 21 V.R. 526, at [118]–[119].
[48] [2004] UKHL 30; [2004] 2 A.C. 557, at [31]–[32].
[49] [2009] VSC 381; (2009) 24 V.R. 415.
[50] Direct use immunity prevents compelled incriminating testimony from being used directly against that person. Derivative use immunity prevents compelled incriminating testimony from being used to obtain other evidence against that person.

testify against oneself or to confess guilt.[51] She therefore adopted the 'special rule' approach of Nettle JA in *RJE*. The relevant provision, construed in accordance with ordinary principles of statutory construction, limited Charter rights by failing to provide derivative use immunity and was not justified under s.7(2) on the evidence before the court. However, Warren CJ held that it could be re-interpreted to provide derivative use immunity.[52] She did not find it necessary to consider whether s.32(1) embraced the *Ghaidan* approach in order to reach this conclusion.

The Victorian Court of Appeal's decision in *R. v Momcilovic*[53] marked a definitive rejection of the 'special rule' approach and a retreat from the earlier tentative embrace of foreign jurisprudence in the application of ss. 32(1) and 7(2). *Momcilovic* concerned a conviction under the Drugs, Poisons and Controlled Substances Act 1981 (Vic) (the Drugs Act). Section 5 deemed drugs found on a person's premises to be in their possession, unless they satisfied the court to the contrary. Section 73(2) provided that possession of a traffickable quantity of a drug of dependence was prima facie evidence of trafficking. Section 71AC made it an offence for a person to 'traffick' in a drug of dependence. The s.32(1) issue was whether, in accordance with the right to a presumption of innocence,[54] s.5 should be interpreted as imposing a lesser, evidential burden, rather than a legal burden of proof.[55]

The Court of Appeal emphatically rejected the 'special rule' approach taken in the Supreme Court in *RJE* and *DAS*, holding that:

> [T]he inclusion of the purpose requirement made it unambiguously clear that nothing in s 32(1) justified, let alone required, an interpretation of a statutory provision which overrode the intention of the enacting Parliament.[56]

Section 32(1) therefore had the same status as other legislative provisions and common law principles of statutory construction. The Court of Appeal set out a new methodology for determining whether a statutory provision infringed a Charter right:

> Step 1: Ascertain the meaning of the relevant provision by applying s 32(1) … in conjunction with the common law principles of statutory interpretation and the *Interpretation of Legislation Act 1982* (Vic);

[51] Charter, ss. 24 and 25(2)(k).
[52] [2009] VSC 381; (2009) 24 V.R. 415, at [167]–[169].
[53] [2010] VSCA 50; (2010) 25 V.R. 436.
[54] Charter, s.25(1).
[55] The Court recognised but declined to follow the approach adopted in the UK case of *R. v Lambert* [2001] UKHL 37; [2002] 2 A.C. 545. Instead the Court preferred the jurisprudence of New Zealand superior courts that had refused to interpret 'until the contrary is proved' as 'unless sufficient evidence is given to the contrary' on the basis that this would be giving the legislation a strained and unnatural meaning: at [117]–[118].
[56] [2010] VSCA 50; (2010) 25 V.R. 436, at [74].

Step 2: Consider whether, so interpreted, the relevant provision breaches a human right protected by the Charter;

Step 3: If so, apply s 7(2) of the Charter to determine whether the limit imposed on the right is justified.[57]

This differs from the *Hansen/Fearnside* approach in that the interpretive mandate is not 'special' (that is, it does not allow departure from the intention of the enacting Parliament) and in that the reasonable limits enquiry is distinct from and follows the interpretive exercise rather than forming part of it.[58] Applying these steps, the Court of Appeal held that s.5 was clearly intended to impose a legal burden of proof on the defendant.[59] The Court held that this was 'not so much an infringement of the presumption of innocence as a wholesale subversion of it'[60] and went on to find that there was no 'reasonable justification, let alone any "demonstrable" justification [and in fact no evidence had been led in relation to this at all], for reversing the onus of proof in connection with a possession offence'.[61] The Court of Appeal thus proposed to make a declaration of inconsistent interpretation in accordance with s.36(2) to the Charter[62] that s.5 could not 'be interpreted consistently with the presumption of innocence under s.25(1) of the Charter'.[63]

An appeal to the High Court of Australia followed. Ultimately it was successful on largely non-Charter grounds. However, the judgment (which runs to more than 250 pages) has major implications for the interpretation and validity of ss. 32(1), 7(2) and 36(2) and we discuss them in the broader context of Australian constitutionalism in the next section of this essay.

The Court of Appeal's narrower reading of the interpretive mandate in *Momcilovic* has not stripped the provision of all effect. It has been relied upon in post-*Momcilovic* cases both to broaden a statutory provision so as to avoid rights incompatibility[64] and to construe a statutory discretion of a public authority narrowly to avoid 'drastic interference' with human rights.[65]

[57] [2010] VSCA 50; (2010) 25 V.R. 436, at [35].

[58] The *Hansen/Fearnside* approach may require iterative cycles of re-interpretation and justification: see Evans and Evans, *Australian Bills of Rights: The Law of the Victorian Charter and the ACT Human Rights Act*, pp.99–100.

[59] [2010] VSCA 50; (2010) 25 V.R. 436, at [119].

[60] [2010] VSCA 50; (2010) 25 V.R. 436, at [152].

[61] [2010] VSCA 50; (2010) 25 V.R. 436, at [152].

[62] Notice provisions in ss. 36(3) and 36(4) prevented it from being made immediately.

[63] [2010] VSCA 50; (2010) 25 V.R. 436, at [157].

[64] *DPP v KW* [2011] VCC (2 May 2011) (a prohibition on a third party 'us[ing]' a listening device to record a private conversation without a warrant extended to a prohibition, not just on a third party activating the listening device, but to police who obtained evidence in an investigation by having the complainant telephone the accused from the police station from a telephone fitted with a recording device).

[65] *PJB v Melbourne Health (Patrick's case)* [2011] VSC 327.

However, both of these decisions contain residues of the view that the interpretive mandate allows a departure from the intention of the enacting parliament. Whether they survive the scrutiny of the Court of Appeal remains to be seen. More representative, perhaps, of the *Momcilovic* approach to the interpretive mandate is *Castles v Secretary to the Department of Justice*,[66] in which the Charter was relied upon to confirm an interpretation of a provision already reached on the ordinary principles of statutory construction. This outcome was not, however, necessarily entirely a product of *Momcilovic*. *Castles* was, in fact, consistent with earlier Charter cases, in which there was a tendency to reason that rights-consistent interpretive conclusions could be justified by reference to the principle of legality and that the Charter could, if necessary, be called in aid as an *additional* reason for the conclusion.[67] The full explanation of this treatment of the interpretive mandate, as well as its implications, depends on understanding the legal and political setting in which the Charter was enacted.

Australian Exceptionalism?

Australian Bills of Rights operate in a very different legal and political setting from the other exemplars of the new Commonwealth model—the UK HRA, the New Zealand Bill of Rights Act 1990 (NZ) (NZBORA) and the Canadian Charter—despite shared common law and parliamentary traditions. The setting is sub-national rather than national; in Victoria, the legislature charged with scrutiny of Bills and holding government to account has two elected chambers; there is no supranational tribunal adjudicating over the same set of rights, let alone one to which affected citizens can have resort; and there is a century-old tradition of strong judicial review of federal and structural constitutional questions mirrored by 'considerable restraint' in review of administrative decisions.[68] We cannot elaborate the full significance of all these and other more subtle differences in this essay. Instead, we focus on Australia's strong cultural and constitutional commitment to legalism and to the separation of powers, and the profound effects of these commitments on the Charter

[66] [2010] VSC 310; (2010) 28 V.R. 141.

[67] *RJE v Secretary to the Department of Justice* [2008] VSCA 265; (2008) 21 V.R. 526 (Maxwell P and Weinberg JA); *WBM v Chief Commissioner of Police* [2010] VSC 219; (2010) 27 V.R. 469; *C v Chief Commissioner of Police & Anor* [2008] VSC 51; (2008) 20 V.R. 174; *Director of Public Transport v XFJ* [2010] VSC 319; *DPP v Piscopo* [2011] VSCA 275.

[68] M. Taggart, "'Australian Exceptionalism' in Judicial Review" (2008) 36 *Federal Law Review* 1, 5.

(and effectively the ACT HRA) in the recent High Court decision in *R. v Momcilovic*.[69]

The Role of the Courts and the Separation of Powers

Perhaps the most quoted aphorism in Australian legal writing is Sir Owen Dixon's remark on the occasion of his swearing in as Chief Justice:

> Close adherence to legal reasoning is the only way to maintain the confidence of all parties in federal conflicts. It may be that the court is thought to be excessively legalistic. I should be sorry to think that it is anything else. There is no safer guide to judicial decisions in great conflicts than strict and complete legalism.[70]

The legalistic judicial method epitomized by these remarks has waxed and waned but has never been entirely absent.[71] Most judges have favoured a formalist style of constitutional adjudication that avoids anything that 'would plunge them into deciding questions better left for political rather than judicial determination'.[72] This has the effect of isolating Australia from the development of rights-protective jurisprudence in other jurisdictions, perhaps not always for reasons that are fully persuasive.[73]

The commitment to a legalistic method reinforces and is reinforced by the constitutionally entrenched separation of powers at the federal level. Under the established doctrine, federal courts cannot exercise non-judicial power (except when strictly incidental to their judicial functions), and only federal courts and state courts in which the Federal Parliament has vested federal jurisdiction can exercise federal judicial power.[74] Open-ended discretions cannot be conferred by the Federal Parliament on such courts, nor can they or their judges decide questions based on entirely open-ended criteria.[75] Moreover, federal courts exercising federal jurisdiction can only exercise judicial power in 'matters', that is concrete disputes in which 'there is some immediate right, duty or liability to be established by the determination of the

[69] [2011] HCA 34; (2011) 280 A.L.R. 221.

[70] (1952) 85 C.L.R. xi, xiv. See also J. Gava, "Dixonian Strict Legalism, *Wilson v Darling Island Stevedoring* and Contracting in the Real World" (2010) 30 O.J.L.S. 519.

[71] See, for example, J. Gava, "The Rise of the Hero Judge" (2001) 24 *University of New South Wales Law Journal* 747.

[72] Sir Anthony Mason, "The Role of a Constitutional Court in a Federation: A Comparison of the Australian and the United States Experience" (1986) 16 *Federal Law Review* 1, 12.

[73] See, for example, Adrienne Stone, "Comparativism in Constitutional Interpretation" (2009) *New Zealand Law Review* 45. For commentary on related developments in administrative law, see Taggart, "'Australian Exceptionalism' in Judicial Review".

[74] See, generally, L. Zines, *The High Court and the Constitution* 5th edn (Annandale, NSW: Federation Press, 2008), chs 9 and 10.

[75] See, for example, *Yanner v Minister for Aboriginal and Torres Strait Islander Affairs* [2001] FCA 36; (2001) 108 F.C.R. 543.

Court'.[76] The Federal Parliament cannot authorise federal courts or state courts 'to make a declaration of the law divorced from any attempt to administer that law'.[77] As a result, courts exercising federal jurisdiction cannot decide abstract questions or issue advisory opinions.[78] Further, while there is a constitutionally entrenched right of appeal to the High Court from state Supreme Courts exercising state jurisdiction, there is no such appeal unless there is a 'matter'.[79]

This federal constitutional doctrine limits the powers that may be conferred upon state courts *by state Parliaments* as well, notwithstanding the absence of any formal doctrine of separation of powers under the state constitutions. These courts must be of a character competent to receive federal jurisdiction conferred on them by federal legislation.[80] Thus, a state Parliament cannot confer upon a state court non-judicial functions 'of a nature that might lead an ordinary reasonable member of the public to conclude that the Court was not independent of the executive government of the State'.[81] The High Court now firmly insists that the states cannot confer non-judicial functions on state courts in a way that is incompatible with the 'institutional integrity of the State court' and its capacity to exercise federal jurisdiction.[82]

It seems unlikely that rights adjudication, of *its very nature*, is a non-judicial function that cannot be conferred on a federal court and that threatens the institutional integrity of state and territory courts. The High Court still recognises and applies the freedom of political communication, implied from the text and structure of the *Constitution* by the Mason court in the 1990s.[83]

[76] *In re Judiciary and Navigation Acts* [1921] HCA 20; (1921) 29 C.L.R. 257, 265.
[77] *In re Judiciary and Navigation Acts* [1921] HCA 20; (1921) 29 C.L.R. 257, 266. See also *Mellifont v A-G (Qld)* [1991] HCA 53; (1991) 173 C.L.R. 289, at 303 ('*Mellifont*').
[78] *In re Judiciary and Navigation Acts* [1921] HCA 20; (1921) 29 C.L.R. 257, 265–66; *Croome v Tasmania* [1997] HCA 5; (1997) 191 C.L.R. 119, 135–36. It may also be that all jurisdiction exercised by territory courts is federal jurisdiction: see *Re Governor, Goulburn Correctional Centre Ex p Eastman* [1999] HCA 44; (1999) 200 C.L.R. 322, at [37]–[39] (Gaudron J), at [62]–[63] (Gummow and Hayne JJ).
[79] *O'Toole v Charles David Pty Ltd* [1991] HCA 44; (1991) 171 C.L.R. 232, 282; *Mellifont* [1991] HCA 53; (1991) 173 C.L.R. 289, 302–03.
[80] *Kable v DPP (NSW)* [1996] HCA 24; (1996) 189 C.L.R. 51; *North Australian Aboriginal Legal Aid Service Inc v Bradley* [2004] HCA 31; (2004) 218 C.L.R. 146, 161–64, at [24]–[32] (applying the principle to territory courts); *R. v Baker* [2004] HCA 45; (2004) 223 C.L.R. 513, at [5]–[6], [51]; *Gypsy Jokers Motorcycle Club Inc v Commissioner of Police* [2008] HCA 4; (2008) 234 C.L.R. 532, at [10].
[81] *Kable v DPP (NSW)* [1996] HCA 24; (1996) 189 C.L.R. 51, 117 (McHugh J).
[82] See, for example, *South Australia v Totani* [2010] HCA 39; (2010) 242 C.L.R. 1; *Wainohu v New South Wales* [2011] HCA 24; (2011) 243 C.L.R. 181.
[83] For recent examples, see *Coleman v Power* [2004] HCA 39; (2004) 220 C.L.R. 1; *Mulholland v Australian Electoral Commission* [2004] HCA 41; (2004) 220 C.L.R. 181; *APLA Ltd v Legal Services Commissioner (NSW)* [2005] HCA 44; (2005) 224 C.L.R. 322; *Hogan v Hinch* [2011] HCA 4 ; (2011) 275 A.L.R. 408.

Furthermore, although the legitimacy of the implication is regularly debated,[84] there appears to be little doubt that bodies exercising federal judicial power are capable of applying a test that asks whether limits on freedom of expression are 'reasonably appropriate and adapted to achieving an end in a manner that is compatible with the system of representative government enshrined in the Constitution'.[85] Australian courts have also interpreted and applied anti-discrimination statutes for more than three decades with no sensible suggestion that the rights conferred by those statutes are inherently non-justiciable.

The more credible arguments focused on three specific features of the Australian Bills of Rights: the interpretive mandate which might require more judicial discretion, and usurpation of the constitutional function of the legislature to make the law, than could be reconciled with the separation of powers; the power to grant declarations of inconsistent interpretation which might, because of the abstractness of the question determined, not amount to conferral of jurisdiction in a 'matter'; and the ability to appeal declarations of inconsistent interpretation to the High Court which might be precluded for want of a 'matter'. Members of the High Court raised these issues in the course of the application for special leave to appeal the Victorian Court of Appeal's decision in *Momcilovic*.[86]

Impact on the Interpretive Mandate

In *R. v Momcilovic*, the High Court (with Heydon J dissenting) allowed Ms Momcilovic's appeal and quashed her conviction on the basis that the deeming provision in s.5 of the Drugs Act did not apply to the relevant offence,[87] or, on the basis that although it did apply there had been a misdirection,[88] or on the basis that the provision under which she was charged was inconsistent with an overriding federal law.[89] All the majority judges agreed that the plain meaning of the deeming provision, placing an evidential burden on the

[84] See, for example, *Australian Broadcasting Corporation v Lenah Game Meats Pty Ltd* [2001] HCA 63; (2001) 208 C.L.R. 199, at [347]–[348] (Callinan J); *Roberts v Bass* [2002] HCA 57; (2002) 212 C.L.R. 1, at [285] (Callinan J). More generally, see Adrienne Stone, "The Limits of Constitutional Text and Structure Revisited" (2005) 28 *UNSW Law Journal* 842; Nicholas Aroney, "Justice McHugh, Representative Government and the Elimination of Balancing" (2006) 28 *Sydney Law Review* 505.

[85] *Coleman v Power* [2004] HCA 39; (2004) 220 C.L.R. 1, at [97] (McHugh J).

[86] *R.* v *Momcilovic* [2010] HCATrans 227 (3 September 2010) (French CJ, Crennan and Bell JJ).

[87] *R. v. Momcilovic* [2011] HCA 34; (2011) 280 A.L.R. 221 ('*Momcilovic (HCA)*'), at [72]–[73] (French CJ), at [197]–[198] (Gummow J), at [280] (Hayne J), and at [581] (Crennan and Kiefel JJ). For French CJ and Gummow J, this conclusion was reinforced by the Charter's interpretive mandate: at [73], [199]; cf. [613] (Crennan and Kiefel JJ).

[88] *Momcilovic (HCA)*, at [699]–[701] (Bell J). Heydon J dissented: see at [370]–[371].

[89] *Momcilovic (HCA)*, at [280] (Hayne J).

accused, was not displaced.[90] The clarity of outcome for Ms Momcilovic was not, however, matched by clarity in the High Court's conclusions about the interpretation and indeed constitutional validity of the Charter. In this section we consider the Court's reasoning about the interpretive mandate contained in s.32; in the next section we consider the power to make declarations of inconsistent interpretation under s.36.

The Court addressed three interlocked issues in relation to s.32 of the Charter. The first was whether the interpretive mandate was qualified by the reasonable limits provision in s.7(2). On this issue, the six-member majority was evenly divided, posing a real difficulty for the future application of the Charter.

The second issue was the 'strength' of the interpretive mandate. Here at least the result was clear, if disappointing for proponents of the new Commonwealth model. Six justices (with Heydon J disagreeing) held that it gave effect to ordinary principles of interpretation including the principle of legality, removing one possible pillar of a claim that the Charter (and ACT HRA, given the substantially identical interpretive mandate) qualify as exemplars of the new Commonwealth model.

The third issue was the constitutional validity of the interpretive mandate. Heydon J alone had concluded that s.32 gives effect to a strong form of interpretation and was therefore invalid. The remainder of the Court, following their conclusion that s.32 gave effect to ordinary principles of interpretation, held that it was valid.

In the following we unpick the reasoning behind these conclusions in more detail.

The Interpretive Mandate and s.7(2)

The majority was evenly split on whether the interpretive mandate was required to include a reasonable limits or proportionality analysis. French CJ and Crennan and Kiefel JJ (the latter two in a joint judgment) held that the interpretive mandate *was not* qualified by s.7(2); Gummow (with whom Hayne J agreed on these issues) and Bell JJ held that it was. Heydon J, who dissented, held (like Gummow, Hayne and Bell JJ) that the interpretive mandate was qualified by s.7(2) but that that led to its invalidity (and the invalidity of the whole Charter). The rejection of a proportionality analysis would be consistent with a general Australian reticence about the concept. That reticence draws in part on ideas about the special significance of the separation of powers to Australian constitutionalism. In several contexts, including rights-

[90] *Momcilovic (HCA)*, at [62] (French CJ), at [191] (Gummow J) (semble), at [581] (Crennan and Kiefel JJ), and at [685] (Bell J).

related contexts, the High Court asks whether an impugned law is 'appropriate and adapted' to a legitimate legislative purpose. Occasionally that test is said to be equivalent to a proportionality test but that language is also deprecated by some. A former Chief Justice cautioned:

> [I]nappropriate use of the concept of proportionality may amount to an invitation to the judicial branch of government to impose its own ideas of policy upon the legislature. The separation of powers works in more than one direction. It prevents the legislature and the executive from exercising judicial power. It also prevents the judiciary from exercising legislative power.[91]

Proportionality is also, and rather implausibly, said in the Australian context not to involve any element of balancing.[92] The Court has not elaborated the test to any significant degree. Moreover, the Court adheres to the *Wednesbury* line in administrative review. It rejects even the modest and halting development of a proportionality test in UK administrative law as inconsistent with the Australian separation of powers and driven in the United Kingdom by European and human rights influences absent in Australia.[93]

The reasoning of French CJ and Crennan and Kiefel JJ emphasises the structure and language of the Charter rather than these more general concerns about proportionality analysis. They saw s.7(2) as detached from the rights in Pt2 (though both appear in Pt2 and both refer to compatibility or incompatibility)[94] and noted that in South Africa and Canada (on whose limitation provisions s.7(2) is modelled) limitations analysis goes to validity and not interpretation.[95] Both judgments also emphasised that a proportionality analysis forms no part of traditional approaches to interpretation, that it follows rather than forms part of an interpretive process, and that the language of the Charter did nothing to displace the traditional approach to interpretation.[96]

On the other hand, Gummow J (with whom Hayne J agreed) did not provide extended reasons for applying s.7(2) in the interpretive process. It appeared self-evident to him that the assessment called for by s.7(2) was linked to the interpretive process in much the same way as it was under the NZ BORA.[97] For Bell J, 'compatibility with human rights'—a concept that linked the interpretive mandate, the scrutiny process and the obligation on public

[91] *Vasiljkovic v Commonwealth* [2006] HCA 40; (2006) 227 C.L.R. 614, at [41] (Gleeson CJ).

[92] S. Evans and A. Stone, "Balancing and Proportionality: A Distinctive Ethic?", conference paper presented at VIIth World Congress of the International Association of Constitutional Law Athens, 11–15 June 2007.

[93] See Taggart, "'Australian Exceptionalism' in Judicial Review", 24–27.

[94] *Momcilovic (HCA)*, at [26] (French CJ), at [574] (Crennan and Kiefel JJ).

[95] *Momcilovic (HCA)*, at [26].

[96] *Momcilovic (HCA)*, at [34] (French CJ), and at [574] (Crennan and Kiefel JJ).

[97] *Momcilovic (HCA)*, at [168].

authorities—consistently meant 'compatibility with the rights as reasonably limited under s 7(2)'.[98]

It was therefore only Heydon J who rested his conclusion on constitutional grounds, holding that s.7(2) involved the courts in performing an essentially legislative task.[99]

The Strength and Validity of the Interpretive Mandate

All members of the majority agreed that the Charter did not displace the traditional approach to interpretation and was therefore valid. Only Heydon J accepted that s.32 required or authorised 'remedial' interpretation and that led to its invalidity. The decision of the House of Lords in *Ghaidan* was front-and-centre in the argument before the High Court. (Gummow J noted sardonically that 'the House of Lords decisions upon the UK Act exercised a fascination to the point of obsession in the preparation and presentation of much of the submissions in the present appeal').[100] The majority judges emphasised a variety of factors in rejecting *Ghaidan* as a guide to the interpretation of s.32(1).

The *Ghaidan* approach—assumed to allow a departure from the intention of the enacting legislature—was seen to depart from fundamental Australian constitutional assumptions about interpretation and the legitimate role of the courts. The High Court held that the role of the courts in interpretation was to give effect to the intent of the enacting legislator, determined from text, context and purpose. The interpretive task begins with the text because '[t]he language which has actually been employed in the text of legislation is the surest guide to legislative intention'.[101] Moreover, 'in performing its functions, a court should never stray too far from the text, for it constitutes the authentic voice of the constitutionally legitimate lawmaker'.[102] There is the usual uneasy balance between the insistence on the one hand that context, canons of construction, purpose and consequences can sometimes displace the literal or grammatical meaning[103] and the equal insistence on the other hand that, for example, '[h]istorical considerations and extrinsic materials cannot be relied

[98] *Momcilovic (HCA)*, at [678].
[99] *Momcilovic (HCA)*, at [430]–[436].
[100] *Momcilovic (HCA)*, at [160].
[101] *Alcan (NT) Alumina Pty Ltd v Commissioner of Territory Revenue* [2009] HCA 41; (2009) 239 C.L.R. 27, at [47].
[102] *Australian Finance Direct Limited v Director of Consumer Affairs Victoria* [2007] HCA 57; (2007) 234 C.L.R. 96, at [34]. For a particularly narrow view, see *Momcilovic (HCA)*, at [442] (Heydon J).
[103] *Project Blue Sky Inc v Australian Broadcasting Authority* [1998] HCA 28; (1998) 194 C.L.R. 355, 384.

on to displace the clear meaning of the text'.[104] It is hard to see that either formulation dictates an outcome in cases where there is a constructional choice to be made. Whatever the problems with the metaphor of intent, the principle is said to have constitutional status:

> It has been said that to attribute an intention to the legislature is to apply something of a fiction. However, what is involved here is not the attribution of a collective mental state to legislators. That would be a misleading use of metaphor. Rather, judicial findings as to legislative intention are an expression of the constitutional relationship between the arms of government with respect to the making, interpretation and application of laws ... [T]he preferred construction by the court of the statute in question is reached by the application of rules of interpretation accepted by all arms of government in the system of representative democracy.[105]

One of the animating ideas is a formal sense of the rule of law: an interpretive methodology that gives primacy to text can be seen as

> dictated by elementary considerations of fairness, for, after all, those who are subject to the law's commands are entitled to conduct themselves on the basis that those commands have meaning and effect according to ordinary grammar and usage.[106]

Finally, the traditional approach includes a commitment to the principle of legality, 'the presumption that, in the absence of unmistakable and unambiguous language, the legislature has not intended to interfere with basic rights, freedoms or immunities'.[107]

In *Momcilovic*, the majority judges held that there was nothing in the Charter's interpretive mandate that suggested a departure from the traditional intention-seeking approach to interpretation, let alone the clear statement that would be required for such a profound change.[108] Indeed, as held by the Court of Appeal, the traditional approach was reinforced by the proviso in s.32(1), absent from the corresponding provision in the HRA, that human rights consistency in interpretation was subject to preserving consistency with legislative purpose[109] and also by the requirement to 'interpret' rather than

[104] *Alcan (NT) Alumina Pty Ltd v Commissioner of Territory Revenue* [2009] HCA 41; (2009) 239 C.L.R. 27, at [47]. In most Australian jurisdictions, statute authorises recourse to extrinsic materials, including parliamentary materials, to determine meaning at least in a case of ambiguity.

[105] *Zheng v Cai* [2009] HCA 52; (2009) 239 C.L.R. 446, at [28].

[106] *Corporate Affairs Commission (NSW) v Yuill* [1991] HCA 28; (1991) 172 C.L.R. 319, 340, quoted in *Alcan (NT) Alumina Pty Ltd v Commissioner of Territory Revenue* [2009] HCA 41; (2009) 239 C.L.R. 27, at [4] (French CJ).

[107] *Project Blue Sky* [1998] HCA 28; (1998) 194 C.L.R. 355, 384 n.56. See, for example, *Evans v New South Wales* [2008] FCAFC 130; (2008) 168 F.C.R. 576. The principle is traced back to *Potter v Minahan* [1908] HCA 63; (1908) 7 C.L.R. 277.

[108] *Momcilovic (HCA)*, at [50] (French CJ).

[109] *Momcilovic (HCA)*, at [50] (French CJ), at [170] (Gummow J) (Hayne J agreeing at [280]), at [544] (Crennan and Kiefel JJ), and at [684] (Bell J).

'read and give effect' to legislation.[110] By contrast, the *Ghaidan* approach came close to requiring the courts to legislate rather than interpret[111] or to confer a choice on the courts regarding the content of the law.[112] The judgments thus reflect more confidence that the distinction between interpretation and legislation satisfactorily defines the scope of permissible interpretation than seems justified.[113] Section 32 was held to give effect to the principle of legality, and no more than that,[114] although perhaps in somewhat more robust form than contemplated in *Watkins v Home Office*.[115]

Impact on the Power to Make Declarations of Incompatibility/Inconsistent Interpretation

The second question was whether making 'declarations of inconsistent interpretation'[116] under s.36 of the Charter involves an exercise of judicial power. This issue was always likely to be genuinely contentious. The equivalent provision (UK HRA, s.4) is central to the UK version of the new Commonwealth model, signalling parliamentary responsibility for addressing rights incompatibilities that cannot be resolved within the bounds of judicial interpretation of legislation. But in the Australian context, it is argued, it divorces the making of the declaration from the resolution of the concrete dispute presented by the parties, giving the declaration a hypothetical or abstract character and engaging the courts in the legislative process in a way that is inconsistent with their institutional integrity.[117] The hypothetical character could be seen to be underscored by the fact that the inability to reach a rights-consistent interpretation and the making of a declaration do not affect the validity or operation of the legislation in question[118] so the declaration has no effect on the rights of the litigants. The engagement in the legislative process could be seen to be manifested in the obligation on the Court to cause

[110] *Momcilovic (HCA)*, at [151] (Gummow J), and at [544]–[545] (Crennan and Kiefel JJ).
[111] *Momcilovic (HCA)*, at [537] (Crennan and Kiefel JJ).
[112] *Momcilovic (HCA)*, at [169] (Gummow J). Cf. French CJ's comments on 'constructional choice' at [43], [50] and [73].
[113] See A. Kavanagh, "The Elusive Divide between Interpretation and Legislation under the Human Rights Act 1998" (2004) 24 O.J.L.S. 259.
[114] *Momcilovic (HCA)*, at [51] (French CJ); cf. at [387], [411] (Heydon J); *R. v Momcilovic* [2010] VSCA 50; (2010) 25 V.R. 436, at [55]–[56].
[115] [2006] UKHL 17; [2006] 2 A.C. 395. See also *Evans v NSW* [2008] FCAFC 130; (2008) 168 F.C.R. 576.
[116] Charter, s.36(5).
[117] See J. Stellios, "State/Territory Human Rights Legislation in a Federal Judicial System" (2008) 19 *Public Law Review* 52. See also M. McHugh, "A Human Rights Act, the Courts and the Constitution", presentation given at the Australian Human Rights Commission, 5 March 2009.
[118] Charter, ss. 32(3) and 36(5).

the declaration to be communicated to the Attorney-General, triggering further obligations on the Attorney-General to provide the declaration and ministerial response to the Parliament.[119]

One of us had argued, prior to *Momcilovic*, that the better view is that declarations of inconsistency are not incompatible with the separation of powers doctrine.[120] It is not possible under the ACT HRA or the Victorian Charter to seek a declaration of inconsistency outside the context of substantive proceedings between parties involving the legislative provision in relation to which a declaration might be made. The declaration is an incident of determining the meaning of that provision, following the requirement of the relevant Human Rights Act that legislation be interpreted consistently with protected human rights.

On the other hand, the contrary conclusion is open and would be consistent with Australian constitutional formalism and a distancing of Australian constitutional arrangements—particularly as regards the separation of powers—from human rights jurisprudence in other jurisdictions.[121]

This is the debate that played out in *Momcilovic*. In short, four justices upheld the validity of s.36; of them two held that it requires consideration of s.7(2) (but its use had to be carefully quarantined from federal matters), two that it did not (and they would not use s.36 in at least some criminal matters). Two of the majority justices (and Heydon J) held that s.36 was invalid.

More fully, French CJ (with whom Bell J agreed on this) and Crennan and Kiefel JJ held that s.36 was valid.[122] They reached this conclusion despite the fact that they also held that making a declaration of inconsistent interpretation was *not* an exercise of judicial power.[123] (They also observed that '[a] 'dialogue' is an inappropriate description of the relations between the Parliament and the courts'[124] and that s.36(2) 'effects a novel alteration to the customary interchange between courts and Parliament').[125] For Crennan and Kiefel JJ the power to make a declaration was nonetheless valid because it was *incidental* to the s.32(1) interpretive question that was integral to the matter before the court.[126] It was possible, therefore, for a declaration to be

[119] Charter, ss. 36(6)–(7) and 37.
[120] Evans and Evans, *Australian Bills of Rights: The Law of the Victorian Charter and the ACT Human Rights Act*, pp.150–53. To describe the contrary argument as 'implausible', as we did, now seems hyperbolic in light of *Momcilovic (HCA)*.
[121] See, for example, *Al-Kateb v Godwin* [2004] HCA 37; (2004) 219 C.L.R. 562, at [3] (Gleeson CJ), at [51] (McHugh J), and at [237]–[240] (Hayne J).
[122] *Momcilovic (HCA)*, at [574]–[575] (Crennan and Kiefel JJ).
[123] *Momcilovic (HCA)*, at [88]–[91] (French CJ), at [584] and at [586] (Crennan and Kiefel JJ). Their reasons for the latter conclusion were much the same as those given by Gummow J.
[124] See French CJ (Bell J agreeing) to similar effect: *Momcilovic (HCA)*, at [95] (French CJ).
[125] *Momcilovic (HCA)*, at [534] (Crennan and Kiefel JJ).
[126] *Momcilovic (HCA)*, at [584]; see also at [535] (Crennan and Kiefel JJ).

made in a federal matter or for the power to be conferred on a federal court. French CJ (and perhaps Bell J)[127] disagreed. The making of a declaration was not incidental to the interpretive question. A declaration could not be made in a federal matter, nor could the power be conferred on a federal court.[128] However, the power could be validly conferred on a state court,[129] which could make a declaration even in a federal case provided the federal elements were at an end.[130]

Critical to the conclusion of all four justices was a finding that the making of declarations was not incompatible with the institutional integrity of the court.[131] The court was not being 'enlist[ed] ... to give effect to any pre-determined conclusion on the part of the legislature or the executive'.[132] The making of the declaration did not have a close connection with the political branches of government.[133] It occurred independently of any 'instruction, advice or wish of the Legislature or the Executive Government'.[134] It did not 'implement any policy or action of the executive or the legislature'.[135] This was an instance of the familiar practice of courts 'pass[ing] comments upon conclusions they have reached about defects in legislation in the course of their reasons' rather than advising on law reform.[136]

It is worth noting that French CJ and Bell J on the one hand and Crennan and Kiefel JJ on the other disagreed about the applicability of s.7(2). For Crennan and Kiefel JJ, if the Court were required to consider s.7(2) in deciding whether or not to make a declaration, s.36 might have been invalid: 'it may well have been said that the Court was being asked to consider an abstract question of law ... which has no legal consequence'[137] because s.7(2) forms no part of the interpretive exercise.[138] This left them puzzling whether s.7(2) had any consequences at all—perhaps, they suggested, '[i]t might operate as a statement of principle directed to the legislature'.[139] For French CJ, s.7(2) was not relevant to the determination of whether a law was inconsistent with human rights (applying his reasoning in relation to s.32), but:

[127] The extent of her agreement with French CJ is not clear: see *Momcilovic (HCA)*, at [661].
[128] *Momcilovic (HCA)*, at [100] (French CJ).
[129] *Momcilovic (HCA)*, at [95]–[97] (French CJ).
[130] *Momcilovic (HCA)*, at [101] (French CJ).
[131] *Momcilovic (HCA)*, at [97] (French CJ), and at [603] (Crennan and Kiefel JJ).
[132] *Momcilovic (HCA)*, at [597] (Crennan and Kiefel JJ).
[133] *Momcilovic (HCA)*, at [597] (Crennan and Kiefel JJ).
[134] *Momcilovic (HCA)*, at [597] (Crennan and Kiefel JJ), quoting *Wilson v Minister for Aboriginal and Torres Strait Islander Affairs* [1996] HCA 18; (1996) 189 C.L.R. 1, 17.
[135] *Momcilovic (HCA)*, at [602] (Crennan and Kiefel JJ).
[136] *Momcilovic (HCA)*, at [600] (Crennan and Kiefel JJ).
[137] *Momcilovic (HCA)*, at [590] (Crennan and Kiefel JJ).
[138] *Momcilovic (HCA)*, at [568], and at [576] (Crennan and Kiefel JJ).
[139] *Momcilovic (HCA)*, at [575] (Crennan and Kiefel JJ).

> Section 7(2) could still have a role to play in informing the discretion of the Court to decline to make a declaration of inconsistent interpretation under s.36(2). There would, after all, be no point in advising the Parliament of an inconsistency founded on a limitation that was 'reasonable' according to the criteria in s.7(2).[140]

Gummow J (with Hayne J again agreeing) held that the power to make declarations was incompatible with the institutional integrity of the Supreme Court and therefore invalid.[141] (Heydon J too held it was invalid along with the rest of the Charter.) The declaration was not an exercise of judicial power because 'the Court's declaration will produce no foreseeable consequences for the parties'.[142] It amounted to an advisory opinion on a question of law.[143] It 'formally set in train a process whereby the executive branch of government may or may not decide to engage legislative processes to change existing legislation', something equally outside the judicial power.[144] It was not 'an integral part of the process of determining the rights and obligations of the parties which [were] at stake in the proceedings'.[145] The reasoning of the majority is preferable on these issues.

Impact on the Power to Appeal a Declaration of Incompatibility to the High Court

Although French CJ and Crennan, Kiefel and Bell JJ concluded that s.36 was valid, their finding that it was not an exercise of judicial power[146] had important consequences for whether a declaration of inconsistent interpretation will in the future be able to be appealed to the High Court. The appellate jurisdiction of the High Court is defined by s.73 of the Constitution, which provides, relevantly, that the High Court has jurisdiction 'to hear and determine appeals from all judgments, decrees, orders and sentences ... of the Supreme Court of any State'. The phrase 'judgments, decrees, orders and sentences' has been interpreted by the High Court as confined to decisions made in the exercise of judicial power.[147] Thus, for a decision of any kind to fall within the appellate jurisdiction of the High Court it must be made in the

[140] *Momcilovic (HCA)*, at [36] (French CJ).
[141] *Momcilovic (HCA)*, at [188] (Gummow J).
[142] *Momcilovic (HCA)*, at [179] (Gummow J), quoting *Ainsworth v Criminal Justice Commission* [1992] HCA 10; (1992) 175 C.L.R. 564, 581–82.
[143] *Momcilovic (HCA)*, at [183] (Gummow J), citing *Wilson v Minister for Aboriginal and Torres Strait Islander Affairs* [1996] HCA 18; (1996) 189 C.L.R. 1, 18–19.
[144] *Momcilovic (HCA)*, at [184] (Gummow J).
[145] *Momcilovic (HCA)*, at [187] (Gummow J).
[146] *Momcilovic (HCA)*, at [101] (French CJ), [584] (Kiefel and Crennan JJ), [661] (Bell J).
[147] *Mobil Oil Australia Pty Ltd v Victoria* (2002) 211 C.L.R. 1, at 38 [63] (Gaudron, Gummow and Hayne JJ).

exercise of judicial power. The finding of French CJ (with Bell J agreeing), that a declaration of inconsistent interpretation was not an exercise of judicial power, automatically placed such declarations outside the appellate jurisdiction of the High Court. Although Kiefel and Crennan JJ held that a declaration of inconsistent interpretation was incidental to the exercise of judicial power, their Honours ultimately held that '[a] statement or conclusion, made incidentally to the exercise of judicial power, which induces a change in the legislation, is not an exercise of judicial power'.[148] Thus their judgment also placed declarations of inconsistent interpretation outside the appellate jurisdiction, reflecting and reinforcing their diminished status as something less than curial orders made in the exercise of judicial power.

Implications

What then are the implications of the decision in *Momcilovic*? In short, the Charter continues to operate in Victoria, both in state matters and in federal jurisdiction, though significant uncertainty remains about the relationship of s.7(2) to the interpretive mandate, the strength of that mandate and the relationship of s.7(2) to the power to make declarations of inconsistency. It does not signal the death knell for federal charters of rights in Australia, though politically they remain a distant prospect and it does add significantly to the drafting challenges.

Heydon J predicted:

> In future the decision that s 32(1) is valid will be remembered. Not so the narrow interpretation on which the conclusion of validity rests. In numerous minds forensic oblivion will be its portion. Most of those who will remember it will silently suppress it. Any protest about this will be silenced by a reference to the blessed vagueness of the word 'purpose' in s 32(1).[149]

He may be right. The majority judgments certainly confirm the legitimacy and potential strength of the common law principle of legality, even in Australian jurisdictions without a Charter of Rights.[150] But the limits of

[148] *Momcilovic (HCA)*, at [586].

[149] *Momcilovic (HCA)*, at [455].

[150] It is worth noting that in *Evans v State of New South Wales* [2008] FCAFC 130; (2008) 168 F.C.R. 576, at [72], the Full Court of the Federal Court, including French J as he then was, affirmed that '[t]he freedoms associated with personal liberty are not residual'. Contrast the conventional common law conception of these freedoms, identified in Gardbaum, "The New Commonwealth Model of Constitutionalism", at 733. In *South Australia v Totani* [2010] HCA 39; (2010) 242 C.L.R. 1, at [31], French CJ wrote that the principle of legality 'imposes something approaching a formal requirement of clear statutory language'. But note the sharp division of opinion in *Al Kateb v Godwin* [2004] HCA 37; (2004) 219 C.L.R. 562 about the implications of the principle of legality.

permissible interpretation remain opaque, shrouded in metaphor. Perhaps more problematic is the obfuscation of the reasonable limits analysis if s.7(2) is treated as irrelevant to interpretation. It seems implausible that courts will seek to interpret legislation in conformity with some absolute conception of the relevant rights. But without s.7(2) the analysis does not have a statutory anchor or structure. And *Momcilovic* may well be seen as casting doubt on the use of a non-statutory proportionality analysis of the kind employed in the United Kingdom. The position is even less clear in relation to rights that are expressed to have internal limits.[151] Do they survive *Momcilovic*? As for declarations of inconsistency, given the absence of a clear majority on whether s.7(2) analysis is involved and a likely majority for invalidity if it is, it is very unlikely that s.36 will be applied in future. Moreover a majority would invalidate a federal power to grant declarations of inconsistent interpretation, constraining the drafting options for any future national Bill of Rights.[152]

Finally, it is worth pausing to consider the explanatory power of the constitutional text and structure that underpinned the decision in *Momcilovic*. The separation of powers and rule of law are not uniquely Australian. Arguments for a range of interpretive approaches can be, and indeed have been, made in the United Kingdom and elsewhere on the basis of these principles.[153] Members of the High Court noted that the interpretive approach they preferred was not unlike that adopted in *Wilkinson*.[154] What is distinctively Australian is that a particular, perhaps narrow and rigid, version of these principles has assumed entrenched, overriding constitutional status.

Review and Repeal

The Charter was a policy of the long-serving Australian Labor Party government of Victoria. Members of the opposition Liberal and National parties

[151] For example, s.15 (the right to freedom of expression is 'subject to lawful restrictions reasonably necessary' to achieve various ends) and s.13(1) (the right to privacy may not be 'unlawfully or arbitrarily interfered with').

[152] Judges can signal their interpretive conclusions in other less formal ways. (Indeed Penfold J did so in one case: *In the matter of an application for bail by Islam* [2010] ACTSC 147; (2010) 4 A.C.T.L.R. 235, at [401].) And other bodies (notably the Equal Opportunity and Human Rights Commission) can alert the executive and legislature to the courts' comments, as recommended in the National Human Rights Consultation.

[153] See, for example, A. Young, *Parliamentary Sovereignty and the Human Rights Act* (Oxford: Hart Publishing, 2009); A. Kavanagh, *Constitutional Review under the UK Human Rights Act* (Cambridge: Cambridge University Press, 2009); Philip Sales and Richard Ekins, "Rights-consistent Interpretation and the Human Rights Act" (2011) 127 L.Q.R. 217.

[154] *R. (Wilkinson) v Inland Revenue Commissioners* [2005] UKHL 30.

had voted against it and threatened to repeal it if and when they formed government. The Liberal and National parties formed government after the November 2010 state election and it fell to the new government to commission the review of the first four years of operation of the Charter required by s.44. The task was given to the Scrutiny of Acts and Regulations Committee (SARC) with wide-ranging terms of reference.

The Committee reported on 14 September 2011, less than a week after the decision of the High Court in *Momcilovic*.[155] It was split on whether the key provisions of the Charter should be retained or modified. A majority of SARC recommended the repeal of the interpretive mandate, the power to make declarations of inconsistent interpretation and the conduct obligation for public authorities, the first two both central to the claim that the Charter embodies weak-form judicial review.[156] The majority recommended:

> [O]nly Division 1 of Part 3 of the Charter (scrutiny of new laws) be retained, with the modifications recommended in this Report, and that Divisions 3 (interpretation of laws) and Divisions 4 (obligations of public authorities) be repealed.[157]

A minority of SARC recommended that all the Charter's operative provisions be retained, but subject to modifications, some significant (see below).

If the operative provisions were to be retained, the whole Committee made wide-ranging recommendations for modifications, including the following in relation to interpretation, reasonable limits on rights, and the power to make a declaration of inconsistent interpretation.[158]

Interpretation

Even if the minority recommendations were accepted (thus retaining the interpretive mandate), SARC recommended that 'consideration be given to whether Charter s. 32 is necessary, in light of common law principles of statutory interpretation'.[159] This recommendation reflects the assertion in the cases and commentary that s.32 does little more than give effect to the common law principle of legality, perhaps across a wider set of rights.

[155] Scrutiny of Acts and Regulations Committee, Parliament of Victoria, *Review of the Charter of Human Rights and Responsibilities Act*, tabled 14 September 2011 ('SARC Report'), http://www.parliament.vic.gov.au/images/stories/committees/sarc/charter_review/report_response/20110914_sarc.charterreviewreport.pdf. Under its terms of reference it was obliged to report by 1 October 2011. The Attorney-General was obliged under s.44 to table the report by that date.

[156] SARC Report, recommendation 35.

[157] SARC Report, recommendation 35.

[158] Given the scope of this essay, we cannot canvass the many other recommendations.

[159] SARC Report, recommendation 24.

The Committee further recommended that if s.32 were to be retained that it be 'redrafted in a manner that both clarifies that it is limited to traditional approaches to interpretation and makes its meaning accessible to local users, without undue recourse to overseas judgments'[160] and that it be expressly made subject to the statutory requirement that interpreters prefer a purposive interpretation of legislation.[161] The desire to make provisions 'accessible to local users' and to avoid use of international comparators recurs in a number of recommendations.[162] The Committee recommended that if s.32(1) were retained, s.32(2) (which permits recourse to international and comparative material in interpretation) be repealed, while preserving 'existing common or statutory law on the relevance of non-Victorian judgments or laws to the interpretation of Victorian statutory provisions'.[163]

Reasonable Limits

We discussed earlier in this essay the complex constitutional issues that arose in *Momcilovic* because of the presence of s.7(2) of the Charter—the reasonable limits provision. The Committee avoided addressing these issues by recommending that the interpretive mandate be amended in a way that would require preference to be given to a construction that was compatible with human rights, but would not require a court to consider whether limits on rights were reasonably justified.[164] However, SARC also addressed s.7(2) directly, recommending that if it were retained that it 'be redrafted to state the test for limiting rights in plain language that is accessible to Victorians without reference to comparative jurisprudence'.[165] We wonder whether the suggestion that the provision ask whether a law is 'reasonably appropriate and adapted to serve a legitimate end',[166] a test used in Australian constitutional jurisprudence, would in fact be any more accessible; it certainly would not have appeased the members of the High Court in *Momcilovic* who objected to use of this kind of test in the interpretive process, though of course this was not the focus of SARC's recommendation.[167]

[160] SARC Report, recommendation 24.
[161] *Interpretation of Legislation Act 1984* (Vic), s.35(a); SARC Report, recommendation 25.
[162] SARC Report, recommendations 2, 13 and 23.
[163] SARC Report, recommendation 27.
[164] SARC Report, 116. The Committee also took the view that when s.38 (the public authority obligation) was properly construed, it may not engage s.7(2): 110.
[165] SARC Report, recommendation 13.
[166] SARC Report, 91.
[167] See above, p.235ff.

Declarations of Inconsistent Interpretation

The Committee did not have the same anxieties as members of the High Court in *Momcilovic* about describing the Charter model as involving an inter-institutional dialogue. Nonetheless, consistently with the concerns expressed in *Momcilovic* about declarations of inconsistent interpretation, SARC recommended that Parliament should consider whether 'an independent non-judicial body' such as the Human Rights Commission rather than the courts should have the function of triggering executive and legislative review of statutory provisions that the courts had interpreted inconsistently with human rights.[168]

The government's initial response to the Report was cautious, noting that the views of SARC were not necessarily those of the government and that SARC and submissions had argued that the Charter had delivered benefits and should not be repealed.[169] The formal government response was delivered on 14 March 2012.[170] The government agreed with a number of minor recommendations of SARC to improve and clarify the operation of the Charter.[171] In relation to SARC's recommendations that the interpretive mandate and the obligation on public authorities be repealed, however, the government's position was as follows:

> The Government believes that there is an ongoing place for the courts in protecting rights in relation to the Charter but acknowledges the concerns raised by the SARC majority as to the role of the courts and the obligations of public authorities. These are important questions for the Charter ... [that] are not appropriately or adequately addressed by responding to the series of discrete recommendations provided by SARC. The government has determined that it should seek specific legal advice regarding the questions raised by the SARC majority [and respond to these questions] ... on the basis of clear evidence.[172]

The government specifically noted that further analysis of the issues raised by SARC was appropriate because *R. v Momcilovic*, as well as *Director of Housing v Sudi*[173]—an important decision on the obligations on public author-

[168] SARC Report, recommendation 31.
[169] Ted Baillieu, Premier of Victoria, Charter of Human Rights SARC Report Media Release, 14 September 2011, at http://www.premier.vic.gov.au/media-centre/media-releases/1966-charter-of-human-rights-sarc-report-.html.
[170] Parliament of Victoria, Scrutiny of Acts and Regulations Committee, Review of the Charter of Human Rights and Responsibilities Act 2006, Government Response, 14 March 2012 ('SARC Report Government Response').
[171] Such as improvements to the parliamentary scrutiny process and to the internal complaints processes, clarification of the legal status of certain processes and documents and the repeal of the parliamentary override provision. See SARC Report Government Response, p.2.
[172] SARC Report Government Response, pp.2–3, see also pp.23–24.
[173] [2011] VSCA 266.

ities—were handed down immediately prior to the delivery of the SARC Report, and as such SARC had not been able to consider the implications of these decisions in its review. The position of the government in relation to the operative provisions of the Charter thus remains to be determined.

Conclusions

Mark Tushnet conjectured that systems of weak-form judicial review may be unstable in practice, susceptible to being 'transformed in either direction', retreating back into systems of parliamentary supremacy or accreting power to the courts so that they converge on strong-form judicial review systems.[174] Arguably the former is what has happened in *Momcilovic* given the High Court's rejection of rights enforcement that 'goes beyond ordinary modes of statutory interpretation'. It is interesting to observe, however, that the High Court Justices' rationales for this decision appear to involve a strategic retreat of a different kind from that suggested by Tushnet. Rather than a retreat from weak-form judicial review and enhanced interpretive powers in order to preserve the validity and legitimacy *of the Charter*,[175] the retreat seems, for most of the judges, to be a reflection of a deep commitment to a particular conception of the judicial method and the separation of powers that underpins the wider integrity and legitimacy of the Australian judicial system. There is an irony in this: the hypertrophic development of the separation of powers in Australia, alongside a formalist methodology, supports the legitimacy of strong-form judicial review on structural and federal (mostly non-rights oriented) constitutional grounds in a system otherwise committed to parliamentary supremacy. But in *Momcilovic* it sharply limited an attempt sanctioned by Parliament to enhance enforcement of rights that did not disturb the legislature's formal power to have the final word on the law of the land.

Of course, the Court's rejection of a strong interpretive mandate does not mean that the Charter model is now indistinguishable from the old Commonwealth model of parliamentary supremacy. The interpretive mandate survives and extends the reach, if not the force, of the common law principle of legality. Even if the interpretive mandate collapses back into the common law principle of legality, the declarations power survives, albeit in attenuated form, and provides some differentiation of the Charter model from the old Commonwealth model.

[174] M. Tushnet, "New Forms of Judicial Review and the Persistence of Rights- and Democracy-based Worries" (2003) 38 *Wake Forest Law Review* 813, 824ff.

[175] Though perhaps this is the case for the s.7(2) and s.36 analysis in the High Court, and perhaps for the Court of Appeal's decision more generally.

However, there is some risk that *Momcilovic* circumscribes the declarations power in such a way that collapse into parliamentary supremacy is inevitable. The High Court has deprecated the language of institutional dialogue. The status of a declaration of incompatibility is reduced by the inability to appeal its making to the High Court. If the Charter is amended to shore up the validity of the declarations power by requiring the Equal Opportunity and Human Rights Commission, rather than the courts, to communicate declarations to Parliament, the status of declarations will be further undermined. Furthermore, if the reasonable limitations analysis is not relevant to the decision to issue a declaration, the power to issue such a declaration does little to shift the institutional balance away from parliamentary supremacy because government and Parliament can readily confess the incompatibility but assert that the limitations are justified.[176]

It is too early to write the obituaries for statutory Bills of Rights in Australia. It is clear, however, that the Charter's survival, and by extension that of the ACT HRA, as exemplars of the new Commonwealth model lie in the balance. We await with interest the inevitable series of cases working through the implications of *Momcilovic*, the ongoing response of the Victorian government to the issues raised by the SARC Report and the approach of the Parliament to both.

Note. The treatment of the separation of powers in this essay forms part of a project supported by the Australian Research Council on executive power under the Australian Constitution: DP1092671.

[176] Contrast Gardbaum, "The New Commonwealth Model of Constitutionalism", at 748 (suggesting that courts might be emboldened in their interpretations and making of declarations if they were not responsible for the ultimate limitations analysis).

11

Cross-fertilisation of Constitutional Ideas: The Relationship between the UK Human Rights Act 1998 and the New Zealand Bill of Rights Act 1990

PETRA BUTLER

Introduction

THIS ESSAY EXPLORES HOW THE HUMAN RIGHTS ACT 1998 (HRA) and jurisprudence of the United Kingdom have influenced New Zealand's legal landscape. In the United Kingdom, the HRA introduced not only greater protection of substantive rights and freedoms, but also a perceived shift in the constitutional balance between the judiciary and legislature. The judiciary has taken on an expanding role as protector of rights, and with that a (perceived) more significant role in holding the state to greater account. These developments have been viewed with interest in New Zealand, though this country has not followed completely in the United Kingdom's footsteps. This essay discusses the impact of the HRA on New Zealand's constitutional framework and jurisprudence, or the lack thereof.

The first part of the essay discusses the passage to enactment of the New Zealand Bill of Rights Act 1990 (BORA). This background is important to understand the differing political and constitutional forces which have shaped the form and content of the two statutes. The second part discusses two key areas of jurisprudence which demonstrate the extent to which the HRA has influenced New Zealand law. The first focuses on the extent to which New Zealand has followed the United Kingdom in its approach to interpreting legislation consistently with guaranteed rights and freedoms. The second focuses on remedies and, in particular, on declarations of inconsistency. These two issues relate to one another because from a widely held New Zealand perspective the UK judiciary takes a more 'adventurous' approach to achieving rights-consistent interpretation and gives a stronger response in the event of finding an inconsistency. On this basis, it could be argued that the judiciary in

Proceedings of the British Academy, **183**, 251–278. © The British Academy 2013.

the United Kingdom takes a stronger stance towards protection of rights[1] than its New Zealand counterpart, which is only partially explained by legislative authorisation. While New Zealand has not followed the suit of the United Kingdom, HRA jurisprudence is valuable both as a point of reference and offering a possibility for future reform. Lastly, the essay surveys the use of UK jurisprudence in regard to the interpretation to substantive rights under the BORA.

Journey to Enactment: The Case of the Bill of Rights Act

In 1985, the (then) Minister of Justice, Sir Geoffrey Palmer, tabled in Parliament a White Paper entitled "A Bill of Rights for New Zealand" ('White Paper').[2] This document proposed to give effect to many of the rights stated in the International Covenant on Civil and Political Rights 1966 (ICCPR) and to affirm the rights of Maori under the Treaty of Waitangi.[3] The White Paper drew influence from other national and international instruments. In particular, the Canadian Charter of Rights and Freedoms 1982 ('Canadian Charter')[4] and the ICCPR were of 'major importance'.[5] The Canadian Charter substantially alters the balance of power between the judiciary and the legislature: the Canadian courts have the power to invalidate legislation that is considered inconsistent with Charter rights.[6] In addition, where a claimant's Charter rights are found to have been infringed, the courts may apply a wide range of remedies to address the breach.[7] The White Paper advocated a similar shift in the powers of the organs of government, by the Bill of Rights being enacted as supreme law[8] with a double entrenchment provision[9] to protect it from ordinary repeal.

[1] *Re application by AMM and KJO* [2010] N.Z.F.L.R. [29]; (2010) 30 B.H.R.C. 471 (HC) where Simon France J and Wild J observed, 'it was apparent that the UK Courts, in relation to a similarly worded provision [s.3] in the Human Rights Act … had adopted an approach that showed greater willingness to massage the statutory language in order to achieve a rights-consistent outcome'. See also J. F. Burrows and R. Carter, *Statute Law in New Zealand*, 4th edn (Wellington: LexisNexis, 2009), p.367.

[2] Sir Geoffrey Palmer, "A Bill of Rights for New Zealand: A White Paper" [1985] A.J.H.R.A. 6.

[3] White Paper, cl.4(1) provided 'The rights of Maori under the Treaty of Waitangi are hereby recognised and affirmed.'

[4] Enacted as part of the Constitution Act 1982 (Canada).

[5] White Paper, at [10.1].

[6] Constitution Act 1982, s.52(1) provides that courts may invalidate laws which breach the constitution (including the Canadian Charter) and s.24(1) gives the judiciary powers to place obligations on the government where a claimant's rights are held to be violated.

[7] Constitution Act 1982, s.24(1) provides that the court may order 'such remedy as the court considers appropriate and just in the circumstances'.

[8] White Paper, cl.1.

[9] White Paper, cl.28 proposed that a provision of the Bill of Rights could only be repealed or amended by a majority of 75% of Members of Parliament or a simple majority of a referendum.

The White Paper was examined by a Select Committee, which engaged in widespread public consultation over a substantial period. The Select Committee noted in its Report[10] that there was significant public opposition to several aspects of the White Paper. The entrenchment provisions were opposed due to the proposed redistribution of power from elected representatives to the appointed judiciary.[11] The Select Committee recommended removing the provision establishing the legislation as supreme law, the entrenchment provisions and the references to the Treaty of Waitangi. It considered that as an ordinary statute, a Bill of Rights could have valuable moral and educative functions,[12] as well providing a check on executive action.[13]

After these amendments were made, the draft legislation was introduced to the House as the New Zealand Bill of Rights Bill 1989. Sir Geoffrey, by this time Prime Minister, said this at the Bill's introduction:

> How best to protect basic rights and freedoms is an issue of fundamental importance to all New Zealanders, and, as lawmakers, parliamentarians have a special responsibility in the matter. The New Zealand Bill of Rights and associated proposals for changes to the Standing Orders will encapsulate the role of Parliament as a guardian of fundamental rights and freedoms in New Zealand. In that sense the Bill is very much a parliamentary Bill of Rights.[14]

The Bill was enacted as the New Zealand Bill of Rights Act 1990. The Act upholds parliamentary sovereignty; s.4 provides that legislation is not rendered invalid merely by reason of inconsistency with the BORA. Judging by the public's wariness of allowing the judiciary to strike down legislation, Parliament was not viewed as a threat to civil liberties; rather, it was considered a guardian of rights.[15] The nod to the ICCPR carried through to the final

The provision is referred to as providing 'double-entrenchment' because had that provision been enacted, a 75% majority would also be required to amend or repeal the entrenchment provision itself.

[10] Justice and Law Reform Committee, "Final Report of the Justice and Law Reform Committee on a White Paper on a Bill of Rights for New Zealand" [1987–90] A.J.H.R.I. 8C 2–3.

[11] Justice and Law Reform Committee, "Final Report of the Justice and Law Reform Committee on a White Paper on a Bill of Rights for New Zealand".

[12] The Committee was concerned about New Zealanders' lack of understanding of human rights and was of the view that such legislation could play an important role in furthering public education. See Justice and Law Reform Committee, "Final Report of the Justice and Law Reform Committee on a White Paper on a Bill of Rights for New Zealand".

[13] Justice and Law Reform Committee, "Final Report of the Justice and Law Reform Committee on a White Paper on a Bill of Rights for New Zealand".

[14] Rt Hon. Sir Geoffrey Palmer, "New Zealand Bill of Rights Bill: Introduction" (10 October 1989) 502 N.Z.P.D. 13038.

[15] Rt Hon. Sir Geoffrey Palmer, "New Zealand Bill of Rights Bill: Third Reading" (21 August 1990) 510 N.Z.P.D. 3760. This perception is not universal. For instance, unlimited parliamentary sovereignty is perceived as a threat rather than a virtue in Germany: see Stefan Oeter, "Fundamental Rights and Their Impact on Private Law—Doctrine and Practice Under the German Constitution" (1994) 12 *Tel Aviv University Studies in Law* 7, 31–32.

version of the legislation,[16] but the Act differed markedly from the Canadian Charter in terms of the judiciary's ability to hold the executive to account. These aspects of the BORA are explored further below with regard to subsequent developments in the United Kingdom.

New Zealand Responses to the Human Rights Act

As discussed above, the BORA retains both parliamentary sovereignty and supremacy of legislation. The following section discusses New Zealand jurisprudence with the view to ascertain how far the New Zealand and the UK judicary are in tune with each other. Thomas J stated in *Pora* that when confronted with a difficult provision, 'the courts make do by filling the gap, if there be a gap, or by otherwise adopting an interpretation which accords with the purpose of the statute'.[17] New Zealand has followed the suit of the United Kingdom in some respects, such as in the recognition of remedies. New Zealand, on a widely held view, has departed from the United Kingdom, however, in the approach to interpretation of legislation. This departure seems to signal a greater willingness on the part of New Zealand courts to defer to parliamentary intention at the cost of upholding the rights and freedoms in the BORA. However, it is argued that the difference might not lie with the courts but with the respective Parliaments.

Judicial Interpretation of Legislation

Section 6 of the BORA directs the courts to interpret an enactment in the manner most consistent with the rights contained in the BORA. Similarly, s.3 HRA provides that legislation must, 'as far as it is possible', be interpreted consistently with rights set out in the European Convention on Human Rights (ECHR). While both pieces of legislation appear to champion rights contained in the legislation, they operate rather differently.[18] New Zealand jurisprudence

[16] The Long Title provides that the Bill of Rights Act 'affirm[s] New Zealand's commitment to the [ICCPR]'.

[17] *R. v Pora* [2001] 2 N.Z.L.R. 37 (CA), at [122] (Thomas J).

[18] It has to be noted that the New Zealand judiciary is divided on the question of how different s.3 HRA and s.6 BORA are. See, for example, Elias CJ in *R. v Hansen* [2007] 3 N.Z.L.R. 1, at [13]: 'I am unable to accept that there is any material difference between the New Zealand and United Kingdom models' (hereafter '*R. v Hansen*'). And Lord Cooke in *Ex p. Kebilene* [2000] 2 A.C. 326, at 374: '[s.3 HRA] read as a whole, conveys, I think, a rather more powerful message'. Lord Steyn expressed the view that 'the draftsman of the 1998 Act had before him the model of the New Zealand Bill of Rights Act which imposes a requirement that the interpretation to be adopted must be reasonable. Parliament specifically rejected the legislative model of requiring a reasonable interpretation': see *Ghaidan v Mendoza* [2004] 3 All E.R. 411, at [44]. See also Burrows who

in regard to the courts' mandate under s.6 has been significantly shaped by the presence of s.5 BORA, which provides that rights may be subject to limits that are 'demonstrably justified in a free and democratic society'. There is no equivalent in the HRA (although there are similar types of statements to be found in some of the provisions of the ECHR which are incorporated in the Schedule of the HRA). The existence of s.5 has had considerable weight in the discussion of the approach to s.6.[19]

New Zealand Case Law: The Early Cases

In New Zealand, while there was early judicial flirtation with the notion that s.6 could allow legislation to bear new, unintended meanings that gave effect to fundamental rights and freedoms, the courts have since confirmed that 'there are some real limits on the extent to which the Court can act under s 6 so as to remove inconsistency'[20] and that s.6 authorises consistent meanings only where they can be 'reasonably' given,[21] 'tenable'[22] or 'properly'[23] given; s.6 does not authorise a 'strained interpretation'.[24] Conversely, UK courts have held that a strained interpretation may result in order to give effect to Convention rights.[25]

The following gives an overview of the case law where the courts gave some direction in regard to the interpretation of legislation and which forms the basis of the widely held view that the UK courts are 'activist' in regard to HRA-consistent interpretation of legislation whereas New Zealand courts adhere to and preserve parliamentary sovereignty.

who on the one hand seems to agree with Lord Cooke that there is a significant difference between the two sections—s.3 being stronger (Burrows and Carter, *Statute Law in New Zealand*, p.365). However, Burrows then considers s.6 gives the courts room to advance the purpose of the legislation 'to enhance and preserve citizens' fundamental rights' (Burrows and Carter, *Statute Law in New Zealand*, p.367).

[19] See, for example, *R. v Hansen* at [57], [88], [190] and [266]; *Moonen v Film and Literature Board of Review* [2000] 2 N.Z.L.R. 9, at [16].

[20] *Re application by AMM and KJO* [2010] N.Z.F.L.R. 629, at [31].

[21] Tipping J in *R. v Hansen*, at [158] and [159], Anderson J in *R. v Hansen*, at [290]: 'reasonably possible'; McGrath J in *R. v Hansen*, at [252] 'reasonably possible'. *Ministry of Transport v Noort* [1992] 3 N.Z.L.R. 260, 272 (CA) (Cooke P); *Police v Herewini* [1994] 2 N.Z.L.R. 306, 313 (CA) (Cooke P).

[22] Tipping J in *R. v Hansen* [2007] 3 N.Z.L.R. 1, at [149].

[23] *Quilter v Attorney-General* [1998] 1 N.Z.L.R. 523, 581; (1997) 4 H.R.N.Z. 170, 232 (CA) (Tipping J); *Moonen v Film and Literature Board of Review* [2000] 2 N.Z.L.R. 9 (CA), at [17].

[24] See *Simpson v Attorney-General (Baigent's case)* [1994] 3 N.Z.L.R. 667 (CA), at 674 (Cooke P); *R. v Phillips* [1991] 3 N.Z.L.R. 175 (CA), at 177; *Quilter v Attorney-General* [1998] 1 N.Z.L.R. 523 (CA), at 542 (Thomas J) and *Bailey v Whangarei District Court* (1995) 2 H.R.N.Z. 275, at 289–90 (HC).

[25] *R. v A (No.2)* [2002] 1 A.C. 45 (HL), at [44] (Lord Steyn).

In the Court of Appeal's first BORA case, *Flickinger v Crown Colony of Hong Kong*,[26] the Court relied on s.6 to overturn an established interpretation of a statutory provision that was not ambiguous. The appellant argued that the provision should be given a BORA-consistent meaning, which would depart from previous case law. The Court noted that the provision had not been read in the way advocated by the appellant because 'statutory context and [legislative] history led to a different conclusion'. Despite this, the Court held that the provision was to bear a meaning consistent with the BORA.[27] In a similar fashion, Cooke P (as he then was), in *Herewini v Ministry of Transport*,[28] regarded s.6 as an 'emphatic direction' to the courts as to the proper role of rights and freedoms in the interpretation process.[29]

Following early trends, in *Simpson v Attorney-General*[30] (commonly referred to as *Baigent's case*), the Court of Appeal read down apparently clear legislation to recognise the right to be free of unreasonable search and seizure.[31] In *Baigent's case*, police officers searched the plaintiffs' house with a warrant issued on wrong factual assumptions and continued the search despite knowing it was the wrong address. The Court considered the scope of statutory immunities given to police officers executing warrants in light of the right to be free from unreasonable search. Cooke P held that the broad wording of the immunities meant that unreasonable acts committed in bad faith were not protected, but unreasonable acts carried out in good faith were.[32]

However, in *Knight v Commissioner of Inland Revenue*, Hardie Boys J considered that s.6 could be invoked only in cases of 'ambiguity or uncertainty'.[33] The judge held in a later case that the BORA signalled that it was 'Parliament's intention that the rights and freedoms … should be upheld unless there is clear legislative intention to the contrary'.[34] Those two contrary approaches were resolved with the enactment of the Interpretation Act 1999, which provides principles of legislative interpretation. One of the most oft-cited principles is that the meaning of a provision 'must be ascertained from its text and in the light of its purpose'.[35] While a previous incarnation of the

[26] [1991] 1 N.Z.L.R. 439 (CA).
[27] [1991] 1 N.Z.L.R. 439 (CA), at 440 (Cooke P).
[28] [1994] 2 N.Z.L.R. 306.
[29] [1994] 2 N.Z.L.R. 306, at 313 (Cooke P).
[30] [1994] 3 N.Z.L.R. 667 (CA).
[31] BORA, s.21.
[32] [1994] 3 N.Z.L.R. 667 (CA), at 674.
[33] [1991] 2 N.Z.L.R. 30.
[34] *Ministry of Transport v Noort* [1992] 3 N.Z.L.R. 260 (CA), at 287 (Hardie Boys J).
[35] Interpretation Act 1999, s.5.

legislation[36] contained a similar direction, the new phrasing emphasises the importance of parliamentary purpose when interpreting legislation.[37]

R. v Poumako[38] and *R. v Pora*[39] demonstrate both the approach taken in New Zealand and the difficulties caused by the procedural provisions of the BORA. The decisions deal with the interpretation of amending legislation which provided for increased penalties for so-called 'home invasion' offending and which was intended to operate retrospectively.[40] Confusingly, another provision in the same legislation provided that no penalty was to have retrospective effect.[41] The retrospective provision was on its face inconsistent with s.25 BORA, which provides that a person convicted of an offence in respect of which the penalty has varied between the commission of the offence and sentencing has the right to the lesser penalty. The issue was whether the legislation should be interpreted to uphold its retrospective application so that offenders who committed home invasions prior to the enactment of the legislation would be subject to the increased penalties. Since the decisions were handed down shortly after the HRA came into force, there was at that time little UK jurisprudence to guide the approach to the interpretation of legislation in light of the direction for consistency with rights where possible.

In *Poumako*, the Court found it desirable for Parliament to reconsider the issue, holding that the legislation was inconsistent with fundamental rights.[42] However, the majority dealt with that issue only in an obiter dictum as the decision was based on other grounds. The judges looked at the drafting history of the retrospective clause. The clause was introduced late in the legislative process and so was not subject to a report by the Attorney-General under s.7 BORA for compliance with rights and freedoms in the Act. According to the judges, that history did not reveal an indication that Parliament was aware of the inconsistency. Thomas J was of the view that, in such circumstances, 'a

[36] Acts Interpretation Act 1924, s.5(j) provided 'Every Act ... shall accordingly receive such fair, large, and liberal construction and interpretation as will best ensure the attainment of the object of the Act and of such provision or enactment according to its true intent, meaning, and spirit.'

[37] *R. v Rongonui* [2000] 2 N.Z.L.R. 385 (CA), at [161].

[38] *R. v Poumako* [2000] 2 N.Z.L.R. 695 (CA), at [80].

[39] [2000] 2 N.Z.L.R. 37 (CA).

[40] Criminal Justice Amendment Act (No.2) 1999, s.2(4) provided: 'Section 80 of the principal Act [which provided for increased penalties] applies in respect of the making of any order under that section on or after the date of commencement of this section, even if the offence concerned was committed before that date.'

[41] Criminal Justice Act 1985, s.4(2) provided: '[N]otwithstanding any other enactment or rule of law to the contrary, no court shall have power, on the conviction of an offender of any offence, to impose any sentence or make any order in the nature of a penalty that it could not have imposed on or made against the offender at the time of the commission of the offence, except with the offender's consent.'

[42] *R. v Poumako* [2000] 2 N.Z.L.R. 695 (CA), at [42] (Gault J).

firm indication of the Court's opinion can be expected to be of constructive assistance to Parliament'.[43]

The majority considered that it was not Parliament's intention for the provision to have retrospective effect and interpreted it narrowly, concluding that the section could be given effect only back to the date on which the amendments commenced. While still conflicting with s.25 BORA, a narrow retrospective reading of this type was the most consistent available interpretation.[44] Conversely, the dissenting judges found that the section was unambiguous and certain, and s.6 could not support an interpretation which was not Parliament's intent.[45]

The Court of Appeal had to address the same issue in *Pora*. The judges agreed that both provisions were clear in their meaning but were irreconcilable, so that one had to yield over the other. The Court was divided as to whether a right could be limited by later legislation.[46] Three of the judges held that the doctrine of implied repeal meant that the statute enacted later in time had effect and, therefore, that the retrospective provision stood. Those judges acknowledged that their interpretation resulted in a serious breach of a fundamental right. While dissatisfied with the outcome, their Honours held that having regard to the text of the provision and evidence from the parliamentary debates, parliamentary intention was so clear that the inconsistency could not be removed by judicial interpretation.[47] Conversely, the other judges held that Parliament's intention could be located in the earlier provision, except where Parliament had expressly indicated that it intended to cease protecting the right in question.[48] The judges also noted that they were following Parliament's own direction in s.6 so that 'Parliament must speak clearly if it wishes to trench upon fundamental rights'.[49] They held that the significance of the inconsistency was such that it was inconceivable that Parliament could have 'acted so casually' in removing the right.[50] Accordingly, it would draw the bow too far to presume that Parliament intended the retrospective provision to prevail.[51]

[43] *R. v Poumako* [2000] 2 N.Z.L.R. 695 (CA), at [101].
[44] *R. v Poumako* [2000] 2 N.Z.L.R. 695 (CA), at [37] and [40] (Gault J).
[45] *R. v Poumako* [2000] 2 N.Z.L.R. 695 (CA), at [55] (Henry J) and [80] (Thomas J).
[46] Richardson P did not address the issue in his judgment, so the bench of seven judges was split 3:3.
[47] *R. v Pora* [2001] 2 N.Z.L.R. 37, at [109]–[116] (Keith J, Gault J, McGrath J (delivered by Keith J)).
[48] *R. v Pora* [2001] 2 N.Z.L.R. 37, at [48] and [49] (Elias CJ and Tipping J (delivered by Elias CJ)); [140]–[157] (Thomas J).
[49] *R. v Pora* [2001] 2 N.Z.L.R. 37, at [156] (Thomas J).
[50] *R. v Pora* [2001] 2 N.Z.L.R. 37, at [48] (Elias CJ and Tipping J).
[51] *R. v Pora* [2001] 2 N.Z.L.R. 37, at [48] (Elias CJ and Tipping J).

UK Case Law

Early UK jurisprudence declined to follow the approach in *Knight*,[52] instead favouring a rights-consistent interpretation over an interpretation which is rights-inconsistent and might be said to uphold parliamentary intention in respect of the statutory provision under the spotlight. Executive support for that divergence can be found in the Commentary to the Human Rights Bill, which considered that the future s.3

> goes far beyond the present rule which enables the courts to take the Convention into account in resolving any ambiguity in a legislative provision. The courts will be required to interpret legislation so as to uphold the Convention rights unless the legislation itself is so clearly incompatible with the Convention that it is impossible to do so.
>
> This 'rule of construction' is to apply to past as well as to future legislation. To the extent that it affects the meaning of a legislative provision, the courts will not be bound by previous interpretations. They will be able to build a new body of case law, taking into account the Convention rights.[53]

One of the leading cases in this regard is *R. v A (No.2)*.[54] The House of Lords was required to interpret a provision which severely restricted cross-examination of rape complainants about the kind of sexual conduct that could be relevant to a defence alleging consent.[55] The Court accepted that the legislative purpose was to keep unnecessary evidence of a complainant's previous sexual behaviour out of trials,[56] but held that the provision had to be read subject to s.3 if at all possible. Lord Steyn, in the leading speech, quoted the Lord Chancellor who observed, while the Human Rights Bill was progressing through Parliament, that 'in 99 per cent of the cases that will arise, there will be no need for judicial declarations of incompatibility', and the Home Secretary who stated '[w]e expect that, in almost all cases, the courts will be able to interpret the legislation compatibly with the Convention'.[57] Lord Steyn concluded, 'In accordance with the will of Parliament as reflected in section 3 [of the HRA] it will sometimes be necessary to adopt an interpretation which linguistically may appear strained.'[58] His Lordship held that the provision in question should be read as subject to the 'implied provision' that cross-examination on sexual matters would be allowed if required to ensure a fair

[52] *Knight v Commissioner of Inland Revenue* [1991] 2 N.Z.L.R. 30.
[53] *Rights Brought Home: The Human Rights Bill*, Cm. 3782 (October 1997), at [2.7] and [2.8].
[54] *R. v A (No.2)* [2002] 1 A.C. 45 (HL).
[55] Youth Justice and Criminal Evidence Act 1999, s.41.
[56] *R. v A (No.2)* [2002] 1 A.C. 45, at [144]–[145] (Lord Hutton).
[57] *R. v A (No.2)* [2002] 1 A.C. 45, at [44] (Lord Steyn).
[58] *R. v A (No.2)* [2002] 1 A.C. 45, at [44] (Lord Steyn).

trial.[59] Relevant sexual experiences between a complainant and an accused would be admissible where ruled as necessary by a trial judge.[60]

Lord Hope took a different approach, but reached the same conclusion. He stated that s.3 was merely a rule of interpretation and did not entitle judges to act as legislators.[61] However, Lord Hope noted that when the Bill was passing through the House of Commons the responsible minister stated that it was compatible with the HRA,[62] which was evidence to suggest that Parliament intended to adhere to Convention rights.[63] On that basis it was legitimate to read the section so as to uphold the right to a fair trial.

R. v Lambert[64] is widely held to illustrate the House of Lords' divergence from New Zealand in respect of the approach to interpretation. The core question the House of Lords had to decide was whether 'prove' in terms of the Misuse of Drugs Act 1971—imposing an onus on the defendant to prove that he had no intention to supply drugs—meant 'proof', i.e. on a balance of probabilities, or merely imposed an evidentiary burden. The House of Lords held that s.3 HRA required, in light of art.6(2) ECHR, that the reverse onus provision be read as merely imposing an evidential burden (discharged by raising a reasonable doubt) rather than a legal burden (requiring a defendant to satisfy the court on the balance of probabilities), as had been held previously.[65] In reaching that decision, Lord Steyn discussed the interpretive approach available to the courts:

> So far as possible judges should seek to achieve the same attention to detail in their use of language to express the effect of applying section 3(1) as the parliamentary draftsman would have done if he had been amending the statute. It ought to be possible for any words that need to be substituted to be fitted in to the statute as if they had been inserted there by amendment. If this cannot be done without doing such violence to the statute as to make it unintelligible or unworkable, the use of this technique will not be possible. It will then be necessary to leave it to Parliament to amend the statute and to resort instead to the making of a declaration of incompatibility.[66]

Lord Steyn held that the courts were not bound by previous authorities as to the interpretation of legislation. The courts could state the effect of the provision without altering the ordinary meaning of the words, or translate a provision from wording that is incompatible to wording that is compatible, or

[59] Pursuant to EHCR, art.6.
[60] *R. v A (No.2)* [2002] 1 A.C. 45, at [45] (Lord Steyn).
[61] *R. v A (No.2)* [2002] 1 A.C. 45, at [108] (Lord Hope).
[62] *R. v A (No.2)* [2002] 1 A.C. 45, at [69] (Lord Hope).
[63] *R. v A (No.2)* [2002] 1 A.C. 45, at [69].
[64] *R. v Lambert* [2002] 2 A.C. 545 (HL).
[65] *R. v Lambert* [2002] 2 A.C. 545 (HL), at [42].
[66] *R. v Lambert* [2002] 2 A.C. 545 (HL), at 585.

read words in to a provision. However, his Lordship noted that 'interpretation of a statute by reading words in to give effect to the presumed intention must always be distinguished carefully from amendment. Amendment is a legislative act. It is an exercise which must be reserved to Parliament.'[67]

The UK courts have, however, stepped back from the perceived constitutional abyss of judicial law-making, as demonstrated in *Re S (Care Order: Implementation of Care Plan)*.[68] The House of Lords had to examine the Court of Appeal's interpretation of the Children Act 1989, in which the Court of Appeal proposed a new procedure for final orders whereby, at trial, milestones of a care plan would be identified and elevated to 'starred status'. Lord Nicholls questioned whether the courts had the power to introduce rights and liabilities not sanctioned by legislation. His Lordship observed that courts must be mindful that the HRA reserved the amendment of legislation to Parliament, holding that s.3 preserved parliamentary sovereignty.[69] If a meaning departed substantially from a 'fundamental feature' of legislation, it is likely to have 'crossed the boundary between interpretation and amendment'.[70] Parliament had entrusted the responsibility for looking after children who are the subject of care orders to local authorities, not the courts. The Court of Appeal, the House of Lords said, had gone too far as the starring system amounted to amendment, rather than interpretation of, legislation.[71]

In *R. (on the application of Wilkinson) v Inland Revenue Commissioners*[72] the House of Lords emphasised the need for s.3 HRA to result in interpretation that did not depart from the 'context' of legislation. In the leading speech, Lord Hoffmann said:

> I do not believe that s 3 … was intended to have the effect of requiring the courts to give the language of statutes acontextual meanings. That would be playing games with words.[73]

The emphasis on context was developed further by the House of Lords in *Ghaidan v Godin-Mendoza*.[74] The House of Lords was called on to consider whether 'spouse' in the Rent Act 1997 could include long-standing same-sex relationships, so that the Convention rights to a private and family life and

[67] *R. v Lambert* [2002] 2 A.C. 545 (HL), at 586.
[68] *Re S (Care Order: Implementation of Care Plan)* [2002] 2 W.L.R. 720 (HL).
[69] *Re S (Care Order: Implementation of Care Plan)* [2002] 2 W.L.R. 720 (HL), at [39] (Lord Nicholls).
[70] *Re S (Care Order: Implementation of Care Plan)* [2002] 2 W.L.R. 720 (HL), at [40] (Lord Nicholls).
[71] *Re S (Care Order: Implementation of Care Plan)* [2002] 2 W.L.R. 720 (HL), at [43] (Lord Nicholls).
[72] [2003] 1 W.L.R. 1718.
[73] [2003] 1 W.L.R. 1718, at [17].
[74] *Ghaidan v Godin-Mendoza* [2004] 2 A.C. 557; [2004] UKHL 30.

freedom from discrimination were given full effect. Previous interpretations of the legislation had held that 'spouse' included those living as 'wife or husband' but excluded same-sex relationships.[75] Their Lordships held that, following the HRA, courts had a duty to consider whether a new, rights-consistent interpretation was possible. Lord Nicholls held that the direction to interpret legislation consistently with the ECHR where 'possible' gave rise to ambiguity and that it was for the courts to separate the 'sheep from the goats',[76] that is, to decide where legislation was capable of being rendered compliant with the ECHR. Ambiguity was not required in order to interpret a provision consistently with the ECHR.[77] While an interpretation should not depend upon the 'particular words adopted by the parliamentary draftsman',[78] it must be compatible with the 'underlying thrust' of the legislation.[79] In the result, 'spouse' was interpreted to extend to same-sex partners as it did not contradict fundamental principles of the legislation.[80]

In 2011 the *Ghaidan* approach continued to govern the operation of s.3 as to the proper constitutional bounds between the judiciary and legislature in the United Kingdom. The Supreme Court affirmed the statement in *Ghaidan* that the courts should not adopt a meaning that is inconsistent with a fundamental feature of legislation because it would 'cross the constitutional boundary that section 3 … seeks to demarcate and preserve'.[81] Lord Phillips noted that s.3 applies to all legislation, whether pre-existing or post-dating the HRA. His Lordship added that so far as that applicability alters the interpretation of legislation before the HRA came into force, the HRA 'has the effect of amending legislation'.[82]

Anthony Lester QC has observed that the absence in the HRA of the equivalent of s.4 BORA (which preserves legislation in the face of inconsistency) avoids the problems faced by the New Zealand courts.[83] Lester argues:

> It has avoided the risk that the Courts would have applied the doctrine of implied repeal to the interpretation of the [HRA], with the result that a future

[75] *Fitzpatrick v Sterling Housing Association Ltd* [2001] 1 A.C. 27.

[76] *Ghaidan v Godin-Mendoza* [2004] 2 A.C. 557; [2004] UKHL 30, at [27].

[77] *Ghaidan v Godin-Mendoza* [2004] 2 A.C. 557; [2004] UKHL 30, at [29] (Lord Nicholls), [44] (Lord Steyn) and [67] (Lord Millett).

[78] *Ghaidan v Godin-Mendoza* [2004] 2 A.C. 557; [2004] UKHL 30, at [31] (Lord Nicholls).

[79] *Ghaidan v Godin-Mendoza* [2004] 2 A.C. 557; [2004] UKHL 30, at [33] (Lord Nicholls).

[80] *Ghaidan v Godin-Mendoza* [2004] 2 A.C. 557; [2004] UKHL 30, at [128] (Lord Roger).

[81] *Hounslow London Borough Council v Powell* [2011] 2 W.L.R. 287; [2011] UKSC 8, at [62] (Lord Hope).

[82] *Hounslow London Borough Council v Powell* [2011] 2 W.L.R. 287; [2011] UKSC 8, at [98] (Lord Phillips).

[83] Anthony Lester QC, "The Magnetism of the Human Rights Act 1998" (2002) 33 V.U.W.L.R. 53, 63.

> Parliament would have been deemed to have intended, by implication, to depart from Convention rights in a later statute. Such an approach would have undermined the effectiveness of the Act in securing compatibility between future legislation and Convention rights.[84]

Lester suggests that removal of s.4 would allow New Zealand courts to interpret legislation more consistently with the rights and freedoms in the BORA.[85] However, this suggestion has not been adopted by Parliament.

New Zealand Case Law: The Response?

The most recent decision in which the New Zealand Supreme Court had the opportunity to adopt the UK approach to legislative interpretation was *R. v Hansen.*[86] The Supreme Court was called on to rule on the interpretation of a provision of the Misuse of Drugs Act 1975 (comparable to the UK Misuse of Drugs Act 1971), which required defendants charged with possession with intent to supply to 'prove' they did not have the requisite intention in order to escape conviction.

The case therefore concerned a reverse onus provision, with the central question whether 'prove' referred to an evidential or legal burden. The case represented a salient opportunity to follow the House of Lords' approach in *Lambert.* However, the Supreme Court decided to stay the course. The Court unanimously declined to follow *Lambert*, holding that 'prove' was not ambiguous; it referred to a legal burden. To hold that 'prove' meant 'evidential burden' was strained and was therefore not available as an interpretation.[87]

However, the Court was split as to the approach to be taken to interpretation. The majority, Blanchard J, Tipping J, McGrath J and Anderson J, stressed that the starting point was Parliament's intended meaning, and only if that meaning was inconsistent with rights and freedoms did the question arise whether a rights-compliant meaning could be ascertained.[88] Therefore, Parliament's intended but inconsistent meaning was to be preferred to a meaning which was reasonably possible and protected fundamental rights, but was unintended by Parliament.[89] Tipping J explicitly declined to follow the UK approach, seeing it as 'mandating a judicial override of Parliament, if Parliament's meaning is inconsistent with a right or freedom'.[90]

[84] Lester QC, "The Magnetism of the Human Rights Act 1998", 63.
[85] Lester QC, "The Magnetism of the Human Rights Act 1998", 63.
[86] *R. v Hansen* [2007] 3 N.Z.L.R. 1 (SC).
[87] *R. v Hansen* [2007] 3 N.Z.L.R. 1 (SC), at [256] (McGrath J).
[88] *R. v Hansen* [2007] 3 N.Z.L.R. 1 (SC), at [89] (Tipping J).
[89] *R. v Hansen* [2007] 3 N.Z.L.R. 1 (SC), at [90].
[90] *R. v Hansen* [2007] 3 N.Z.L.R. 1 (SC), at [158].

Elias CJ disagreed with the majority and considered that the direction to interpret legislation consistently with the BORA should not be made subject to reasonable limitations under s.5. To do so would distort the Court's role from finding 'a meaning consistent with the rights and freedoms ... to one of preference for consistency with the rights as limited by a s 5 justification'.[91] The Chief Justice considered that the approach of the majority supported the existence of 'reasonable rights', which risked rights erosion.[92] An approach similar to that of the United Kingdom was justified because 'apparent meaning yields to less obvious meaning under common law presumptions protective of bedrock values'.[93] The judge considered that s.6 BORA and s.3 HRA were materially similar, as the direction to apply a consistent interpretation where one 'can' do so is a similar direction to do so where 'possible'.[94] This view has been endorsed by academics.[95]

The reasons behind Elias CJ's unwillingness to follow the majority are echoed in Claudia Geiringer's analysis of the effect of *Hansen*. Geiringer considers that after *Hansen* there is no real difference between the judiciary's interpretative approach under the BORA and the pre-existing common law 'principle of legality', which posits that where possible legislation is to be interpreted consistently with fundamental rights recognised by common law.[96] Other commentators have suggested *Hansen* establishes that s.6 BORA is subservient to s.5(1) of the Interpretation Act 1999.[97]

In New Zealand, rights-consistent interpretations must be 'fairly open'[98] and 'tenable',[99] based on Parliament's intended meaning. *Quilter*[100] and *Hansen* illustrate the courts' willingness to avoid stepping on Parliament's constitutional toes. New Zealand courts have held that the interrelationship

[91] *R. v Hansen* [2007] 3 N.Z.L.R. 1 (SC), at [6].

[92] *R. v Hansen* [2007] 3 N.Z.L.R. 1 (SC), at [6].

[93] *R. v Hansen* [2007] 3 N.Z.L.R. 1 (SC), at [13].

[94] *R. v Hansen* [2007] 3 N.Z.L.R. 1 (SC), at [13].

[95] See, for example, Andrew Butler "Interface between the Human Rights Act 1998 and Other Enactments: Pointers from New Zealand" (2000) 3 E.H.R.L.R. 249, 251: 'Both sections use strong mandatory language in expressing the nature of the rights-compatible interpretation exercise ... Where something can be done, then it is possible to do it; where it is possible to do something then it can be done. To my mind, these provisions evince no different emphasis or intention on their face.'

[96] Claudia Geiringer "The Principle of Legality and the Bill of Rights Act: A Critical Examination of *R. v Hansen*" (2008) 6 NZ Jnl Pub & Int L 59, at 73.

[97] Interpretation Act 1999, s.5(1) reads: 'The meaning of an enactment must be ascertained from its text and in the light of its purpose.' See P. Joseph, *Constitutional and Administrative Law in New Zealand*, 3rd edn (Wellington: Brookers, 2007), at [27.4.6]; Burrows and Carter, *Statute Law in New Zealand*, p.367. See also Elias CJ in *Morse v Police* [2011] N.Z.S.C. 45, at [12].

[98] *Ministry of Transport v Noort* [1992] 3 N.Z.L.R. 260, 286 (CA) (Hardie Boys J).

[99] *Moonen v Film and Literature Board of Review* [2000] 2 N.Z.L.R. 9 (CA), at [16].

[100] See the discussion of *Quilter* below, p.266.

of the procedural provisions is such that, where there are two possible interpretations, a tenable interpretation which accords with Parliament's legislative intention, but which is inconsistent with rights and freedoms, is to be preferred over a strained rights-consistent interpretation. This seems rather different to the UK courts' willingness to find a rights-consistent meaning so long as it accords with the 'underlying thrust' of legislation.

UK jurisprudence has been keenly observed by the New Zealand judiciary and it is a widely held view, as noted above, that the New Zealand courts have declined to follow suit. Not everyone would put it as drastically as John Burrows and Ross Carter:

> The Supreme Court in *Hansen* made it fairly clear that the New Zealand courts are not prepared to follow the *radical*, *strongly assertive*, and sometimes *startling* line of their UK counterparts.[101]

However, a closer examination of the four judgments often used as examples, illustrating the different approaches—namely *Lambert*,[102] *Hansen*,[103] *Ghaidan*[104] and *Quilter*[105]—suggests that the approaches the courts take might not be as 'at the opposite end of the spectrum' as Burrows and Carter contend.

The House of Lords in *Lambert* in 2001 could take some heart that its view that the word 'prove' in the UK Misuse of Drugs Act 1971 could legitimately be held to impose only an evidentiary not a legal burden on an accused by dint of the parliamentary reaction to a comparable holding on the burden of proof in a counter-terrorism offence in its earlier decision in *Kebilene*.[106] Parliament had responded to *Kebilene* by stating in subss. 118(1) and 118(2) of the Terrorism Act 2000 that 'the reverse onus of proof is satisfied if the person adduces evidence which is sufficient to raise an issue with respect to the matter unless the prosecution can prove the contrary beyond reasonable doubt'.[107] The Supreme Court in *Hansen* did not have such indication from the New Zealand Parliament. In fact, since the decision in *Hansen*, the New Zealand Parliament has continued to enact legislation containing reverse onus provisions.[108] This could be an indication that the New Zealand courts have been astute as to the political environment.

[101] Burrows and Carter, *Statute Law in New Zealand*, p.365 (emphasis added).
[102] [2002] 2 A.C. 545 (HL).
[103] [2007] 3 N.Z.L.R. 1 (SC).
[104] [2004] 2 A.C. 557 (HL).
[105] [1998] 1 N.Z.L.R. 523 (CA).
[106] [2000] 2 A.C. 326 which already held that proof needed to be interpreted as evidentiary burden, see at [373] (Lord Cooke).
[107] *R. v Lambert* [2002] 2 A.C. 545, at [40] (Lord Steyn).
[108] For example, the Misuse of Drugs (Classification of BZP) Amendment Act 2008; Misuse of Drugs Amendment Act (No.2) 2011—all amendments had negative s.7 reports by the Attorney-General. Note that Sch.5 to the Criminal Procedure (Reform and Modernisation) Bill 2010 proposes to repeal s.67(8) Summary Proceedings Act 1957 which reads: 'Any exception, exemption,

Similarly, in *Quilter*, three lesbian couples who wanted to get married had asked the Court of Appeal to interpret 'marriage' in the Marriage Act 1955 (which itself contained no definition of the term) consistently with the right to be free from discrimination under s.19 BORA so as to include same-sex couples. The Court rejected the claim. It held that the BORA could not be used to reinterpret the Marriage Act 1955 in a way that Parliament had not intended. Tipping J stated, 'We may interpret, but we cannot rewrite or legislate.' The judge looked to legislation that had been enacted since the BORA,[109] finding that it disclosed Parliament's intention to continue to apply the 'traditional' concept of marriage, that is between a man and a woman.[110] In contrast, the House of Lords in *Ghaidan* could resort to two Bills then before Parliament—the Housing Bill and the Civil Partnership Bill—which contained provisions that would have the effect of confirming on the face of legislation that the survivor of a cohabitating homosexual couple is to be treated in the same way as the survivor of a heterosexual couple.[111]

One decision which on first sight could be argued to disprove this essay's argument is *R. v A (No.2)*.[112] The decision concerned the then newly enacted rape shield law embodied in s.41 of the Youth Justice and Criminal Evidence Act 1999 which prohibits the giving of evidence and cross-examination about any sexual behaviour of the complainant except with leave of the court. Section 41 extensively describes the extent of the discretion of the judge. The House of Lords had to determine whether the extensive definition of the discretion infringed the right to a fair trial. It concluded that it could do. So the majority read into s.41 in conjunction with s.3 HRA and art.6 ECHR a further discretion allowing evidence to be given if otherwise the fair trial rights of the accused would be infringed. In other words, they added a further exception to the discretion-defining sections.[113] Some considered this radical, especially since s.41 was intended to be a response to a difficult problem concerning criminal procedure. However, it has to be noted that s.41 had only then

proviso, excuse, or qualification, whether it does or does not accompany the description of the offence in the enactment creating the offence, may be proved by the defendant, but, subject to the provisions of *section 17*, need not be negatived in the information, and, whether or not it is so negatived, no proof in relation to the matter shall be required on the part of the informant.' This is the first indication that Parliament has taken note of the fact that reverse onus provisions infringe the BORA.

[109] For instance, the Births, Deaths and Marriages Registration Act 1995 and the Marriage (Forms) Regulations 1995 proceeded on the basis that marriage was between a man and a woman, as s.55 required forms to be signed 'by the husband, the wife and two other witnesses to the solemnisation'.

[110] [1998] 1 N.Z.L.R. 523 (CA), at 580.

[111] See reference to the Bills: [2004] 3 All E.R. 411, at [22] (Lord Nicholls).

[112] *R. v A (No.2)* [2002] 1 A.C. 45.

[113] *R. v A (No.2)* [2002] 1 A.C. 45, at [45] (Lord Steyn). Lord Hope dissenting.

recently been inserted into the Act as a response to the far broader judicial discretion of s.2(2) of the Sexual Offences (Amendment) Act 1976. There was overwhelming evidence that that Act had not achieved its object of preventing the illegitimate use of prior sexual experience in rape trials. In respect of sexual experience between a complainant and other men, which can only in the rarest cases have any relevance, it created too broad an inclusionary discretion. Moreover, it left wholly unregulated questioning or evidence about previous sexual experience between the complainant and the defendant even if remote in time and context. Therefore, as Lord Steyn points out, 'There was a serious mischief to be corrected.'[114] The House of Lords agreed that Parliament's intent had been to correct the 'mischief'. The issue became whether their Lordships could correct Parliament's 'over-correction'.[115] The majority in effect concluded that it could; and doing it was not acting inconsistently with the thrust of the legislation in issue. In that regard it is clear from their Lordships' opinions that Parliament's intent played a major role in their decision-making. It also should be noted that Parliament has not amended the legislation to reverse the impact of the Appellate Committee's decision.

Therefore, even though the House of Lords has in its analysis of s.3 HRA emphasised that 'it will sometimes be necessary to adopt an interpretation which linguistically may appear strained'[116] on the occasions where one could argue that the Court had adopted such a linguistically 'strained interpretation', in fact the Court did have a considerably clear indication from Parliament that its 'strained' interpretation was at least within the range of the politically acceptable if not 'not contrary' to Parliament's intent.[117]

The cautious approach of the New Zealand Court of Appeal in *Quilter* and the New Zealand Supreme Court in *Hansen* demonstrates the same willingness to adhere to the boundaries of perceived parliamentary intent (as judged by the political/legislative environment).[118] The difference between the

[114] *R. v A (No.2)* [2002] 1 A.C. 45, at [28].

[115] See Lord Hope (dissenting), *R. v A (No.2)* [2002] 1 A.C. 45, at [109].

[116] *R. v A (No.2)* [2002]1 A.C. 45, at [44] (Lord Steyn). See also the comprehensive analysis by Aileen Kavanagh of s.3 HRA's meaning and function in "Choosing between Sections 3 and 4 of the Human Rights Act 1998: Judicial Reasoning after *Ghaidan v Mendoza*", in H Fenwick, G Phillipson and R Masterman (eds), *Judicial Reasoning under the UK Human Rights Act* (Cambridge: Cambridge University Press, 2007) and "The Role of Parliamentary Intention in Adjudication under the Human Rights Act 1998" (2006) O.J.L.S. 179.

[117] See *Bellinger v Bellinger* [2003] 2 A.C. 467 where the House of Lords came to the conclusion that the far-reaching ramifications of the proposed interpretation for many areas of the law meant that it was more appropriate for Parliament to tackle the issue of transsexual marriage than the courts. The Court issued a declaration of incompatibility under s.4 HRA.

[118] See, in regard to the relationship between Parliament and the courts on human rights issues, P. Butler "It Takes Two to Tango—Have They Learned Their Steps", available at http://ssrn.com/abstract=2022681 or http://dx.doi.org/10.2139/ssrn.2022681. Butler explores the way the dialogue model works in New Zealand using some empirical research.

approaches of the UK courts and the New Zealand courts, therefore, might not lie in their approaches to parliamentary sovereignty but rather in the speed and willingness with which the Parliament have been able to focus on and embrace their respective human rights legislation and the signals the respective Parliaments have thereby been sending to the judiciary. Whether the UK courts' language—i.e. their statements of their willingness 'to adopt an interpretation which linguistically may appear strained'[119]—has spurred Parliament to embrace human rights, whether the Joint Committee on Human Rights has helped to create a culture more amicable to human rights issues, or whether the UK membership of the European Union[120] and the Council of Europe is responsible for Parliament's proactive legislative activity at the time (or whether it was pure chance) are matters beyond the scope of this essay.

The Provision of Remedies

The White Paper originally provided that individuals whose rights had been breached could apply to the courts to 'obtain such remedy as the court considers appropriate and just in the circumstances'.[121] Sir Geoffrey Palmer stated at the Bill's Second Reading that it 'creates no new legal remedies for courts to grant. The judges will continue to have the same legal remedies as they have now.'[122] In its final form, however, the BORA omitted the remedies clause. Nevertheless, that does not mean that Parliament intended the legislation to be 'toothless'[123] or 'watered down',[124] as some opponents described the Bill.

Very early in its BORA jurisprudence, the Court of Appeal held that it had the mandate to develop remedies, such as the inadmissibility of evidence and the stay of proceedings where breaches were found to have occurred.[125] The Court further acknowledged the existence of remedies in *Baigent's case*.[126] The plaintiffs brought a claim on the basis of a breach of the right in the

[119] *R. v A (No.2)* [2002] 1 A.C. 45, 68.

[120] Burrows and Carter, *Statute Law in New Zealand*, p.365: 'And the New Zealand Parliament has not modified its sovereignty by joining a larger unit.'

[121] White Paper, cl.25.

[122] Rt Hon. Geoffrey Palmer MP, "New Zealand Bill of Rights Bill: Second Reading" (14 August 1990) 510 N.Z.P.D. 3450.

[123] Paul East MP, "New Zealand Bill of Rights Bill: Third Reading" (21 August 1990) 510 N.Z.P.D. 3762.

[124] Paul East MP, "New Zealand Bill of Rights Bill: Third Reading" (21 August 1990) 510 N.Z.P.D. 3762.

[125] See, for example, *Ministry of Transport v Noort* [1992] 3 N.Z.L.R. 260 (CA); *Martin v Tauranga District Court* [1995] 2 N.Z.L.R. 419 (CA). See pre-BORA in regard to exclusion of evidence: *R. v Kirifi* [1992] 2 N.Z.L.R. 8, 12 (CA) (Cooke P).

[126] *Simpson v Attorney-General (Baigent's case)* [1994] 3 N.Z.L.R. 667.

BORA to be free from unreasonable search and seizure, but statutory immunities barred the awarding of damages against the Crown and police officers in civil proceedings. The majority of the Court held that the statutory immunities did not apply to an action based on the BORA, since this was an action in public law and not in tort, at which the immunities were aimed.

Casey J noted that it would be strange for Parliament to accept that New Zealand citizens could go to the United Nations Human Rights Committee under the Optional Protocol to the ICCPR but could not obtain redress against human rights abuses under domestic law implementing the ICCPR.[127] The Court was of the view that it would fail in its duty if an effective remedy was not awarded to a claimant whose rights had been breached.[128] Casey J stated:

> I do not regard the absence of a remedies provision in the Act as an impediment to the Court's ability to 'develop the possibilities of judicial remedy' as envisaged in art 2(3)(b) [of the ICCPR].[129]

Cooke P held that the 'ordinary range of remedies will be available' to remedy a breach of the BORA.[130] However, a definitive list of available remedies was not attempted.

Baigent's case prompted the question of whether the subject of remedies under the BORA should be left to be further developed judicially, or whether legislative reform might be desirable. The government requested the Law Commission to consider the common law development from *Baigent's case*. The Commission endorsed the approach taken by the Court of Appeal,[131] and Parliament has abided by those recommendations. The New Zealand courts have continued to develop jurisprudence relating to remedies for breaches of the BORA. However, as McLay has pointed out, the revolutionary action of the Court of Appeal to construct public law compensation had not led to a revolution but, on the contrary, the record in regard to awarding *Baigent* damages is very thin.[132] There is one major exception and a reasonable number of minor awards.[133] The exception is *Taunoa v Attorney-General*,[134] where the

[127] *Simpson v Attorney-General (Baigent's case)* [1994] 3 N.Z.L.R. 667, 691.

[128] *Simpson v Attorney-General (Baigent's case)* [1994] 3 N.Z.L.R. 667, 676 (Cooke P) and 702 (Hardie Boys J).

[129] *Simpson v Attorney-General (Baigent's case)* [1994] 3 N.Z.L.R. 667, 691.

[130] *Simpson v Attorney-General (Baigent's case)* [1994] 3 N.Z.L.R. 667, 676 (Cooke P).

[131] New Zealand Law Commission, "Crown Liability and Judicial Immunity: A Response to *Baigent's Case* and *Harvey v Derrick*" (N.Z.L.C. R37, Wellington, 1997), pp.26–29.

[132] Geoff McLay, "Damages for Breach of the New Zealand Bill of Rights" [2008] N.Z.L.R. 333, 334 and 345 with suggestions why *Baigent* damages have not become a major remedy for breaches of the BORA.

[133] McLay, "Damages for Breach of the New Zealand Bill of Rights", 334, 335 with n.3 citing comparative material and other articles reviewing the case law on public law damages.

[134] (2004) 7 H.R.N.Z. 379; (2004) 8 H.R.N.Z. 53; *Attorney-General v Taunoa* [2006] 2 N.Z.L.R. 457 (CA); *Taunoa v Attorney-General* [2008] 1 N.Z.L.R. 429 (SC).

Supreme Court of New Zealand awarded damages to prisoners who had been subjected to the Department of Corrections' 'Behaviour Management Regime' which was held in parts to violate s.23(5) BORA for not treating the prisoners 'with humanity and with respect for their inherent dignity'. The decision to award damages to prisoners provoked immense public outcry[135] and resulted in the government ameliorating the effect of the decision by passing legislation designed to make the fruits of the prisoners' court actions available to the victims of their crimes.[136]

Baigent's case was decided prior to the enactment of the HRA. When the HRA came into existence, the United Kingdom avoided the uncertainty faced in New Zealand by enacting specific remedies provisions. The court may 'grant such relief or remedy, or make such order, within its powers as it considers just and appropriate'.[137] In addition, the HRA allows courts to make declarations of incompatibility where legislation is found to be incompatible with a Convention right.[138] The HRA thus sanctions judicial remedies and avoids the difficult debate experienced in New Zealand as to the proper constitutional boundaries in respect of judicial remedies.

The New Zealand courts have not accepted that the BORA is purely interpretative and have recognised the possibility of remedies. However, there has not been any suggestion made that s.6 BORA might be remedial as has been made by the House of Lords.[139] While damages are accepted as awardable, the availability of a declaration of inconsistency is less certain. The HRA's explicit provision for remedies significantly departs from the BORA model. That difference has resulted in distinctive New Zealand jurisprudence which observes but does not have full congruence with the position in the United Kingdom.

The Rationale and Appropriateness of Damages

The Court of Appeal created a public law compensatory remedy in *Baigent's case.*[140] Compensation was said to 'affirm the right'.[141] The High Court in *Manga v Attorney-General*[142] discussed the rationale for awarding remedies under the BORA. Hammond J stated that the remedies addressed public as

[135] The total award was NZ $86,000. Mr Taunoa received NZ $35,000.
[136] See Prisoners' and Victims' Claims Act 2005.
[137] HRA, s.8(1).
[138] HRA, s.4.
[139] For a full discussion, see Kavanagh, "Choosing between Sections 3 and 4 of the Human Rights Act 1998", pp. 127, 128.
[140] *Simpson v Attorney-General (Baigent's case)* [1994] 3 N.Z.L.R. 667.
[141] *Simpson v Attorney-General (Baigent's case)* [1994] 3 N.Z.L.R. 667, 703 (Hardie Boys J).
[142] [2000] 2 N.Z.L.R. 65 (HC).

well as private dimensions, because not only was an individual applicant aggrieved, but the claim has a 'distinct interface with public administration, and indeed, the governance of a given jurisdiction'.[143]

By contrast, the UK courts have stated that in awarding damages the goal is to compensate the victim for the harm caused,[144] rather than denouncing the breach more generally. In that respect, the United Kingdom treats the assessment of damages for breach of the HRA in a similar way to that undertaken in tort law, where damages correspond to specified loss, or in equity, where compensatory damages restore claimants to the position they would have been in but for the breach.[145] Juliet Philpott has observed:

> [T]he New Zealand judiciary has a more rights-focused view of the purpose of remedies for rights violations than the United Kingdom … perhaps this approach is a consequence of the fact that the availability of [BORA] damages was authorised by the courts in the first place.[146]

While the rationales as to *why* damages are awarded for breaches of rights differ, there are similarities between the jurisdictions as to *when* damages will be appropriate. The HRA provides that damages should be awarded only where 'necessary'[147] to remedy a breach. Damages are not awarded as of right. And in its 2006 report the Law Commission described the UK approach as follows:

> [D]amages are available where there has been a breach of a victim's [ECHR] rights, but those damages are discretionary and modest, allowing the court to tailor the remedies to fit the particular circumstances of the case. Although complaints certainly have been made about the limiting of damages in this way, others may see this flexible approach as an appropriate model for damages in a public law context.[148]

The New Zealand courts have developed a similar approach. For instance, in *P F Sugrue Ltd v Attorney-General* the Court of Appeal held that damages should be awarded only where necessary to give effect to the claimant's

[143] [2000] 2 N.Z.L.R. 65 (HC), at [82].

[144] *R. (KB) v Mental Health Review Tribunal* [2004] Q.B. 936, 959 (Stanley Burton J).

[145] See Juliet Philpott, "Damages under the United Kingdom's Human Rights Act 1998 and the New Zealand Bill of Rights Act 1990" (2007) 5 N.Z.J.P.I.L. 211, 217.

[146] Philpott, "Damages under the United Kingdom's Human Rights Act 1998 and the New Zealand Bill of Rights Act 1990", 219.

[147] HRA, s.8(3) provides: 'No award of damages is to be made unless, taking account of all the circumstances of the case, including—(a) any other relief or remedy granted, or order made, in relation to the act in question (by that or any other court), and (b) the consequences of any decision (of that or any other court) in respect of that act, the court is satisfied that the award is necessary to afford just satisfaction to the person in whose favour it is made.'

[148] Law Commission for England and Wales, *Damages under the Human Rights Act 1998*, Law Commission Report No.266 (October 2000), at [2.13].

rights.[149] One observation is, as McLay points out, that the United Kingdom and the New Zealand courts 'appear to be moving away from the idea that an award of damages under either the HRA or under *Baigent*, is an appropriate remedy for procedural failings'.[150]

Declarations of Inconsistency

The HRA differs from the BORA by providing for the courts to grant a declaration where a provision is deemed incompatible with a Convention right.[151] There is no equivalent provision in the BORA, apart from one exception which came into being in 2001. That exception is in respect of s.19, which prohibits freedom from discrimination. Under that provision, Pt1A of the New Zealand Human Rights Act 1993 applies, forming the basis of a declaration of inconsistency.[152] The availability of declarations of incompatibility in the HRA served as a useful precedent for the inclusion of the remedy under the NZ Human Rights Act 1993.[153]

The UK courts have awarded declarations of incompatibility on several occasions.[154] While the European Court of Human Rights has indicated that declarations of incompatibility are not effective remedies under the ECHR because they are not binding on the parties,[155] this view is not shared universally. Commentary to the Human Rights Bill summarised the effect of these provisions:

[149] [2004] 1 N.Z.L.R. 207 (CA), 233 (Blanchard J).

[150] McLay, "Damages for Breach of the New Zealand Bill of Rights", 341.

[151] HRA, s.4.

[152] Human Rights Act 1993 (NZ), s.92J, which was enacted through the Human Rights Amendment Act 2001. The Human Rights Review Tribunal and, on appeal, courts, can issue declarations of inconsistency in regard to unjustified limitations of s.19 of the BORA. Case law is still sparse under Pt1A Human Rights Act 1993. So far there have been four decisions by the Human Rights Tribunal: *Ministry of Health v Atkinson*, HC Auckland CIV-2010-404-000287, 7 March 2011; *CPAG v Attorney-General*, HC Wellington CIV-2009-404-273, 10 September 2010; *Attorney-General v Howard* [2011] 1 N.Z.L.R. 58; *Smith v Air New Zealand Ltd* [2011] 2 N.Z.L.R. 171.

[153] See the approving comments in *Re-evaluations of Human Rights Protections in New Zealand* (Wellington, Ministry of Justice, 2000), at [50].

[154] For example, *R. (on the application of H) v Mental Health Review Tribunal for the North and East London Region & The Secretary of State for Health* [2001] EWCA Civ 415; *International Transport Roth GmbH v Secretary of State for the Home Department* [2002] EWCA Civ 158; *R. (on the application of Anderson) v Secretary of State for the Home Department* [2002] UKHL 46; *A and others v Secretary of State for the Home Department* [2004] UKHL 56; *R. (on the application of Sylviane Pierrette Morris) v Westminster City Council & First Secretary of State* [2005] EWCA Civ 1184. See also http://webarchive.nationalarchives.gov.uk/+/http://www.dca.gov.uk/peoples-rights/human-rights/pdf/decl-incompat-tabl.pdf.

[155] *Burden v United Kingdom* (2008) 47 E.H.R.R. 38.

> Although the courts will not, under the proposals in the Bill, be able to set aside Acts of the United Kingdom Parliament, the Bill requires them to interpret legislation as far as possible in accordance with the Convention. If this is not possible, the higher courts will be able to issue a formal declaration to the effect that the legislative provisions in question are incompatible with the Convention rights. It will then be up to the Government and Parliament to put matters right. The Bill makes a 'fast-track' procedure available for the purpose of amending the law so as to bring it into conformity with the Convention.[156]

Declarations would spur Parliament into action through political pressure, rather than judicial compulsion. Anthony Lester QC has also argued that a declaration is of 'powerful support' to those taking a claim against the United Kingdom to the European Court.[157]

The express legislative authorisation for declarations of incompatibility has meant that the UK courts have not had to go down the same jurisprudential road as the New Zealand courts. While declarations of illegality have long been accepted as available in judicial review, jurisprudence regarding declarations of inconsistency in the BORA context has not produced a clear way forward.

It is arguable that Cooke P's statement in *Baigent's case* that courts could award the 'ordinary range of remedies'[158] included declarations of inconsistency, as declarations of illegality already existed under traditional judicial review.[159] Following *Baigent's case* the courts discussed declarations of inconsistency on several occasions, but no judgment has reached a definitive conclusion. The first judicial mention of a declaration was made by Cooke P in *Temese v Police*.[160] Cooke P observed that a declaration of inconsistency could be viewed as a gratuitous criticism of Parliament. However, the judge did not rule out the possibility of awarding a declaration.[161] In his dissenting judgment in *Quilter*,[162] Thomas J considered that it would be a 'serious error' for a court to refrain from making a declaration where an inconsistency is found to exist.[163]

A few months before the Court of Appeal handed down the decision *Moonen v Film and Literature Board of Review*,[164] the HRA was enacted.

[156] Secretary of State for the Home Department, *Rights Brought Home: The Human Rights Bill*, Cm.3782 (October 1997), Introduction and Summary.
[157] Anthony Lester QC, "The Magnetism of the Human Rights Act 1998" (2002) 33 V.U.W.L.R. 53, 67.
[158] [1994] 3 N.Z.L.R. 667 (CA), 676 (Cooke P).
[159] Claudia Geiringer, "On the Road to Nowhere: Implied Declarations of Inconsistency and the New Zealand Bill of Rights Act" (2009) 40 V.U.W.L.R. 613, 632.
[160] (1992) 9 C.R.N.Z. 425, 427.
[161] (1992) 9 C.R.N.Z. 425, 427.
[162] *Quilter v Attorney-General* [1998] 1 N.Z.L.R. 523 (CA).
[163] *Quilter v Attorney-General* [1998] 1 N.Z.L.R. 523 (CA), 554.
[164] [2002] 2 N.Z.L.R. 754 (CA).

Tipping J, writing the judgment of the Court, held that the courts had a duty to 'indicate that although a statutory provision must be enforced according to its proper meaning, it is inconsistent with the Bill of Rights'.[165] As Claudia Geiringer observes, it is 'perhaps not unreasonable to assume that this United Kingdom constitutional reform was not far from the mind of Tipping J when he wrote the *Moonen* decision'.[166] His Honour considered that a 'judicial indication' would be valuable to claimants taking a case to the UN Human Rights Committee and of interest to Parliament.[167] However, his Honour refrained from clarifying whether formal declarations of inconsistency were possible. While Tipping J considered that courts should 'declare' inconsistencies, it is not clear whether his Honour was referring to formal declarations or informal 'judicial indications'.[168]

Thomas J in the Court of Appeal took the opportunity to discuss whether a declaration of inconsistency could be awarded in light of the HRA in *Poumako*. While the majority of the Court avoided discussing this question, Thomas J in his dissenting judgment observed that the UK Parliament had not considered there was a contradiction between retaining supremacy of legislation and enabling declarations of incompatibility.[169] His Honour concluded that, in the New Zealand legislation, 'a declaration and s 4 can stand together'[170] and indicated that he would have issued a declaration of inconsistency in respect of the retrospective penalty clause in the Criminal Justice Amendment Act 1999. He considered that to fulfil their judicial function, the courts needed to be able to declare legislation inconsistent. A declaration would alert Parliament to unjustified limitations on rights that may have been missed in the legislative process. Thomas J considered that Parliament would welcome such an indication, rather than considering it in danger of being 'gratuitous' as Cooke P had cautioned in *Temese*.

The latest authority which discusses declarations of inconsistency is *R. v Hansen*.[171] The Supreme Court has accepted that the judiciary has jurisdiction, and indeed a responsibility, to indicate if it finds an inconsistency with the BORA.[172] While Tipping J hinted at the possibility in his judgment,[173]

[165] [2002] 2 N.Z.L.R. 754 (CA), at [20]. See also at [19] where Tipping J states that if the Court finds that a limitation on a right is not justified under s.5, 'there is an inconsistency with s5 and the Court may declare this to be so, albeit bound to give effect to the limitation in terms of s4'.

[166] Geiringer, "On the Road to Nowhere", at 618.

[167] [2002] 2 N.Z.L.R. 754 (CA), at [20].

[168] See, generally, Geiringer, "On the Road to Nowhere", at 619.

[169] *R. v Poumako* [2000] 2 N.Z.L.R. 695, at [106].

[170] *R. v Poumako* [2000] 2 N.Z.L.R. 695, at [106].

[171] *R. v Hansen* [2007] 3 NZLR 1 (SC).

[172] *R. v Hansen* [2007] 3 NZLR 1 (SC), at [253]–[254] (McGrath J).

[173] *R. v Hansen* [2007] 3 NZLR 1 (SC), Tipping J held at [107]: 'How far is the majority able to go in legislating to restrict the rights and freedoms of minorities? The point is essentially the same whether the Courts have power to strike down legislation or whether, as in New Zealand, they do

again the Court refrained from concluding whether a formal remedy of a declaration of inconsistency was available.

The provision for declarations of incompatibility in the HRA has not been thoroughly explored by the New Zealand jurisprudence in respect of the possibility of a similar remedy in New Zealand. Case law in this area is thin on the ground for several reasons. First, where appellants seeking declarations of inconsistency have failed to seek that remedy in the court of first instance, courts have considered that to be ground for refusing the remedy on appeal.[174] Secondly, a declaration of inconsistency is a civil remedy, and has been held to be unavailable in criminal proceedings.[175] Thirdly, much of the case law has been preoccupied with ascertaining the proper interpretative approach to the BORA. The courts have not yet had to answer definitively the question of awarding a declaration, so the impact of the HRA in this area remains to be seen.[176]

Influence on Rights

Recent research has shown that the New Zealand Supreme Court engages with international jurisprudence in 41 per cent of its judgments.[177] Judgments of the UK courts are generally relied on most frequently after Australia and Canada. In regard to rights jurisprudence the Supreme Court relies mostly on Canadian precedent.[178] The use of Canadian precedent rather than reliance on UK jurisprudence can be explained by the fact that the drafting of the individual guarantees in the BORA was significantly influenced by the Canadian Charter.[179]

---

not, and can only declare that certain legislation, although operative, is inconsistent with the Bill of Rights.'

[174] See, for example, *R. v Chatha (No.2)* [2008] N.Z.C.A. 466, at [32] (Glazebrook J); *McDonnell v Chief Executive of the Department of Corrections* [2009] N.Z.C.A. 352, at [129]–[130].

[175] *Belcher v Chief Executive of the Department of Corrections* [2007] N.Z.C.A. 174.

[176] See Williams J in *Zaoui v Attorney-General* [2004] 2 N.Z.L.R. 339, where his Honour states that he was bound by Court of Appeal jurisprudence that despite not having ever issued a declaration of inconsistency had accepted that a declaration was a possible remedy. However, his Honour also held (at [167]) that a declaration was a remedy of last resort and that the case before him did not warrant a declaration since there were sufficient other remedies available for Mr Zaoui. For a general discussion, see Geiringer, "On the Road to Nowhere".

[177] P. Butler, "The Use of Foreign Jurisprudence in the New Zealand Supreme Court", in A. Buechler and M. Mueller-Chen (eds), *Private Law, National–Global–Comparative*, Festschrift Ingeborg Schwenzer zum 60. Geburtstag (Bern: Staempfli, 2011), pp. 305 and 307.

[178] Butler, "The Use of Foreign Jurisprudence in the New Zealand Supreme Court", pp. 305 and 308.

[179] White Paper, at [10.1].

Further, New Zealand courts are aware that the New Zealand legal landscape can be unique. Recently, the Court of Appeal noted the authorities of *London Borough of Lewisham v Malcolm*[180] and *Kay v London Borough of Lambeth*[181] (referred to by counsel), which grappled with the issue of whether the County Court is entitled to refuse a possession order on the grounds of discrimination under s.22 of the UK Disability Discrimination Act 1995 or breach of art.8 ECHR. However, the Court held that 'care must be taken with these authorities where the legislative background is quite different from our own'.[182]

A database search reveals that the HRA has been cited 43 times.[183] In the most recent example the High Court rejected reliance on *R (Mahmood) v Secretary of State for the Home Department*[184] and the European Court of Human Rights decision in *Advic v United Kingdom*,[185] arguing for the existence of a right to family life.[186] Similarly, in *P v Attorney-General*,[187] the High Court had to examine whether the plaintiff had a right to compensation under either the Bill of Rights Act 1688, the Universal Declaration of Human Rights, the ICCPR or the BORA for sexual assault while in the Navy. The Court cited *Jones v Saudi Arabia*,[188] where, in a claim in the United Kingdom for compensation for torture in prison in Saudi Arabia, the House of Lords distinguished between international law establishing a universal criminal jurisdiction over alleged torturers and the absence of such universal jurisdiction in a civil claim for compensation, to reject the claim.[189]

The rights which have received the most scrutiny in New Zealand in recent years have been freedom of expression and freedom from discrimination. In regard to the latter the question of how to determine the comparator group has been particularly prominent. In *Ministry of Health v Atkinson* the High Court found it helpful to consider the approach of the House of Lords[190] in *Lewisham London Borough Council v Malcolm*.[191] In *Simunovich Fisheries Ltd*

[180] *London Borough of Lewisham v Malcolm* [2008] 1 A.C. 1399 (HL).
[181] *Kay v London Borough of Lambeth* [2006] UKHL 10; [2006] 2 A.C. 465.
[182] *Winther v Housing Corporation of New Zealand* [2010] N.Z.C.A. 601, at [46]. See also *Child Poverty Action Group (CPAG) v Attorney-General*, H.R.R.T. 41/05, 16 December 2008, at [113] where the Human Rights Review Tribunal, having been referred to comparative jurisprudence, emphasised that New Zealand had to find its own solution.
[183] Between 2000 and 5 September 2011 using Brief Case (the New Zealand legal database).
[184] *R (Mahmood) v Secretary of State for the Home Department* [2001] 1 W.L.R. 840 (CA).
[185] *Advic v United Kingdom* [1995] E.C.H.R. 57.
[186] *M v Minister of Immigration*, HC Auckland CIV-2011-404-2913, 5 September 2011 (Courtney J).
[187] HC Wellington CIV-2006-485-874, 16 June 2010 (Mallon J).
[188] [2007] 1 A.C. 270, at [71].
[189] HC Wellington CIV-2006-485-874, 16 June 2010, 199 (Mallon J).
[190] *Lewisham London Borough Council v Malcolm* [2008] 1 A.C. 1399 (HL).
[191] *Ministry of Health v Atkinson*, HC Auckland CIV-2010-404-000287, 7 March 2011, at [88].

v Television New Zealand Ltd,[192] a defamation case, the Court of Appeal did consider UK authority. However, it pointed out that earlier New Zealand case law had already cautioned in regard to the use of English precedent under the HRA.[193] But in any event the Court used the UK jurisprudence to strengthen its argument.[194] UK authorities were considered extensively in *Hosking v Runting*.[195] The case concerned the publication of photographs taken covertly of the twins of a celebrity couple and published in a women's magazine. The question arose whether New Zealand recognised a tort of invasion of privacy. The Court of Appeal held that New Zealand would acknowledge a tort of privacy rather than following the English route of 'breach of confidence'.[196]

Conclusions

Undoubtedly, the New Zealand judiciary, legal profession and academia have keenly observed developments in the United Kingdom from the enactment of the HRA.[197] However, New Zealand has refrained from adopting many of those developments. The HRA was enacted with the benefit of hindsight, eight years after entry into force of the BORA. While there are significant legislative differences, there are also different political forces at work behind the respective pieces of legislation, which have influenced the way the statutes are applied.

In New Zealand, Parliament is viewed as a protector of rights, and judicial attempts to chip away at its sovereignty are viewed with suspicion. Generally, judges are acutely aware that they are not to wander into Parliament's arena. That has resulted in an interpretative approach which is much more cautious. The courts can be understood as supplementing Parliament's intention by filling gaps in legislation. Case law has demonstrated a judicial willingness to find an inconsistency rather than adopt a strained interpretation which gives greater effect to rights. By contrast, the UK judiciary has stipulated that it would uphold rights-consistent interpretations

[192] [2008] N.Z.C.A. 350 (CA).
[193] *Simunovich Fisheries Ltd v Television New Zealand Ltd* [2008] N.Z.C.A. 350 (CA), at [91].
[194] *Simunovich Fisheries Ltd v Television New Zealand Ltd* [2008] N.Z.C.A. 350 (CA), at [91]–[92].
[195] [2005] 1 N.Z.L.R. 1 (CA), at [23]–[53] (Gault J with whom Blanchard J agrees); at [200]–[201] (Keith J).
[196] *Hosking v Runting* [2005] 1 N.Z.L.R. 1 (CA); see, for example, at [248] (Tipping J): 'It is inherent in what I have already written that I prefer a different structural path to that which the House of Lords followed in that case. The English approach is nevertheless instructive from the substantive point of view.'
[197] Travel between both countries for the participation at conferences, sabbaticals, lectures etc. is extensive.

at the cost of adopting strained interpretations. This boldness may be due to the constitutional tradition of the courts as a bastion of rights protection or the influence of Strasbourg, for the legislative provisions directing consistent interpretation are not significantly different between the jurisdictions. However, a closer examination of key decisions suggests that the House of Lords and Supreme Court have in the cases where one could speak of a strained interpretation done so with the knowledge that the interpretation was not foreign to Parliament.

While both New Zealand and the United Kingdom recognise the availability of damages for breaches of rights, the New Zealand judiciary reached that conclusion prior to (and so independently of) the HRA. There has, however, been substantial uncertainty in New Zealand regarding declarations of inconsistency. The judiciary has been rather hesitant about recognising it has such a power. The UK has avoided that problem due to Parliament's express provision for declarations of incompatibility. That may reflect both the United Kingdom's interest in being seen by the wider European community to be promoting rights and a lesson learned from observing the New Zealand experience.

The HRA provides a valuable point of reference for New Zealand, but at present this country has not taken the same path as the United Kingdom. As more countries adopt Bills of Right which shift the balance of power between Parliament and the judiciary, the New Zealand public—and Members of Parliament—may become more comfortable with the notion that a Bill of Rights can (and should) constrain legislative action. We may then see a sea-change towards greater promotion of rights with increased congruence between the approaches of New Zealand and the United Kingdom.

Note. I would like to thank Catherine Harwood for her assistance with this essay and the editors for their very helpful comments. As always, the views expressed and any errors made in this essay are mine alone.

Part V

Amendment, Repeal or a Bill of Rights for the United Kingdom?

12

A Bill of Rights for the United Kingdom? Lessons from Overseas

ALICE DONALD

Introduction

THE UK COALITION PARTIES ENTERED THE 2010 general election with divergent positions on human rights. The Conservatives pledged to repeal the 1998 Human Rights Act (HRA) and replace it with a UK Bill of Rights, without expressly committing to an alternative mechanism for incorporating the European Convention on Human Rights (ECHR) into domestic law. The Liberal Democrats were committed to the HRA and to extending and entrenching it within a written constitution. The roots of this divergence stretch back decades and have been starkly visible since the Conservatives first pledged to repeal the HRA in 2001.[1]

Conservative discourse has centred on the purported impact of the HRA on efforts to tackle terrorism and crime, such as the erroneous claim that the Act bars police from publishing photographs of fugitives.[2] Another motif has been the intention to decouple a Conservative-designed Bill of Rights from the jurisprudence of the European Court of Human Rights by weakening s.2 HRA, which requires domestic courts to 'take account of' Strasbourg case law.[3] The Act has also been blamed for creating an infantilising and individualistic culture and, paradoxically, for failing to protect fundamental liberties.[4] The Liberal Democrats deplored the conduct of the debate about human

[1] D. Erdos, "Ideology, Power Orientation and Policy Drag: Explaining the Elite Politics of Britain's Bill of Rights Debate" [2009] 44 *Government and Opposition* 20.
[2] See, for example, PM's statement on violence in England, 10 August 2011. For a refutation of this claim, see K. Starmer, "Public Prosecution Service Annual Lecture—The Role of the Prosecutor in a Modern Democracy", Public Prosecution Service Annual Lecture, Royal Society of Medicine, London, 21 October 2009.
[3] D. Grieve, "European Convention on Human Rights: Current Challenges", speech at Lincoln's Inn, 24 October 2011. On which, see Chapter 13, this volume.
[4] D. Cameron, "Balancing Freedom and Security—A Modern British Bill of Rights", speech to the Centre for Policy Studies, London, 26 June 2006.

Proceedings of the British Academy, **183**, 281–307. © The British Academy 2013.

rights by the two larger UK parties.[5] Indeed, the party's manifesto omitted its long-held commitment to a Bill of Rights since, a senior party source said, 'it would not be difficult to use the Orwellian language of a UK Bill of Rights to water down the HRA'.[6]

After negotiating these apparently incompatible positions, the Coalition stated:

> We will establish a Commission to investigate the creation of a British Bill of Rights that incorporates and builds on all our obligations under the European Convention on Human Rights, ensures that these rights continue to be enshrined in British law, and protects and extends British liberties. We will seek to promote a better understanding of the true scope of these obligations and liberties.[7]

This Commission was established in March 2011.

While much commentary has focused on the possible content of a UK Bill of Rights,[8] the process by which it might be created has invited less scrutiny. To rectify this omission, the Equality and Human Rights Commission (EHRC) commissioned research in 2009 to examine the processes that had been used to develop Bills of Rights (or proposed Bills) in comparable jurisdictions.[9] The methodology consisted primarily of 43 semi-structured interviews with individuals who had designed, implemented, advised or studied Bill-of-Rights processes in Canada, New Zealand, Australia and Northern Ireland.[10] The interviewees did not constitute a representative sample of opinion on particular approaches to legal reform. Rather, they were selected for their knowledge and experience of the political and methodological dilemmas confronting those designing a Bill-of-Rights process once the political decision has been made to undertake it.[11] The views of participants

[5] N. Clegg, "The Attacks on Liberty", *New Black Magazine*, 23 December 2008.

[6] F. Klug, "Why Lib Dems Reject Bill of Rights", *Guardian*, 14 April 2010.

[7] HM Government, *The Coalition: Our Programme for Government* (2010), p.11. Note that the Coalition agreement speaks of a 'British Bill of Rights' while the Commission on a Bill of Rights established as a result of the agreement refers consistently, and properly, to a 'UK Bill of Rights'. This essay uses the term 'UK Bill of Rights' except where the term 'British' is used in citation.

[8] See, for example, Joint Committee on Human Rights, *A Bill of Rights for the UK?* Twenty-ninth report of Session 2007–08, vol.1. Report, together with formal minutes (London: Stationery Office, 2008); JUSTICE Constitution Committee, *A British Bill of Rights: Informing the Debate* (London: JUSTICE, 2007).

[9] A. Donald, with the assistance of P. Leach and A. Puddephatt, *Developing a Bill of Rights for the UK* (Manchester: Equality and Human Rights Commission, 2010).

[10] Interviews were also conducted with architects of the Bill-of-Rights process in South Africa. While their experience bears comparison with the transitional context in Northern Ireland, the unique circumstances in post-apartheid South Africa make it difficult to draw conclusions that might be applicable in a country like the United Kingdom and therefore evidence from South Africa is not considered in this essay.

[11] For a socio-political explanation of the origins of Bills of Rights in advanced, industrialised democracies, see D. Erdos, *Delegating Rights Protection: The Rise of Bills of Rights in the Westminster World* (Oxford: Oxford University Press, 2010).

were also sought on the extent to which the process had helped to engender a sense of democratic legitimacy in the outcome.[12]

This essay draws on evidence from this research and updates it. The first section discusses the nature of Bills of Rights and the trend towards participatory methods for their creation. The second section examines key aspects of the design of Bill-of-Rights processes. The third examines the context for creating a UK Bill of Rights, including the work of the Commission on a Bill of Rights. The fourth and final section concludes by reflecting on the challenges facing the Commission in the light of experience overseas.

Bills of Rights and 'Process-driven Constitutionalism'

Philip Alston proposes three essential characteristics of Bills of Rights: they provide protection for those human rights which are considered, at a given historical moment, to be of particular importance; they are binding upon governments and can only be overridden with significant difficulty; and they provide some form of redress in the event that violations occur.[13] Documents with these characteristics are also called 'Charters of Rights' or, as in the United Kingdom, a 'Human Rights Act'.

Some of the best-known Bills of Rights were part of constitutional settlements following conflict or political upheaval (France, the United States, South Africa and the proposed Northern Ireland Bill of Rights). Elsewhere, they were the product of considered political debate about the value of such legislation in a modern democracy (Canada, New Zealand, Australia and the UK HRA) with, as Erdos argues, distinct political 'triggers' for their (attempted) creation in each context.[14] Bills of Rights created in the post-war era have been based on, or strongly influenced by, international human rights treaties. They vary from the US model of constitutional supremacy,

[12] Fabienne Peter defines democratic legitimacy as 'the normative concept that establishes under what conditions the members of a democratic constituency ought to respect a democratic decision'; F. Peter, *Democratic Legitimacy* (New York and Abingdon: Routledge, 2009), p.4. It is beyond the scope of this essay to examine alternative conceptions of democratic legitimacy; for example, procedural conceptions that focus purely on the decision-making process and substantive conceptions which also include criteria that relate to the quality (e.g. rationality or justness) of the decisions made. This essay follows Peter's preferred (procedural) conception; this states that what is important for democratic legitimacy is that the normative and empirical premises of proposals are subjected to 'the scrutiny of an inclusive process of public deliberation'; Peter, *Democratic Legitimacy*, p.3.

[13] P. Alston, *Promoting Human Rights through Bills of Rights* (Oxford: Oxford University Press, 1999), p.10.

[14] Erdos, *Delegating Rights Protection: The Rise of Bills of Rights in the Westminster World*, pp.5–7.

which entrenches fundamental rights as supreme law, to statutory models which give primacy to parliamentary sovereignty and involve some form of constitutional dialogue between judicial and legislative institutions.[15]

In 2007, Kader Asmal argued that 'the process by which a bill of rights is drawn up is as important as the end product'.[16] Asmal spoke from experience of drafting the South African constitution and addressed himself to the framers of a Bill of Rights for Northern Ireland. His argument reflects a broader post-war trend towards what Hart calls 'process-driven constitutionalism'. Vivien Hart suggests that participation has emerged as both a right and a necessity in the formation of constitutional documents:

> Process has joined outcome as a necessary criterion for legitimating a new constitution: how the constitution is made, as well as what it says, matters.[17]

The United Nations body which monitors civil and political rights recognises a specific right to participate in choosing or changing a constitution.[18] Jennifer Nedelsky argues that in order to justify constitutionally entrenched rights as constraints on democratic decision-making 'the processes by which [rights] are defined must themselves be universally recognized as legitimate'.[19] Colin Harvey extends this argument, suggesting that, whether or not a Bill of Rights is constitutionally entrenched, the process of adoption is paramount:

> The principled reason is that deliberation is always an essential aspect of reflective law and policy formation in a political community ... The pragmatic consideration is that if ... the Bill of Rights is to assume the exalted status of the 'sacred' text in a secular society then its shape (not simply the choice to accept or reject it) must be determined by a broadly-based process of popular participation.[20]

In addition to democratic legitimacy, participatory constitutional development has been associated with other benefits. Writing about the transition from authoritarian to democratic systems in Europe, Andrew Arato argues

[15] These models of constitutionalism have also been characterised as 'strong-form' and 'weak-form' judicial review; see M. Tushnet, "Alternative Forms of Judicial Review" [2003] 101 *Michigan Law Review* 2781.

[16] K. Asmal, "Designing a Bill of Rights for a Diverse Society" [2007] 6 E.H.R.L.R. 607.

[17] V. Hart, *Democratic Constitution Making, Special Report No 107* (Washington: US Institute of Peace, 2003), p.12.

[18] Committee on Civil and Political Rights, *The Right to Participate in Public Affairs, Voting Rights and the Right of Equal Access to Public Service (Art. 25)* (1996), 12/07/96, CCPR General Comment No.25, at [6].

[19] J. Nedelsky, "Reconceiving Rights and Constitutionalism" (2008) 7 *Journal of Human Rights* 162.

[20] C. Harvey, "The Politics of Rights and Deliberative Democracy: The Process of Drafting a Northern Irish Bill of Rights" [2001] 1 E.H.R.L.R. 61.

that 'it is unthinkable that legitimate constitution making bypass extended public discussion', one benefit being that such discussion permits the main actors to 'advance and defend positions for which normatively convincing arguments can be devised'.[21]

Roland Penner notes that the 1982 Canadian Charter of Rights and Freedoms was forged in a 'democratic crucible'. During nationally televised hearings of a joint parliamentary committee, more than 1,000 individuals and 300 groups petitioned for changes and additions, and the committee, after 60 days of hearings, successfully proposed to Parliament some 65 substantial amendments to the government draft.[22] Penner argues that the judiciary has generally 'taken rights both seriously and creatively ... no doubt influenced by the popular support which led both to the eventual passage of the Charter and to the Charter's inclusion of substantial community and equality rights'.[23] Geoffrey Leane interprets the Canadian experience differently, describing the creation of the Charter as a largely top-down process driven by elite negotiation: 'the creature of a highly motivated Prime Minister [Pierre Trudeau] and often reluctant Premiers of the various provinces, but never "of the people"'.[24] Trudeau championed the Charter as the centrepiece of his project to patriate the constitution (that is, to make it amendable by Canada only, with no role for the UK Parliament) and as a source of unity to counter Quebecois separatism.[25] However, Penner notes that provincial governments, jealous of their jurisdictions and, in some instances, ideologically opposed to a constitutional Bill of Rights, were 'prodded and persuaded' towards reform by a domestic human rights movement formed of groups representing, among others, women, aboriginals, the disabled, and religious, ethnic and language minorities.[26] Thus, social movements had a degree of influence over the process of elite negotiation as well as the content of the Charter.

Such popular momentum was lacking in the creation of the New Zealand Bill of Rights Act 1990 (BORA). This was a partisan measure promoted by the Labour government without the support of the (then) opposition or of many Labour ministers, and with minimal public engagement.[27] The BORA

[21] A. Arato, *Civil Society, Constitution, and Legitimacy* (Lanham, MD: Rowman & Littlefield, 2000), p.250.

[22] R. Penner, "The Canadian Experience with the Charter of Rights: Are There Lessons for the United Kingdom?" [1996] P.L. 107.

[23] Penner, "The Canadian Experience with the Charter of Rights", 123.

[24] G. Leane, "Enacting Bills of Rights: Canada and the Curious Case of New Zealand's 'Thin' Democracy" (2004) 26 *Human Rights Quarterly*, 155.

[25] Canada already had a non-entrenched Bill of Rights enacted in 1960, which applied only to federal law as it lacked the requisite provincial consent.

[26] Penner, "The Canadian Experience with the Charter of Rights", 107.

[27] P. Joseph, "The New Zealand Human Rights Experience", in P. Alston (ed.) *Promoting Human Rights through Bills of Rights* (Oxford: Oxford University Press, 1999).

followed unsuccessful moves in 1985 to create a constitutionally entrenched Bill of Rights similar to the 1982 Canadian Charter. A Justice and Law Reform Select Committee of Parliament held hearings over two years and analysed more than 400 submissions, the majority of which focused on the controversial issue of abortion. Submissions suggested that there was little public support for an entrenched Bill.[28] In 1990, and with little additional public consultation, the BORA was enacted as ordinary legislation with subordinate status which can be overridden by a simple majority in Parliament.[29] Interviewees for the EHRC-commissioned research attributed the BORA's unpopularity (or at least obscurity) partly to this unpromising beginning; nevertheless, there have been no moves to repeal it.

JUSTICE notes that processes to create Bills of Rights in the post-war era have grown steadily 'in their breadth, inclusiveness, sophistication and general effectiveness'.[30] The more recent processes to develop Bills of Rights in Australia and Northern Ireland placed a greater premium on public involvement than in either Canada or New Zealand. Since 2002, several Australian states or territories have conducted inquiries into how human rights could be better protected. In Victoria, Tasmania, Western Australia and the Australian Capital Territory (ACT) the inquiries recommended the adoption of some kind of Bill of Rights. Each was run by an independent committee and involved concerted forms of public engagement with a strong emphasis on face-to-face contact with communities in preference to relying on interest groups or legal professionals.[31] George Williams, who chaired the Human Rights Consultation Committee in Victoria, stated:

> I felt strongly the real danger of introducing a major democratic reform that had not been preceded by a significant period of consultation and engagement … That led me to believe that one of the key principles had to be that an instrument of this type … had to be generated by a very inclusive process to give the outcome legitimacy.[32]

The ACT and Victoria took action: the ACT passed the Human Rights Act 2004 and Victoria passed the Charter of Human Rights and Responsibilities

[28] S. Glazebrook, "The New Zealand Bill of Rights Act 1990: Its Operation and Effectiveness", paper prepared by Justice Susan Glazebrook, New Zealand Court of Appeal, for the South Australian State Legal Convention, 22–23 July 2004.

[29] Leane, "Enacting Bills of Rights: Canada and the Curious Case of New Zealand's 'Thin' Democracy", 171.

[30] JUSTICE Constitution Committee, *A British Bill of Rights*, p.98.

[31] Inquiries were also conducted in Queensland and New South Wales by parliamentary committees; both rejected legislation and recommended other measures to protect human rights. See A. Byrnes, H. Charlesworth and G. McKinnon, *Bills of Rights in Australia: History, Politics and Law* (Sydney: University of New South Wales Press, 2008).

[32] Interview with Professor George Williams, 27 October 2009.

Act 2006. Tasmania and Western Australia deferred action pending the outcome of a National Human Rights Consultation. This was completed in September 2009 and recommended the adoption of a federal Human Rights Act broadly similar to the ACT and Victoria model. This was based on majority support for a Human Rights Act among the 35,000 submissions generated by the consultation, the largest response to any public inquiry in Australia.[33] Despite this, in April 2010, the Australian government said it would not introduce a federal Human Rights Act on the grounds that it would be 'divisive', and deferred reconsideration of the measure until 2014.[34] Instead, it initiated other reforms in the areas of education and pre-legislative scrutiny against human rights standards.[35]

The Northern Ireland process shared the emphasis on community participation but was considerably more protracted and necessarily reactive to political circumstances.[36] The 1998 Belfast (Good Friday) Agreement provided for a Northern Ireland Human Rights Commission (NIHRC) with a mandate to

> consult and to advise on the scope for defining, in Westminster legislation, rights supplementary to those in the European Convention on Human Rights, to reflect the particular circumstances of Northern Ireland, drawing as appropriate on international instruments and experience.[37]

The following decade saw an extensive process of public consultation led by the NIHRC and involving numerous other actors.[38] A key development was the establishment in 2006 of the Bill of Rights Forum, a negotiating body comprising political parties and civil society representatives under an international chair whose deliberations took place in public.[39] Consensus proved

[33] Of the 35,000 submissions, 83% supported a Human Rights Act. In independent opinion polling, 57% supported an Act and 14% were opposed. See National Human Rights Consultation Committee, *National Human Rights Consultation Report* (Canberra: Commonwealth of Australia, 2009), p.6.

[34] The Hon. Robert McClelland MP, Attorney-General for Australia, "Address to the National Press Club of Australia—Launch of Australia's Human Rights Framework", 21 April 2010.

[35] E. Santow, "The Act That Dares Not Speak Its Name: The National Human Rights Consultation Report's Parallel Roads to Human Rights Reform" (2010) 33 *U.N.S.W. Law Journal* 8.

[36] C. Harvey and A. Schwartz, "Designing a Bill of Rights for Northern Ireland" (2009) 60 N.I.L.Q. 181.

[37] NIHRC, *A Bill of Rights for Northern Ireland: Advice to the Secretary of State for Northern Ireland* (Belfast: NIHRC, 2008), p.8.

[38] NIHRC, *Making a Bill of Rights for Northern Ireland* (Belfast: NIHRC, 2001).

[39] Bill of Rights Forum, *Final Report: Recommendations to the Northern Ireland Human Rights Commission on a Bill of Rights for Northern Ireland* (Belfast: Bill of Rights Forum, 2008), pp.7–8.

elusive and the Forum's recommendations to the NIHRC expressed divergent views on many issues. Informed by these recommendations and its own consultations, the NIHRC submitted its advice on a Northern Ireland Bill of Rights to the UK government in December 2008.[40] Each proposed right (including social and economic rights, environmental rights and victims' rights) was explained and justified with reference to a detailed methodology.[41]

In November 2009, the Northern Ireland Office (NIO) responded with a consultation paper which accepted only two of the proposed rights for inclusion; other rights and enforcement issues were either discarded or left open for consultation.[42] The NIHRC criticised the three-month consultation as belated and inadequate for a constitutional enterprise of such significance.[43] The NIO received 36,492 responses to the consultation. It noted that there was 'considerable support from human rights and community groups for a wide-ranging Bill of Rights' along the lines of that recommended by the NIHRC but that the consultation also demonstrated 'opposition to a wide-ranging Bill of Rights and support instead for a more limited set of rights that reflected the particular circumstances of Northern Ireland'.[44] The NIO did not quantify the weight of opinion on each side. The Minister of State for Northern Ireland, Hugo Swire MP, later indicated that the Coalition would subsume the Northern Ireland Bill of Rights within the architecture of a UK-wide Commission lest it become, as he put it, a 'stand-alone sideshow'.[45]

Designing a Bill-of-Rights Process

Once conditions are considered propitious to invite public engagement in the formation of a Bill of Rights, what form should it take? This section identifies aspects of the design of process that participants in our research considered to be of greatest importance and to be transferable between national contexts.

[40] NIHRC, *A Bill of Rights for Northern Ireland: Advice to the Secretary of State for Northern Ireland.*

[41] Harvey and Schwartz, "Designing a Bill of Rights for Northern Ireland", 190–91.

[42] NIO, *Consultation Paper—A Bill of Rights for Northern Ireland: Next Steps* (London: NIO, 2009). The rights proposed for inclusion were the right to vote freely in and be elected at genuine periodic elections held by secret ballot (p.35) and the right of the people of Northern Ireland to identify themselves and be accepted as Irish or British or both (p.42).

[43] "Commission Rejects NIO Consultation on a Bill of Rights", 17 February 2010.

[44] NIO, *Publication of Responses to Consultation: A Bill of Rights for Northern Ireland: Next Steps* (16 December 2010).

[45] HC Debs, vol.512, col.850, 30 June 2010.

Terms of Reference

All modern Bills of Rights have been designed to incorporate international human rights into domestic law and/or to strengthen existing human rights protection.[46] No processes under review permitted even the possibility of regression, either in terms of standards or mechanisms and institutions for protecting human rights.[47] The way in which governments initiated reform, either through a draft Bill and/or through the terms of reference or mandate established for public consultation, expressly excluded this option.[48]

Defining certain areas as non-negotiable might appear to conflict with the principle of democracy. George Williams noted that in recommending significant reform such as a Bill of Rights, the question always needs to be asked:

> How will that reform be assisted—or not—by the openness of the terms of reference and will there be any lingering questions of illegitimacy?[49]

However, interviewees for the EHRC-commissioned research understood the democratic imperative as requiring not a blank sheet in which all possible options are given equal consideration—including that of regression—but rather transparent terms of reference which state clearly the parameters of the discussion in relation to existing human rights protections and international obligations. This approach is consistent with the principle of non-regression established by UN bodies that monitor states' compliance with their international human rights obligations. In broad terms, this requires

[46] The Canadian Charter of 1982 built upon the existing (non-entrenched) Bill of Rights enacted in 1960, itself largely based on the International Covenant on Civil and Political Rights (ICCPR). The New Zealand Bill of Rights Act 1990 expressly affirmed New Zealand's commitment to the ICCPR. The South African Bill of Rights built upon the Canadian Charter, the ICCPR and the International Covenant on Economic and Social Rights (ICESCR). Bills of Rights which have been enacted or recommended in Australia have drawn explicitly on the ICCPR and in some cases the ICESCR and on models of enforcement from jurisdictions including the United Kingdom.

[47] An exception is the review by a parliamentary committee of the Victorian Charter of Human Rights and Responsibilities in 2011. The Scrutiny of Acts and Regulations Committee recommended against repeal of the Charter but was split on whether key provisions should be retained or modified. A majority recommended, among other steps, that the courts should have no role or a substantially reduced role in enforcing human rights and providing remedies when they are breached and that public authorities should have no, or reduced, obligations to act compatibly with the Charter. See Scrutiny of Acts and Regulations Committee, Parliament of Victoria, *Review of the Charter of Human Rights and Responsibilities Act*, tabled 14 September 2011, http://www.parliament.vic.gov.au/images/stories/committees/sarc/charter_review/report_response/20110914_sarc.charterreviewreport.pdf.

[48] See Donald, Leach and Puddephatt, *Developing a Bill of Rights for the UK*, pp. 22–25 for detailed discussion of the terms of reference of the processes under review.

[49] Interview, 27 October 2009.

that standards of protection that have been adopted should not be undone at a later date without compelling justification.[50] The principle of non-regression goes to the heart of the relationship between human rights and democracy and reflects a view of Bills of Rights as not only negative instruments to constrain the state, but also positive instruments to enable relatively powerless groups to exert influence in the democratic process. By this account, a utilitarian calculus that justifies the weakening of human rights protection (or countenances that possibility) on the grounds that it expresses the majority will, or protects society at large, is spurious. Rather, the democratic imperative is to construct a process which facilitates participation by groups whose rights are most vulnerable to abuse.

Statements of Intent

Bill-of-Rights processes are necessarily constrained by what is considered legally and politically feasible in terms of possible outcomes. Interviewees differed as to how these constraints should be managed. Some favoured a clear statement of intent from government about what options it favours, since it may be disempowering for people to be consulted about outcomes that are politically unattainable. Others favoured casting the net wider to encompass options that do not necessarily have elite support.

Some noted that meaningful engagement tends to come around contested areas: a key aspect of the process, then, is to identify areas where interest groups and the political elite do not agree and put these at the heart of the consultation. Victoria provides a salient example. The Victorian government's statement of intent was prescriptive in ruling out the inclusion of socio-economic rights, yet the weight of community engagement convinced the government to provide for a review of the Charter by 2011 to determine, among other things, whether it should be expanded to include these rights.[51] The Victorian process, then, combined relatively unconstrained community discussion with a commitment from the government to act within certain parameters.

Northern Ireland presents a contrasting experience. Interviewees for the EHRC-commissioned research concurred that the decade-long process had

[50] See, for example, Committee on Economic, Social and Cultural Rights, *The Nature of States Parties Obligations (Art 2, par 1)* (1990) 14/12/90, CESCR General Comment No.3, at [9].

[51] G. Williams, "The Victorian Charter of Human Rights and Responsibilities: Origins and Scope" (2006) 30 *Melbourne University Law Review* 880. In September 2011, the parliamentary committee charged with reviewing the Charter recommended that no further rights be added to it; see Scrutiny of Acts and Regulations Committee, Parliament of Victoria, *Review of the Charter of Human Rights and Responsibilities Act*.

been unduly protracted. This was partly due to lack of clarity at the outset on the time-frame, procedure, mandate and terms of reference of both the NIHRC and the Bill of Rights Forum. These were contested throughout, hindering progress on substantive issues. Also lacking was a clear procedural commitment from the UK government about what action it would take after the NIHRC presented its advice. One interviewee in Northern Ireland, who wished to remain anonymous, noted:

> Before you even step into this arena you need to tie down more carefully a clear line about what happens after [the consultation] because there's a real danger of creating expectations among communities that are vulnerable and marginalised.

This risk is also present in Australia, where the government chose not to act on the preference expressed during the consultation for a federal HRA.[52] Interviewees emphasised that if a government appears to disregard the outcomes of public consultation, both the process itself, and subsequent government actions, risk being viewed as illegitimate. This risk is likely to be compounded if the reasons for the decision are not transparent or suggest that the consultation was undertaken in bad faith.

Running the Process

In Australia, most Bill-of-Rights processes were run by independent committees, typically comprising four people nominated by all parties. Most were not human rights experts, with the exception of the committee chairs in Victoria and ACT. The federal committee included a prominent broadcaster, a former police officer specialising in counter-terrorism and an indigenous barrister, with a Jesuit priest and lawyer, Frank Brennan, as chair. The Victoria committee included a basketball player; the ACT committee, a poet. Some interviewees were uncomfortable about the idea of appointing members primarily for their public profile. Most added that it was important for independent bodies consulting on a Bill of Rights to include at least one member with human rights expertise so that it was not wholly reliant on external legal advice. Interviewees familiar with the Australian experience broadly endorsed the model and considered it transferable to other contexts. Chris Sidoti, an Australian human rights advocate who chaired the Northern Ireland Bill of Rights Forum, argued:

> The credibility of the process has to be designed right up front … Human rights are an emotive issue [and] attract a high level of irrational responses … so it's far better for such a consultation to be undertaken by a group of 'clean skins'.[53]

[52] F. Brennan, "Human Rights Act Door Still Swinging" [2010] 20(11) *Eureka Street*.
[53] Interview, 28 November 2009.

A review of the Northern Ireland process reveals the particular difficulties facing national human rights institutions (NHRIs) charged with leading a Bill-of-Rights process. Anne Smith views the Northern Ireland experience as a 'stellar illustration' of the challenges facing NHRIs, which must carve out a space between government and civil society and remain independent of government while being reliant on state funding.[54] One interviewee noted that the NIHRC's role had created suspicion among some communities that a 'maximalist approach was intended from the start'. Interviewees suggested that more appropriate roles for NHRIs were to influence and monitor the process; champion key principles; generate community engagement; speak authoritatively about human rights; and engage in 'myth-busting'.

No interviewee favoured public consultations on a Bill of Rights being run by a government department or solely by a parliamentary committee because these have tended to be more conventional and static in their methods than independently-run processes and significantly less able to generate community engagement. It was noted that such processes may also be more vulnerable to becoming a proxy for other political battles than in the relative 'safe haven' of an independent exercise.

Achieving Political Consensus

The premium placed on achieving political consensus around a Bill of Rights varies with the context. Constitutional reform like that in Canada and South Africa is commonly perceived as requiring substantial consensus, since partisan initiatives are unlikely to achieve legitimacy or longevity. Statutory Bills of Rights developed in settled times have rarely achieved cross-party consensus. In Australia, the conservative Liberal Party has consistently opposed Bill-of-Rights processes initiated by Labor administrations at federal and state level. The UK HRA is another salient example.

A key question arises in relation to process. How should it seek to build political consensus if this is lacking at the outset? The experience of Northern Ireland is pertinent. One interviewee, who wished to remain anonymous, suggested that it was unrealistic to expect the NIHRC to achieve cross-party consensus:

> There was no express requirement in the mandate to achieve consensus around the proposals … Ultimately if you ask a human rights commission to do this, all you can really expect … is that it will provide you with solid human rights advice. If your dominant concern is party political consensus, then give it to a body that is set up to do that.

[54] A. Smith, "The Unique Position of National Human Rights Institutions: A Mixed Blessing?" (2006) 28 *Human Rights Quarterly* 904.

Some interviewees suggested that the Bill of Rights Forum provides a model that could be used in other contexts. While it came too late in the Northern Ireland process and was inadequately resourced, it had increased the knowledge and understanding of decision-makers, overcome some political obstructions and established precisely where agreement and disagreement lay.[55] It had also provided an arena for politicians to be challenged by community groups to defend their positions, thereby educating all players.

Interviewees suggested that the achievement of political consensus is not reducible to this or that procedural initiative but is dependent also upon the nature of the constitutional 'moment' and on having champions in the legislature and (as in Canada) sustained political leadership. Nor does cross-party consensus, desirable as it may be, necessarily create a sense of popular ownership. Rather, interviewees argued that forums for political negotiation should co-exist with consultative bodies that engender trust by being demonstrably non-partisan and offering multiple opportunities for public participation.

Participation, Consultation and Deliberation

Consultation refers to a process intended to elicit the views and preferences of the public, with the aim of informing policy-makers.[56] Deliberation is a process by which, typically, randomly sampled citizens are intensively educated to permit them to hold informed discussion of a policy question and reach a considered judgment.[57] A process is generally described as participatory when it involves a significant proportion of those targeted and includes people who are hard to reach because of discrimination or disadvantage. Post-war Bill-of-Rights processes have been primarily consultative rather than deliberative and, as we have seen, have varied in the extent to which they were participatory.

In relation to consultation, interviewees recommended combining qualitative and quantitative methods in order to insulate the process from allegations that it is confined to a self-selecting audience. Frank Brennan noted that the multi-stranded nature of the national consultation in Australia had bolstered its credibility:

[55] Donald, Leach and Puddephatt, *Developing a Bill of Rights for the UK*, p.33.

[56] For discussion of consultative and deliberative methods, see G. Smith, *Beyond the Ballot: 57 Democratic Innovations from Around the World—A Report for the Power Inquiry* (London: Power Inquiry, 2005); A. Runswick, *A Guide to Involving Citizens in Constitutional Reform* (London: Unlock Democracy, 2007).

[57] Involve and the National Consumer Council, *Deliberative Public Engagement: Nine Principles* (London: National Consumer Council, 2008).

> We were always aware that those who came to community meetings were likely to have a grievance or personal agenda, so it was also important to have rigorous independent research to capture general opinion.[58]

Some Australian processes used social networking and other online forums, email and text messaging to generate submissions, as well as conducting 'town hall' meetings, opinion polls, focus groups and targeted conversations with community groups. In Northern Ireland, methods included training some 400 community-based facilitators; independent thematic advisory groups; advertising campaigns on television, radio, billboards and bus-shelters; and opinion polls and educational work conducted jointly with civil society networks.[59] Also available (though not used in a Bill-of-Rights process to date) are innovations that provide anonymous, secure virtual spaces for groups that would be unlikely to participate effectively via conventional means.[60]

Deliberative methods have not been used in any Bill-of-Rights process outside the United Kingdom except that in ACT, where some 200 randomly chosen citizens held two days of televised deliberation during which they were exposed to competing views.[61] In common with most deliberative polls, the process produced statistically significant changes both to levels of understanding and opinions: support for a Bill of Rights grew, but support for a constitutionally entrenched Bill fell.[62] The consultative committee's recommendations reflected this outcome in proposing a statutory HRA.

Proponents of deliberative methods argue that they offer advantages over the use of consultative methods alone.[63] The outcomes of deliberation can be promoted as a legitimate proxy for the conclusions the public would reach if everyone had the opportunity to become fully informed. However, even proponents of deliberative forums argue that they should not be used in isolation from other participatory approaches. Rather, their impact comes in part from being communicated to, and scrutinised within, the wider public sphere. Moreover, targeted consultative methods may also be required to ensure that the views of relatively powerless groups are given privileged status in the process. A hallmark of the Australian and Northern Ireland processes was

[58] Interview, 20 November 2009.

[59] NIHRC, *Progressing a Bill of Rights for Northern Ireland: An Update* (Belfast: NIHRC, 2004), pp.145–48; NIHRC, *Views on a Bill of Rights for Northern Ireland: Results from a 2004 Opinion Survey* (Belfast: NIHRC, 2004).

[60] An example in the United Kingdom is Womenspeak, a virtual space for consultation with survivors of domestic violence. See Smith, *Beyond the Ballot: 57 Democratic Innovations from Around the World*, pp.90–104.

[61] Issues Deliberation Australia, *The ACT Deliberates: An ACT Bill of Rights? A Territory Deliberative Poll—Final Report* (Canberra: Issues Deliberation Australia, 2002).

[62] Issues Deliberation Australia, *The ACT Deliberates*, pp.20–21.

[63] Smith, *Beyond the Ballot: 57 Democratic Innovations from Around the World*, p.55.

the effort to elicit opinions and experiences from groups identified as socially excluded or disadvantaged rather than those already motivated and equipped to make submissions. Some Australian committees worked in partnership with community law centres and front-line service providers systematically to facilitate hundreds of submissions from individuals who would otherwise have been unlikely to participate: for example, older people, homeless people, prisoners and ex-prisoners; people with disabilities or mental health problems; and refugees and asylum seekers.[64]

Translating Process into Content

Many interviewees placed great value on 'traceability', that is the visible imprint of the process on the final outcome in the form of a draft Bill or (as in Northern Ireland and Australia) recommendations as to its content. It is notable that, in jurisdictions where there has been a significant degree of public participation in creating a Bill of Rights, its effect has been to give popular weight to legislative options for change and/or to expand or strengthen the government's proposed legislative model in specific ways. This has partly been a numbers game: the recommendations of committees in Australia and of the NIHRC in Northern Ireland were wholly or partly justified in terms of the volume of submissions received, the results of opinion surveys and, in the ACT, the majority preference in the deliberative poll.

However, interviewees concurred that the consultation should not be a majoritarian exercise. Indeed, Bills of Rights derive largely from the imperative to protect individuals and minorities from the consequences of majority rule.[65] To counter this danger, consultative bodies in Australia and Northern Ireland gave additional weight to the views of less powerful groups. Consultation committee reports in Australia are suffused with stories of abuse or neglect, adding authenticity and urgency to their recommendations. Yet synthesising thousands of diverse stories along with submissions from expert bodies is challenging, as Frank Brennan acknowledged:

[64] National Human Rights Consultation Committee, *National Human Rights Consultation Report*, p.130; Consultation Committee for a Proposed WA Australia Human Rights Act, *The WA Human Rights Act: Report of the Consultation Committee for a Proposed WA Human Rights Act* (Perth: Government of Western Australia, 2007), Appendix F; Victorian Human Rights Consultation Committee, *Rights, Responsibilities and Respect: The Report of the Human Rights Consultation Committee* (Melbourne: Victorian Human Rights Consultation Committee), pp.165–67.

[65] See A. Kavanagh, "The Role of a Bill of Rights in Reconstructing Northern Ireland" (2004) 26 *Human Rights Quarterly* 956.

> Trying to balance the contributions that reflect lived experience and those of a more theoretical or abstract nature was problematic … was an ongoing and irresolvable tension in drafting our report.[66]

Interviewees suggested that consultative bodies need to assess submissions qualitatively as well as quantitatively: for example, to give appropriate significance to detailed submissions and those from organisations with large memberships as compared to 'tick box' responses from individuals. Mindful of these tensions, interviewees concurred that consultative bodies should be scrupulous in justifying the rationale for their recommendations and how these relate both to community preferences and to international standards. The national consultation committee in Australia presented the case for and against each legislative and other option for strengthening human rights protection and specified how many submissions supported or opposed each option (including how many were the product of orchestrated campaigns). When an option attracted strong support and the committee considered that its advantages outweighed any disadvantages, it was generally recommended.[67]

The Role of Civil Society

In Australia and Northern Ireland, civil society networks were influential in initiating, energising and informing Bill-of-Rights processes and remain instrumental in lobbying for the implementation of the outcomes of consultation. The origins of the Australian consultation lie in the New Matilda campaign initiated in 2005 and relaunched in 2008 as the Human Rights Act for Australia Campaign. Some 25,000 of the 35,000 submissions to the national consultation were generated through civil society-led campaigns.[68] In Northern Ireland, the Human Rights Consortium, established in 2000 to encourage public involvement, grew into a coalition of more than 100 community groups, NGOs and trade unions campaigning for a 'strong and inclusive' Bill of Rights. Interviewees noted that initiatives to involve community networks need to start well before any public consultation in order that civil society groups can influence the design of the process and inform their own constituencies.

[66] Interview, 20 November 2009.

[67] National Human Rights Consultation Committee, *National Human Rights Consultation Report*, p.343.

[68] National Human Rights Consultation Committee, *National Human Rights Consultation Report*, pp.5–6.

Education

Intensive education of participants is an integral feature of deliberative methods. However, in broader public consultations, the objective of raising public knowledge and understanding is harder both to achieve and to measure. Interviewees in Northern Ireland noted that the protracted process there had succeeded in raising human rights 'literacy' through initiatives such as the training of facilitators and mentoring of community projects by those with human rights expertise. Those who designed the consultative processes in Australia placed a high premium on avoiding legalistic terms and using human rights-compatible language that resonated with communities, such as 'not letting people fall through the cracks'. Interviewees were generally dubious about how far a time-limited consultation could fulfil a serious educational function in relation to human rights; rather, a minimum requirement was the provision of impartial, accessible information in appropriate formats and languages and a commitment by all parties to correcting myths and misperceptions.

Time-frame

The processes under review involved varying timescales: from three months in Tasmania to a decade in Northern Ireland. Interviewees suggested that once the decision has been taken to invite public engagement the process must not be protracted or indeterminate because this can breed disillusionment and dissipate momentum. Most recommended a defined period of consultation of six months to a year. Where consultation is preceded by a period of civil society activism, as in Australia, momentum is likely to be greater. Where the impetus is largely top-down, as in the United Kingdom, the chances of achieving meaningful engagement within a limited time-frame are correspondingly reduced.

Resources

The resources required to run a consultation will vary between jurisdictions. The Australian national consultation had a budget of A$2.8 million (around £1.8 million) and a secretariat of around 20 people. Resource issues surfaced in Northern Ireland where, in 2002, two commissioners resigned because, among other concerns, the Bill-of-Rights process 'had not received the internal allocation of resources (in time, thought or money) it requires'.[69] Yet where

[69] NIHRC, *Progressing a Bill of Rights for Northern Ireland: An Update*, p.8.

public involvement was limited, as in New Zealand and Canada, interviewees did not attribute this to a shortage of resources as such. Rather, they suggested, it is the political intent behind a Bill-of-Rights process that determines its ambition. Several interviewees noted that a public-facing process to create a Bill of Rights is 'better not done at all than done badly', especially where trust in the sincerity of public consultation is fragile.

Responsibilities

Debates about the merits, or dangers, of connecting rights and responsibilities are well-rehearsed.[70] No Bill-of-Rights process outside the United Kingdom has included questions about personal responsibilities in its terms of reference.[71] In one revealing snapshot, more than 40 per cent of Australians surveyed during the national consultation agreed that if members of a group abused the wider community's rights then it was reasonable to restrict the rights of the entire group, while 57 per cent agreed that it was reasonable to reduce or remove an individual's rights if they did not respect those of the community.[72] This example illustrates how social anxieties can surface during processes which invite debate about human rights, along with notions of rights being contingent on personal behaviour, particularly in relation to unpopular groups. It suggests that giving prominence to responsibilities in a Bill-of-Rights process requires careful management in the context of low public understanding about, or antipathy towards, human rights. For this reason, interviewees suggested that responsibilities should be introduced into consultation processes, if at all, as a matter of education about the duty to respect the rights of others, rather than as the basis for substantive legislative provisions.

Creating a UK Bill of Rights

Before assessing the work of the Commission on a Bill of Rights in the light of international experience, it is worth exploring the recent history of the Bill-of-Rights project in the United Kingdom.

[70] L. Lazarus, B. Goold, R. Desai and Q. Rasheed, *The Relationship between Rights and Responsibilities* (Ministry of Justice Research Series No.18/09, 2009).

[71] In Victoria, 'responsibilities' appear in the title and preamble of the Charter but not its substantive content.

[72] National Human Rights Consultation Committee, *National Human Rights Consultation Report*, p.347.

A striking feature of debate about a UK Bill of Rights has been the lack of acknowledgement that the HRA is itself widely viewed as a Bill of Rights. It has been referred to as such by academic commentators,[73] former UK government ministers[74] and actors in other jurisdictions who have sought to emulate the UK legislative model.[75] As Francesca Klug notes, notwithstanding the absence of judicial strike-down powers, the HRA exhibits many features of a 'higher law' to which other law and policy should conform.[76] Yet, Klug argues, the Act has failed in its symbolic requirements: it has not been viewed by the UK public as '*their* bill of rights'.[77]

The unpopularity of the HRA is widely assumed but should not be overstated or misconstrued. In broad terms, evidence from quantitative and qualitative surveys over the past decade suggests that negative attitudes towards human rights and/or the HRA are not immutable and that people tend to become more positive about human rights and the HRA the more they know about them.[78] Polling data suggest that hostility towards the HRA is due not to its content (or its very existence) but to the way in which it is perceived to be implemented so as to protect 'undesirable' groups more than others.[79] There is evidence that the specific rights enshrined in the HRA are almost universally popular. For example, in the Liberty Human Rights Act poll in 2010, 95 per cent of respondents believed the right to a fair trial is vital or important; 94 per cent believed that respect for privacy and family life is vital or important; and 96 per cent supported the existence of a law 'that protects rights and freedoms in Britain'.[80] A survey commissioned by the Ministry of Justice produced similar results.[81] This survey also indicated very low levels of public awareness about the HRA.[82]

[73] For example, Alston, *Promoting Human Rights through Bills of Rights*, p.11.

[74] Jack Straw, who was Home Secretary when the HRA came into force, described it as 'the first Bill of Rights this country has seen for three centuries'; see J. Straw MP, speech to the Institute of Public Policy Research, 13 January 2000.

[75] For example, National Human Rights Consultation Committee, *National Human Rights Consultation Report*, p.263.

[76] F. Klug, "A Bill of Rights: Do We Need One or Do We Already Have One?" [2007] P.L. 701, 708.

[77] Klug, "A Bill of Rights: Do We Need One or Do We Already Have One?", 713 (emphasis in original).

[78] For an analysis of this evidence, see A. Donald, P. Leach and J. Watson, *Human Rights in Britain since the Human Rights Act 1998: A Critical Review* (Manchester: Equality and Human Rights Commission), pp.161–83.

[79] Donald, Leach and Watson, *Human Rights in Britain since the Human Rights Act 1998: A Critical Review*, pp.174–77.

[80] See http://www.comres.co.uk/polls/Liberty_HRA_poll_27.09.10.pdf.

[81] Ministry of Justice, *Human Rights Insight Project* (London: Ministry of Justice, 2008).

[82] Ministry of Justice, *Human Rights Insight Project*, p.27.

The relative unpopularity of the HRA has been attributed to several factors. These include: the lack of public engagement in the HRA's creation combined with the absence until 2007 of a human rights commission to promote understanding and implementation of it; a lack of government leadership combined with ministerial discomfort at the challenge the HRA has sometimes posed to executive power; hostile and erroneous media reports; and political discourse which has sometimes distorted the HRA's impact.[83]

Opinion surveys on a Bill of Rights are inconsistent. In 2006, an ICM State of the Nation survey reported that 77 per cent of those polled agreed that 'Britain needed a bill of rights to protect the liberty of the individual'.[84] However, the Hansard Society's 2008 Audit of Political Engagement found that the issue of 'whether Britain needs a new Bill of Rights' scored third lowest out of 11 constitutional issues for public understanding at 28 per cent.[85] The 2006 ICM poll gauged support for a Bill of Rights in the context of specific rights it might contain, including, for example, the right to hospital treatment on the National Health Service within a reasonable time (supported by almost 90 per cent). The Hansard survey did not discuss specific rights; it found that, compared with other constitutional issues, the question of whether Britain needs a new Bill of Rights is 'among the most technical and the vaguest' and lacks 'real resonance, at least when stated in these terms'.[86] We may infer that popular enthusiasm for a new Bill of Rights in the abstract is unproven.[87] As the Joint Committee on Human Rights noted in 2008, any UK government will have an 'uphill task to stimulate and inspire public debate'.[88]

One such attempt to generate debate was the Labour government's 11-month consultation on its 2009 Green Paper on a Bill of Rights and Responsibilities.[89] The consultation was styled 'People, Power and Politics' and run by civil servants in the Ministry of Justice. It consisted partly of a series of deliberative events held around Britain, at which a total of around

[83] Donald, Watson and Leach, *Human Rights in Britain since the Human Rights Act 1998: A Critical Review*, pp.178–81; F. Klug, "'Solidity or Wind?' What's on the Menu in the Bill of Rights Debate?" (2009) 80 *Political Quarterly* 420.

[84] Joseph Rowntree Reform Trust, *State of the Nation 2006: Summary Results* (York: JRRT, 2006).

[85] Hansard Society, *Audit of Political Engagement 5: The 2008 Report with a Special Focus on the Constitution* (London: Hansard Society, 2008), p.5.

[86] Hansard Society, *Audit of Political Engagement 5*, p.39.

[87] See also P. Vizard, *Should Economic and Social Rights Be Included in a Bill of Rights? An Analysis of Public Attitudes* (Centre for the Analysis of Social Exclusion, London School of Economics, 2010).

[88] Joint Committee on Human Rights, *A Bill of Rights for the UK?*, p.79.

[89] Ministry of Justice, *Rights and Responsibilities: Developing Our Constitutional Framework* (London: Stationery Office, 2009).

500 randomly selected participants debated national identity and values, a Bill of Rights and Responsibilities and a written constitution.[90] The Ministry also held round-table discussions with, among others, representatives of faith communities and disability organisations; and established a website and Twitter feed. It observed that the consultation

> shows a strong public appetite for further debate of these profoundly important issues, and broad support for adoption of a Statement of Values and a Bill of Rights and Responsibilities as part of a suite of constitutional changes.[91]

The assertion that public appetite was 'strong' is contestable: the consultation process in fact took place largely unnoticed by the media and the wider public. While the consultation 'reached' a combined total of 2,500 people, including some 600 Twitter followers, only 123 submissions were received, including 35 online comments.[92] This lacklustre response appears to bear out interviewees' observations as to the deficiencies of government-administered processes. The Labour government's exercise had, one interviewee noted, made a UK Bill of Rights appear to be 'just another piece of legislation'. Moreover, it had failed to overcome a sense of unease and disengagement with the Bill-of-Rights project in the devolved nations.

Devolution presents potential obstacles to the creation of a UK Bill of Rights that must be negotiated sensitively.[93] JUSTICE argues that if the HRA were amended or repealed and/or if a Bill of Rights were enacted covering the devolved jurisdictions, the devolution statutes would need to be amended.[94] Any such decision would almost certainly require the consent of the Scottish Parliament and the Northern Ireland Assembly, as well as being likely to breach both the Belfast (Good Friday) Agreement and treaty obligations owed to the Republic of Ireland as a guarantor of that Agreement.[95] Further, a UK-wide process or one that emphasises 'Britishness' could inflame sections of opinion in the devolved nations. There is no consensus on the seriousness of these problems. Former Labour ministers spoke of 'tricky' drafting issues,

[90] Donald, Leach and Puddephatt, *Developing a Bill of Rights for the UK*, pp. 58–65; Ministry of Justice, *People and Power: Shaping Democracy, Rights and Responsibilities* (London: Stationery Office, 2010); Ministry of Justice, *Rights and Responsibilities: Developing Our Constitutional Framework: A Summary of Responses* (London: Stationery Office, 2010).

[91] Ministry of Justice, *Rights and Responsibilities: Developing Our Constitutional Framework: A Summary of Responses*, p.6.

[92] Ministry of Justice, *Rights and Responsibilities: Developing Our Constitutional Framework: A Summary of Responses*, p.9.

[93] For discussion of the legal, constitutional and political obstacles posed by devolution, see JUSTICE, *Devolution and Human Rights* (London: JUSTICE, 2010).

[94] JUSTICE, *Devolution and Human Rights*, p.3.

[95] JUSTICE, *Devolution and Human Rights*, p.23.

rather than matters of principle, arising from devolution.[96] Conversely, JUSTICE argues:

> Amendments to the HRA or legislating for a Bill of Rights would be dangerous and risky—to the protection of rights, to the constitution of the United Kingdom, and to the Union itself.[97]

Certainly, there is an onus on the consultative process to create a UK Bill of Rights to take account of the sensitive and dynamic context created by devolution. Interviewees suggested that this should involve tailored consultations in each devolved nation, with terms of reference and a methodology agreed between the UK government and the devolved authorities—an objective the Labour government's 2009 consultation singularly failed to achieve.

The Commission on a Bill of Rights

The Commission on a Bill of Rights held its first meeting in May 2011 and is due to report by the end of 2012. It is comprised of nine people, eight of whom are Queen's Counsel.[98] It is supported by a full-time secretariat of five,[99] with members committed to working three days per month.[100] The Commission's programme budget for 2011–12 was £97,500 plus £66,000 for the Commissioners' remuneration.[101]

The Commission has been criticised for its lack of diversity: it is comprised of eight white men and one white woman, with two Scots and no one based in Wales or Northern Ireland.[102] Giving evidence to the Political and Constitutional Reform Committee, one Commission member, Lord Lester of Herne Hill QC, responded to the accusation that the body was too 'pale, stale and male':

> [W]e have to have extremely good outreach; we have to compensate for our lack of diversity ... We are really essentially of the legal class and that has advantages but also serious disadvantages. We are going to have to go out and listen and discuss with an enormous range of people to overcome these disadvantages.[103]

[96] Joint Committee on Human Rights, *A Bill of Rights for the UK?*, p.28.
[97] JUSTICE, *Devolution and Human Rights*, p.27.
[98] In March 2012, one of the original members of the Commission, Dr Michael Pinto-Duschinsky, resigned and was replaced by Lord Faulks QC.
[99] Information provided by Commission on a Bill of Rights Secretariat by email, 18 October 2011.
[100] Minutes of the meeting of the Commission on a Bill of Rights, 26 January 2012, p.3.
[101] Information provided by Commission on a Bill of Rights Secretariat by email, 18 October 2011.
[102] See, for example, Society of Black Lawyers, "Lawyers Criticise Coalition Government's 'All White' Bill of Rights Commission", 4 July 2011.
[103] HC Debs, vol.1049-ii, Q62, 16 June 2011.

Members of the Political and Constitutional Reform Committee voiced concerns about the potential for the Commission to become deadlocked, given that its eight members (excluding the chair, Sir Leigh Lewis) are equally split between avowed supporters and detractors of the HRA.[104] Lord Lester responded by suggesting that

> contrary to what the outside world thinks, my view is that members of this Commission can secure a high common factor of agreement and are not going to split on party lines and argue like cats in a bag.[105]

Commission members agreed in February 2012 that they 'would wish to strive for the maximum degree of unanimity in the Commission's final report'.[106]

The Commission launched its formal public consultation in August 2011 with a discussion paper inviting responses to the question of whether the United Kingdom needs a Bill of Rights and, if so, what it should contain and how it should apply to the devolved nations.[107] Perhaps mindful to avoid the proverbial cat fight, the document provides a factual description of the United Kingdom's human rights and constitutional architecture but omits any discussion of what a Bill of Rights might entail, why it might be needed or how it might relate to the HRA. The consultation elicited some 900 responses.[108] In July 2012, the Commission issued a second consultation, which is more substantial and discursive than the first.[109] For example, it raises the question of new rights which might be included in a Bill of Rights, including socio-economic rights, children's rights, environmental rights, and rights to equality, trial by jury and administrative justice.

In addition, the Commission has held discussions with the judiciaries of England and Wales, Northern Ireland and Scotland, as well as with the Justices of the Supreme Court.[110] It has also co-hosted two seminars with academics, legal practitioners and other interested parties. In January 2012, members of the Commission noted that it 'would benefit from carrying out further consultation with the wider public'; however, proposals put forward

[104] Explaining his decision to resign from the Commission in March 2012, Dr Michael Pinto-Duschinsky stated that it had 'sidelined parliament and the Prime Minister' and that after one year in operation it was clear that 'it has been intended all along to issue a report in favour of the status quo'; "Bill of Rights Commissioner Resigns over Bypass of Commons", *Guardian*, 11 March 2012.

[105] HC Debs, vol.1049-ii, Q58, 16 June 2011.

[106] Minutes of the meeting of the Commission on a Bill of Rights, 29 February 2012, p.2.

[107] Commission on a Bill of Rights, *Discussion Paper: Do We Need a UK Bill of Rights?* (Members of the Commission on a Bill of Rights, 2011).

[108] See http://www.justice.gov.uk/downloads/about/cbr/cbr-respondents.pdf.

[109] Commission on a Bill of Rights, *A Second Consultation* (Members of the Commission on a Bill of Rights, 2012).

[110] See http://www.justice.gov.uk/about/cbr/consultation-prog.

by one (unnamed) member for a 'substantially augmented work programme', including 50 public hearings, were considered to 'substantially exceed the resources available to the Commission'.[111] In February 2012, Sir Leigh Lewis noted that he had authorised the issue of an Invitation to Tender for 'proposals for carrying out a consultation exercise with the UK public on the issue of whether we need a UK Bill of Rights and related issues'. He added, however, that no decision had been taken on whether to proceed with this work.[112]

Sir Leigh had previously noted that the Commission was 'acutely conscious' of the devolution dimension.[113] In November and December 2011, members of the Commission met representatives of the devolved administrations and legislatures of Northern Ireland, Wales and Scotland and other interested parties in two-day visits to each nation.[114] The Commission also established an Advisory Panel formed of individuals nominated by the devolved administrations.[115] Members of this panel from Scotland and Wales ventured that a UK Bill of Rights was being conceived primarily to address what were perceived as 'English problems' and

> there was no view in Scotland and Wales that a UK Bill of Rights was necessary or desirable in order to address a perceived lack of public confidence in the current human rights system.[116]

Achieving Democratic Legitimacy for a UK Bill of Rights: Lessons from Overseas

While the right to participation is becoming established in law and theory, the means of realising that right in the formation of Bills of Rights, and the consequences for democratic legitimacy, are matters of debate and experimentation. Reflecting on the Canadian experience, Leane argues that it is a moot point whether broad community participation is a prerequisite for achieving democratic legitimacy for a Bill of Rights, or whether elite support and an absence of widespread resistance suffice.[117] General prescriptions are perilous

[111] Minutes of the meeting of the Commission on a Bill of Rights, 26 January 2012, pp.2–3.
[112] Minutes of the meeting of the Commission on a Bill of Rights, 29 February 2012, p.2.
[113] HC Debs, vol.1049-i, Q31, 9 June 2011.
[114] See http://www.justice.gov.uk/about/cbr/consultation-prog.
[115] The Welsh government nominated Clive Lewis QC and Revd Aled Edwards, and the Scottish government nominated James Mure QC and Professor Alan Miller on behalf of the Scottish Human Rights Commission. By January 2012, no nomination had been made by the devolved administration of Northern Ireland. See Minutes of the meeting of the Commission on a Bill of Rights, 26 January 2012, p.6.
[116] Minutes of the meeting of the Commission on a Bill of Rights, 26 January 2012, p.13.
[117] Leane, "Enacting Bills of Rights: Canada and the Curious Case of New Zealand's 'Thin' Democracy", p.156.

since each national experience is particular: for example, the Canadian Charter benefited from Trudeau's charismatic leadership, exercised at a heightened constitutional moment. In the three decades since the Charter was enacted, expectations have increased that the process of creating a human rights instrument will at least attempt to be participatory. This expectation is fuelled by the development of consultative and deliberative approaches and technology that permit ever more sophisticated forms of public engagement.

No single method of consultation or deliberation is a 'magic bullet' for achieving democratic legitimacy (and associated benefits such as a sense of popular ownership and enhanced public understanding of human rights). Methods may legitimately vary between jurisdictions. However, those with experience of designing and implementing such processes concur that the form of consultation or deliberation and the institutions used are likely to affect what it is possible to achieve in this regard. In summary, they suggest that:

- Governments should issue a clear statement about the purpose of a Bill of Rights and the terms of reference for the process of creating it. This should include a procedural commitment to act on the results of that process within clearly stated parameters.
- A Bill-of-Rights process should be non-regressive. No process to create a Bill of Rights has permitted even the possibility of regression, either in terms of human rights standards or mechanisms and institutions for enforcement. A process premised on weakening human rights protection would disturb norms established across the democratic world and set a damaging precedent internationally.
- The body running the process should be capable of facilitating community-level discussions as well as eliciting expert opinion. Community discussion should be as unconstrained as possible whilst being informed to the greatest possible extent about existing human rights protections and options for building upon them.
- The credibility of the process is likely to be enhanced if it is independent of government and has no vested interest in the outcome, and if it combines both qualitative and quantitative approaches.
- The process should place a high premium on eliciting the views and experiences of groups whose human rights are most vulnerable to being breached.
- It is desirable for the process to have a clear time-frame with, at some point, a momentum-building phase with the aim of generating interest even among those who were previously unengaged.
- The process should be adequately resourced so as to be appropriately ambitious for the stated purpose.

- The outcome of the process should be transparent about the rationale for specific provisions and how these relate both to consultative or deliberative processes and international standards.

In the light of these insights, how may we assess the work of the Commission on a Bill of Rights and the challenges it faces? At the time of writing in July 2012, a definitive assessment of the Commission's methodology is premature. However, the signs are not promising that it is well-equipped to negotiate the considerable hurdles strewn in its path.

When interviewed in 2009 and early 2010, participants in the EHRC-commissioned research who are familiar with the UK context argued that conditions for creating a new Bill of Rights were unfavourable. The polarised and frequently ill-informed political discourse surrounding the project was incommensurate with its gravity; public enthusiasm was not assured; and there was virtually no momentum behind the idea from civil society. No convincing case had been made for the need for a new Bill of Rights, beyond 'rebranding' the HRA or tinkering with its provisions.

There are few grounds for revising this assessment in 2012. Indeed, opportunistic attacks on the HRA as a contributory cause of the English riots of August 2011 might be seen as a nadir of domestic human rights debate.[118] Proponents of the HRA must welcome the Coalition's commitment (expressed in the Commission's terms of reference) to create a Bill which 'incorporates and builds on' all the United Kingdom's obligations under the ECHR and ensures that these rights continue to be enshrined in UK law. However, a member of the Commission on a Bill of Rights, Baroness Kennedy, writing before her appointment, expressed concern that 'the rights agenda is going to be a source of real tension' within the Coalition; she argued that human rights 'have to be non-negotiables in this new political landscape'.[119] The Commission has been widely viewed as a means of deferring for as long as possible this contentious area of policy. The Coalition has issued no clear statement about the purpose of a UK Bill of Rights; nor has it given any commitment to act upon the outcome of the Commission's recommendations within certain parameters. These are significant obstacles to achieving an outcome which might enjoy democratic legitimacy, in the sense of having been subject to inclusive and informed public deliberation. As we have seen, much political (and especially Conservative) discourse about the need for a new 'British' or 'UK' Bill of Rights is predicated on the assertion that we do not already have

[118] See, for example, "David Cameron: Human Rights in My Sights", *Sunday Express*, 21 August 2011.

[119] H. Kennedy, "Human Rights Must Not Be Subject of Coalition Deals", *Guardian*, 19 May 2010.

one. This assertion obscures both the origins and the nature of the HRA and produces ill-informed debate about the options available.

The Attorney-General, Dominic Grieve, has stated that one of the most compelling reasons given for introducing a new Bill of Rights is 'so that all British citizens of different backgrounds feel ownership of it'.[120] This is a laudable aim. However, it is not evident why a new Bill of Rights that fulfils the Commission's non-regressive mandate will necessarily enjoy a greater sense of popular ownership than the HRA, unless the underlying reasons for the unpopularity and misunderstanding of the Act are addressed. Cosmetic 'rebranding' of the Act (for example, as being based on 'British' values) is unlikely to change public attitudes or understanding and would, in any event, be an insufficient reason to embark on constitutional reform of such significance.

Neither the Commission's rather arid discussion paper of August 2011, nor its belated second consultation of July 2012, provides the basis for the kind of ambitious community outreach that Commission members originally aspired to conduct. Further, the Commission's relatively protracted timescale, combined with its modest resources, appear likely to frustrate the achievement of momentum behind a UK Bill of Rights—and with it any wider objective to design a process which becomes, as one interviewee in the EHRC-commissioned research put it, 'an exercise in building citizenship rather than just market research'. Nor is it evident at the time of writing that the Commission has the intention or resources to engage with marginalised or disadvantaged groups whose rights are most centrally at stake.

One means of enhancing political discussion would be a concordat that would commit parties to refrain from using language or bringing stories into the public domain that knowingly distort the impact of human rights and the HRA.[121] While this appears a distant prospect, it is to be hoped that the Commission at least fulfils its mandate to 'consider ways to promote a better understanding of the true scope' of the United Kingdom's human rights obligations. An improved understanding of human rights among both politicians and the public would be a considerable achievement for the Commission given the inauspicious circumstances of its birth.

[120] D. Grieve, "Liberty and Community in Britain", speech for Conservative Liberty Forum, 2 October 2006.

[121] I am grateful to Francesca Klug, Professorial Research Fellow at the London School of Economics, for this suggestion.

13

Conservative Anti-HRA Rhetoric, the Bill of Rights 'Solution' and the Role of the Bill of Rights Commission

HELEN FENWICK

Introduction

IN RESPONSE TO THE RIOTS IN AUGUST 2011, British Prime Minister David Cameron was quick to attack the Human Rights Act 1998 (HRA) on the basis that 'phoney human rights concerns' must not get in the way of dealing with rioters.[1] Some days later, in his analysis of the causes of the riots, he fleshed out his view that the HRA was linked to the riots, and his solution—a British Bill of Rights:

> As we consider these questions of attitude and behaviour ... we inevitably come to the question of the Human Rights Act and the culture associated with it ... We're working to develop a way through the morass by looking at creating our own British Bill of Rights. And we will be using our current chairmanship of the Council of Europe to seek agreement to important operational changes to the European Convention on Human Rights ... the interpretation of human rights legislation has exerted a chilling effect on public sector organisations, leading them to act in ways that fly in the face of common sense, offend our sense of right and wrong, and undermine responsibility ...[2]

Deep dissatisfaction with the HRA and a determination to repeal it was also reflected in Conservative pronouncements in the run-up to the 2010 general election, and in the Conservative manifesto.[3] But when the Coalition government was formed this became, for obvious political reasons, a much more difficult issue, given the differing stances taken on it by the Conservatives and Liberal Democrats[4] prior to the general election. The notion that a rapid

[1] Speech to House of Commons, 11 August 2011.
[2] In a speech to his constituency, 15 August 2011.
[3] The Conservative Party manifesto promised to 'Replace the Human Rights Act with a UK Bill of Rights'.
[4] The Liberal Democrats' manifesto promised to 'Ensure that everyone has the same protections under the law by protecting the Human Rights Act'.

Proceedings of the British Academy, **183**, 309–342.

repeal of the HRA might be undertaken, based on David Cameron's pledge to that effect to the *Sun* in 2006,[5] had to be put to rest. A partial and temporary solution—obviously unsatisfactory from a Conservative viewpoint—was found by consigning this issue to a Commission to examine the possibility of creating a British Bill of Rights (BoR). This allowed the uneasy compromise adopted by the two parties to subsist, for a time.

However, the Commission is in the position of dealing with near-irreconcilable aims since the underlying concern, from the Conservative perspective, clearly appears to be to enhance the autonomy of the Westminster Parliament at the expense of both Strasbourg's influence and the maintenance of European Convention on Human Rights (ECHR) standards, as interpreted at Strasbourg. The aim of the Conservative leadership, this essay argues, is to utilise the BoR to create a change from the balance the HRA creates between parliamentary and judicial power: a theme constantly recurring in the speeches of Conservative HRA sceptics relates to weakening the influence of both the Strasbourg Court and of domestic judges. That aim is likely to influence both the outcome of the Commission's deliberations, bearing in mind the fact that David Cameron nominated four of the members, and the reception of the proposals in 2012–13.

The background to the appointment of the BoR Commission and the stances taken towards the HRA by its members reveal the contradictions inherent, this essay argues, in its remit, especially when compared to the stance taken by Cameron on this issue since 2006. The remit has nothing to say about complete withdrawal from the ECHR, or repeal of the HRA. But, at the same time, senior Conservatives and the Conservative nominees on the Commission appear to consider that the attempt should be made under the BoR to weaken the ties to Strasbourg created by the HRA. The idea, it is argued, appears to be to seek to utilise the BoR to increase the autonomy of the Westminster Parliament in human rights matters. The extent to which that is the case and to which the BoR could be used (if at all) to achieve that aim forms a key theme of this essay.

Bearing that context in mind, this essay considers what a Bill of Rights under the Coalition government (or a future Conservative government) might look like, in contrast to the HRA, taking account of ideas expressed by Conservative spokespersons prior to and after the 2010 general election,[6] and of answers given by members of the Bill of Rights Commission to the

[5] He told the *Sun*, 12 May 2006, that it was wrong to allow 'the human rights of dangerous criminals to fly in the face of common sense'.

[6] In "Balancing Freedom and Security—A Modern British Bill of Rights", speech to the Centre for Policy Studies, London, 26 June 2006, David Cameron stated that the HRA should be repealed. See also in particular the Rt Hon. Dominic Grieve QC in a speech to the Human Rights Lawyers Association, 23 March 2010 (which has not been published).

Commons Select Committee on Political and Constitutional Reform in 2011.[7] It considers what role, if any, the Commission is likely to play in framing any BoR. This essay also touches on the second aspect of the Commission's remit, its advisory role on reform of the European Court of Human Rights (ECtHR)[8]; comments from the Conservative-nominated Commission members[9] indicate that they view the role as related to the enterprise of handing autonomy back to the Westminster Parliament by creating a more circumscribed role for the Court. Dominic Grieve has proposed reform of the Strasbourg Court via adoption of a much stronger principle of subsidiarity.[10] Such reform has been trailed by senior Conservatives as creating a context within which utilising a BoR to tailor decisions on the scope of rights to the perceived needs of the United Kingdom with minimal interference from Strasbourg has realisability. However, this essay questions whether adopting a BoR on the lines favoured by the Conservative leadership, combined with the Strasbourg reforms recently determined on,[11] would be likely to realise the aims of creating divergence from Strasbourg and enhancing parliamentary autonomy.

The Bill of Rights Commission

The Coalition's Programme for Government stated that a Commission was being established to investigate the creation of a 'British Bill of Rights that incorporates and builds on all our obligations under the European Convention on Human Rights'. After May 2010 there was an uneasy silence on the issue of the HRA or a BoR. Almost a year later, nothing was known as to the Commission; it was eventually set up in March 2011 and will report before the end of 2012.[12] Its full remit is:

[7] See Commons Select Committee on Political and Constitutional Reform, *UK Bill of Rights Commission—Oral and Written Evidence—9 and 16 June 2011* (19 July 2011). Below this evidence is referred to in relation to the Question number to which the answer relates.

[8] It has already given interim advice on such reform, by way of a letter to Nick Clegg and Kenneth Clarke, on 28 July 2011.

[9] For example, Martin Howe QC in relation to *UK Bill of Rights Commission—Oral and Written Evidence—9 and 16 June 2011*, Q82.

[10] In intervening in *Scoppola v Italy (No.3)*, Application no.126/05, in a statement indicative of the government's plan for reform of the Strasbourg Court in chairing the Council of Europe; in his speech, "European Convention on Human Rights—Current Challenges", 24 October 2011, at Lincoln's Inn, London.

[11] See discussion below of the draft declaration for the 2012 High Level Conference at Brighton.

[12] The Commission is headed by former Permanent Secretary, Sir Leigh Lewis. Eight members were appointed: Martin Howe QC, Anthony Lester QC, Jonathan Fisher QC, Helena Kennedy QC, Anthony Speaight QC, Philippe Sands QC, Michael Pinto-Duschinsky and Sir David Edward.

> To investigate the creation of a UK Bill of Rights that incorporates and builds on all our obligations under the European Convention on Human Rights, ensures that these rights continue to be enshrined in UK law, and protects and extends our liberties. To examine the operation and implementation of these obligations, and consider ways to promote a better understanding of the true scope of these obligations and liberties. To provide advice to the Government on the on-going Interlaken process to reform the Strasbourg court ahead of and following the UK's Chairmanship of the Council of Europe. To consult, including with the public, judiciary and devolved administrations and legislatures ...

Apart from its interim advice on reform of the ECtHR,[13] it has produced so far one discussion paper—of a brief, descriptive and markedly bland nature—entitled *Do We Need a Bill of Rights?*[14] No indication as to the possible forms any Bill of Rights might take have emerged from the Commission as a whole.

It appears, it is argued, that the setting up of the Commission kept matters in stasis, perhaps in anticipation of the possibility that unfolding events and the political reaction to them might affect the public mood and possibly create a build-up of feeling in which the repeal of the HRA became unavoidable. Cameron's reaction to the riots suggests that that is the case. In other words, events might well allow political capital to be made by adopting an anti-HRA stance in relation to unpopular minority groups—prisoners, suspected terrorists, the poor and disaffected—thus allowing the Conservatives' stance towards the HRA to dominate, and placing the Liberal Democrats in a difficult political position on the issue.

The BoR Commission is divided between Liberal Democrat nominees who support the HRA[15] and Conservative nominees who want to see it repealed and replaced by an instrument that could appear to offer aid to the government in terms of escaping from the demands of the Strasbourg Court and the ECHR.[16] It has been argued that 'the deadlocked membership of the commission confirms the widespread expectation that it will spend most of its time producing rival dissenting papers that will be the basis of Conservative and Liberal Democrat manifesto commitments at the next election'.[17] Lord Lester, however, has said that the Commission is 'not going to split on party lines and argue like cats in a bag'.[18]

[13] Published 28 August 2011.

[14] Published August 2011, available at http://www.justice.gov.uk/about/cbr/consultation-prog.

[15] Kennedy, Lester, Sands, Edward.

[16] Speaight, Howe, Pinto-Duschinsky (now resigned from the Commission), Fisher.

[17] See *Guardian*, 18 March 2011.

[18] See answers to the Commons Select Committee on Political and Constitutional Reform, *UK Bill of Rights Commission—Oral and Written Evidence—9 and 16 June 2011*, answer to Q58.

Repeal of the Human Rights Act

Repealing the HRA would obviously be a major, highly controversial and politically very difficult step. The terms of reference of the Commission make no mention of its repeal since the Commission has been asked only to consider the creation of a BoR. But the HRA is inevitably the elephant in the room: the Commission can hardly decide on the issue of the creation of a BoR without considering the fate of the HRA. It is understandable that some resiling from the position taken by Cameron in 2006—whereby creation of a BoR was inevitably accompanied by repeal of the HRA—occurred when the Coalition government came to power. As mentioned, the Liberal Democrats made a manifesto pledge in 2010 to retain the HRA, as did Labour.[19] Clearly, Cameron would (depending on the timetable that eventually emerges) want to get the repealing legislation through Parliament without damaging the Coalition and without facing combined Labour and Lib Dem opposition. The stance of the Scottish National Party, Ulster Unionists and Plaid Cymru would presumably depend on the stance taken as regards the devolution arrangements affecting the Northern Ireland Assembly, the Welsh Assembly and the Scottish Parliament—which adds a range of further complications (this issue is briefly touched on below).

The members of the Commission appear to take diverging stances on the question of repeal of the HRA, and it can probably be assumed that Helena Kennedy, Philippe Sands and Anthony Lester at the least would have to be convinced that the BoR would deliver the same degree of rights protection as the HRA, before they would recommend repeal. In giving evidence to the Constitutional Reform Select Committee one of the Conservative members of the Commission[20] was asked about the differing Liberal Democrat and Conservative stances, and whether in reality the purpose of the Commission was to give the two Coalition parties options at the end of 2012 enabling them to include different proposals in their manifestos for the next election, based on the expert advice from their own party members on the Commission.[21] Anthony Speaight replied that that was not the case and that the parties did not differ as much as was supposed. As to the question of accompanying

[19] The Labour Party manifesto stated: 'We are proud to have brought in the Human Rights Act, enabling British citizens to take action in British courts rather than having to wait years to seek redress in Strasbourg. We will not repeal or resile from it.'

[20] It may be noted that Speaight had produced a pamphlet—*The Human Rights Act: Legal Pathways* (2007)—considering implications of replacing it with a British Bill of Rights.

[21] See answers to the Commons Select Committee on Political and Constitutional Reform, *UK Bill of Rights Commission—Oral and Written Evidence—9 and 16 June 2011*, answer to Mr Chope, Q37.

creation of the BoR with repeal of the HRA, he said: '[M]y favoured option would be that, that in place of the Human Rights Act there would be a new statute—let's call it a UK Bill of Rights for want of a better label.'[22]

Martin Howe, a further Conservative nominee, also appeared to favour repeal of the HRA, stating:

> There is a perception at the moment, I believe, among a section of the country, that the Human Rights Act is an alien import that comes in from abroad … The Human Rights Act, obviously in a sense it can be said to constrain or conflict with parliamentary sovereignty.[23]

On this point, Lord Lester, in contrast, said: '[one] approach would be to keep the Human Rights Act as it is but perhaps have a political declaration with it. Another approach would be to amend or replace the Human Rights Act. That would be fraught with some difficulty …'[24]

Clearly, the collective view of the Commission—if one emerges—is not yet known, but, bearing in mind the stance Cameron has taken on this issue, it would be surprising if, as leader of the Coalition government, he were prepared to take action to implement proposals that did *not* include the replacement of the HRA by the BoR. The terms of reference of the Commission could be interpreted as impliedly including the possibility of merely retaining the HRA, possibly with some modifications, but it is reasonably clear that such an outcome would not have the support of the Conservative Party.

Devolution Issues[25]

The exact relationship between a BoR and the devolved legislatures is clearly going to be a complex and problematic issue, one that at present has received little attention. It would appear that renegotiation of the devolution settlements might be necessitated. This issue is one of those that the BoR Commission raised in its 2011 discussion paper, *Do We Need a Bill of Rights?*,[26] and the devolved legislatures have appointed members to an advisory panel,

[22] See A. Speight in answers to the Commons Select Committee on Political and Constitutional Reform: *UK Bill of Rights Commission—Oral and Written Evidence—9 and 16 June 2011*.
[23] See *UK Bill of Rights Commission—Oral and Written Evidence—9 and 16 June 2011*, answers to Q77 and Q80.
[24] See *UK Bill of Rights Commission—Oral and Written Evidence—9 and 16 June 2011*, answer to Q58.
[25] See further Chapter 4 and Chapter 12, this volume.
[26] Published August 2011, available at http://www.justice.gov.uk/about/cbr/consultation-prog.

lawyers rather than politicians, to provide advice to the Commission on legal and technical aspects of devolution matters.[27]

Unlike the Westminster Parliament, the devolved legislatures are not free to disregard the ECHR. Under the Scotland Act 1998, actions by members of the Scottish government and legislation enacted by the Scottish Parliament must be compatible with the Convention. Under the terms of the Northern Ireland Act 1998, ministers and Northern Ireland departments must act compatibly with the ECHR, and the Northern Ireland Assembly does not have competence to legislate in a manner incompatible with the Convention. The same is true of the Welsh Assembly under the Government of Wales Act 2006. As far as these legislatures are concerned the ECHR is entrenched. Presumably the Commission will need to consider whether those requirements as to compatibility should be revisited under a BoR.

There is also the question of the relationship with a Northern Ireland Bill of Rights. The Northern Ireland Human Rights Commission (NIHRC) was set up in 1999 and required to advise the Secretary of State for Northern Ireland on the scope for defining rights additional to the ECHR ones in a Bill of Rights for Northern Ireland. The Belfast (Good Friday) Agreement of 1998 states that the Bill should reflect the particular circumstances of Northern Ireland. In 2008, the NIHRC presented its advice on a Bill of Rights for Northern Ireland to the government. The government published its paper, *A Bill of Rights for Northern Ireland: Next Steps*, for consultation, and the NIHRC made a written response to that paper in 2010, in which it found that the response demonstrated a lack of understanding of the purpose and functions of a Bill of Rights; failed to take appropriate account of international human rights standards; and appeared to be suggesting the lowering of existing human rights standards in Northern Ireland.[28]

The question of the Northern Ireland BoR will obviously be one that the BoR Commission will have to tackle. The key issues will no doubt be whether Northern Ireland should have its own BoR and, if so, what should the relationship be between the Northern Ireland Assembly and the BoR. But in general a key question will be whether the devolved legislatures should be subject to the rights listed in the BoR, as they are currently to the ECHR. If the agenda which, it is argued below, the Conservatives appear to be pursuing eventually prevails, it would be possible for the devolved legislatures to be able to legislate contrary to such rights.

[27] See Speaight, *UK Bill of Rights Commission—Oral and Written Evidence—9 and 16 June 2011*, answer to Q50.

[28] *A Bill of Rights for Northern Ireland: Next Steps*, Response to the Northern Ireland Office (February 2010).

Reconciling Parliamentary Sovereignty with Rights Protection

A seminal constitutional decision involving a choice between judicial and parliamentary checks on executive power, and therefore as to the allocation of power, had to be taken regarding the choice of model for the enforcement of the ECHR when the Human Rights Bill was being considered. The choice made was to afford the HRA no special constitutional protection and to leave the ultimate task of checking executive power to Parliament; so judicial rulings remain (at least as a matter of constitutional theory) subject to primary legislation. The HRA therefore sought to reconcile rights protection placed to a significant extent in the hands of the courts with parliamentary sovereignty. Although the Convention contains the familiar list of rights usually found in a number of Bills or Charters of Rights, the HRA was not intended to be a Bill of Rights on the models provided by the Amendments to the US Constitution or the Canadian Charter: under the HRA, laws that conflict with the rights cannot be struck down. Further, unlike the German Basic Law or the US Amendments, the HRA can simply be expressly repealed or amended like any other statute and it is, therefore, in a far more precarious position.

However, although parliamentary sovereignty was preserved as a matter of constitutional theory, ss. 3, 4 and 2 HRA effected, as discussed below, a significant transfer of power to the judiciary; but the HRA also apparently imposed limitations on its use. On a face-value reading of the HRA, legislation incompatible with the Convention can be passed and is binding on public authorities[29] unless s.3 can be relied upon to read the provision in question compatibly with the ECHR. Legislation declared incompatible with the ECHR under s.4 remains valid[30] and the executive may, but need not, bring amending legislation before Parliament if a declaration of incompatibility is made.[31] Legislation can be presented to Parliament which may be incompatible with the ECHR.[32] It is readily apparent, then, that there was a contradiction between the liberal aim of affording the Convention rights efficacy in domestic law in order to aid in reversing the effects of the over-centralisation of power, and the aim of preserving the key feature of the constitution—parliamentary sovereignty combined with the dominance of Parliament by the executive—which gave rein to that power. The factors underlying this contradiction form one of the central themes apparent in the human rights

[29] HRA, s.6(2).
[30] HRA, ss. 6(2) and 4(6).
[31] HRA, s.10.
[32] HRA, s.19.

field over the last 12 years—the search for a means of giving efficacy to the rights in the face of hostile legislation, including post-HRA Labour legislation, such as the Terrorism Act 2000, as amended, and the Anti-Terrorism, Crime and Security Act 2001 (ACTSA).

This essay argues that while there have been serious tensions between the ECHR and government criminal justice or counter-terrorist policy in the years 2000–12, the particular resolution of the tension between rights protection and parliamentary sovereignty created by the HRA has *not* in general been utilised by the executive in the sense of seeking to defy the ECHR openly. The particular constitutional choices reflected in the HRA have on the whole *not* been exploited to allow the government, as dominant within Parliament, to disregard or limit the Convention rights to an extent that the ECHR itself does not allow. As Keith Ewing wrote in 1999:

> [W]e should be careful about distinguishing form from substance, principle from practice. As a matter of constitutional legality, Parliament may well be sovereign, but as a matter of constitutional practice, it has transferred significant power to the judiciary [under the HRA].[33]

The methods of recognising the doctrine of parliamentary sovereignty utilised in the HRA—ss. 3(2) and 6(2)—have *not* been the most significant factors in determining the balance between the exercise of governmental power and rights. Thus, a doctrinal analysis of the status of the ECHR in domestic law is inadequate to explain its impact, since such an analysis has been superseded by the political stance taken by the previous government.

For example, after the derailing in 2004 of the Labour government's counter-terror detention-without-trial measure in *A and others*[34] it could, as a matter of constitutional theory, have sought to rely on the parliamentary sovereignty-preserving HRA provisions, ss. 6(2) and 3(2)(b), allowing Parliament to pass legislation regardless of the Convention rights, which public authorities, including courts, must then apply. Had that occurred, the judiciary would, according to Lord Scott in the 2009 case of *AF (No.3)*,[35] have loyally accepted Parliament's decision. Sections 6(2) and 3(2) have nothing to say about the necessity or proportionality of the measures needed to avert the crisis, as art.15 ECHR does,[36] and do not overtly demand that an emergency must be in being. (After the decision in *A and others* the government appeared reluctant to risk seeking a derogation in 2005.) But the political reality was that the government would have doubted its ability to persuade

[33] K. D. Ewing, "The HRA and Parliamentary Democracy" (1999) 62 M.L.R. 79, 92.
[34] [2004] UKHL 56.
[35] [2009] UKHL 28, at [97].
[36] They also place no restrictions on the Articles that could be violated. In contrast, under art.15, only certain rights are capable of derogation.

Parliament to accept a scheme that openly failed to adhere to either art.6 or 5, unless it claimed that that was necessitated by the crisis, and clearly the question would have arisen as to why it did not seek a derogation if so certain that the crisis demanded repudiation of art.5 or 6 standards. Further, open defiance of the ECHR after receiving it into domestic law under the HRA would have been politically difficult, and an eventual adverse decision at Strasbourg would have forced the government to revisit the issue. Obviously, the United Kingdom would have remained constrained by the ECHR at the international level and probably would have found itself eventually in breach of its Treaty obligations.

So, instead of relying on the HRA provisions allowing Parliament to pass legislation in breach of the ECHR, the government brought forward legislation—the Prevention of Terrorism Act 2005—which was apparently ECHR-compliant but did not fully deal with the problem of being unable to prosecute or deport a certain group of persons suspected of terrorist activity.[37] It should be noted that s.6(2) *was* relied upon by the government as part of the response to the declaration of incompatibility in *A and others*: the declaration did not affect the validity of the offending legislation—Pt4 ACTSA—and therefore those detained under its provisions remained lawfully in detention. However, s.6(2) was relied upon only as a temporary expedient—to create a period of time (around three months) within which to prepare and bring forward the replacement legislation.

An important exception to the point above as to the use of s.6(2) HRA arises in respect of prisoners' voting rights. The Labour government did not respond to the ruling at Strasbourg in *Hirst v UK*[38] to the effect that the failure of the United Kingdom to allow such rights breached art.3 of the First Protocol. The declaration of incompatibility by the Court of Session in *Smith v Scott* on this matter was not acted on[39]; in 2011, Parliament voted to continue to disregard the *Hirst* decision.[40] In *Greens and MT v United Kingdom*,[41] the Court had ordered the United Kingdom to bring forward, within six months of the judgment becoming final in April 2011, appropriate legislative

[37] See further on this episode H. Fenwick, "Recalibrating ECHR Rights, and the Role of the Human Rights Act Post 9/11: Reasserting International Human Rights Norms in the 'War On Terror'?" (2010) 63 C.L.P. 153.

[38] *Hirst v UK* (2004) 38 E.H.R.R. 825; *Hirst v UK (No.2)* (2004) 38 E.H.R.R. 40.

[39] *Smith v Scott* [2007] SC 345. In those proceedings by prisoners in Scotland, in Northern Ireland (*R. v Secretary of State Ex p. Toner and Walsh* [1997] N.I.Q.B. 18) and in England and Wales (*Chester v Secretary of State for Justice* [2010] EWCA Civ 1439) the relevant Secretary of State expressly accepted that the ban on prisoner voting is incompatible with the ECHR.

[40] The Tory backbencher David Davis and former Labour Home Secretary Jack Straw tabled the 10 February 2011 motion opposing reform, which was accepted by a majority of MPs (234 to 22).

[41] Judgment of 23 November 2010.

proposals to implement *Hirst*. Since the *Hirst* ruling the offending provisions of s.3 of the Representation of the People Act 1983 have remained legally valid and applicable despite their incompatibility with the ECHR. Further, in *Tovey & Ors v Ministry of Justice*,[42] the High Court struck out a claim for compensation by a prisoner in respect of his disenfranchisement under the blanket ban. The ruling confirmed that as a matter of English law, taking account of the HRA, a prisoner cannot succeed before a court in England and Wales in any claim for damages or a declaration. In April 2011 a panel of the Grand Chamber refused to hear the United Kingdom's appeal on the issue,[43] and ordered compliance with the *Hirst* ruling by 11 October 2011—although the period has been extended.[44]

This is an unresolved matter that is creating a direct clash between parliamentary autonomy and the authority of the ECtHR; it is clearly likely to influence consideration of the BoR. But this is an exceptional situation and the current government clearly does not view the HRA as providing an answer to it merely on the basis that the HRA allows for departure from the ECHR, if consented to by Parliament. Similarly, the Labour government was in general reluctant to bring legislation before Parliament unaccompanied by a declaration of its compatibility with the ECHR. It did so once—in the Communications Act 2003. But the provision in question, continuing the ban on political advertising, was not as controversial as the matters of non-prosecution counter-terror measures or the issue of prisoners' voting rights. More importantly, its compatibility with art.10 was viewed as uncertain; the government did not accept that there was incompatibility, and its stance was for the time being vindicated by the House of Lords in *Animal Defenders*.[45]

Departing from the ECHR under a Bill of Rights?

Preserving 'Soft' Entrenchment?

So consideration of the potential relationship between a BoR and parliamentary sovereignty is likely to take account of a political reality in which *overt* disregard of the ECHR has so far largely been avoided. An important driver for change, from the Conservative viewpoint, is to hand greater power to Parliament to determine human rights issues. David Cameron has said that the HRA

[42] [2011] EWHC 271 (Q.B.) (18 February 2011).
[43] On 12 April 2011.
[44] Due to the hearing in the Italian voting rights case—*Scoppola v Italy (No.3)* (2011), Application no.126/05.
[45] *R. (on the application of Animal Defenders International) v Secretary of State for Culture, Media and Sport* [2008] UKHL 15; [2008] 1 A.C. 1312.

should be repealed and replaced by the BoR, 'so that Britain's laws can no longer be decided by unaccountable judges'.[46] How far the 2012 Commission proposals might cover the possibility of creating greater autonomy for Parliament in the BoR is obviously unclear, but it appears highly unlikely that there would be Conservative support for weakening parliamentary sovereignty.[47]

Pronouncements from senior Conservatives prior to the 2010 general election, and statements from the Conservative members of the BoR Commission, indicate that the BoR is not likely to be given a stronger constitutional status than that of the HRA.[48] For example, Martin Howe said in evidence to the Select Committee:

> [W]ould a Bill of Rights for the United Kingdom represent a stronger constraint on Parliament than the existing mechanism, which I think some people call 'soft entrenchment' under the HRA? ... That is certainly not something I favour.[49]

Michael Pinto-Duschinsky[50] has written (prior to being appointed to the Commission) that the HRA weakened parliamentary sovereignty because it

> obliged British judges to accept the interpretations of the very broad terms of the European Convention on Human Rights before their own interpretations. It obliged them to place these interpretations from Strasbourg before the meaning of the legislation passed at Westminster.[51]

Thus it seems highly probable that in a BoR put forward by a Conservative-dominated government, sovereignty would be preserved by equivalents to ss. 3(2) and 6(2), probably combined with a s.4 equivalent, rather than allowing judges a strike-down power. Obviously each of these possibilities offers opportunities to revisit the sections in the light of the experience of the HRA over the last 12 years, and the jurisprudence that has emerged. In particular, the Coalition government might be tempted to remove or weaken s.4, which has come to be viewed as creating a de facto obligation upon the executive to

[46] "Rebuilding Trust in Politics", 8 February 2010.

[47] See s.18 of the European Union Act 2011 for clear endorsement of parliamentary sovereignty.

[48] Grieve has said that it will 'be possible to repeal or override part or all of a Bill of Rights in exactly the same way as the Government has routinely done to Habeas Corpus and Magna Carta': "Liberty and Community in Britain", speech, 2006.

[49] See *UK Bill of Rights Commission—Oral and Written Evidence—9 and 16 June 2011*, answer to Q81.

[50] He was a Commission member but resigned from the Commission in March 2012, reportedly because the Commission had 'sidelined parliament and the prime minister' (*Guardian*, 11 March 2012).

[51] *Bringing Rights Back Home: Making Human Rights Compatible with Parliamentary Democracy in the UK* (London: Policy Exchange, 2011).

act, even though technically a s.4 declaration can be disregarded.[52] It is possible that the 'fast-track' procedure for amending incompatible legislation will be removed,[53] and it would be consistent with the aspiration of the Conservatives to weaken the link with Strasbourg not to include the provision in s.10(1)(b) HRA to the effect that the power to take remedial action can be triggered by a finding of the Strasbourg Court. But creating greater parliamentary autonomy in a radical and more far-reaching sense clearly depends more on reform to the ECtHR, rather than on any changes effected under a BoR.

The parliamentary sovereignty-preserving mechanisms in the HRA might in effect be bolstered when their equivalents are considered for the BoR as a concomitant to possible changes to the mechanisms affording the judges power to determine the interpretation and application of the rights. So it appears possible that the section of the HRA which, it is argued, handed a very significant measure of power to judges—s.3—might appear in the BoR in a modified and weakened form.[54] Grieve has said in relation to the use of the interpretative obligation under s.3 that it is wrong that courts should 'have power to stand a statute on its head'.[55] The new s.3 would presumably refer to creating compatibility between the list of rights in the BoR, which would no doubt reflect all the ECHR obligations (without necessarily including the text of the ECHR itself). One possibility would be that *a* new replacement for s.3 could state that in the event of a conflict between decisions of the Strasbourg Court (as opposed to domestic decisions as to the interpretation of provisions of the BoR list of rights) and provisions in legislation, the latter *must* prevail, but a declaration of the incompatibility can be made. That in itself would not fully solve the problem—for Conservatives—of Strasbourg interventionism, at the parliamentary level. But, combined with the possible changes to s.2 HRA that have been mooted as discussed below, it would prevent courts absorbing Strasbourg decisions into domestic law, allowing 'read-down' of legislation via s.3 HRA, without affording the executive an opportunity to

[52] See, for example, the Chamber judgment in *Burden v United Kingdom* (2006), Application no.93378/05. It was found that the applicants had not needed to exhaust the remedy of obtaining a s.4 declaration, since it was a remedy that was dependent on the discretion of the executive and so ineffective on that ground. The Court expressed the view, however, that it was possible that, at some future date, evidence of a long-standing and established practice of ministers giving effect to the courts' declarations of incompatibility might be sufficient to persuade it of the effectiveness of the procedure.

[53] See Dominic Grieve: 'I am certainly intent on getting rid of the fast track procedure for primary legislation to be struck down in the event of declarations of incompatibility' ("Proposals for a British Bill of Rights", speech to a British Academy/AHRC Forum, 8 March 2010).

[54] For example, the term 'reasonably' could be included on the lines of the equivalent provision in the Canadian Charter.

[55] Conservative Home blog, 14 April 2009.

make a determination as to the favoured response. Such a change would not deal with the inroads made into parliamentary sovereignty by the Strasbourg Court itself, again currently perceived as a serious problem by Conservative HRA sceptics.

Jeffrey Jowell has argued that under the HRA the courts were 'charged by Parliament with delineating the boundaries of a rights-based democracy'.[56] This view of the HRA, often termed that of 'liberal constitutionalism', which can be referred to as reflecting an incorporationist stance, finds that the HRA created a shift of power from Parliament to the judges, removing human rights from the political realm. An opposing view[57] finds that courts, under the HRA, are able to engage in a constitutional dialogue between themselves, Parliament and the executive as to the interpretation of the ECHR[58]: the HRA asks courts to examine a legislative interference with a right, and, if it is deemed inappropriate to create compatibility between the interfering measure and the right under s.3 HRA, it asks them to inform Parliament via s.4 HRA that it has breached the Convention. The role the BoR may be intended to play from a Conservative perspective can be contrasted with that of the HRA, in terms of these opposing models, well established in public law literature, of dialogic constitutionalism or incorporationism.

As a number of commentators have pointed out, s.3 HRA has tended to be used to a greater extent than anticipated, a stance that obviously does not comport fully with furtherance of the dialogic model.[59] The BoR appears likely to resemble the HRA in creating an appearance of adhering to a constitutional dialogic model, while in actuality its parliamentary sovereignty-preserving mechanisms are probably no more likely than those of the HRA to be utilised—in terms of *open* defiance of the ECHR. In other words, whatever form such mechanisms take in a BoR, no government as a matter of constitutional reality is likely to announce that it intends to introduce legislation in deliberate breach of its Treaty obligations. Thus, under a BoR, Parliament is likely to continue to tend to rely on the ECHR exceptions and derogation system rather than on the equivalents of ss. 3(2) and 6(2). However, although open defiance of the ECHR would be unlikely, and the BoR Commission's remit does not include leaving the ECHR system completely, the BoR could be used to limit and blunt the impact of decisions at Strasbourg as far as the UK courts are concerned.

[56] J. Jowell, "Judicial Deference: Servility, Civility or Institutional Capacity" [2003] P.L. 592, 597.
[57] See, for example, T. Hickman, *Public Law after the Human Rights Act* (Oxford: Hart, 2010), pp.58–63.
[58] See F. Klug, "The HRA—A 'Third Way' or a 'Third Wave' Bill of Rights" [2001] E.H.R.L.R. 361.
[59] See, for example, A. Kavanagh, *Constitutional Review under the UK Human Rights Act* (Cambridge: Cambridge University Press, 2009), pp.121–32.

Senior Conservatives appear to consider that departures from the ECHR could occur under a BoR in comparison with the HRA. But it follows from the discussion that such departures are unlikely to come about due to the creation of radically stronger measures to protect parliamentary sovereignty. As discussed, the sovereignty-protecting measures have not been extensively utilised under the HRA to allow for departures from the ECHR, except in the sense that s.6(2) has applied to allow incompatible measures to continue to take effect for a time, as in the instance of prisoners' voting rights or in respect of the three-month gap between the declaration of incompatibility in *A and others* and the repeal of Pt 4 ACTSA. But governments have in general sought to stay within the ECHR, rather than openly repudiate it, as the HRA allows—with Parliament's consent. If strengthening the parliamentary sovereignty-preserving measures of the HRA in the BoR is unlikely to hand determinations as to human rights matters to Parliament to a significantly greater degree, then the underlying purpose of the BoR, from the Conservative perspective—to set the United Kingdom largely free from the influence of Strasbourg—might appear to be unlikely to be realised, except in the sense that determinations as to acceptance of ECtHR decisions might be made more frequently by Parliament than by the courts. However, it is argued below that there is another possible method of minimising the impact of the rights recognised under the ECHR without necessarily appearing to do so, which is favoured by Conservative HRA sceptics.

Changing the Relationship between Strasbourg and the Domestic Courts

There are signs that, prior to the 2010 election, senior Conservatives intended to use the BoR to seek to sever or weaken the connection with Strasbourg created by s.2 HRA. Dominic Grieve has argued that the HRA had been 'interpreted as requiring a degree of deference to Strasbourg that I believe was and should be neither required nor intended'. Instead, he said, a new BoR would make it clear that British courts could allow for UK common law to take precedence over decisions by the ECtHR in Strasbourg.[60] That could be achieved by requiring the domestic courts to take a different stance from Strasbourg, possibly in specified circumstances. There are some signs that certain Commission members have sympathy with a stance of that nature. Anthony Speaight said in evidence to the Select Committee:

> [T]he court ... makes decisions that something or other is a human right that would not by the average Briton be regarded as a human right ... To be told—to take the current example that is uppermost in one's mind—that this country's

[60] Dominic Grieve's Guest Lecture, Middle Temple Hall, 30 November 2009.

> penal policy, supported overwhelmingly by its legislators, is incompatible with human rights just strikes most Britons as nonsense.[61]

The replacement for s.2 HRA in the BoR could play a role in the hunt for 'greater subsidiarity' and, from the point of view of the Conservatives on the Commission and the Conservative Party generally, this is clearly a key aspiration underlying this project.

Currently, in seeking to interpret the Convention rights under the HRA, the domestic judiciary 'must take into account' any relevant Strasbourg jurisprudence, under s.2. Those words appear to indicate that the jurisprudence is non-binding, but they do not reflect the dominant stance taken towards the Strasbourg jurisprudence in domestic courts. It was found in *Ullah*[62] in the House of Lords that the judges must follow any clear and constant jurisprudence of the Strasbourg Court. In the counter-terrorism case of *AF*[63] the stance taken by Lord Carswell, and accepted by the majority, was to the effect that a Strasbourg decision, *A v UK*[64]—upholding a higher due process standard than the previous House of Lords decision in *MB*[65] had done—had to be applied. It was considered by the majority that there was no leeway under s.2 HRA to do otherwise. Lord Carswell found (reluctantly) that the principle espoused by the Grand Chamber in *A v UK* differed from that adopted by the majority in *MB*, but whatever 'latitude' might be permitted to the courts by the duty to take Strasbourg judgments into account under s.2(1) HRA, 'the authority of a considered statement of the Grand Chamber is such that our courts have no option but to accept and apply it'.[66] The Strasbourg Court had upheld a higher standard of fair trial rights (demanding minimum disclosure of the evidence against him to the person to whom preventive measures had been applied) than the House of Lords had upheld in *MB*, meaning that despite the HRA and the reliance on the Strasbourg jurisprudence demanded by s.2, the Lords had failed to interpret the Strasbourg jurisprudence in the way with which Strasbourg would have concurred.

In *R. v Horncastle*,[67] also in the context of art.6, the Supreme Court considered that departure even from clear jurisprudence was exceptionally

[61] See *UK Bill of Rights Commission—Oral and Written Evidence—9 and 16 June 2011*, in reply to Q36.

[62] *R. (on the application of Ullah) v Special Adjudicator* [2004] UKHL 26. See further J. Lewis, "The European Ceiling on Human Rights" [2007] P.L. 720.

[63] See *Secretary of State for the Home Department v AF (No.3)* [2009] UKHL 28.

[64] (2009) 49 E.H.R.R. 29.

[65] [2008] A.C. 440.

[66] 'Views may differ as to which approach is preferable, and not all may be persuaded that the Grand Chamber's ruling is the preferable approach. But I am in agreement with your Lordships that we are obliged to accept and apply the Grand Chamber's principles in preference to those espoused by the majority in *MB*', at [108].

[67] [2010] 2 W.L.R. 47.

acceptable under s.2 HRA, as s.2 originally intended. The domestic provisions in question, the Court found, struck the right balance between the imperative that a trial must be fair and the interests of victims in particular and society in general. In other words, the Strasbourg test did not strike the right balance and therefore was not applied. The Supreme Court decided that the European Court's decision insufficiently accommodated aspects of the domestic process, and determined that in those rare circumstances it could decline to follow the decision, as it did. But the Supreme Court in *Cadder v HM Advocate (HM Advocate General for Scotland and another intervening)*[68] found that s.2 HRA required it to apply the decision of the ECtHR in *Salduz v Turkey*.[69] Thus, in effect, the Strasbourg jurisprudence, although not technically binding on domestic courts, may be viewed as coming close to having a binding impact via s.2 HRA, if it is clear and consistent.[70]

Clearly, the effect of s.2 HRA under its current interpretation from *Cadder* does not in formal terms limit parliamentary sovereignty. But in terms of constitutional reality it can do. If, as in *AF*, a court follows a Strasbourg ruling and accordingly 'reads down' legislation under s.3 HRA, then for a period of time (until and if amending or replacement legislation changes the position) the legislation assumes a form that differs from that which Parliament had determined upon. Thus, an area of law is interpreted and applied according to Strasbourg norms, rather than according to norms accepted by the Westminster Parliament.

Given that this position under s.2 HRA is viewed as wholly unsatisfactory from the point of view of the Conservative HRA sceptics, what options would be available in terms of reframing the s.2 equivalent in the Bill of Rights? The idea, as expressed by Dominic Grieve, appears to be to make provision in a BoR s.2 replacement that would allow or require the judges in effect to apply the *Horncastle* principle in a range of circumstances, *not* as an exception:

> [W]e could positively provide for a right of rebuttal ... which allows the Supreme Court to be able to say to the Strasbourg court that it has not made the principle clear, or that it has not applied the principle consistently, or that it has misunderstood national law or the impact of its decisions on the UK legal system.[71]

[68] [2010] 1 W.L.R. 2601. See, in particular, [33], [40], [41] and [47], referring to [55] in *Salduz*.
[69] (2008) 49 E.H.R.R. 421.
[70] The Court in *R. (on the application of Quila) v Secretary of State for the Home Department* [2011] UKSC 45 did decline to follow the elderly Strasbourg case of *Abdulaziz*, but on the basis that there was no 'clear and consistent jurisprudence' to follow (at [43] (Lord Wilson)).
[71] See Dominic Grieve QC, Attorney-General, "European Convention on Human Rights—Current Challenges", speech at Lincoln's Inn, London, 24 October 2011.

That could mean that in certain circumstances the domestic jurisprudence would diverge from that of Strasbourg. In order to achieve this it could be considered necessary to include a list of circumstances under which departure from Strasbourg should occur. An obvious instance would be where there is a gap in the jurisprudence or where the instance in question was within the state's margin of appreciation. Far more controversially, such a list could include instances where Parliament had recently decided to strike a balance between competing rights or between rights and societal concerns differing from that struck at Strasbourg, reflecting the *Horncastle* stance.

Under art.46 ECHR, states must abide by decisions of the Strasbourg Court. Grieve's proposals would not contravene that Article but would not address a head-on clash between a legislative provision and a Strasbourg decision. A changed s.2 equivalent might make it less likely that the courts would absorb a Strasbourg decision into domestic law, as in *AF*, but Parliament would still be faced with the need to respond to it, as in the prisoners' voting rights instance. This point illustrates the limitations, from the anti-HRA Conservative perspective, of seeking to use a BoR to enhance the autonomy of the Westminster Parliament in human rights matters.

The Liberties and Obligations to be Protected/Recognised under the BoR?

The pronouncements made by senior Conservatives prior to the election showed a striking lack of clarity as to the respects in which the BoR might differ from the HRA; as a result Erdos argued that any changes might be largely cosmetic.[72] Under the terms of reference for the Commission the British BoR is intended to incorporate and build on 'all the obligations under the European Convention on Human Rights, and protect and extend British liberties'. The terms indicate that the Commission is not being asked to consider the introduction of a completely new set of rights in a tailor-made British BoR, although additional rights could be added. That at least is the understanding of the Chair of the Commission, Sir Leigh Lewis.[73]

It would be tempting to see the introduction of a BoR as an opportunity to adopt a more comprehensive list of rights, relevant in the 21st century. From today's perspective, the 60-year-old ECHR looks very much like a

[72] See D. Erdos, "Smoke but No Fire? The Politics of a 'British' Bill of Rights" (2010) 81 *Political Quarterly* 188.

[73] See *UK Bill of Rights Commission—Oral and Written Evidence—9 and 16 June 2011*, answer to Q8 from Mr Chope.

creature of its period,[74] with its provision against slavery[75] and its long lists of exceptions to certain fundamental rights. Its out-of-date feel has led a number of commentators to echo the plea put forward some years ago by Adam Tomkins and Brian Bix for 'a document of principle for the 1990s and not a document of exceptions from the 1950s'.[76] David Feldman has made a similar point: the Convention rights are 'by no means a comprehensive basis for a modern system of protection for [individualistic and public] values'.[77] The far more thorough South African Bill of Rights provides an example of such a system. Liberty's *Manifesto for Human Rights* put forward in 1997 proposed that a domestic Bill of Rights could be drawn up, based on the ECHR, but using more up-to-date language and addressing certain of the inadequacies of the ECHR.[78] In particular, Liberty criticised the lack of minimum conditions for detention outside art.5, and the lack of a right to jury trial. The Equality and Human Rights Commission (EHRC) found on the question of a more comprehensive instrument in 2010: 'The government should incorporate in any Bill of Rights a fully enforceable free-standing right to equality.'[79] The EHRC advocated inclusion of a right to dignity and 'measures to increase participation and representation of particular groups such as women, ethnic minorities, disabled persons and older persons as provided for in relevant international conventions and principles'.[80] It has also often been pointed out that the Convention contains no specific rights for children.[81]

The HRA has been criticised on the basis that the opportunity was lost to include certain social, environmental and economic rights,[82] including some

[74] The Convention was drafted in 1949 and based on the United Nations Declaration of Human Rights. The Declaration was adopted on 10 December 1948 by the General Assembly of the UN.

[75] Slavery in the sense of human trafficking is still a live issue in Europe. See *26th Report of the JCHR on Human Trafficking 2005–06*, HL Paper 245-1, HC Paper 1127-1 (13 October 2006).

[76] A. Tomkins and B. Bix, "Unconventional Use of the Convention" (1992) 55 M.L.R. 721, 725. See also A. Ashworth, "The European Convention on Human Rights and English Criminal Justice: Ships which Pass in the Night?", in M. Andenas (ed.), *English Public Law and the Common Law of Europe* (London: Key Haven, 1998), p.215.

[77] See D. Feldman, "The Human Rights Act 1998 and Constitutional Principles" (1999) 19 L.S. 165, 170.

[78] National Council for Civil Liberties 1997 (now Liberty). See also the Bill drawn up by the Institute for Public Policy Research: Constitution Paper No.1, "A British Bill of Rights", 1990.

[79] That would of course mean including Protocol 12 ECHR or utilising it as a basis for including such a right.

[80] EHRC, *HRA PLUS Human Rights for 21st-century Britain* (Spring 2010).

[81] J. Fortin "Rights Brought Home for Children" (1999) 62 M.L.R 350. The inclusion of children's rights is likely to be argued for in relation to the BoR proposal; see Children's Rights Alliance press release, "Bill of Rights Could Strengthen the Rights of Children", 20 May 2010.

[82] See K. D. Ewing and C. A. Gearty, "Rocky Foundations for Labour's New Rights" (1997) 2 E.H.R.L.R. 149.

of those protected under the International Covenant on Social, Economic and Cultural Rights. Obviously, if the opportunity arises, various interest groups are likely to put forward arguments for specific additions to the current Sch.1 rights. On socio-economic rights the EHRC said in 2010:

> The government [the previous Labour government] should consult ... in relation to all the key socio-economic rights: the right to an adequate standard of living including housing; the right to physical and mental health; the right to education; the right to work, and the right to social security.[83]

But it is readily apparent that under a Conservative-dominated Coalition government the addition of such rights is highly unlikely. Speaight commented in 2011: 'I am more inclined towards a more minimalist statement of rights than one that goes in the direction of environmental rights and socio-economic rights.'[84]

When listed rights have been referred to by senior Conservatives prior to the 2010 general election and recently by Commission members, the references have been, it appears, to the list of rights in Sch.1 HRA, with some additions—most obviously a right to jury trial[85]—and possibly with the creation of limits on the power of the state to impose administrative sanctions without due process of law—such as fines for speeding. None of the speeches of Conservative spokespersons prior to the election made mention of the possibility of protecting the further rights under the later Protocols. Speaight said to the Select Committee that a new BoR 'would set out as the rights every single word that is in the European Convention but also some extra things, jury trial being one of my candidates for addition'.[86] It appears likely at present that the list of rights would echo those of the ECHR with a few additions. Thus, any radical movement away from Strasbourg would not be likely to be effected by substantive changes to the list of rights covered.

Determining the 'True Scope of These Obligations and Liberties'

The BoR has been constantly trailed by Conservatives as a panacea for the ills created by the HRA. If change is not to be effected by changing the wording of the rights, other methods of redefining them appear to be in contemplation. The remit of the BoR Commission does not appear to cover complete

[83] EHRC, *HRA PLUS Human Rights for 21st-century Britain* (Spring 2010).

[84] See *UK Bill of Rights Commission—Oral and Written Evidence—9 and 16 June 2011*, Q49.

[85] See Grieve, "Proposals for a British Bill of Rights".

[86] See *UK Bill of Rights Commission—Oral and Written Evidence—9 and 16 June 2011*, answer to Q47.

withdrawal from the ECHR. Sir Leigh Lewis, Chair of the Commission, was asked in giving evidence to the Constitutional Reform Committee whether the Commission's options were too limited by its terms of reference, which prevent it arguing for such withdrawal. He did not completely rule out consideration of the possibility: '[I]f some members take a different view of what the terms of reference might cover ... we will need to look at that.'[87] That issue is clearly distinct from that of the question of the content of the BoR. However, other ways of creating a distance between the impact of the rights protected under a BoR and those under the ECHR were mentioned a number of times by David Cameron, Dominic Grieve and Jonathan Fisher prior to the 2010 general election, and recently by Speaight.

Civic Responsibilities?

The idea of creating civic obligations in a BoR has been a recurring theme. In 2006, Cameron said that a modern British Bill of Rights would balance rights with responsibilities.[88] Jonathan Fisher,[89] one of the Conservative nominees on the BoR Commission, has written that the ECHR is 'a fundamentally flawed and lop-sided document ... with an entrenched bias in favour of individual rights. The document is hopelessly unbalanced by its omission to incorporate any notion of civil obligation into the text.' He noted that art.29 UDHR—'(1) Everyone has duties to the community in which alone the free and full development of his personality is possible'—was omitted from the text of the ECHR. Therefore he concluded that civil obligations should be included in a British Bill of Rights to 'unambiguously declare to each and every British citizen the importance of individual responsibility and promote societal cohesion ... [and] notions of good citizenship'.[90] The connections between these ideas and those expressed by Cameron in 2011 in the context of the riots are readily apparent. Such ideas might also appear attractive from a Conservative perspective in relation to the prisoners' voting issue. The possibility of referring to both rights and responsibilities in the BoR was raised in the Constitutional Reform Select Committee in relation to the obligations citizens could be expected to fulfil in order to access the rights,[91] and it was agreed that that was one of the issues for consideration.

[87] See *UK Bill of Rights Commission—Oral and Written Evidence—9 and 16 June 2011*, answer to Q6.
[88] "Balancing Freedom and Security—A Modern British Bill of Rights".
[89] Director of Research, Society of Conservative Lawyers.
[90] *A British Bill of Rights and Obligations* (Conservative Liberty Forum, 2006).
[91] See *UK Bill of Rights Commission—Oral and Written Evidence—9 and 16 June 2011*, Q49, from Mr Chope. He said: 'The biggest political problem seems to arise when people seek justice under the European Convention where they themselves have contributed to their own problems.'

If a BoR did impose both rights and responsibilities that could imply that citizens would be placed under an obligation to *qualify* for rights protection by discharging such responsibilities. For example, prisoners could be excluded in certain circumstances from seeking to claim a right to vote, or possibly other democratic rights (aspects of arts 10 and 11 ECHR) due to their failure to abide by civic responsibilities by committing criminal offences. Obviously such a provision would contradict the notion that rights inhere automatically in humans. The EHRC's position on this issue is:

> [H]uman rights can never be made contingent on the exercise of responsibilities. This position reflects requirements under international human rights treaties to which the UK government is a party. However, there may be merit in recognising in any Bill of Rights the responsibilities we have to protect each others' human rights. This could help to promote mutual respect, tolerance and a more cohesive society.[92]

This issue is returned to below.

Rebalancing or Interpretation Clauses in the BoR?

David Cameron as Prime Minister has indicated on a number of occasions that he sees a BoR as a means of allowing the United Kingdom to escape from human rights constraints that he considers offensive and as flying in the face of common sense. He has continually held out a BoR as the cure for an over-expansive use of human rights laws. He made that point in relation to prisoners' voting rights (see above) and the finding in 2010 of a breach of art.8 in respect of the requirement that certain sex offenders must be subject indefinitely to 'notification requirements', without a prospect of change if they had reformed.[93] The BoR Commission was established in response to that decision.[94]

Dominic Grieve has mentioned the possibility of including 'interpretation clauses' in a BoR a number of times[95]: 'There is certainly a degree of interpretation where there would be greater flexibility in the Bill of Rights than there is, currently in the ECHR.'[96] Cameron has spoken of the BoR solu-

[92] EHRC, *HRA PLUS: Human Rights for 21st-century Britain* (Spring 2010).

[93] The decision of the Supreme Court in *R. (F) v Secretary of State for the Home Department* [2010] UKSC 17.

[94] The comment was made at Prime Minister's Questions on 15 February 2011; Mr Cameron was responding to Tory MP Phillip Davies who complained about the Supreme Court ruling that sex offenders could appeal against having to register with the police for life.

[95] See "Proposals for a British Bill of Rights"; "Liberty and Community in Britain". Such interpretation clauses were also referred to in his Guest Lecture, Middle Temple Hall, 30 November 2009.

[96] He continued: 'That I think is feasible. It would be quite wrong to suggest that it would completely transform the situation [in relation to the deportation of suspected terrorists at risk

tion as 'one which … enables a British Home Secretary to strike a common-sense balance between civil liberties and the protection of public security'.[97] Jonathan Fisher has echoed the idea that a BoR would give the Home Secretary greater flexibility in making a judgment in the public interest, in relation to deportation in particular.[98] Lord Hoffman has said that the 10 original Member States of the Council of Europe did not agree to 'uniformity of the *application* of the Convention rights in each of their countries'; he went on to say that the Strasbourg Court has 'been unable to resist the temptation to aggrandise its jurisdiction and to impose uniform rules on member states'.[99] Dominic Grieve in 2009 welcomed this criticism of the Court and said that the Conservative approach to a BoR would be to create compatibility with the ECHR; 'But there is no reason why our courts should be bound by Strasbourg Court jurisprudence, if their own interpretation is different, particularly where rights should be balanced by responsibilities.'[100]

This issue arose in evidence to the Commons Select Committee in 2011 from BoR Commission members, although in much less stark and melodramatic terms. Speaight said:

> [W]hat could be done in a UK Bill of Rights is some tweaking of rights. In the Human Rights Act, there was one attempt by Parliament to tweak by section 12, which in effect said where there is a conflict between privacy and free speech under articles 8 and 10, free speech is very, very important. [It meant] let the free speech end [of the seesaw] win. In my view the English judges have simply ignored that, so tweaking may not work very well. But that is a precedent showing that tweaking can be done, and it certainly is a possibility in a UK Bill of Rights that extra text can be added to a repeat of the wording of the Convention.[101]

The idea of interpretation clauses has, unsurprisingly, not been referred to by Baroness Kennedy, Lord Lester or Philippe Sands in evidence to the Committee.

The references from Conservative HRA sceptics are to including a rebalancing provision in the BoR going beyond the exceptions and derogation system of the ECHR. Such a provision could, depending on its nature, shift the balance towards greater protection for certain societal interests than

---

of torture in the receiving country]' (Dominic Grieve, Radio 4, 'Westminster Hour', 25 June 2006). See, further, JUSTICE, *A British Bill of Rights: Informing the Debate* (19 November 2007), http://www.justice.org.uk/publications/listofpublications/index.html.

[97] "Balancing Freedom and Security—A Modern British Bill of Rights".

[98] *A British Bill of Rights and Obligations.*

[99] In his Judicial Studies Board lecture, 2009 (emphasis in original).

[100] Conservative Home blog, 14 April 2009.

[101] See *UK Bill of Rights Commission—Oral and Written Evidence—9 and 16 June 2011*, answer to Q45.

would occur under the ECHR system. One obvious possible model for such a rebalancing clause would be s.1 of the Canadian Charter of Rights and Freedoms which 'guarantees the rights and freedoms set out in it subject only to such reasonable limits prescribed by law as can be demonstrably justified in a free and democratic society'.[102] This idea has already attracted criticism. Jean-Paul Costa, then President of the ECtHR, said of the BoR proposal:

> Introducing a British bill of rights could create a complex situation ... it could mean that most rights [in the Convention] are protected to more or less the same extent, but not 100% of them. This could create divergences between the case law [from Strasbourg] and the law in the UK.[103]

An 'interpretation clause' creating exceptions going beyond those expressly present does not appear in the HRA, except impliedly, insofar as it arises from Strasbourg jurisprudence,[104] and influences domestic law via s.2 HRA. This second possibility would have to be accompanied by the changes to the replacement for s.2 in a BoR discussed above since otherwise the courts would merely tend to apply the Strasbourg jurisprudence, meaning that the balance struck between individual rights and societal interests, or between competing rights, would continue in general to echo that struck at Strasbourg. Three possible uses of such a clause are considered below.

Article 8 and Deportation

Article 8's protection for family life has been relied upon to resist deportation. Its second paragraph allows for deportation if justified as necessary in a democratic society on grounds of national security and prevention of crime.[105] This can be a difficult issue for states, partly because if a breach of art.8 is likely to arise in the receiving country due to deportation, it may be the case that no state action is likely to remedy it (e.g. because it would be unacceptable to make an exception to sharia law), whereas diplomatic assurances can, in the view of the UK government, House of Lords[106] and Strasbourg,[107] remedy the situation where it is alleged that a breach of arts 3 or 6 (a 'flagrant' breach of art.6) could arise in the receiving country.

[102] Jonathan Fisher, in *A British Bill of Rights and Obligations*, suggested that a rebalancing clause could also make reference to civic responsibility.
[103] *Guardian*, 27 June 2010.
[104] See, on the possibility of departure from art.6 standards where absolutely necessary, *Rowe v United Kingdom* (2000) 30 E.H.R.R. 1, at [61]; *Botmeh and Alami v United Kingdom*, Application no.15187/03 (2007), at [37]; *Van Mechelen v The Netherlands* (1997) 25 E.H.R.R. 647, at [58].
[105] See *Norris v Government of USA* [2010] UKSC 9.
[106] See *RB (Algeria) (FC) and another (Appellants) v Secretary of State for the Home Department OO (Jordan) (Original Respondent and Cross-appellant) v Secretary of State for the Home Department (Original Appellant and Cross-respondent)* [2009] UKHL 10.
[107] *Othman v UK*, Application no.8139/09, judgment of 17 January 2012.

In 2011, Home Secretary Theresa May told the Commons Home Affairs Select Committee that she was concerned that foreign criminals could use the 'right to a family life' under art.8 as a way of successfully fighting deportation. She said that in the last three months of 2010, 99 foreign prisoners had successfully claimed that deporting them would breach their right to a family life under art.8(1) in Britain. She went on to say that Home Office officials are examining the definition to see if there is scope to limit its use:

> [W]e are looking at ... a better definition within Article 8 to see if that's a way in which we can provide greater ability for us to be able to ensure people are removed when it's appropriate to do so.[108]

She was referring to the Home Office Consultation on Family Migration,[109] which begins by referring to the balance created under art.8 between rights and societal interests, and continues by referring to the creation of a British BoR as a means of clarifying the balance. Legislation is proposed to allow use of art.8 in such cases only in exceptional instances. A decision that has greatly exercised Grieve is that in *EM v Lebanon*,[110] in which a woman was not deported due to the violation of her art.8 right to respect for her family life she would suffer in Lebanon due to sharia law. Grieve views the decision in *EM* as one that has resulted from a judicial desire to shadow Strasbourg in the HRA—and go beyond Strasbourg—and one which could damage security in the United Kingdom if suspected terrorists could not be deported in similar circumstances. He has already indicated that he sees this as a problem that could be remedied under a BoR.[111]

The principle captured in *EM v Lebanon* could be overturned via legislation on family migration, possibly aided in future by provisions in a BoR. But clearly Parliament might invite successful applications to Strasbourg in so doing, since Strasbourg has accepted that deportation may be in breach of art.8, in circumstances hard to view as exceptional, depending on the question of the disproportionality of the impact on family life in relation to the aim pursued.[112] Further, Parliament would be unlikely, even under a BoR with a changed s.2, to have an assurance that the courts would disregard the Strasbourg stance on this matter.[113]

[108] *Daily Telegraph*, 6 July 2011.
[109] Home Office, July 2011. The consultation paper is available on the UK Border Agency website, www.ukba.homeoffice.gov.uk/policyandlaw/consultations.
[110] [2008] UKHL 64.
[111] Conservative Home blog, 14 April 2009. He also highlighted the case in 2010: "Proposals for a British Bill of Rights".
[112] See *Boultif v Switzerland* (2001) 33 E.H.R.R. 1179; *Üner v The Netherlands* (2006) 45 E.H.R.R. 421.
[113] See *Secretary of State for the Home Department v Masih* [2012] U.K.U.T. 46.

Non-materially Qualified Rights

The non-materially qualified Convention rights create particular problems, especially in the context of counter-terrorism, from the Conservative viewpoint. Employment of an 'interpretation clause' could have far-reaching effects since the intention of certain senior Conservatives appears to be to allow for the redefinition of non-materially qualified rights to suit the specific situation in the United Kingdom. A rebalancing clause introduced in a BoR could be used to introduce proportionality-based arguments into non-materially qualified rights, limiting the scope and effect of the right. It could affect arts 2 and 3, but it would be most likely to apply to arts 5 and 6 since arts 8–11 already contain exceptions based on a broad range of societal interests if the interference is necessary and proportionate. Articles 5 and 6, in contrast, make no provision for exceptions, apart from those already set out in the Articles (which are very limited in the case of art.6, applying only under art.6(1) to excluding the public and press from the hearing on national security grounds). Under the Strasbourg jurisprudence the scope for placing limitations on the standards to be applied is limited—it can occur only on a 'strictly necessary' basis where national security (or another pressing interest) demands it, so long as the hearing overall is fair.[114]

The British government, in *A v UK*,[115] put forward an argument for widening the exceptions to art.5 via introduction of a proportionality-type argument:

> The Government relied upon the principle of fair balance, which underlies the whole Convention, and reasoned that sub-para.(f) of Article 5(1) had to be interpreted so as to strike a balance between the interests of the individual and the interests of the state in protecting its population from malevolent aliens. Detention struck that balance by advancing the legitimate aim of the state to secure the protection of the population.[116]

The idea of creating a balance—going beyond express exceptions—between the needs of society and individual rights in relation to arts 5 and 6 has

[114] See *Rowe v United Kingdom* (2000) 30 E.H.R.R. 1, at [61]; *Botmeh and Alami v United Kingdom*, Application no.15187/03 (2007), at [37]; *Van Mechelen v The Netherlands* (1997) 25 E.H.R.R. 647, at [58]. Thus, limited departures from certain aspects of a fair hearing, including full disclosure of the material on which suspicion is based or equality of arms, may be permissible, provided that these are strictly necessary to protect other vital interests, such as the safety of witnesses or national security. Article 5 does not allow people to be detained indefinitely even for the most pressing national security reasons, without a derogation.

[115] (2009) 49 E.H.R.R. 29.

[116] (2009) 49 E.H.R.R. 29, at [148]. Sub-para.(f) referred to provides that one of the permitted exceptions to the right to liberty is: 'the lawful arrest or detention of a person to prevent his effecting an unauthorised entry into the country or of a person against whom action is being taken with a view to deportation or extradition'.

emerged in a number of instances.[117] In the public protest case of *Austin*,[118] the House of Lords unanimously concurred with Lord Hope's findings to the effect that in making a determination as to the ambit of art.5(1), the *purpose* of the interference with liberty could be viewed as relevant; if so, he found that it must be to enable a balance to be struck between what the restriction sought to achieve and the interests of the individual.[119] Lord Hope also found, in *R. v A*,[120] that in the context of art.6 a fair balance must be struck 'between the demands of the general interest of the community and the requirements of the protection of the individual's fundamental rights', relying on *Sporrong and Lönnroth v Sweden*.[121]

If this idea were to emerge as an aspect of the BoR Commission proposals, or, eventually, as part of a Conservative proposal for a BoR, it would be of very doubtful compatibility with the remit of the Commission to protect all the Convention rights. The *Sporrong and Lönnroth v Sweden* principle might be relied upon to seek to show that an interpretation clause was in accordance with the ECHR. But obviously this possibility would be highly controversial and likely to lead to successful applications to Strasbourg. The decision in *A v UK*[122] offered little encouragement to the idea that greater flexibility could be introduced into arts 5 and 6; the Strasbourg Court expressly rejected the idea that exceptions could be read into art.5 going beyond those already accepted. Lord Hoffmann, in *AF*, said on *A v UK* that the decision

> was wrong and ... may well destroy the system of control orders which is a significant part of this country's defences against terrorism [but the United Kingdom] is bound by the Convention, as a matter of international law, to accept the decisions of the ECtHR on its interpretation. To reject such a decision would almost certainly put this country in breach of the international obligation which it accepted when it acceded to the Convention.[123]

Some softening of the stance taken in *A v UK* has more recently become apparent: in *Austin v UK*,[124] Strasbourg gave some acceptance to the rebalancing argument accepted in the House of Lords in relation to art.5, but rejected it when put forward by the UK government in the context of art.3 in *Babar*

[117] See, further, Fenwick, "Recalibrating ECHR Rights, and the Role of the Human Rights Act post-9/11: Reasserting International Human Rights Norms in the 'War On Terror'?"
[118] *Austin v Commissioner of Police for the Metropolis* [2009] UKHL 5.
[119] [2009] UKHL 5, at [27].
[120] [2001] UKHL 25, at [91].
[121] (1982) 5 E.H.R.R. 35, at [69].
[122] (2009) 49 E.H.R.R. 29.
[123] [2009] UKHL 28, at [70].
[124] Judgment of 15 March 2012, Applications nos. 39692/09, 40713/09 and 41008/09. See in particular at [59].

Ahmad and others v UK.[125] Nevertheless, uncertainty remains not only as to the likely reception at Strasbourg of domestic decisions based on a general rebalancing provision, but also as to the outcome of such decisions themselves. The leeway that would be left to domestic judges as to manipulation of proportionality analyses, with international human rights standards in mind, could well mean that the hoped-for advantages of introducing rebalancing clauses in a BoR would not materialise.[126]

Competing Rights, especially Articles 8 and 10

An interpretation clause could be employed to create a new balance between competing rights. The most obvious area that could be affected would be the current balance between arts 8 and 10 in the context of privacy rights against the press, obviously a matter that sections of the press are extremely concerned about, arguably for the reason put forward by Lord Lester to the Select Committee:

> [T]here is a commercial reason why some newspapers do not like the European Convention or the HRA. That is because they don't like restrictions on their right to invade personal privacy and they rightly see the Act, and the Convention, as a restriction on that particular way of earning money.[127]

Dominic Grieve has said on this:

> Where rights are qualified and not absolute and a balance has to be struck between competing rights, as must happen in relation to many of the Articles of the ECHR, we should also consider if we wish through interpretation clauses to give a more detailed guide consonant with our own legal and political traditions than does the ECHR text itself as to the weight to be given to each of them.[128]

Specifically, Grieve has shown interest in creating a new balance between arts 8 and 10, one which would be likely to give presumptive priority to art.10, departing from the balance created in *Von Hannover*.[129] The Chair of the Select Committee clearly views this as an important issue for the BoR Commission: 'I am desperately hanging on to not asking you about the First Amendment right to tackle the questions about privacy.' Anthony Speaight said on this to the Commission that the role of the HRA 'has been beneficial. There is one significant area where I do not think that is the case, and that is privacy cases.' Lord Lester, in contrast, said: 'some sections of the media …

[125] Judgment of 10 April 2012.

[126] See Benjamin Goold et al., *Public Protection, Proportionality and the Search for Balance* (Ministry of Justice, 2007).

[127] See *UK Bill of Rights Commission—Oral and Written Evidence—9 and 16 June 2011*, answer to Q65.

[128] See "Proposals for a British Bill of Rights".

[129] *Von Hannover v Germany* (2005) 40 E.H.R.R. 1.

like to take the benefit of article 10 on free speech but not the burden of article 8 on privacy'.[130]

Promoting a Better Understanding of the Rights, but Rejecting the European Aspect of the HRA?

Part of the remit of the Commission refers to promoting a better understanding of rights. Sir Leigh Lewis, when asked about this aspect of the Commission's mission by the Chair of the Commons Select Committee, said that the Commission would attempt to ensure that more informed debate on rights could occur.[131] However, one of the themes mentioned a number of times by Conservatives has referred less to creating a more accurate understanding of the HRA, or human rights in general, than to rejecting a 'European human rights culture' as an alien import to the United Kingdom.

Negative Perceptions of the HRA as Protecting Alien European Human Rights

The perception of the ECHR in the popular consciousness has posed a continuing problem for human rights advocates in the United Kingdom post-HRA. As has often been pointed out, the inception of the HRA was not accompanied by the kind of popular debate that preceded the US Bill of Rights in 1789, or that accompanied the adoption of the Canadian Charter of Fundamental Rights and Freedoms as part of the patriation of the Canadian constitution in 1982. Although in 1998 the new Labour government commanded widespread popular support—and the HRA was passed during its honeymoon period—it did not seek to make the case for the HRA to the British people. That proved eventually to create problems, after 9/11, when the HRA came under pressure in relation to counter-terrorist strategy, and the war in Iraq led to a rapid diminution of the Labour government's popularity. As Francesca Klug put it, 'if the world hadn't shifted on its axis after 11 September 2001, the HRA may well have bedded down to become an accepted part of the legal and constitutional landscape of the UK'.[132]

[130] See *UK Bill of Rights Commission—Oral and Written Evidence—9 and 16 June 2011*, answer to Q59.

[131] See *UK Bill of Rights Commission—Oral and Written Evidence—9 and 16 June 2011*, answer to Q27.

[132] F. Klug, "A Bill of Rights: What For?", in C. Bryant MP (ed.), *Towards a New Constitutional Settlement* (Smith Institute, 2007), p. 133.

Clearly, the hostility of parts of the media has been fuelled by the use of the HRA to aid in creating a tort of misuse of personal information. Lord Lester said on this issue to the Commons Select Committee in 2011:

> [S]ome sections of the media—self-interested, God bless them—have campaigned vigorously against the Human Rights Act, totally unscrupulously, completely unfairly, mischaracterising everything as being a result of the Human Rights Act. That I expect to continue and I have already seen that they seek to rubbish the Human Rights Commission as part of their campaign.[133]

He indicated that the hostility might spring from restrictions 'on their right to invade personal privacy' created by the HRA.[134]

It was possible in the post-HRA years for popular ignorance of and lack of adherence to the HRA to be exploited and manipulated by the Conservative Party and a hostile media.[135] The Labour government after 9/11 also appeared remarkably reluctant to defend its own instrument. As Klug put it:

> After the 2005 London bombings in particular, the Prime Minister sometimes sounded like a cheer-leader for this negative spin, threatening to 'amend' the Human Rights Act in respect of the interpretation of the ECHR.[136]

The appeal to fear of terrorism was effective in creating a misleading image of the HRA. A false dilemma was created by parts of the media, suggesting that the only alternatives were rights protection under the HRA or security, so repeal of the HRA would destroy the main barrier to introducing effective counter-terrorist measures. Further, various media myths were promulgated: police had to supply fried chicken to a suspected car thief under the HRA[137]; and 'Serial killer, Dennis Nilsen, 60, received hardcore gay porn in jail thanks to human rights laws.'[138]

A British Instrument Reflective of Traditional Liberties rather than European Human Rights?

As a result of the negative perception of the HRA, discussions about a BoR have involved references to British values rather than European ones, and to a shared cultural understanding of principles. In 2006, David Cameron spoke of 'a new solution that protects liberties in this country that is home-grown

[133] See *UK Bill of Rights Commission—Oral and Written Evidence—9 and 16 June 2011*, answer to Q59.
[134] See *UK Bill of Rights Commission—Oral and Written Evidence—9 and 16 June 2011*, answer to Q65.
[135] See Department of Constitutional Affairs, *Review of the Implementation of the Human Rights Act* (July 2006).
[136] Klug, "A Bill of Rights: What For?".
[137] *Sun*, 7 June 2006.
[138] *Sun*, 13 May 2006.

and sensitive to Britain's legal inheritance, that enables people to feel they have ownership of their rights'.[139] One Conservative member of the Commons Select Committee which questioned members of the BoR Commission in 2011 spoke of 'one of the biggest conflicts [as being] between what might be described as Continental jurisprudence and British jurisprudence'.[140] Creating a break under the BoR with the 'European' aspect of the HRA is seen from the Conservatives' perspective as important in terms of 'selling' the new instrument to the British people. Anthony Speaight said on this: 'it is a great pity that the HRA is necessarily perceived to have based our rights on a charter of rights that comes from elsewhere. It is not perceived as being part of Britain's heritage.'[141] Covering the same obligations as the ECHR does not necessarily involve using the terminology of the ECHR. Speaight suggested that different wording could be used, more redolent of English heritage, including wording from the Magna Carta and the term 'habeas corpus'.[142] In contrast, Helena Kennedy said:

> [I]t has to be told to the public: the people who were at the heart of creating the European Convention on Human Rights were British lawyers, and they drew on common law values.[143]

If the view expressed by Speaight prevails that might mean that changes to the wording used to express the Convention rights could be employed to create a distinctively 'British' feel to the instrument. For example, the free speech clause might not be labelled 'Article 10' or use the exact wording of art.10. The effects of any such change would not be radical, but might be viewed as necessary to generate popular support for the BoR and possibly form part of an attempt to persuade the judges to adopt interpretations of the rights differing from those of the Strasbourg Court.

Reform of the European Court of Human Rights?

The ideas of including interpretation clauses—which the author has discussed in detail elsewhere[144]—and of a 'right of rebuttal' of Strasbourg decisions are

[139] "Balancing Freedom and Security—A Modern British Bill of Rights".
[140] Mr Chope.
[141] See *UK Bill of Rights Commission—Oral and Written Evidence—9 and 16 June 2011*, answer to Q36.
[142] *UK Bill of Rights Commission—Oral and Written Evidence—9 and 16 June 2011*, answer to Q39, http://www.publications.parliament.uk/pa/cm201012/cmselect/cmpolcon/1049/11060903.htm.
[143] See *UK Bill of Rights Commission—Oral and Written Evidence—9 and 16 June 2011*, answer to Q109.
[144] See H. Fenwick, "The Human Rights Act or a British Bill of Rights: Creating a Down-grading Recalibration of Rights Against the Counter-terror Backdrop?" [2012] P.L. 468–90.

clearly ones that the Conservative leadership wishes to pursue. They appear to harmonise with the enterprise of distancing the UK courts from Strasbourg, and returning autonomy in human rights matters to the Westminster Parliament. But, as discussed, even if a BoR could be utilised to achieve these objectives—which itself is clearly open to doubt[145]—applications could still be made to Strasbourg, and the United Kingdom would still be bound to respond to its decisions. The prisoners' voting rights and Qatada sagas[146] illustrate the problem: in effect, the HRA did not block the outcome preferred by the government in each instance. But the Conservative approach was given at least a colourable plausibility by placing reliance on the idea of introducing a BoR on the lines discussed as part of a *dual* strategy which also involved reforms of the Strasbourg Court, based on a principle of enhanced 'subsidiarity'. In the aftermath of David's Cameron's speech on the riots (see above), the Ministry of Justice stated that Kenneth Clarke would be seeking 'important operational changes' to the Court when Britain took over the chair of the Council of Europe in November 2011. It was stated that Clarke would try to redraw the relationship with national courts to see if more issues could be handled nationally.[147] Those changes were, it appeared, intended to emerge in the 2012 High Level Conference at Brighton, following the Interlaken and Izmir conferences, on the future of the Court.[148]

A 'leaked'[149] draft declaration for the Brighton conference gave some credibility to the Conservative 'enhanced subsidiarity' approach. It focused on the grave problem of the backlog of cases facing the Court and made proposals intended to create greater acceptance of the ECHR at national level, to allow the Court to focus on the more significant claims, and to avoid it being faced with claims that should be dealt with at national level. But among laudable proposals for dealing with the backlog, it included the following—at para.19:

> (a) The conference therefore welcomes the development of the Court within its case-law of principles such as subsidiarity and the margin of appreciation doctrine … and encourages the Court to give great prominence to these principles in its judgements; (b) Concludes that the transparency and accessibility of the

[145] The author has considered the possibility elsewhere that the judges might incline towards more, not less, 'activist' decisions, under an instrument termed a 'Bill of Rights': see Fenwick, "The Human Rights Act or a British Bill of Rights: Creating a Down-grading Recalibration of Rights Against the Counter-terror Backdrop?".

[146] See *Othman v UK*, Application no.8139/09, 17 January 2012. The House of Lords had found that Qatada could be deported despite the possibility that torture-tainted evidence might be used at his trial; the Strasbourg Court disagreed.

[147] See A. Travis, article on the HRA, *Guardian*, 17 August 2011, p.8.

[148] 19 and 20 April 2012.

[149] 23 February 2012.

> principles of the margin of appreciation and subsidiarity should be enhanced by their express inclusion in the Convention, and invites the Committee of Ministers to adopt the necessary amending instrument within one year.

Para.23(b), on options for amending the admissibility criteria, proposed that an application should be declared inadmissible if it is the same in substance as a matter that has already been determined by the national courts *unless* the Court considers that the national court 'clearly erred in its application or interpretation of the Convention rights or the application clearly raises a serious question concerning the application and interpretation of the Convention'.

The declaration, however, emerged from the Brighton conference in somewhat weakened form—unsurprisingly. It determined that

> a reference to the principle of subsidiarity and the Brighton doctrine of the margin of appreciation as developed in the Court's case law should be included in the Preamble to the Convention.[150]

As to admissibility it stated that an application should be regarded as manifestly ill-founded if it

> raises a complaint that has been duly considered by a domestic court applying the rights guaranteed by the Convention in light of well-established case law of the Court including on the margin of appreciation as appropriate, unless the Court finds that the application raises a serious question affecting the interpretation or application of the Convention.[151]

Further, as originally drafted, an advisory opinion would 'ordinarily' have prevented the individual in whose case the opinion was sought from making an application to the Court on the same matter. But now, in para.12(d), the 47 member states will have to consider whether this procedure should be introduced; individual states will then have to decide whether to accept it; further, advisory opinions will not be binding on other states.

This declaration, then, may mean that if domestic courts appear to have taken account of Convention principles, or where an advisory opinion has been given, some applications may be declared inadmissible. It may mean that the Court retreats to an extent from a more interventionist stance in the name of subsidiarity or the margin of appreciation doctrine. But this position falls short of the approach trailed by the Conservative leadership prior to the Brighton conference. Thus, the Conservative rhetoric on ECtHR 'reform', like its BoR rhetoric, seems likely to fail to accord with reality.

[150] Para.12(b).
[151] Para.15(d).

Conclusions

The timetable for the BoR Commission set out at the beginning of this essay lends credibility to the notion that its proposals are unlikely to be implemented before another general election: once it presents proposals at the end of 2012 they will need to be debated and it appears, at the time of writing, unlikely that agreement will be reached on them under Cameron's leadership, taking account of the general views of the Conservative Party, given the interest in repealing the HRA and creating divergence from Strasbourg. When a general election occurs in 2015, the possibly divergent proposals may well form part of the different election manifestos, bearing in mind the likelihood that by that time the Conservative Party will no doubt have formed more radical proposals of its own. So the proposals from Commission members opposed to the ECHR—involving cutting or weakening the 'anchor' to the Strasbourg Court created by the HRA by the means described above, as part of a means of diminishing the general influence of the Strasbourg Court—might be expected to appear in the Conservative manifesto. If the Conservatives were returned with an increased majority, then the public would be viewed as having given the party a mandate to repeal the HRA and put those proposals into effect in the BoR. The setting up of this Commission is, fairly clearly, merely a device to avoid confronting for a time the different stances taken on the HRA of the Liberal Democrats and Conservatives.

This essay concludes on a depressing note. The appetite of a number of senior Conservatives for repeal of the HRA and diminution of Strasbourg influence appears undiminished, even enhanced, in the context of the Coalition. The Prime Minister has reiterated a number of times his view that the BoR can provide a remedy for the damage he views the human rights culture under the HRA has done, and has referred approvingly to the setting up of the Commission, implying that it will produce proposals for an instrument fulfilling the aims he has set out for it. Yet the government has set up the Commission with a remit almost completely at odds with those aims. The contradiction between the role David Cameron claims the Commission will play and the role it seems likely to play is now becoming much more apparent. Thus an air of unreality pervades the deliberations of the Commission: possibly its eventual proposals will prove merely irrelevant in the coming battle over the fate of the Human Rights Act. Similarly, the expectations raised by the Conservative leadership as to the role to be played by a BoR or by Strasbourg reform in addressing the problem of 'phoney human rights concerns' increasingly seem unlikely to be realised.

Index

BoR = Bill of Rights   BORA = Bill of Rights Act
ECHR = European Convention on Human Rights
ECtHR = European Court of Human Rights   HRA = Human Rights Act 1998